LAST STAND

LAST STAND

Ted Turner's Quest to
Save a Troubled Planet

TODD WILKINSON

LYONS PRESS
Guilford, Connecticut
An imprint of Globe Pequot Press

Lyons Press is an imprint of Globe Pequot Press.

All insert photos by Turner Works, LLC, unless otherwise noted.

Project editor: Meredith Dias
Layout: Justin Marciano

ISBN 978-1-4930-0650-2

Printed in the United States of America

The Library of Congress has previously catalogued an earlier (hardcover) edition as follows:

Wilkinson, Todd.
  Last stand : Ted Turner's quest to save a troubled planet / Todd Wilkinson.
      p. cm.
  Includes index.
  1. Turner, Ted. 2. Businesspeople—United States—Biography. 3. Capitalists and financiers—United States—Biography. 4. Environmental responsibility—United States. I. Title.
  HC102.5.T86W538 2013
  333.72092—dc23
  [B]
                                                                    2012044122

10 9 8 7 6 5 4 3 2 1

CONTENTS

A Time to Rally

Foreword by Ted Turner

Some people may view this book, *Last Stand,* as me pulling back the curtain that has blocked public view of my "other life"—the one that has existed all these years parallel to my involvement with media and racing yachts. They're probably right. It does.

But in all honesty, there has never been a master plan, never a strategy for mapping out how to get rich, and I'm not talking in monetary terms. There was no single enlightening moment when I started buying land and building a bison herd in the Wild West, or getting behind the efforts of the United Nations, or aspiring to eradicate nuclear weapons from the face of the Earth, or accepting the fact that as a so-called "plutocrat" and member of the 1 percent, I feel a moral obligation to give back to society.

There are many ways to live a rich life that have nothing to do with the material. The fact is, I never aspired to become a Gilded Age tycoon. I had instincts, sure, but, in large part, I winged the course that brought me here and adapted as more information became available. Ultimately you have to listen to your heart. I wish that I had done that more often, earlier in my life. What I do know is that I'm listening to it now.

Today, as I look back, I can tell you this: Most people don't become "environmentalists" or "humanitarians" or "eco-capitalists" overnight and certainly not by accident. Just as becoming "successful" and being good at making money involves an evolution in thinking, so, too, does the compulsion to act on your conscience. Trust me: You don't need to have a fortune to make a difference in leaving the world a little better off. All that's required is a will and a belief that you can. What money can give you, if you're willing to part with it, is an ability to operate at scale.

I had a passion for sailing and sought to connect the world through CNN and TBS, which became known as the SuperStation. But I also owned a professional baseball club, the Atlanta Braves. I learned a lot in our (successful) attempt to win a World Series. I learned to put faith in the collective power of good people both on and off the field, to recognize the intangible rewards that come from true teamwork and selflessness. I learned that amazing positive achievements can happen when you join others in digging deep and finding a common confidence that enables you to prevail—when your backs are against the wall and others have sold you short. America and the world love to cheer for underdogs.

One of my biggest discoveries, however—an insight that guides me today—was witnessing the influence that fans can have in changing the momentum of a game. I saw it happen over and over again. When fans believe that great things are possible—yes, please apply the same metaphor to *citizens and their governments* and to *employees and their innovative companies*—players *feel* it and breakthroughs can happen.

We live in an age when we desperately need miraculous breakthroughs. Allow me, then, to invoke a sports analogy that I hope you'll think about as you begin Todd Wilkinson's book, *Last Stand*.

The world is in peril and it's time for all of us to put our rally caps on. This isn't a liberal or conservative issue. Don't believe it when the folks on television try to portray it that way. To set the context, imagine that it's the bottom of the seventh inning and the home team—that's the side playing for preservation of Mother Earth and civilization—is down by a couple of runs.

The opposing team has an imposing lineup. The names on the backs of the jerseys are: Apathy, Cynicism, Greed, Sloth, Violence, Cruelty, Hatred, Intolerance, and Selfishness.

All is not lost—yet—but in order to win, we as citizens watching from the bleachers need to rise to our feet. It's time that we band together, make some noise, suit up and become heroes, and remind others who are trying to mount a comeback that we're on the same side.

We can't commit any more serious errors. Instead of doing dumb things, we need to play smarter because this is the one game we can't afford to lose. If there's anything that *Last Stand* does, I hope that it will inspire you to consider that, by working together—as neighbors, as businesspeople, as citizens and inhabitants of the only planet in the cosmos known to contain life—we have the capacity to change the trajectory of the world. Of course, we have no other choice.

Over many years, I've given probably thousands of interviews. My first impression of Todd Wilkinson when he arrived on my ranch doorstep in Montana was that he'd probably be just another reporter looking for just another superficial story to tell.

I came to discover that's not how he works. He's as tenacious as I am. A good journalist doesn't come at you with just a single smart question. He is prepared to follow up with a great second and third question, and then, fourth, fifth, and sixth. As the interviewer, he knows that you have to make your subjects feel uncomfortable sometimes.

During our many conversations, he kept after me. He didn't accept pat responses. "Ted, people say that you're *unreflective*. Are you?" he asked.

The questions he presented forced me to think. I'll admit: He made me feel uneasy by pressing me about personal areas of my life that I had held close to the chest, aspects that I still am trying to make sense of, stories that I've never shared in detail with anyone. He wasn't doing it to pry,

I came to realize. He wanted me to reflect on decisions I've made, and the reasons why being an environmentalist, eco-capitalist, humanist, father, granddad, and landowner matter to me.

He delves into terrain that's never been covered in other books, including some of the most meaningful parts of my life. You'll read about my painful relationship with my dad, my marriage to Jane Fonda, my mentorship by Jacques Cousteau, and friendships with people like Mikhail Gorbachev. You'll know why I find power in reciting the verse of Thomas Babington Macaulay's epic poem, "Horatius at the Bridge," which serves as a parable for our time.

My first interview with Todd happened back in 1992. I hadn't been in the West all that long. I remember him asking, "What is your *vision*?" I explained part of it that day. The rest was a work in progress. I was impressed by his knowledge and command of environmental and political topics. He grasped the big picture I was trying to create, of how it all melded together.

Somewhere between then and now, I started to trust him in ways that I seldom do with writers or even other people. I granted him unlimited access and I agreed that there would be no preconditions set about what he could write or ask me. I put faith in his instincts as a respected old-school journalist and I became curious, frankly, where those instincts would lead him. I opened myself up and the result is this open book.

You'll notice that the subtitle of *Last Stand* is "Ted Turner's Quest to Save a Troubled Planet." What's before us now is not *my* quest; it's our shared character-defining test and our opportunity. We're in this together; while the threats are formidable and many, what I like about the subtitle is that it implies there still is hope.

My friend Tom Brokaw routinely points to the sense of shared sacrifice, embraced on behalf of country and the world by members of "the Greatest Generation" during World War II. We can choose to rally together, as they did, or we can sit back, unrustled by the stirrings of our conscience and be remembered by our grandchildren as "the Lamest Generation." We as a civilization have epic challenges before us; our survival isn't at this moment assured. I don't have to tell you that. You feel the dissonance and uncertainty in the air. Given the current path, if it isn't changed, we will be the first generation in modern times that won't deliver our kids and grandkids a better world. Throughout my career as a businessman, I've come to realize that capitalism isn't the problem, but it's how we practice capitalism—how we approach it as a proposition based only on depleting finite resources. Such thinking is wreaking havoc and is the root cause of lots of misery in the world.

Some have described me as a lefty. But I'm pro-business and I'll flaunt my credentials before anybody: I've lectured at some of the nation's top business schools, regularly attended the World Economic Forum in Davos, I've testified before Congress about the need for sensible not overbearing regulation, and I'm a member of Rotary Club, the National Restaurant Association, the National Bison Association, the Montana Stockgrowers Association, and several different chambers of commerce. I also value, equally as much, clean air and water, habitat necessary to sustain wildlife, and open space. I'm a hunter, angler, hiker, horseback rider, mountain biker, military veteran, and sailor. As a bumper sticker on my car says, "I Brake for Butterflies."

Those who claim that one can't hug a sheltering tree and simultaneously aspire to have economic prosperity and strive to give all people a decent quality of life are being disingenuous. On my lands, I have set out to prove that the polemic of environment versus economy is a false dichotomy, that you can be a tree hugger and still have your name appear in *Forbes*.

I've always looked to the future as a realm full of boundless possibility. But I'm worried. Never before has humanity confronted so many epic issues—nuclear proliferation, swelling human population, a vast gulf between haves and have nots, the biodiversity crisis, social tensions, environmental degradation, and climate change—converging at once. The chances that we might fail in our endeavor to save ourselves are high. The scientific evidence is clear and putting our heads in the sand doesn't change reality.

I've had the good fortune of living on this planet for three quarters of a century. For all of us, it's home ground.

Henry David Thoreau, one of my favorite American thinkers, once wrote: "None are so old as those who have outlived enthusiasm." Another man I studied, as my investments in CNN and TBS started paying off, was the Gilded Age tycoon and philanthropist Andrew Carnegie, who warned against hoarding of wealth. He said, "As I grow older, I pay less attention to what men say. Just watch *what they do*."

I believe in the power of the free enterprise system and the genius of democracy. I believe in freedom and liberty and private property rights. I am a patriot. On so many different levels, the private sector is able to foster innovation and act faster, better, and more cheaply than governments, but governments have a crucial role. And we must remember that, just as humankind is not separate from nature, we are indivisible from government. Nature is us; so too is government.

Those around us who claim that plundered environments are a necessary consequence of wealth creation have it wrong, the same as those who insist that government regulation is the bane of business. Again, we need a new model for thinking about capitalism and our obligation as global citizens.

The noted American actor/director Orson Welles remarked: "If you want a happy ending, that depends, of course, on where you stop your story." Today, in a world surging toward ten billion, one thing is certain about the current narrative being written: We won't and can't consume our way out of the mess we're in.

Long ago, when I was a young man and reeling from my father's suicide, I embraced the "me-first" ideology of Ayn Rand, who preached that we should worship the self before country and local community. She rejected spirituality and held up greed as a virtue. Rand was wrong, dead wrong, and it is precisely that kind of twisted logic that has sown division in our world. Our strength as a species resides with our ability to empathize—and in using our good fortune to minimize the pain and suffering of others, including other species. How we treat the Earth is the biggest expression of our success or failure as a society.

As a septuagenarian, I believe that responsible grandparents care about what kind of world they are leaving their grandkids. There's no retirement age that lets you off the hook from that. I don't say this to sound melodramatic, but the duty of citizenship never goes away, especially when one becomes an elder. We need to lead by example and young people need to step up to the plate. The search is on for new heroes. It's now the bottom of the seventh and it's our turn to bat.

PROLOGUE

Rewilding—Foreplay

"Ted is one of the most switched-on environmentalists I've ever met. From his understanding of bison and mega fauna to nukes, he is able to grasp the full magnitude of different moving parts like few others I know. Why? Because he's not a passive participant as a global citizen. He has earned his credibility."

—TIM FLANNERY, AUTHOR OF *THE WEATHER MAKERS*

The first vision of the wild wolf comes in a dream. The temporal context: autumn 2008. A stressful time, a period when one of the superstructures holding the world together—the global financial markets—is literally falling apart at the seams.

In his dream, Turner walks through a fog. Wearing a beaver-felt fedora and denim jacket, longer in the tooth and with a few wrinkles in his face, he looks older than some might remember him being. Yet, for a septuagenarian, he still moves at a brisk clip.

Whenever he's on one of his fifteen ranches scattered across seven western states, and no matter the season, Turner leaves his bedroom windows cracked open at night. The years have left him hard of hearing—the result, he says, of chronic exposure to the deafening strikes of waves pounding the hulls of sailboats he raced as a young man. Rest assured, those around him know he takes in far more than he lets on. His antennae pick up natural acoustics, and those sounds from the wilds, he says, fuel imagery that float through his dreams. Last night, while falling asleep, he could have sworn that he detected a succession of sonorous, low-decibel wails. They weren't the usual yips of coyotes or the bugling of bull wapiti. They were something else.

Within the dream, he climbs across one of the sagebrush-coated hillsides that rise above his Montana home. Wrapped in a low-hanging bank of October clouds, the scenery resembles the moody Munros of Scotland during the rainy season. His old Labrador, Blackie, is nowhere to be found.

The path he's on, a game trail, cuts between bunches of juniper and treeless meadow. About a mile in, he finds hoofprints of elk and moose in the mud. Off to the side of his route stands the muted form of a bison bull. It lifts its massive head in acknowledgment of the interloper's approach, and then, following a couple of chesty groans that send steam billowing into the air, lowers its horns to feast again on a multihued salad bar of native brome.

Turner just saunters by, nodding with satisfaction. He gave the beast its home.

Confronting a shifting wind now, the breeze blows directly into his face, and his eyes water. At this senescent stage, thanks to therapy, he is trying to absorb whatever finds him *in the moment*—forcing himself, often against his stir-crazy habits, to shed his notorious restlessness. To slow down.

Pausing to catch his breath, he peers southward. A weather inversion has pressed cirrus clouds down tight upon the Spanish Peaks. He has never taken these mountains for granted, not since he first spied them. It was in the year leading to his fiftieth birthday, the year he took up fly fishing, the year he courted his third wife, the year that he believes he started to let go of others' expectations of him.

Back around that time, during an interview with a local newspaper reporter in Bozeman, he had insinuated how he intended to escape his fishbowl existence in the city known as the Big Peach. He's always loved Atlanta, but he was tired of being the Mouth of the South. He aspired to be somebody else. "I bought [this] place [the Flying D Ranch] to get away from people. If I wanted to be around people, I would have stayed in Atlanta. The only way to get access to a place like this is to do like I did and work hard forty or fifty years and make twenty-two million dollars and then go buy it for yourself. Me. I want to live as far away as I can from everybody. I am becoming a hermit. There is nothing wrong with that."

We will visit the hermit allusion again, later. But now consider Turner's geographical coordinates in his dream. All of the capacious expanse between the Spanish Peaks and where he stands is within the actual deed to the Flying D, one of the finest ranches in the world, a property that he often says, in hindsight, radically changed his life. It renewed him. Once, he regarded the D as a trophy to mark his financial success; now it's simply *home*—and it's wilder and less cluttered with the trappings of a human footprint than when it first became his. He feels belonging.

Turner returns to the march, and even in reverie he feels sweat beads on his forehead. He strides methodically, head down, watching his feet, careful not to trip on slippery scree.

And then once again there *it* is. A wail catches his ear. He halts. The sound hovers in the air and blends into the howling wind. He twists to survey the misty panorama. Had he just been hearing things?

In his peripheral vision, he sees an advancing blur. Bearing down, ambling downwind in a trot that will intersect his path, the black figure obviously does not know he's there.

His first thought? *Grizzly*. His second thought: I am unarmed. The anxiety shocks him nearly awake. But then a split second later, he notes this animal's size and shape, its coat the tint of coal. Not a bear but a large wolf.

The wolf walks toward Turner, and doesn't halt until it has ventured close. Seeing Turner, it freezes, holding perfectly still. Each creature studies the other, awaiting a sign of intention. Turner is close enough to see even the moistness on the animal's nostrils. The way the wind ruffles its fur. The glow of its eyes.

"Okay wolfie," he says softly in his baritone southern twang. "Okay fella, tell me what you want to do. Tell me what you're thinking, boy. Has anyone ever told you that you're a handsome looking wolf? I'm not going anywhere. Now, it's your move."

A *real* moment—an encounter strikingly similar to that one—will soon be counted among Turner's most memorable accomplishments: his first bona fide run-in with a wild wolf at short range, and it will take place behind his house. For years, he had wistfully mused about how such a meeting with *Canis lupus* might come to pass on land he owned. He *thought* it would occur, but feared it might not happen before he died. "I can relate to wolves," he would simply say when friends asked him why he would welcome lobos on his back doorstep.

Consummate underdogs forced to navigate the fringes of society—archetypes of controversy, beloved and reviled, charismatic and misunderstood—Turner holds wolves to be, along with bison, his totem creatures. "We only malign people and things we don't understand," he says. "We won't harm the things that we regard as our friends. Sometimes, we just need to change the perspective on who our friends, and who our enemies, are."

Later on that day in 2008, having woken from his wolf dream, Turner waded into a Montana stream, casting for trout. Global financial markets *were* teetering on the brink of collapse, raising the specter of a coming Great Depression. Lehman Brothers, weeks before, was already gone. And Turner had just received a phone call, telling him that he'd lost millions in the meltdown of a bank. Though distracted, all he could think about was the provocative image of the wolf.

Biologists whom Turner employs have advised him that in the remote possibility he ever stumbles upon a lobo or mountain lion on his forays at close range, he should raise his voice, shout at the top of his lungs to assert a dominant presence. He doesn't know why, but in his dream he refrained from adhering to the protocol. He wasn't afraid. He remembered why he had craved surges of adrenaline as a young businessman and mariner stalking opportunity.

Soon enough, Turner will see a lone wolf in the flesh barely a stone's throw from where this one visited him in his sleep.

———

It is twenty years earlier. Nothing about *this* moment could be misconstrued as imaginary. Ted Turner's pedal is pressed to the metal. He's antsy, in a bother about how the day is getting away from him. He is on the run, full throttle, fueled by high-octane kinetic energy. As an instinct of survival embedded in his constitution, he will not allow himself to remain in one location longer than half a week. He is already anticipating his next move.

His *modus operandi* is never stand still. Don't over-romanticize that which cannot be undone. Don't stand idle because it could allow feelings of personal pain to catch up. Don't dwell on the past. Keep it at a safe distance by remaining in motion. Go. Go. Go.

Always, the Turner of midlife is gazing forward into a future he believes he can create as a self-made man. He is known for being madcap yet brilliant, using intuition to uncannily look around corners and recognize business opportunity. He never edits the verbal articulation of his thoughts. He is direct and blunt and candid. He is not encumbered by worries of political correctness. He has caused even world leaders to blush.

Yes, one of his trademark idiosyncrasies is being unpredictable, at least for those who think they have him pegged. Turner, at this moment, is behind the wheel of a white Land Rover fishtailing on a wet clay road in the Red Hills of the Florida panhandle. Also in the vehicle, his youngest son, Beau, and his chief caretaker at Avalon Plantation, Mr. Frank Purvis. Turner's in a hurry. He's crooning the refrain to Andy Williams's song, "Born Free." For good reason.

Giddy, he wants to inspect the designated "release site" before darkness falls. With an early plane to catch out of Tallahassee in the morning, he wants to see the location so that when he's back in Atlanta or on the road in business meetings, he can visualize in his own mind how *the experiment*, his experiment, went down.

Turner does not recall, in hindsight, exactly when the notion of conducting this trial and error project first entered his head. But he was convinced he could succeed doing anything. In the late 1980s, his daring financial bets on cable television, the SuperStation, CNN, and media properties are paying huge dividends. He's rolling in cash and is iconic, in a catbird seat. On a personal level, unbeknownst to most of his business associates, he also has hatched a little plan that he does not intend to circulate for public consumption. He has instructed his property managers to turn loose, in the coming days, two cougars and three black bears into the Avalon backwoods.

The animals are part of a menagerie he assembled at another holding, his historic Hope Plantation in the South Carolina low country near Jacksonboro. Like George and Joy Adamson liberating Elsa the African lioness and restoring her to native ground in Kenya, Turner has similar aspirations for his big cats and bruins.

"We're going to liberate them, guys," he tells Purvis and his son. "They may not have been born free, but they're gonna live free."

He is well aware of the plight of the Florida panther battling extinction, and the fact that cougars have been eliminated from most of the South by centuries of human settlement. He has come to realize that while his pet animals in their caged compounds at Hope are fascinating novelties, and certainly he enjoys showing them off to guests, here they could have an impact. They could bring a raw untamed edge to his quail hunting preserve. And if they propagate, all the better. Believing his deeds noble yet benign, what would it hurt to try? After all, he has *the land.*

⌐⌐⌐

In early March 1988, the plan was executed. The cats and bears were set loose to wander around Avalon. Turner was pleased. The large mammals had never demonstrated any aggression toward people so he wasn't worried they would eat anybody. He felt empowered as he sat in his office in Atlanta. And then the phone rang: One of the cougars had been struck and killed when it tried to cross a highway, shocking the motorist who ran into it. The trail led back to Turner.

"It created quite a little buzz in these parts. Word travels fast," recalls Leon Neel, an internationally recognized forester who specializes in longleaf pine restoration at Tall Timbers Reserve in Georgia, and was then working for Turner on a project at Avalon. "As well-intended as Ted was, I think he was told that you can't just go out and turn a lion loose. Ted so wanted to make Avalon as wild as he could. I think most everyone found it more humorous than anything. I think he was the first to ever try such a thing. I know he was sad, kind of heartbroken, when one of the cougars died."

The incident, because of who Turner was, made national news, running in papers from New York City to Los Angeles. Game wardens wanted Turner to come in for questioning. They interviewed his employees. Turner told authorities that they weren't to blame. They were only following his orders. He was charged with three misdemeanors, fined $1,500, and told in no uncertain terms that if he ever attempted a stunt like that again, he would go to jail. The remaining cougar was trapped and sent back to Hope; the bears were never captured.

Genuinely contrite, Turner says the episode opened his eyes, humbling him but fueling his convictions. He couldn't play God by flouting the law. But owning land gave him a license to act with an alacrity government doesn't possess. He just needed more land. Cougars were on the verge of being declared extinct in the Southeast. And efforts to save the Florida panther were encountering fits and starts. He vowed to himself that he would find a place where large animals could have enough room to wander, where they wouldn't be dodging cars on highways or getting accidentally shot or causing a ruckus. From then on, everything he did would be legit.

Looking back, Mike Phillips has a theory. Phillips is a former government biologist who supervised earlier federal reintroductions of red wolves to the southeastern United States and gray wolves in Yellowstone National Park. Today, he oversees the Turner Endangered Species Fund. Reflecting on Turner's action at Avalon Plantation, he says with a bemused expression. "Obviously, vigilantism is not the way to go and Ted knows it. You don't, with good intentions, just start dumping animals into the backcountry. That's not the way reintroductions are done from a scientific perspective. But you cannot fault his instincts. He sensed the loss of missing pieces and wanted to rectify it. He learned from the episode. If Ted is anything today, he's a man who likes to operate from a sound foundation of science because that's how you can achieve something that lasts."

What's insightful, Phillips notes, is that the incident didn't cause Turner to retreat but instead whetted his appetite. "I interpret it as Ted's ecological foreplay. Here you had a man who was so excited in seeing the power that he had because of his emotional connection to nature, with his opportunities created by television, and owning relatively big pieces of land. His environmental awareness was starting to soar and he wanted to make a difference," Phillips explains. "What happened at Avalon set the stage for what was yet to come. Ted looked west like so many others before him had for opportunity. As his fortune and land acreage grew, he became ready to engage in meaningful restoration and do it right, completely above board. He just had to think about how to take the next steps. I don't think anyone could have realized then how big they'd be."

PART I:

THE MAKING OF A GREEN CAPITALIST

CHAPTER ONE

Empire of Bison

"I am a market fundamentalist just as I know Ted Turner to be a market fundamentalist. But here's how I also understand the market. There are no free lunches. My conception of the free market is you own what you sell, pay for what you take, and choose what you buy . . . Most serious environmental problems involve a violation of all three of those market concepts in one way or the other. People take things that they don't pay for, they sell resources that belong to the commons, and they stick other people with buying things, such as pollution, they didn't choose to own. That is communism packaged under the façade of the free market. Ted is doing far more putting back into the land than he is taking. And he's certainly not asking for preferential treatment the way the cattle industry has with massive subsidies."

—CARL POPE,
FORMER EXECUTIVE DIRECTOR OF THE SIERRA CLUB

CLARENCE "CURLY BEAR" WAGNER HAD BEEN TOLD OFTEN THAT HIS face resembled the man on the buffalo nickel. He took it as high praise. A respected Blackfeet cultural historian, Wagner championed a number of social justice issues during his life. As a youth, he got involved with the fledgling American Indian Movement, joining activists who occupied

Alcatraz Island in protest of government treaties. Later, he fought to have the remains of native people, collected by anthropologists and stored in museums, repatriated to the earth. And he dug dirt on an archaeological project at the Flying D Ranch.

Curly Bear mused how odd it was that events in his life would lead to a convergence of shared passions with a famous businessman. Only in America, he said, could a kid who grew up poor on a reservation find a spiritual connection with a guy known to millions for doing the "tomahawk chop" on national television while rooting for a professional baseball team he owned called the Atlanta Braves.

"That Ted Turner . . . he's not your typical white man," he told me.

It is the summer of 1993. Wagner is next to Turner, who is saddled on a striking palomino horse. The hands of both men are crossed over their pommels. Wagner didn't have to trailer his ride down from Browning, Montana, for the day. A pinto was provided for him by his host.

Native people led by Wagner have arrived, at Turner's invitation, to ceremonially harvest a bison at the Flying D Ranch and show Turner the myriad ways that the bison provides sustenance.

Peeling away from a makeshift encampment of tepees, Turner and Wagner ride to survey the sight. They trot up a hill and stop at the upper lip of a coulee. A ravine trails downward and away, veering into the very heart of the Flying D. Blanketing both sides of the gully across a vista of several hundred acres, a dispersing group of bison cows and calves. The seeds of what will become the largest private bison holding in America.

Wagner, though laconic, grunts his approval. He too imagined a view like this, based on stories told to him by his elders. His lineage in the Blackfeet Nation goes back as far as can be counted. It is possible that his ancestors could have wandered across this exact dale in the years before America was a country. Neither man knows what to say.

Turner is uncomfortable with long awkward pauses in conversation. He will often speak up to fill the void. He and Wagner listen to the sounds of the herd, punctuated by bison calves of the year bawling for their mothers. Without having to admit it, they realize that what was once lost has now been restored, and in a way that many believed could not have happened.

"I imagined this," Turner finally says, his voice trailing off. "Years ago. Before CNN, before TBS, before any of it." He doesn't admit it out loud, but he attributes the making of the scene to kismet.

Turner's attachment to bison started during an admittedly lonely childhood. He was shuttled between Ohio, his birthplace, and boarding schools, as part of his father's regimen for toughening him up. He counts among his favorite memories those spent at a grandfather's farm in Mississippi, and later around the low country near Savannah, Georgia, and Charleston, South Carolina. He chased polliwogs, climbed trees, caught fish, let baby alligators swim in bathtubs, and hunted woodlots with a bb gun. "My closest friend, no matter where I got carted off to, was Jimmy Brown. He was a black man my dad hired to look after me. He had grown up in the back swamps. He was descended from Gullah slaves."

Brown shepherded Turner into the outdoors—and introduced him to sailing, hunting, fishing, and beachcombing. "I could disappear into it, and feel as if I wasn't missing out on anything else in my life. It was where I had my thoughts and not someone else's to answer to. It was one of the few places where I never felt *lonely*," he says.

The first word Turner ever uttered clean, according to his mother, was "pretty"—in response to seeing a butterfly. As a boy, he became a collector of trinkets, a habit that continues to this day. Among his prized possessions were buffalo nickels. He carried them in his trouser pockets. He would rub them together, hoping superstitiously they would give him magical powers and good luck. "Someday, I'm gonna . . ." he would say to himself, closing his eyes and making a wish. Looking back, he realizes the significance of the coins though he was never able to articulate it during the early decades of his business career.

On one side of the nickels was the profile of a bison and, on the other, the silhouette of a plains Native American brave.

Bison are animals that, in too many ways to count, reflect Turner's values, even his convictions on human rights, equality for women, and compulsions as an environmentalist.

"I would feel terrible whenever I went to the movies as a kid and saw a western [film]. The plots never changed. The cavalry or the cowboys would be killing off Indians, who were almost always portrayed as menaces, even though they were the ones trying to hold onto what they had. Nobody ever asked them *why* they were mad. What was it they did wrong, I wondered. They were victims, and I sympathized. Then I realized— I don't remember exactly how old I was—that the same kind of thing had happened to bison."

Turner started to critically ponder—and it's a question that still remains unreconciled—why a great country would deliberately slaughter the animals and the people that were featured on its money? Around the time he turned forty, he vowed that one day he would raise a few bison. "I was aware of the fact they were rare. I just liked the look of them. I've always had an interest in art and I would sketch pictures of them on paper. I mean, how can a person not be magnetized? I wanted to be the first guy on my block to show a few of them off."

But Turner was headquartered in Georgia. In 1976, before he had launched CNN and bought the historic Hope Plantation in South Carolina, he attended a sale of "exotic livestock" and bid on some behemoths coming through the chutes. That purchase altered the course of his life. His inaugural "herd" of bison, three animals strong, was turned out in a makeshift pasture surrounded by a humid cypress swamp. "It took a few years and a hell of a lot of reading before I gained an understanding of what their presence meant for the ecology of the American prairie," he says.

The conditions for raising bison, he soon realized, were not idyllic in the confined spaces. A lot has happened between then and now. Today, in this second decade of the twenty-first century, Turner, with around fifty-six thousand bison in his herd, maintains more of the animals than any person who has ever lived. Of the five hundred thousand bison now alive in the world (compared to, conservatively, thirty-five million that inhabited the United States and Canada prior to the Civil War), roughly one of every nine ranges on Turner lands. The Flying D alone has nearly five thousand, more than the entire bison population of nearby Yellowstone National Park.

Dan Flores has an air of sagacity. In the past, I've encountered the history professor at his cramped office in Missoula on the University of Montana campus and at symposia across the West. I also have a stack of books he's written. Over the years, he's been my go-to guy for sorting out the difference between western mythology, fabricated by Hollywood, and the less sanguine, often brutal, realities of Anglo-European conquest. With hair worn long and tied back in a ponytail, Flores has a walrus mustache and occasionally a beard, the style of which could have been worn by a member of Coronado's troop when it charged north out of Mexico.

In a word, Flores is a historical *revisionist*. "Ted Turner, now that's an interesting topic," he says. "But how will he be interpreted?"

Flores says that Turner has earned a place in history for what he's doing on this side of the Mississippi River. "As a land manager, you could almost describe him as an ecological Thomas Edison," he told me as we visited at a bison conference in downtown Denver. "That he selected bison shows how he thinks outside the box."

Flores does not utter bold overgeneralizations. Before continuing, he notes that it is important to take a moment and ponder the American West, the way generations of citizens have been taught to think about it in the classroom. Turner is not a figure cut from that cloth. "Who are the just and worthy heroes in the textbooks, whose names we can recite by heart?" he asks. Often venerated, Flores asserts, are the "smiteful voices of plunderers" —seldom the latter day healers who followed in the wake of destruction and attempted to put emptied, battered places back together again.

Three individuals over the last 150 years have become supremely synonymous with the American bison: William Frederick (aka "Buffalo Bill") Cody, who famously bragged that he killed thousands of buffalo and is associated with the near annihilation of the species carried out in the name of conquest and prosperity; zoologist William Temple Hornaday, headquartered at the Bronx Zoo, who collaborated with his friend President Theodore Roosevelt and other sportsmen to rescue bison from near extinction at the end of the nineteenth century; and Turner, now a fulcrum in an unprecedented movement to restore the animals to their former indigenous landscapes, starting with his own properties.

Flores says, "What I've come to appreciate about Turner is that there seems to be sophisticated logic informing his decisions. It doesn't matter how Turner started; it's what he has achieved that we need to be mindful of."

Cody has towns, landmarks, and the children of modern lifestyle pilgrims named after him. But for the sake of argument, how many people are conversant with his exploits? Cody's celebrity is based on a dubious achievement and legacy, Flores argues. He earned his colorful sobriquet by slaying, reportedly and by Cody's own estimation, 4,208 bison in a matter of months to feed frontier railroad workers. Later in life, Cody would state his regret how others following in his wake acted with a more insidious purpose to wipe the landscape clean of bison.

"Kill the buffalo and you subdue the Indians." This was the strategic maxim of US general William Tecumseh Sherman. And it is merely a western variation of Sherman's notorious military scorched-earth tactics that he wielded with no remorse as a Union Army commander in his march toward Savannah. Savvy to Sherman's ways, Cody and his contemporaries aided in eliminating bison as a way to deplete the commissary of native peoples. Replacing them, the new coin of the realm, beef cows. While there are innumerable virtuous traits associated with the middle of America as a breadbasket, history often avoids a reference to what's gone missing, Flores says.

Among William Hornaday's dying wishes in 1937 (the year before Turner was born) was to return bison to their rightful place. They had been, after all, the most populous large land mammal on the continent going back to the Ice Age, found eastward in the Carolinas, across the heartland to the Great Basin, and south to north ranging from Mexico to the start of Canada's boreal forest. Francisco Vásquez de Coronado encountered them in the desert and Alexander Mackenzie ran into them in the subarctic muskeg.

Ecologists say they dwarfed the spectacle of today's migration of wildebeest across the Serengeti Plain in Tanzania and Kenya. "Buffalo lived in vast herds that swept over the plains like fish in the sea," writes Tim Flannery in his book *The Eternal Frontier: An Ecological History of North America and Its Peoples*. Some of the groupings were so extensive that Anglo travelers passing through the big open country reported vistas unendingly covered, those same panoramas taking days to traverse all of the animals.

Yes, tens of millions of bison that had been sources of physical and spiritual soul food for Curly Bear Wagner's ancestors were reduced to mere scattered handfuls during Cody's lifetime. Lacking was any profound remorse until it was too late. Flores thinks of Turner as a kind of antipode to Buffalo Bill.

"We pretend as if the history of the West didn't begin until the Conquistadors arrived in the Southwest in the fifteenth century, or when Lewis and Clark passed through Montana in 1804," Turner says. "The natural story of the West is something much bigger and I think it holds important lessons. I've seen the kind of natural destruction that occurred with bison and Indians repeated around the world with different cultures and different abuses of nature."

Flores says America's future—certainly her relationship with nature—spins on how it comes to clearer terms with the past. "Who are the people in the West today who will be looked up to as heroes tomorrow? The reason I ask is that there's an undeniable political nature of history. When I do public talks, I often tell people that I can make a strong guess about how they vote if they will admit which of these two western figures they admire most: John Wayne, or John Muir."

He asks, why is an actor from Iowa who portrayed cowboys in the movies deified? Why is Muir, a real person, who led a conservative movement to save the redwoods and who supported the creation of national parks to serve as sanctuaries guarded against conquest, a partisan lightning rod?

Flores says his profession deserves part of the blame. "I think one of the answers explaining why some of America's population still considers the people who destroyed so much of American nature to be cultural icons is a fault of generations of historians who presented US history as a triumphant march across the continent."

A paragon in pushing for democracy around the world, America still is contending with the long dark shadow of how it treated its own native people and wildlife. Understanding why it happened is essential to preventing the same mindset from cycling back again.

"It sounds a little nuts to many of us, but in this view, Manifest Destiny—seizing the continent from its existing inhabitants, the wholesale depletion of wildlife for fun and profit—became a divinely inspired project," he says. "All sorts of crimes were thus glossed over because they represented inevitable positive gains on behalf of Jesus and civilization and the market. It still goes on. Wildlife was just collateral damage in this great enterprise. This has nothing to do with political correctness. Stewardship, human rights, respect for nature, have roots in the Bible and the

Constitution. What's needed, though, is an honest, adult conversation. I think that Ted Turner, by putting bison back on the land, is trying to broker a larger dialogue."

Flores says he would find it interesting if a new litmus test for assessing virtue were administered to young people: Would they consider Cody or Turner to be a more virtuous figure, and why?

———

In John Neihardt's classic *Black Elk Speaks*, shaman Nicholas Black Elk equates the plight of indigenous peoples to the loss of bison. Black Elk, a Lakota, was alive at the time of the Battle of the Little Bighorn, the assassinations of Crazy Horse and Sitting Bull, and the Wounded Knee Massacre, the latter resulting in part from the Ghost Dance, a spiritual belief that bison would reappear.

"I think I have told you, but if I have not, you must have understood, that a man who has a vision is not able to use the power of it until after he has performed his vision on Earth for the people to see," Black Elk told Neihardt.

Flores makes it clear that he is not attempting to stir up melodrama, or portray the former "media mogul" from Atlanta as a New Age figure, but he believes that Turner and his unmatched modern experiment with bison is Black Elk's words put into practice. "I think that what he is doing with his land and financial resources possesses far greater substance than his better known exploits in the media. This, to me, is what makes Turner 'the bison baron' an interesting character—far greater than anything Cody did."

———

Suppose hypothetically that an ambitious person wakes one morning with aspirations of becoming a *bison baron*—a title that has been bestowed upon Turner by the media.

Precisely what is required? How many animals does one need? How would it differ from being a land baron? Cattle? Oil? How does a rancher employ beasts as "ecological tools" to mend the terrain of former abuses even while trying to promote their conservation as a species, generating if one can, a profit, and delivering healthy food in a safe, reliable way?

The inquiry is presented to Russell Miller, the now-retired general manager of Turner's bison ranches. He stepped down in 2014 after more than a quarter century serving as Turner's right-hand man in the West. Few other ranch managers possess as much accumulated experience.

An English major in college (and occasional cowboy poet), with past lives as a farmer/rancher, agricultural loan officer, and land management consultant, Miller was there at the nebulous beginning of his boss's quest to amass a herd and unleash it as a tool in restoration ecology. Miller saw the experiment move from hypothetical boyhood reverie, based on aesthetics, to assuming substance on an ever-increasing land base.

And, in the beginning, he notes, there was chaos.

"I think that when you work for Ted, and when it involves something that touches him as personally as bison do, you get used to him thinking expansively," Miller says.

He recounts a strategic planning meeting with Turner around the conference room table on the top floor of CNN in Atlanta in the mid-1990s. With Turner's financial advisors in attendance, a meeting had been requested to determine Turner's goals for bison and the ranches—specifically how many animals and acres that Turner had in mind.

"Although he was reluctant to be pinned down, Ted finally asked, 'Well, how many bison could we run on one million acres?' A rough estimate was thrown out, and Ted seemed to be satisfied. The rest of us were relieved that we now knew, at least, where we were headed, which was into the realm of the unprecedented."

Turner wasn't finished ruminating. As he was leaving the room, he turned to the group and queried, "Oh, by the way, how many acres would it take to run one million *bison*?"

"Ted disappeared to another meeting, but his message was clear. We were on a journey, but we were not sure of our destination," Miller shares.

I joined Miller on tours of a few of those destinations that form a larger whole—ranches in Kansas, Oklahoma, Nebraska, and Montana. Turner values government, Miller says as we stroll across Turner's McGinley Ranch in the Sandhills of Nebraska. But he remains perpetually frustrated at the slow pace of bureaucracies and the legislative process of responding to problems. Turner's a do-gooder, Miller says, but he approaches many of the things he does through the instincts he sharpened as a businessman. When I bring it up with Turner himself, he says government and the marketplace, preferably with both working together to achieve virtuous results for society, are the only forces that can deliver change at the systemic level where it has the most impact.

With effusiveness, Turner says he loves national parks such as Yellowstone, but he believes that private landowners, being less hamstrung by politics, funding, and having to appease fractured public constituencies, can move much faster.

So, again, how did his "empire of bison" begin?

Miller says the foundational elements are no mystery. "Well, any good farmer or rancher will tell you: Before you can think about building a herd of any size, you must have a sufficient amount of land and available water; the land needs to have lasting, fertile soil for growing good grass; and for grass to grow you need an adequate amount of precipitation."

Of course, if you abuse one, he says, you harm the rest.

"This isn't revolutionary stuff. It's elemental; it's *evolutionary*," he says, repeating the ingredients again: Ample Land. Fertile Soil. Bountiful Grass. And Clean, Abundant Water. These are the holistic, agrarian building blocks that every rancher and farmer knows at the gut level if one has ambitions of persisting more than a couple of years. With bison, however, achieving the fullest complement of ecological effects requires operating *at scale*.

In Bozeman, Montana, where the western management headquarters of Turner's landholdings are based, Miller has file cabinets brimming with contracts and itemized profit and loss statements, topo maps of the Great Plains, and studies completed by the United States Geological Survey, colleges, and ag extension offices. He has pored over the information, examining historic rainfall and snowpack patterns, flow levels in rivers, studies of underground water tables, soil types, and lengths of growing seasons to try and narrow down the scope of places that meet those four parameters.

"Of course, as the best computer models project, climate change with shifting natural precipitation and hotter temperatures could turn everything on its head, disabusing us of what we think we know and count on," Miller says.

Turner's competitive advantage? Raising native species that, over thousands of years, have weathered fluctuations in climate. But Turner is worried that if temperatures rise as much as scientists expect, droughts and water shortages may become the new norm on the plains.

What started initially as a less than fully formed desire to give bison a home on the range blossomed into one of the world's most fascinating experiments in large mammal wildlife conservation. Turner's adventure with bison and the ranches he's using as laboratories are changing the way agrarians think about sustainable stewardship of grasslands, sharing habitat with predators and other wildlife, the role of locally grown crops in the burgeoning organic food movement, and humane treatment of animals raised for the dinner table.

The mission of Turner Enterprises Inc., the umbrella of Turner's ranching operation, is "to manage the land in an economically sustainable and ecologically sensitive manner while promoting conservation of native species."

It's not hands off, Miller says; it's light on the land as opposed to heavy-handed or industrial. "For the record," he notes, during a tour of the Z Bar Ranch in Kansas, "Ted's goal is not to turn bison into beef cows."

———

In 1992 Turner offered me his first visual reference of what he aimed to achieve with bison. I was at the Flying D at the time, interviewing him for a magazine story.

He and Jane Fonda were newlyweds. They had just built a new home on the ranch and had a layover in Montana amid a hectic schedule of travel. At the time, numerous kinds of provincial suspicions swirled in the rural western hinters about Turner and Fonda.

Danny Johnson, the Flying D's current foreman, was a local teenager when Turner and Fonda showed up in Montana. "I think people were looking for a reason to find fault in them. Jane had a reputation for protesting the Vietnam War and going to Hanoi. Ted was looked upon as a loudmouth. To be honest, I think much of the resentment stemmed from the fact that they were rich outsiders, settling upon a piece of land that all of us wished we could own."

According to some local residents, one of the greatest sins Turner committed, as an affront to "traditional" ranch culture, was selling off the beef cows that came with the Flying D and replacing them with bison, which were looked upon as odd, exotic animals. His coup de grâce was pronouncing to local reporters that cattle were dumber than bison; that they defecate all over themselves; that their hooves trampled the banks of streams in ways that were more harmful than bison; and that they were wimpier, less capable of withstanding the elements, demanding more coddling, artificial feed, and protection from wildlife predators than bison.

When I arrived, Turner's longtime aide-de-camp, a friendly and fit-looking woman named Karen Averitt, answered the door. Averitt, a yoga instructor and gourmet chef, is someone I've come to know fairly well over the years. She plays a role in Turner's life that cannot be exaggerated.

Along with the invaluable Debbie Masterson, Turner's executive assistant in Atlanta who succeeded Dee Woods, these three women, over a span of thirty years, have enabled Turner to be Ted Turner.

Besides managing his schedule in Montana, Averitt coordinates his outdoor activities, choreographs the arrivals and departures of a constant parade of guests, and, on top of it all, delivers savory sustenance for the events that form the highlights of every Turner day—lunches and dinners with friends. But more than that, Averitt and Masterson (and Woods before her) provide emotional coddling and support and stability for Turner, which are vital to his well-being. (Averitt's husband, Jim Averitt, is a nationally known musician and songwriter who, in Montana, helps make sure that the main house is shipshape and handles all of Turner's sizeable travel logistics on the ground.)

I had driven though a spring snowstorm and was running late, waylaid by a bull bison standing in the middle of the dirt road leading to the Turner-Fonda place. Miller had earlier warned me that tardiness could upset Turner and cause him to cancel the interview.

Despite the gossip in southwest Montana, Turner and Fonda had not erected a southern-style mansion equipped with a vanity pool in the backyard. Turner had, in fact, custom engineered a pond out back, which he presented to Fonda as a wedding present. He wanted it to serve as a sanctuary for marsh birds and a waterhole to attract wildlife they could watch from the porch. He worked with engineers so that its surface would perfectly reflect the summits of the Spanish Peaks mountains.

Their home—in contrast to the predominant style of Great Lodge trophy megamansions that have inundated Montana—was surprisingly cozy at 7,288 square feet. Built into the side of a slope, the discreet, unpretentious home site did not lord over its setting. "Before I selected this location, I considered more than half a dozen others and walked them," Turner would explain later. "I wanted the home to sit in deference to the natural beauty of the ranch, not for it to be a monument to me."

Past the doorway splayed across a wooden floor in the living room was a huge tanned bison rug. It was positioned in front of a fireplace column forged of rough native stone. The hearth crackled with flame. On the wall nearby was a stuffed moose head and next to it a massive, original painting by Thomas Moran. Down the hall were aquatints by Karl Bodmer and some 150-year-old high plains scenes by George Catlin.

Over by the south-facing windows, in front of sliding glass doors, a spotting scope was mounted on a tripod for surveying the countryside. Under a glass case nearby were arrowheads, pieces of wildlife bone, and skulls Turner and Fonda had found during hikes.

Meanwhile, across a ceiling beam hovered stuffed animal heads—a bighorn sheep, mountain goat, elk, mule deer, and flying mounts of pheasant and duck—all hunted by the sportsman and his wife. In remembrance next to those trophies was the cougar that had actually been part of Turner's menagerie at a plantation in South Carolina. (It was one of the cougars he attempted to release at Avalon Plantation.) After the cat succumbed to old age, it was preserved by a taxidermist. For Turner it's a reminder of what he's trying to achieve.

In the twenty years that have passed, some of those animals have been removed, symbolizing perhaps the profound, massive leap in thinking that has transformed Turner. Speaking to the couple's insatiable appetite for learning about the natural world, his bookshelves were lined with natural history classics, field guides, and videos of nature documentaries Turner financed for broadcast on TBS and CNN. Finally, on a coffee table, sat rows of photographs, Turner with family members and influential friends whom any student of world events at the time would instantly recognize: former US president Jimmy Carter and former Soviet president Mikhail Gorbachev, Jacques-Yves Cousteau, former Norwegian prime minister Gro Harlem Brundtland, baseball legend Henry Aaron, and others.

In the adjoining dining room with a long rustic banquet table in the middle, chandeliers made of wapiti tines, not crystal, hung from the ceiling, and everywhere windows offered a panoramic view.

Living up to his billing, Turner strolled into the room with frenetic energy. He had guests visiting that he planned to take downhill skiing, then possibly a Turner-led hike into the outback or horseback riding in a lower pasture. They would perhaps finish off the day with a wade in a trout stream.

It was a big interview for me. This was *Ted Turner*. A larger than life figure. He wore jeans, slippers, and a blue Oxford button-down shirt, he said simply, "Hi" with a loud throaty drawl, then reflexively extended a hand. "My name's Ted. What's yours?"

His signature mustache, inspired by actor Clark Gable, star of his favorite movie of all time, *Gone with the Wind*, balanced over his upper lip. His hair still had brown flashes. He looked me over, sizing me up. Although the day was still young in the interior of the outback, Turner was roaring ahead. You could describe his body language as swaggering. At sunrise without hat or gloves, he ventured into the storm on a brisk walk, part of his routine, ready for a sixteen-hour day mixing business, outdoor recreation, and entertaining. There was no delineation between career and avocation, fun and the office. Boundaries were abstractions. He fit the mold of a workaholic, and he was paying whatever price was necessary.

Another thing: Turner has always been a creature of habit. "Early to bed, early to rise, work like hell, and advertise," is a rhyme that defined his work ethic, a mantra taught to him by his father. Confirming his insistence on familiarity, at every one of his residences the same items of rustic wardrobe can be found in the closet. He sees virtue in packing light. Behind it all is a fear of being stranded too long in one place. This was the man who came charging into the living room.

"You can ask me *anything* you want and we'll see if I want to answer it. You got twenty minutes," he said. "*So shooot.*"

Twenty minutes? I had three pages of questions that I had assembled with editors on the other side of the country. I had been told I would have a full hour with Turner.

Fazed, I rifled through pre-prepared questions, scrambling to pare them down.

Five seconds elapsed.

Turner does not like lulls. Two additional seconds expired.

He loudly cleared his throat. "Okay, you got anything for me?"

Fumbling, I dropped my notepad.

Turner's forehead wrinkled, and he sighed.

Ten seconds had passed. Eleven. Twelve.

Turner now was clearly agitated. He cast a lion's glare. One fourth of a minute—fifteen seconds of his time—had expired.

The phone began ringing in the other room. No one was picking it up.

"Karen, could you get that?" Turner called. "It's probably Atlanta."

Averitt was temporarily beyond earshot.

"Karen?" he inquired again. No response. "Kay-ren?!" he repeated. Still nothing.

"KAR-EN!!" he shouted.

Silence.

Averitt, calmly, suddenly appeared. "Yes, Ted?"

"Would you get that?"

"Yes."

"It's probably Atlanta," he said to himself.

Turner listened to Averitt informing the caller that he was in the middle of an interview and would have to call back.

Turner looked at me again. "*Come on*," he said. "What do you have for me? I don't have all day."

With his notorious mercurial temperament, he was primed for a little rhetorical jousting. He had perfected techniques for deliberately putting journalists on edge. If he believed an interview was not going the way he wanted, he would make wisecracks or say something provocative to watch the journalist squirm. Or he might just walk out of the interview. I once saw him respond to a question from another journalist about his wife, Jane Fonda: What did he think about some people calling her a traitor for going to North Vietnam decades earlier? "You know what," he'd said then. "That's a dumb-ass question. I'm not going to dignify it with an answer. I love my wife. You can quote me on that. Too bad for you, you are done. That's my answer. Anybody else got something smarter to ask?"

In Turner's living room, I meekly floated my first question. An easy one, it angled before him like a clay pigeon at the skeet range. "Mr. Turner. You've removed all of the cattle from your ranch, taken down fences, shipped in truckloads of buffalo. You've ruffled the feathers of your neighbors by saying these animals—buffalo—are *better* for the land than beef cows. You've said they're more hygienic and cause less of an environmental impact. What are you hoping to accomplish?"

In control of the clock, Turner created his own pause. A squint crossed his face. He was aware that he was inflicting maximum discomfort.

His head started to move. He nodded. "Well, for starters," he began. "Call me Ted. Mr. Turner was my father. Another thing. God knows I don't like having to correct reporters. Being as smart and full of knowledge as y'all are. I know that most people call the animals 'buffalo' but the official scientific name, in case you didn't know it, is *bison*. I like to be accurate, don't you?"

He walked over to the picture window and bent to peer through the spotting scope. A half hour earlier, the Spanish Peaks had been cloaked behind a curtain of clouds. They now rose clear. Turner was proud of the scene; he owned it, after all.

The vision of what he explained gave him obvious internal joy, for he seemed to lighten up within and started, overtly, to relax. The intensity of his voice and demeanor turned noticeably softer.

Motioning toward his bison herd miles in the distance, which then numbered around twelve hundred, he said it wouldn't be long before the first crop of new calves arrived. They were out there surviving without hay brought in to artificially feed them, and they didn't even blink when a coyote passed by.

"Have you ever eaten bison?" he asked. "Pretty tasty. You ought to try it some time."

Drawing his thoughts back into the room, he gestured toward the Moran, Bodmer, and Catlin paintings. They had been rendered in the throes of the Wild West's last gasp. "Someday, I want my ranch to look something like those."

As the years would reveal, it wasn't physical exactness he was referring to, but the *mood* of the paintings. During his teenage years, Turner had been an amateur artist. He was a romantic, and visually oriented. He said he had compiled a list in his mind of the different wildlife species he'd already seen on the Flying D, and he named many of them—elk, moose, black bears, pronghorn, two kinds of deer, bald and golden eagles, osprey, coyotes. And added that he would eventually like to harbor grizzly bears and a pack of wolves. The chances of that happening seemed laughably remote.

He lamented how the American frontier had been transformed and tamed in less than 150 years. He walked to a table and held up a bison skull, perhaps a few centuries old, that he had found in the mud. He started to riff about the first three bison he ever owned. He grew animated, his posture looser. He espoused the time-tested virtues of bison, that they were hardier and better adapted to handle the harsh winters and hot summers on the prairie. They have less fat and lower cholesterol than most breeds of beef. They are delicious to eat and tender. Bison are better able to ward off predators. "And they are native to North America," he added, "which means they evolved in landscapes like this."

He didn't know it, but he was roughly a decade away from launching a restaurant chain bearing his name, and it would serve bison from his ranches, the first attempt to fully vertically integrate the flow of a native animal from its original habitat to the human plate.

Turner delivered on his promise for a twenty-minute interview, then said, "I've got a few more minutes, what do you say?"

That chat was the genesis of this book. I would come to write five more stories over the years, and with each one Turner would become more trusting, open up a bit more. We never talked about those topics that occupied the tabloids. His relationship with Jane wasn't of much interest to me. And while new biographies about Turner "the media mogul" came and went, nothing was being penned about those endeavors that were consuming far more of his time and resources. What about Ted the environmentalist?

Finally, after years of brushing off overtures from other writers, he consented to the idea of this book, though it took some time before he allowed me to probe his relationship with his father—a topic that those around Turner had warned me to avoid. In fact, that complicated, traumatic chapter could be considered both the lock and key in explaining why Turner was shifting his priorities away from media, even prior to the debacle at AOL Time Warner.

Almost twenty years after that hour-long visit in his living room, Turner's private property holdings in the United States have grown ten times in volume, hovering near two million acres, including three *estancias* in Argentina.

Turner is not the same person he was then, nor are his lands in the same condition as he found them. And whenever he's in the West, his friends say, he's also not the same person as he is in Atlanta.

"Instead of having his foot pressing the gas pedal to the floor and racing 160 miles per hour all the time as he did during the early 1990s, Ted is now going half that fast, which is still way over the speed limit for most human beings," says Turner's longtime friend, financial advisor, and confidant Taylor Glover. "Ted has switched into a different gear, down a different road."

During his halcyon days, Turner took hold of media assets and added value to them, using dynamic tension and an underdog's gatecrasher mentality as a motivating force. There was always an adversary to confront, always a competition going on within himself and against other entities, Glover says. In sailing, it was against other boats and crews. In television, the other networks. He once challenged his media rival Rupert Murdoch of News Corp. to enter the boxing ring to scrap on TV.

"He doesn't see the world that way anymore," Glover says. "He is much more self-reflective and focused on trying to bring people together. He's thinking hard about how he can contribute to resolving human challenges that involve issues far bigger than himself. These passions were always the most important things, but he didn't have the time to act on them."

⌒⌒

When Turner reached the half-century mark in 1988, he owned CNN and TBS, professional baseball and basketball teams, the MGM film library, a handful of properties in the Southeast, and an island. Nevertheless, he felt hemmed in. In his travels between Atlanta and Los Angeles, the inner West was regarded as a "fly-over" region. That perspective changed in 1987. He bought his first ranch, the Bar None, at Toston, near the birthplace of the Missouri River in Montana. At the recommendation of his son, Beau, he had started fly fishing as a way to relax. With a stream running through it, Bar None gave him a great stretch of casting water.

Turner's arrival in Montana coincided with a cultural shift occurring in Big Sky Country. Robert Redford was about to make his movie adaptation of Norman Maclean's novella, *A River Runs Through It*, transforming fly fishing into a national sensation. The film also accelerated a phenomenon that was quietly under way, the changeover of historic working cattle ranches into recreational investment holdings for millionaires and billionaires.

The Bar None whetted Turner's appetite for more land in Montana. He had heard stories of the Flying D from Rob Arnaud, who was working for him as caretaker at the Bar None. A fourth-generation Montanan, Arnaud was also an outfitter conducting commercial hunts on the public land next to the Flying D, and was familiar with its size and beauty.

A handsome, broad-shouldered spread, the Flying D rivals the King Ranch of Texas in mystique. It covers 170 square miles and straddles two counties, girded on one side by the Gallatin River and on the other by the Madison River, both famous blue-ribbon trout meccas. Despite being stocked heavily with cattle and conducting an intensive agricultural operation, the ranch was rumored to have sketchy profit margins. Turner asked the real estate brokers who had found him the Bar None, Joel Leadbetter and Jim Taylor of Hall and Hall, to determine if the Flying D might be available for purchase.

The owners, the Shelton family of Texas, granted a one-person exclusive listing for Leadbetter and Taylor to show Turner the ranch, even though it was "not for sale." However, they indicated a price for the ranch plus all cattle and machinery, a sum that seemed outrageous: twenty-two million dollars. Perhaps they never believed another rancher able to afford it would come forward. They were both right, and much to their dismay, wrong.

Turner was not another would-be rancher. Upon getting the opportunity, he drove through the "D" once, and was instantly smitten. He told Leadbetter, Taylor, and his attorney to do "whatever it took" to close the deal. There would be no dithering around. He correctly ascertained that the Flying D represented a once-in-a-lifetime opportunity.

After intense negotiations over contract details, not the least of which was the value of cattle and machinery, and overcoming sellers' remorse that constantly threatened to torpedo the purchase, the deal was closed. Turner paid $21 million cash and acquired all 107,000 acres, plus the cattle and machinery to operate a legendary ranch. The acquisition made headlines across the West and caused a ruckus. People in Montana only knew Turner for his "Captain Outrageous" reputation in the media. A pervasive fear, for some, was that he would turn the ranch into a massive real estate play, dividing it up and selling the pieces.

His first major decision was to retain the ranch manager, Bud Griffith. Griffith had worked on the Flying D for the Sheltons and, before them, the California-based Irvine Company. "I loved the property and just felt, 'Well, I'll go work for Ted Turner and work for the brand as I always have, no matter who the owner is,'" Griffith said. But Griffith was stunned when Turner issued an edict that bison would replace the D's thousands of cattle, a move that would make "the brand" obsolete. Turner said he would never sear a firebrand into the sides of his bison.

Further changes were already planned. Under decades of intensive grazing by beef cows, both by the Sheltons and Irvine Company, the Flying D suffered from a litany of impacts. Some sections of creek bottom were mud holes. Riparian areas and uplands were denuded of vegetation. The bison would be managed in such a way as to lessen these impacts. "I had never been around bison before and I didn't know a lot about them," Griffith says, chuckling at his own naiveté. "I had no idea what was going to happen next. I got the impression it's just what happens when you work for Ted Turner. He keeps things hopping."

Turner also ordered Griffith to tear down interior barbwire fences that he and other ranch hands had spent decades erecting and maintaining. Down, too, came power poles and lines, corrals, and outbuildings. Turner put a halt to irrigated hay production on an interior portion of the ranch. That portion of ranch had yielded upwards of 1.5 tons of hay an acre but had pulled water out of the streams. Collectively, this was perceived by some of the traditionalists on the ranch as an order to disavow tradition, to turn their backs on their own sweat equity and the codes of the cowboy way.

Turner wanted a free-ranging bison herd within the confines of the ranch, which meant he had to build a perimeter fence to contain his bison. But first he had to locate animals to buy. An old friend of his, Maurice Strong, whom Turner had met through his establishment of the Better World Society and connections to the United Nations, happened to own a ranch in Colorado. Strong recommended a man, Brian Ward, who had experience in the buying and selling of both bison and cattle. Together with Russ Miller, Ward tried to discreetly put word out that Turner was ready to buy some bison. It ended up being one of the worst kept secrets in the New West.

Several months after Turner's first call to start buying, Ward helped facilitate the purchase of one hundred bison from the National Bison Range. They were seed stock. Ward was on hand to watch the first convoys of semi-trailer trucks arrive at the Flying D. As the doors were opened and the clanking of hooves could be heard moving down the metal runways, he remembers thinking to himself, realizing it was a massive understatement: "This should be interesting."

Turner's recolonizing animals charged out of the open metal doors and away from the semis. They got out a ways and stopped, looked warily toward their human liberators, and sensing no harassment, bowed their heads to eat. It was an inspiring sight and at the same time anticlimactic.

"I was so excited," Turner says. "Part of me couldn't believe it was happening. I had goose bumps." He had similar feelings a few years later as he and Wagner sat on their mounts.

It had been well more than a century since the last bison was spotted in this corner of the Gallatin Valley. "I would love to tell you that we knew what we were doing, but in those early years, we were more or less making it up as we went along," Miller says. "I know it sounds hard to believe but in terms of scale of land and size of the herds, no one had done with bison what Ted had in mind."

To illustrate, Miller describes a recent dinner conversation with Turner. "Ted asked if I had any idea when I started with him over two decades ago how big all of this would become? I told him I had no clue. And he replied, 'Neither did I! But hasn't it been fun?' To which I responded, 'Absolutely.'"

In the early 1990s, during a tour across the ranch, I rode with Griffith in a bouncy pickup across the rutted dirt backroads of the ranch. The notes scribbled in my notepad are jumbled but they reveal the essence of the conversation. Griffith expressed dubiousness about Turner's sanguine assertions about bison. He was not happy and didn't believe the bison experiment would work. He stopped short of disparaging his boss, though he was careful not to give me the impression he was an enthusiastic admirer of the animals.

Bison could be unruly, were far less docile than the cattle Griffith was accustomed to, and were dangerous if one wasn't careful in moving through their space. Bulls were known to gore a horse or rider if one ventured too close.

But Ted's feelings about cattle were just as negative. He said they weren't majestic and needed pampering compared to bison, that wildness has been bred out of them, that they were dumb and trashed trout streams by eating all the vegetation and turning streamsides into mud bogs. Neighboring ranchers said it wasn't the domestic bovines that were the problem but how they were managed.

Accustomed to speaking his mind, Turner got himself in hot water with the livestock industry when he demeaned cattle. "The negativity erupted volcanically because Ted is very vocal," Griffith said. "I went to Russ Miller and said Ted needs to back off with his harsh comments about the livestock community and his perception of cattle. We went to

Ted, but Ted said, 'I'm raising bison, not cattle, and look at it this way, every time they complain they're giving us a lot of free advertising for what we want to do.'"

Such pugilism may have worked well in battles Turner waged against media rivals and drumming up publicity for his sports teams, but it didn't sit well in Montana. One morning, Griffith found a bison that had been shot dead.

"Ranchers always talk about what they do on their land is nobody else's business but their own, as long as they're not hurting their neighbors," Turner told me at the time. "Okay, I can live with that. What have they got against me? They've never met me. What have they got against bison? What I'm doing isn't impacting them. How can they judge me if they don't even know who I am?"

Jim Peterson, a cattle rancher from Buffalo, Montana, who oversaw the Montana Stockgrowers Association and later became president of the Montana State Senate, was not amused. "He [Turner] says things that make a guy with a cowboy hat on his head want to scream," he said at the time. He later reflected back on the conflict: "I hate to use the word ridiculous, but it's not far off the mark. Ted was the new biggest guy on the block. The approach we took as stockgrowers is, 'This guy needs some firsthand education.' We made an attempt to reach out to him and set him straight."

The entire stockgrowers board arrived at the Flying D in spring 1994 and spent a day with Turner, Griffith, and Miller in the field—at Turner's invitation. "It was more valuable than anything we did," Peterson said. "And it was educational both ways. Ted had some romantic notions about bison, and he spoke passionately about why he thought they deserved to have a larger place in the West again. He said there seemed to be a bias against bison. We could respect that perception. At the same time, he made some pretty wild extrapolations about cattle. Depending upon what you want your outcomes on the land to be, animals need to be managed.

Even deciding not to manage them, and I don't care what anybody says, is a form of management."

An oft-stated concern from neighboring property owners was that bison might break through the fences and get on their lands. Turner erected fences that kept bison inside the Flying D behind a perimeter fence and yet enabled elk, deer, moose, and pronghorn to move freely back and forth between the ranch and adjacent national forest and other public and private lands.

Some professors in the college of agriculture at Montana State University dismissively told students that Turner's maneuverings with bison were merely experimental—the muses of a hobbyist—and predicted they wouldn't last. The bison's time, they lectured, had come and gone. So would Turner's.

Turner was frustrated. Even though cattle culture was, at most, three or four generations old, people treated it as inviolate. Inside the Flying D, his expanding bison herd was left to wander unshepherded. Bison were indeed hardier than cattle, better able to withstand extreme weather, and they required less babysitting. They didn't depend on the same levels of supplemental feed as cattle, and weren't injected with hormones and antibiotics to help them grow and ward off diseases; they weren't as vulnerable to coyotes, bears, and mountain lions. The females didn't need help giving birth to calves.

By the mid-1990s, a growing herd of fifteen hundred bison had fanned across the Flying D. But they weren't as benign as Turner had presumed; their grazing patterns weren't uniform. They mowed down grasses on some hillsides but not others; they cut trails through the river bottoms and muddied some of Turner's prized fishing areas. Despite all of their operational advantages, Turner realized that if he wanted to achieve a fuller range of desired effects, especially in terms of restoring the health of the cottonwood and willows lining the trout streams, his bison would have to be gently directed.

It meant putting back up some interior fences. When Turner did that, cowboys on call-in radio shows and in letters to the editor in Montana newspapers gleefully accused Turner of backpedaling. Stockmen sensed that Turner was vulnerable to a counterattack. Peterson and the stock-growers invited him to speak at their annual convention in Billings. He accepted. Standing room only, it was among the best-attended cattle meetings in the history of the organization. Many came hoping to hear Turner eat crow.

Turner brought Fonda. Russ Miller advised them that they were entering a room with cattle producers carrying pent-up anger, not only for Turner's earlier remarks but Fonda's involvement with the anti-war movement. Fonda did not want to cower.

The introduction of Turner was made. Some in the audience snig-gered. When he stepped to the podium, he immediately uttered a self-deprecating joke and shot from the hip with a confession: He had been partially wrong about some of his generalized assertions pertaining to bison and cattle. Both animals, he said, need to be husbanded with resource stewardship objectives in mind. As much as he hated fences, he acknowledged a few were needed. Up and down the smorgasbord of plant life that is the Flying D, he learned that bison would congregate, if left to themselves, around certain grasses and not others; they would gobble up "the dessert and not the dinner," as he put it.

Turner also spoke to a perception. Montana, and the West in gen-eral, had a reputation of attracting wealthy outsiders who made no attempt to be part of local communities. He paid higher property taxes because bison were worth more. He spent hundreds of thousands of dollars each year locally buying equipment and supplies for his proper-ties. He assured the room that he had no intention of being an absentee landowner. Any problems with his bison breaking through fences, he said, should be blamed on him. If people had complaints, his number was in the phone book.

He told them he knew that ranching is hard work and that raising cattle is just as legitimate as surrounding himself with bison. "But I must say," he quipped, "that you're missing an opportunity to make some good money. I'm betting on bison."

Mea culpa delivered, he used the pulpit to speak of his own green values. He was determined that the Flying D and his other ranches would be left in better ecological condition than when he found them. And he expressed his wish to one day have wolves on his ranches. And, winking, he said he would welcome grizzlies as long as they didn't eat any people. He confirmed that his ranch hands had been instructed not to shoot coyotes, and he had put a moratorium on killing rattlesnakes unless someone was in imminent peril.

He addressed all kinds of apocryphal rumors, including one that he allegedly gave federal wildlife managers the go-ahead to capture and loose troublesome wayward grizzly bears—"the meaner the better" on a corner of his property. According to these rumors, Turner welcomed man-eating bruins because they'd serve as a deterrent to any would-be trespassers.

As for his trout streams, he confessed that he had a "little beaver problem." The rodents were eating all of the new willows he had planted as part of his riverside restoration. He had ordered some beavers trapped and removed. They would be kept away until the riparian corridor had sufficiently healed.

Like his cowboy counterparts, he told the stockgrowers that he enjoyed riding horses, hunting, and fishing. He said that Fonda had learned to hunt, and had shot a deer, helped clean it, and proudly ate it with friends. Turner espoused his affection for Montana, and suggested that he would run his own ranch his way, and not criticize others for having their own way of doing things. Afterward, as an expression of his contrition, he took out his checkbook and became a lifetime stockgrowers member.

"The thing I remember most, sitting at the table with Ted and Jane, was how nervous they were," Peterson says. "They were outside their comfort zone and in the middle of the lion's den. Everybody politely listened to what he said, and you have to remember that his bride was as controversial a figure as he was. I give him credit for being candid and straightforward. I wouldn't call him disarming."

Half of the membership told Peterson afterward that it had been a positive encounter and the organization needed to have that kind of communication more often. "A significant fraction of others were still mad and didn't have their negative perception of Turner altered in any way. He had insulted their pride," Peterson said. "A small vocal fringe said it was completely inappropriate to even have him in the room. Over the years, the level of tension hasn't faded; nobody has forgotten those days. But I can tell you it was probably one of the most eagerly anticipated conventions we ever had. I give them both a lot of credit for showing up. Others wouldn't have had the courage."

Now, decades later, Peterson says that Turner has changed the way that cowboys think about bison. Observed Bud Griffith, "I know a lot of ranchers who don't have the courage to admit when they make a mistake. Their ego won't let them do it. Ted wasn't afraid. What he always told me is that by being bold sometimes you're gonna fail. When you do, be big enough to acknowledge it and be smart enough to learn."

"Ted dreams large, but he is a realist. He's highly attuned to the nuances of weather and climate," Russ Miller says.

The arid West, with its low precipitation and humidity, represents unique ranching challenges. Where forty acres is often seen as the minimum amount of acreage needed to support a family east of the Mississippi, the geography west of the 100th meridian typically requires a full section of land—640 acres. Russ Miller says that in the Sandhills of Nebraska, where Turner has five ranches, it takes twenty to twenty-five acres to sustain a cow and calf. And at Turner's Armendaris

Ranch in New Mexico, ranching is conducted according to the adage of one cow per section per inch of rainfall, or approximately 120 acres per cow and calf.

"Ted is always calling in, inquiring about the depth of the snowpack and the amount of rainfall," Miller says. "He keeps an eye on the soil and the grass. He's not willing to cut corners and defer maintenance on infrastructure . . . He isn't succeeding at ranching because of his money. He has common sense."

Turner entered the commercial bison business because he wanted to prove it would be economically self-sustaining. "One of the common misperceptions about Ted . . . is that he's so rich he doesn't care about profit and loss with his bison operation. But let me tell you something about Ted Turner," Miller notes. "He does not like to lose money, no matter what business he's in . . . He always says that nothing lasts if it isn't economically sustainable."

When the Flying D ran cattle, it supported seven to eight thousand head. Now it supports around five thousand bison. Turner never has his ranches stocked to full capacity. He builds in a margin of error so that each year certain pastures are rested and others are allowed to recover, especially after years of below-average precipitation. And he makes sure there is enough grass available to feed the public wildlife that roam across the ranch, including an elk herd that fluctuates in size between sixteen hundred and two thousand. When Turner first took ownership of the ranch, there were only hundreds of elk on the property. The previous owners treated them as competitors with their cattle.

"Turner is dealing in large enough numbers—land acreage available to him and the size of his bison herd—in order to be more commercially viable than anyone else could ever hope to be," says rancher and politician Peterson. Envy? Sure there's a lot of that. It's what makes him stand out and sometimes what turns him into a target for criticism. What matters is how he treats the land and nobody can take issue with him for that."

Turner's bison herd is now self-perpetuating. He hasn't bought an animal in decades, although he has steadily increased his land holdings. "I know Ted cultivated a reputation for shrewdly negotiating media deals, but when it comes to buying land, and him knowing what its ownership meant to the families putting it up for sale, he's always insisted that we be fair," Miller says. "I don't think I need to elaborate. It's obvious. Land touches Ted at a deeply emotional level . . . He really does view steward-ship—doing well by the land—as a sacred obligation."

Turner is not a micromanager who hovers. He's not like Steve Jobs was at Apple. His employees and colleagues don't fear him. His genius resides within his uncanny knack—call it a sixth sense or maybe simple gut instinct—for finding the right people to help him carry out visualizations that sometimes, in the beginning, only he can see.

Three of Turner's longest serving ranch managers in the West are Steve Dobrott, Dave Dixon, and Tom Waddell. Dixon, who today over-sees Turner's 13,343-acre Snowcrest Ranch on the Ruby River, is a vet-eran Montana ranch manager who had worked on the Flying D. Dobrott and Waddell are former federal and state wildlife biologists who over-see ranches straddling both sides of the Rio Grande in New Mexico. Dobrott's charge is the 156,000-acre Ladder Ranch, and Waddell's the 358,643-acre Pedro Armendaris Ranch. Add in the 593,000-acre Ver-mejo Park Ranch on the flanks of the Sangre de Cristo Mountains, and well more than half of Turner's holdings are contained in the state that calls itself the Land of Enchantment. All have bison.

In area, Turner's portfolio of land covers 3,125 square miles, spread across those fifteen ranches, five plantations in the Deep South, a coastal barrier island, a trio of estancias in Argentina's Patagonia, a scattering of residential retreats, and an office building crowned by a penthouse in the heart of downtown Atlanta. In the latter, on Luckie Street, a Ted's

Montana Grill restaurant takes up the ground floor with solar panels over the parking lots.

Were Turner's puzzle pieces assembled and placed in a single linear strip of real estate one mile wide, they would span the entire continental United States west to east. If the strip were a quarter of a mile wide, it would be longer than the Great Wall of China; if it were one-eighth of a mile across, the thickness of two city blocks, it would wrap around the Earth.

"What you have to understand about Ted is that many of his endeavors back in Atlanta are examples of him thinking with his head," Waddell tells me. "Out here, in the West, these are examples of him thinking and acting with his heart."

In 1992, Turner and Fonda were entertaining the possible purchase of the historic Gray Ranch. They contacted Dobrott because he had helped to caretake the spread for seven years prior to joining the US Fish and Wildlife Service as a wild quail expert. After Turner passed on buying the Gray, the Ladder came on his radar screen and he enlisted Dobrott, along with Miller and Ward, to inspect it for him.

"The Ladder is, per acre, the finest example of wildlife diversity left in the state. I did not recognize this when I first came to the ranch, but I did discover that this property was a wildlife biologist's dream world," he says.

Dobrott offered an enthusiastic report on the Ladder to Turner and Fonda. Shortly thereafter, he was offered the manager's post. After the purchase was finalized, the couple arrived to inspect the property. The next morning, before sunup, Turner eagerly arrived on Dobrott's doorstep, telling him to put on his hiking boots and take along a pad of paper. It was time for a trek.

His new boss, Dobrott says, had an agenda for how they were going to make the place better than they found it and heal the rolling grasslands of decades of abuse attributed to overgrazing by cattle. They high-tailed with Turner in the lead, straight up a perilous slope of cracked volcanic rock to reach a ridgeline overlook with a five-hundred-foot lethal drop-off on the side.

"I dutifully followed, taking notes along the way," Dobrott says. "After quite a hike filled with multiple 'yes sirs,' we came to a sudden halt. Ted abruptly realized, after enthusiastically gesticulating, that he had led us to the edge of a cliff."

Perched above a chasm, Turner smiled at Dobrott, admired the beauty, and then said, "Oh, maybe you had better lead from here."

"Years later, I thought about how metaphoric the incident was," Dobrott explained to me.

"In his wisdom, Ted leads us all to a precipice of unimaginable responsibility, and then hands over the reins to his caretakers to go forth and fulfill his vision for each property. He knows where he needs to go and he enlists others to accompany him there. It's the same with us as it is with Tim Wirth at the UN Foundation, Mike Finley with the Turner Foundation, and Sam Nunn at the Nuclear Threat Initiative."

Dobrott notes that Turner has amazing recall. His daily life inundates him with financial numbers and statistics relating to his investments, considering proposals for erecting alternative energy arrays, scenarios involving nuclear arsenals, global population trajectories, the number of humans residing in poverty, and the profit-loss statements at his restaurants.

"But out of the blue he will remember down to a specific property how much gas is being used in the vehicles and its corresponding carbon output, the number of bison cows and calves on the ranch, the going rate for bison on the market, and the names of ranch hands," Dobrott says. "Very often, he asks questions that he already knows the answer to."

He pauses, then adds, "He can be hard, kind of obstreperous at times. He has a big ego in that he's proud of his accomplishments, but he isn't threatened by people who know more about subjects than he does. He is a listener, and osmosis is how he learns. Working for Ted, it's not the potential fall that will kill you. It's the personal disappointment of feeling sometimes like you've failed him that hurts. Loyalty develops when people like him believe in you. I don't mean to get too flowery, but he inspires all of us by showing us a view of endless possible horizons, then allows you the freedom to reach a greater height than you thought possible."

Very often, he adds, they also stumble upon startling surprises.

After Turner acquired Vermejo Park Ranch, counted among his new assets was a small and somewhat scraggly herd of bison that inhabited upper-elevation meadows near a geological formation called Castle Rock.

Miller thought those bison, because of their smaller size and unknown health, were expendable, and could be supplanted by bison from other Turner ranches. He consulted Brian Ward, and a recommendation was forwarded to Turner to sell them or turn them into steaks. Miller admits his mistake now: "Ted's response was, 'No, let's keep them.' He wanted us to hold tight and do a little more investigation."

Geneticists at Texas A&M University, led by Dr. James Derr, went to work tracing the Castle Rock herd's provenance. The trail led back to, of all places, Yellowstone National Park. These animals turned out to quite possibly represent one of the few bison herds in existence with no, or at least no detectable, levels of cattle gene introgression. In other words, pure bison.

At the end of the nineteenth century, after tens of millions of wild bison had been reduced to hundreds of individuals in all the West and Canada, the few that remained were often rounded up, sometimes by conservation pioneers, and sometimes to experiment in cross-breeding them with cattle. Recognizing the bison's attributes, the intent ironically was to try and produce hardier beef cows. Although some cross-breeding was successful, development of "upgraded cattle" was not, and the experiments were abandoned.

Unfortunately, a genetic legacy of these experiments has survived through successive generations of bison that exist today. Sadly, many still carry cattle genes in their genetic makeup. Researchers at Texas A&M University have developed technologies to identify both cattle nuclear genes (inherited form both parents) and cattle mitochondrial genes (inherited only from the mother) in these otherwise normal looking bison. Regrettably, almost all bison in public and private herds are now known to be contaminated with either cattle nuclear or mitochondrial genes or in some cases both, Derr says.

Scientists believe only a few existing bison herds were never subjected to these hybridization experiments. To date, no evidence of cattle genes has been found from isolated bison in Yellowstone National Park, Elk Island National Park in Canada, or the Henry Mountains bison herd in Utah (which is thought to be exclusively derived from Yellowstone National Park animals). Also included in this exclusive group is a private herd belonging to Turner. Another entity trying to build a pure genetic herd is the American Prairie Reserve. Turner's Castle Rock herd at the Vermejo Park Ranch, which has existed on this landscape for over 60 years and has expanded to over 1,500 animals, is distinguished by its lineage.

Not with standing his strong commitment to bison conservation, the majority of the more than 50,000 bison owned by Turner are found in his production herds. While it is currently not possible to remove all the cattle nuclear genes from these animals (estimated at less than 1% of the total genes in each animal), researchers at Texas A&M University have developed rapid and reliable technologies to identify animals with cattle mitochondrial DNA from a single tail hair follicle. At significant cost and with substantial effort, Turner is actively reducing the number of bison in his production herds that have cattle mitochondrial DNA. Compared with nuclear genes, cattle mitochondrial DNA is estimated to be present in about 4% of the animals in these herds. The goal is to completely eliminate these cattle genes in all Turner herds over the next few years. Along the way, excess Castle Rock animals are being selected to supplement the breeding stock on these production ranches in addition to genetic testing of all animals selected for breeding stock. In order to further protect the genetic integrity of his herds, animals that test positive for cattle mitochondrial DNA are sold.

Turner also realized that preserving bison was not just a matter of placing animals on properties and allowing them to thrive, but also of taking steps to insure the long term protection and conservation of this uniquely American wildlife species, says Dr. David Hunter, who serves as Turner's on-staff wildlife veterinarian. Turner also partnered with researchers at Texas A&M University who are involved in a genome sequencing project to determine the DNA order of all nuclear genes from a Yellowstone National Park bison. This time, with funding provided through the Turner Foundation, the plan is to sequence the entire bison genome from animals that lived before the major population crash of the late 1800s. The experiments are being done with bone, tooth, and hide samples preserved from historic bison remains housed at the Smithsonian Museum in Washington DC. When completed, this effort will provide a rare insight into what bison genomes were like both before and after the great population crash in the 1880s.

As Dr. Derr points out, "the ability to look at the DNA sequence of genes from bison that lived over one hundred years ago and directly compare their complete genomes with modern bison provides the opportunity to not only understand what bison are today, but to also understand what this species was like back in a time when there were still millions of bison roaming the great plains of North America before any chance of hybridization with cattle."

It's all part of a larger plan, a larger vision, that Turner has for his bison herd. A vision that is idealistic at its roots has been tempered, over time, by the hard truths of the market and modern ecology. Turner has spent more than $300,000 over the years on genetic testing and research. Granted, it is not something that an average "family" rancher could afford, but he says he is applying his largesse to try and do what's best for the species. He's made the results available to other bison ranchers. "He has provided a great baseline for examining bison genetics," says Dave Carter, executive director of the National Bison Association. "If Ted didn't do it, it probably wouldn't get done."

Make no mistake, Turner is interested in bison today for more than their existential value. Just as they represented a plentiful commissary for native people, he believes they can be sustenance for twenty-first-century Americans and give them a deeper philosophical understanding of food. In recent consecutive summers, Turner hosted both the Martha Stewart and Oprah Winfrey shows at his ranches in Montana. One of his purposes was to talk about the health benefits of bison. Over a couple of afternoons, in the company of those influential media women, he reached tens of millions of afternoon viewers wondering what they were going to feed their family for dinner. Many promptly went out and bought bison. Indeed, consumption of bison has been on the rise.

But now it's months later and the middle of winter. Turner is on an inspection of the meat processing plant that handles his bison after they come off his ranches, bound for supermarkets and featured menu items at Turner's restaurant chain, Ted's Montana Grill.

Turner joins a single-file line of men in denim who have donned long white laboratory frocks and beauty parlor hairnets for a tour of Rocky Mountain Natural Meats in suburban Denver. The facility was founded by a New Jersey cowboy named Bob Dineen.

At the front, behind Dineen, Turner wears his hairnet like a beret as he leads ranch hands on a guided tour.

He believes it is important that his field personnel and staff from Turner Enterprises in Atlanta understand how the flow of bison to the marketplace works. Front and center are members of his executive team:

the CEO of Turner Enterprises Taylor Glover, Glover's finance director David Withers, Turner's son-in-law and attorney Rutherford Seydel, and George McKerrow, who presides over the restaurants.

The rooms are bright white with long stainless steel tables—sterile and antiseptic. Turner is pleased that the ideals of health he demands of his ranch managers and stewarding of land are transmitted to the handling and packaging of bison all the way up the food chain. "Most Americans haven't a clue how their food is grown and the route it takes to the neighborhood grocer," Turner says. "This is an important stage."

Every January at the same time that the American cattle industry gathers for the Western Stock Show in Denver, the National Bison Association and Turner Enterprises also converge on the Mile High City for winter meetings. It's an opportunity to exchange notes, go over budgets for the year, and to keep everyone informed of the novel projects being carried out in the western empire. The topics listed on the agenda are wide ranging and progressive. It has included assessments of how much fossil fuel is spent, how much carbon dioxide is being sequestered in healthy grasslands and forests, how to reduce stress on the animals, how to manage them in ways that keep family units together and more closely mimic wild herds, and examinations of how bison cope with the presence of predators.

Turner has said on countless occasions that he doesn't enjoy the idea of his bison having to die. He has often bottle-fed orphaned bison calves. "My involvement with bison has been an education," Turner says. "If you had asked me twenty years ago how a hamburger moves from grass to grocery, I didn't have the knowledge to speak authoritatively on it. But I do today. I read Upton Sinclair's novel about the slaughterhouses of Chicago and it turned my stomach. This is as different from that as the other side of the Moon. I'm not trying to castigate the beef industry. What I am saying is that I'm impressed at all of the measures that are taken by our ranch hands on up to Bob [Dineen at Rocky Mountain Natural Meats] and then to George [McKerrow, operating executive of Ted's Montana Grill] to ensure safety, quality, and humane and respectful handling of the bison."

Temple Grandin, the doctor of animal science, has gained international renown for her work with animals, namely for delving into their thinking and emotional capacity as sentient creatures. She wrote a book, *Animals in Transition*, which explored her personal challenges with autism and her therapeutic work as an animal behaviorist and professor at the University of Colorado. And there was an HBO biopic made about her starring actress Claire Danes. Grandin has served as a consultant to the beef industry and has advised McDonald's and such green-minded grocery chains as Whole Foods, which carries bison meat coming off of Turner ranches.

In 2009, she and Catherine Johnson wrote a well-received book titled *Animals Make Us Human: Creating the Best Life for Animals*. Grandin recounts a reconnaissance inspection she took on behalf of Whole Foods to assess the treatment of animals at an unnamed ranching operation that was to become a potential provider of grass-fed meat.

"I was out on a large bison ranch recently and was very pleased with the handling," she wrote. "Why do they have good handling? Because the boss wants it that way. It's coming down from the top. I have seen this pattern many times. Even back in the bad old days before major customers started doing animal welfare audits of the meat plants, there were always some places that did things right. Every one of these plants or farms had a strong manager who served as the conscience for the employees. Many times I heard employees stop another employee from hurting an animal by saying, 'You can't do that. The boss doesn't allow it.'"

By "boss," Grandin was referring to Turner. She adheres to the principle that landowners are ethically bound to give animals "a life worth living" and Turner, she said, illustrates it. Turner's occasional macho displays aside, his gentle manner around bison, his horses, and the wildlife that share the range with them has rubbed off, infused in his employees.

"We aren't doing what Ted wants only because he is our boss," Miller says. "We do it because he opens our eyes to a better way of seeing things."

Everyone working on his ranches has helped to open Turner's eyes, but none more in pointing about the relationship between animal health and the role of healthy ecosystems than Dr. Hunter. Hunter, the on-staff veterinarian, advisor to the Turner Endangered Species Fund and a figure known internationally for his work in the emerging field of "wildlife conservation medicine," keeps a low profile. "His ability to ensure that the Turner properties avoid some big time problems with infectious disease is legend," says Dr. Derr of Texas A & M University. "He is a pioneer in this field and destined to be an icon."

Hunter wrote an article long ago that was titled "the bison advantage" and spelled out their competitive benefits over domesticated bovines. What Hunter has proved on the ground is that by nurturing and honoring the instincts of wild bison that have made them survivors across eons, Turner can avoid engaging in the kinds of invasive manipulation that are common place within domestic beef production.

"In contrast to the industrial mentality that has been applied to raising cattle, I am most proud of how this organization thinks outside of the box with a variety of native species under its care," Hunter says. "We seek to champion their rightful place on the landscapes where they evolved and yet find ways to steward and safeguard them using minimal inputs, allowing them to exist, as much as possible, as the species God created." In fact, an entire book could be written about the discoveries that Turner, Hunter, and others have made.

Still, Turner struggles with the reality that his bison die to become food on the table. It continues to be difficult for him. When the animals reach Dineen's processing plant, the hides already have been removed, the masses of flesh chilled, cleaned, rinsed, halved, and readied to be turned into choice steaks, roasts, and premium quality hamburger.

Turner always has questions to ask. He stops to chat with Dineen's workers, butchers artfully and efficiently cutting meat, then packaging the cuts and getting them into walk-in coolers to ensure freshness. Safety is a two-fold endeavor involving sanitary handling of the meat in its conversion from being on the hoof to arriving on dinner plates, and in the care given to prevent job-related accidents and injuries that can range from getting cut, slipping on the floor, and throwing out a back to repetitive stress ailments related to meat handling.

Dineen has addressed the former by working with engineers who design state of the art facilities to streamline the flow of bison from the door where it enters the plant to cold storage where it awaits shipping. Unlike the negative stereotype that is sometimes applied to meat plants, Rocky Mountain Natural Meats does not require workers to sumo wrestle with sides of animals through zones of swirling knives and slick floors.

In another room away from the packaging side of the operation, Brian Ward's son, Ty, an employee of Dineen's, is working the phones like a Wall Street stockbroker. Demand for bison has skyrocketed. This is one of the nerve centers for the American bison industry. It's less about frenetic wheeling and dealing than in coordinating supply with grocers and restaurants, the largest buyer being Turner's restaurant chain. Some of the familiar outlets across the country are A&P, Albertson's, Fry's, Hannaford, Kroger, King Soopers, Market Basket, Safeway, Shaw's Shop Rite, Smith's, Stop & Shop, Waldbaum's, Wegmans, and Whole Foods.

"Our goal is not to maximize volume for volume's sake. It is to attain an equilibrium by anticipating demand and matching it with bringing animals off the range. Freshness equates to quality," Dineen says. "If we wanted to be a big player in the American meat industry, we would have built a plant five times as large and our focus would be cattle and hogs and we'd be positioned on the edge of a feedlot."

Operating at scale enables Turner to reduce expenses and enables the cost of bison reaching consumers to be more affordable. Such "vertical integration," which eliminates needless market middlemen, has also enabled Turner and his associates to have a clear-eyed, holistic view of what it takes to grow healthy bison herds on healthy landscapes, and to ensure that the product delivered to consumers maintains its health benefits. He believes society deserves to have a peace of mind in knowing how and where food is produced, rather than having it be shrouded in mystery.

Dr. David Hunter, Turner's valued on-staff wildlife veterinarian, has traveled around the world to advance his understanding of an emerging science called "conservation medicine" that focuses on preventing the spread of zoonotic diseases. Based upon recommendations from Hunter, the Turner management protocol ensures that bison have plenty of room to fan across the landscape, to have an abundance of natural plants and minerals—rather than stuffing them with hay in winter—to feast upon, and are not injected with antibiotics and growth hormones, a practice that is prolific in domestic livestock ranching.

Miller says that Turner could capitalize on demand by flooding his ranches with a lot more bison, but he is guided by ecology and sound resource management. "He's never been interested in imposing the cattle model of production on bison, but neither is it just a hobby. Industrial approaches to agriculture often mean that you are working the land hard. He likes to make money, but making money isn't his only objective."

About four hundred bison move through Dineen's plant each week. A big cattle plant would process that many in an hour, he says. About 125 million cattle annually are raised in the United States.

⌁

At the western headquarters of Turner Enterprises Inc. in Bozeman, a single-story office warren, Miller and assistant general manager John Hansen are in the conference room with intricate budget sheets fanned across a long table. It's crunch time for another year. And during this annum, the West is gripped in drought.

"Under global warming scenarios," Miller says, "what we call drought may become the new norm. It's an issue that is of great concern to Ted and it's one of the reasons why he's been so vigilant not only in pushing Congress to act on controlling CO_2 emissions but increasing his stake in alternative energy as well."

Amid the thousands of pages of spreadsheets that have line item expenses laid out for every ranch, Miller and Hansen track costs for everything from the estimated amount of grass needed for the bison, to engine replacements in pickup trucks to property taxes to health insurance for employees. Row after row of minutiae.

Turner places an emphasis on frugality. "But I can honestly say I've never felt pressure from Ted to cut corners in order to try and turn a profit," Miller says. "He knows that our emphasis is to try and make all of the ranches sustainable by taking care of the land, the bison, and the people. That's why he hired us."

Over the twenty years of Turner's bison operation, only fairly recently have bison returned a multimillion-dollar profit, aided by rising market prices for bison meat (about double the going rate for beef nationally) and rising demand for bison (aided mightily by the heightened profile of bison created by Turner's creation of the Ted's Montana Grill restaurant chain).

Before bison pulled their own financial weight, the diversified income streams from the ranches—commercial hunting and fishing, sustainable timber harvests, and oil and gas royalties—took up the slack. The natural gas royalties at Vermejo Park Ranch in New Mexico are noteworthy in one major regard—Turner doesn't own those mineral rights under the ranch, putting him in the company of thousands of private property owners who are at the mercy of split-estate laws granting energy companies access to their land without payment of royalties or say in whether energy development can occur. But when Turner acquired the ranch, he and his legal team negotiated a progressive mineral extraction agreement that not only dictated environmentally sensitive development of the natural gas by the owner of the gas rights, but also granted Turner a royalty on production. That mineral extraction agreement has served as a national model for government agencies, environmental groups, energy companies, and other private property owners attempting to minimize the ecological impacts of rapidly growing natural gas extraction.

Just as development need not result in massive sacrifice zones, so, too, do preservation and conservation not mean the ability of a landowner to generate an income.

"When Ted attached a conservation easement to the deed of the Flying D, he voluntarily accepted upper limits on the number of animals that could be grazed in order to protect the health of his grasslands," Miller says. "Part of that means setting aside a percentage of the range to feed public wildlife such as elk. Could we be running more bison on the Flying D and the other ranches where there are no easements? Probably. But Ted's not interested in maximizing profit if it comes at the expense of other values."

The ranches are operated by Miller as a confederation of properties under the jurisdiction of individual managers he has hired. Each is allowed to creatively manage his property, so long as he keeps the triple bottom line in mind. Rather than having supplies shipped in from distant cities or countries, Turner has instructed managers to, whenever possible, funnel as much business into local towns. His commerce is significant. The triple bottom line is a principle that encourages business to be approached with broader and longer-term thinking than just focusing on short-term profit or loss. The triple bottom line balance sheet strives to deliver economic profit, ecological benefit, or impacts that are benign, and impart benefits to local and regional communities in terms of quality of life. "How do we save the world?" Turner asks. "The triple bottom line is an important tenet."

Miller says Turner is keenly aware that his legacy, everything he's tried to do with his ranches, will be undermined if they aren't break-even. Running them efficiently, affordably, and sustainably is perceived as a gesture toward the next generation—his children and grandchildren.

"I don't believe that ranching is an either/or proposition," Turner says.

~ ~

Roughly 4,400 ranchers, located in every US state and Canadian province, raise bison. And each year, about sixty thousand bison are processed in North America, a number that continues to rise. But to put it in perspective, Carter notes, the beef industry butchers 125,000 cattle *a day*. Dineen adds: "As a point of comparison, the total output of bison annually is .15 percent of the beef industry."

Flying largely under the radar of public awareness, and as opposed to the cattle industry, the bison industry has voluntarily embraced a system for source verification, led by its largest producer, Turner, in concert with other members of the NBA. "The industry realizes the best way to protect itself is by being vigilant with how ranches are operated, the cleanliness that producers use to process their animals, and those whom we select as our wholesale and retail partners," Dineen of Rocky Mountain Natural Meats says.

Turner and McKerrow have told their waiters at Ted's Montana Grill to take pride in the fact that when diners ask about the birthplace of their bison filet or burger, they can say there's a good chance—one in four—it was grown on a Turner ranch.

"[Turner] is pushing for transparency, and he's not operating his lands with an environmental deficit on his books. He's building green capital. There are some environmentalists who haven't caught up to the pioneering course he is blazing and they need to take a second look," Carl Pope, former executive director of the Sierra Club, says.

"The bison, in the way Ted is ranching them on his own land, pays for itself. I am a fan of what he is doing, not a critic. If he wanted to turn them into cattle and treat them as such, he would raise cattle instead. I don't see him undermining the conservation of the species. He is raising the bison's profile. He is using market forces to enhance their abundance and along the way educating millions of people about the ecological value of having them back in the landscape. Next to maybe Jane Goodall and chimpanzees, name another species that has this kind of champion."

— ⁓ —

"At some time in the relatively near future, we will achieve a 'balance' between what we are consuming and the capacity of the earth's ecosystems to provide those needs, although under existing models of production and consumption, it is likely to be far different and cause far more suffering than we are presently willing to admit," suggests Paul Hawken in *The Ecology of Commerce*, his classic book about triple bottom line accounting. "But rather than look at that balance point as a zero-sum outcome that is distantly achievable, a restorative economy means thinking big and long into the future."

Scaling to achieve greater measures of economic and ecological efficiency is no different for a rancher or restaurateur than it is for a mom and pop retailer peddling a product, or a promoter of wind energy, or a clothing maker like Yvon Chouinard of Patagonia, Doug Tompkins of Esprit, the late carpet manufacturer Ray Anderson, or a large multinational like General Electric headed by Jeff Immelt—all of whom have joined Turner in touting the green revolution.

Dineen says Turner's uncanny understanding about how markets work has influenced him and his decision to expand by betting on the value consumers place on peace of mind in knowing where their food comes from. "One of the things I've learned from Ted, and he is a master at it, is that good ideas work when you are tenacious and hang in there."

— ⁓ —

Turner started placing bison on his lands because he loves *the species*. Anyway he can, whether it's touting the health benefits of eating bison, realizing potential financial dividends by raising them, or employing them as allies in healing natural landscapes, Turner says it fuels the same objective: bringing more back to the wild. It's led the Turner organization down some fascinating rabbit holes.

In 2006, and in concert with the Wildlife Conservation Society, Turner offered up Vermejo Park Ranch to host a gathering of the leading world authorities on bison and conservation. From that meeting, an action plan was formed. The goal was to get wild, free-ranging bison herds, owned and managed by the public, redistributed across as much of their former range as possible.

At a subsequent Denver conference sponsored by the Wildlife Conservation Society, which some called a flashpoint for igniting "the bison renaissance," various scenarios were advanced, practical as well as lofty. One environmental activist spoke of wanting to see tens of thousands of free-ranging bison thundering down a prairie slope in the backdrop of a spectacular sunset. She saw it as a hook for a new era of ecotourism. Travelers from around the world would come, she said, to experience eastern Montana and Wyoming, the Dakotas, Nebraska, and Kansas, just as large numbers of well-heeled adventurers flock to the Serengeti Plain of Kenya and Tanzania.

It's not an uncommon vision of bison nirvana, and one that was once shared by a younger Ted Turner. He dreamed of being so successful in business that he could own large pieces of land and fill them with free-roaming bison. But as attractive as the notion might be, and as Turner discovered, there are a number of problems with free-roaming bison. They are social herd animals, for one thing. They move in groups across landscapes, and they prefer open, lower-elevation areas in winter. Some of the major busy highway thoroughfares in the West run through agricultural valleys where bison would converge. In those places, it isn't practical or safe to have unfenced bison herds flanking highways or interstates.

But because there are many remote, sparsely populated sites, the ideal persists, and has its traceable roots in the vision of two controversial figures, Frank and Deborah Popper. In 1987 the Poppers caused a sensation when they authored an academic paper advocating for a plan they called "the Buffalo Commons." Noting that the treeless interior West was emptying of people due to economic realities, and noting as well the lack of agrarian sustainability, the proliferation of pioneer-era ghost towns, and the troubling draining of the Ogallala Aquifer beneath the Great Plains, they postulated a notion that perhaps the ecological and economic fortunes of the prairie could be revived if large bison herds were allowed to roam free again. They suggested that old homesteads could be purchased by the government and used to expand government landholdings. This, predictably, ignited a firestorm, burning hottest within the circles of government conspiracy theorists who believed Buffalo Commons was a ruse for a land grab. The Poppers received death threats. They were maligned as eastern elitist extremists, and told not to set foot in the West.

As part of Turner's voracious appetite for reading, he studied the Poppers' overview of Buffalo Commons and asked all of his ranch managers to digest it. While he applauded the Poppers for thinking big and rallying behind bison, he didn't believe it could work as proposed. "I think the federal government has other more urgent spending priorities," Turner says. "And even if it didn't, it would never have the resources to buy enough private land to make Buffalo Commons function the way it is explained. If conservation must always rely on government stepping in, and short of nationalization of all land which is a terrible idea, there will never be enough money available to save all the wildlife and landscapes in need of saving.

"I'm a believer in the private sector stepping up and having citizens or business become stakeholders and partners. I'm not against the government, and I'm definitely in favor of restoring bison, but I believe in private enterprise. I think it's more effective, more efficient, and makes things happen faster than government bureaucracies can. If the market is responsible for environmental destruction, I believe it can also be used as a force for good."

The Poppers have come to agree with Turner about the advantages of employing private-property, citizen conservationists rather than using government intervention. They count themselves among his admirers. "I think one of the lines of argument we've heard is that you won't save an animal unless it has commercial value. The ongoing fear was that if bison had commercial value they'd be turned into cattle equivalents. Another premise is that bison on ranches aren't truly 'wild,'" Deborah Popper says. "But it all depends upon what role the rancher envisions for bison in the ecosystem. The relationship between bison and people has always been complex. What's nearly unique with bison, and made vivid by how Turner approaches them, is that they can be commercial and mythic and wildlife symbols all at the same time. I see them as a point of convergence, not divergence, for both indigenous and non-indigenous peoples. The only other animal that comes close to meeting this profile is salmon in the Pacific Northwest, Canada, and Alaska."

"'Wild' is a construct," says Mike Phillips. "I think what most people mean by wild is not how an animal behaves but rather whether it is mostly left to its own devices to handle the challenges of nature and whether it is part of a public herd and therefore owned by citizens. Ted owns his bison herds because, for him, it was the fastest and most effective way he had to grow a herd and address the wrongs that he thought had been committed against the species."

"When we originally proposed the idea of Buffalo Commons in the 1980s," Frank Popper says, "we assumed there could be a federal solution whereby public lands could easily be repopulated with bison. But that was then, and it was also pre-Turner, and we didn't anticipate the impact that someone like him and other buffalo ranchers and tribes and various non-government groups could have. It's not necessary for government to do it, certainly not government alone. Promoting bison conservation through public and private efforts gives the movement a balance and flexibility to move forward with an array of options that didn't exist before."

With affiliations at Rutgers, Princeton, and the City College of New York, Popper explains Turner to his college students this way: "I really see Turner as fitting into the mold of an old-fashioned Romantic capitalist. He likes turning things that are considered broken around, be it baseball teams or relations with the Russians. The spirit was there in the Goodwill Games, the Braves, and in CNN defying its critics when he said the news business needed to exist in real time."

He adds, "I'm trying to think of someone else who qualifies with such a benevolent spirit. Bill and Melinda Gates and Paul Allen and Warren Buffett qualify as great philanthropists but there's no one who, as an enormously successful, self-made capitalist, has made giving away money to environmental and humanitarian causes a standard part of his operating principle. A sense of improvisation has been a hallmark of whatever he's doing. He's been a catalyst for altering how an entire nation thinks about buffalo."

Turner's entry into the bison ranching business did more than alter his perception of stewardship; it altered the perception of others toward him. And while it may have alienated him from the regional livestock industry, it also (unknown to him at the time) gave him a new identity, Bison Baron.

Dan Flores told me, "One of the little-grasped policy decisions made by the federal government and its advisors, the American Bison Society, in saving buffalo a century ago was not allowing them to be wild animals across western public lands. Among all American fauna they, along with wolves and grizzlies, are an exception in that regard. I've liked that Ted has removed fences and attempted to let his herds be wilder. And that he has helped get us to a point where we have more bison now than at any time since the 1880s. Ted has brought bison back into American consciousness and that allows us now to ponder taking next steps."

Montanan Danny Johnson, who grew up a skeptic of Turner only to become the current Flying D manager, says that Turner's earlier aspersions against cattle need to be considered against his record of stewardship, an impulse that is kindred to the beliefs of the good stockmen he knows. "Ted's definitely of the more rural mindset than the city one," Johnson suggests.

Turner is increasingly viewed as an architect of the *New West*. "I think a lot of us know better now, but the lag time for most of the population to being more critical about history seems to be a long one. This is where my idea about our need for new stories, new heroes comes in," Flores says. "History doesn't seem very useful to me when all it does is glorify *the past*. Being critical about the past is how you learn from it. It may take another generation and another step away from frontier veneration, but my own sense is that Ted Turner's bison narrative, still being written, will be regarded as one of the new paradigms that changed history."

As Flores makes clear, Turner is not just a buffalo rancher trying to reconcile ecology and commerce. Indeed, conservationist and Blackfeet Indian Curly Bear Wagner used to call Turner Wovoka, after the Northern Paiute mystic who invented the Ghost Dance, who hoped that the white outsiders would go away and buffalo would miraculously return.

Wagner was a traditionalist. Before he died in 2009, he told me that the promise of Wovoka survived in Turner. "He is a powerful man," Wagner said. "He understands bison as an animal of sustenance that feeds the soul and the body."

Wagner smiled when he was asked if Turner could pass for a Native medicine man. "No," he said, "but Ted has land and money and, while I may never fully understand it, he has an attachment to buffalo. It isn't phony. If there's anything we Indians recognize in white people, it is when they are being deceptive and insincere. Ted Turner isn't that way."

A century and more after Wounded Knee, after the promise of the Ghost Dance died under the bullets of Hotchkiss guns, Ted Turner continues to work to restore bison to the American West.

One evening along a bluff at the Flying D headed toward dusk, he stood thinking of the Blackfeet hunters, of the bison they had once stalked and killed. A few fences from the D's cattle days remained in view, but most of them had been removed. "I try to imagine what it would have been like maybe two hundred years ago to look into this same valley and see the bison out there as they appear to us now," Turner said. "Did they have the same feelings welling up inside of them as I do now?"

He sighed slightly, and turned away, facing instead toward the small city of Bozeman. In one direction, the vast wilderness that he revived, rolling toward Yellowstone. And, in the distance, civilization. Out of sight, but present in his thoughts. An upwelling of big box stores, nondescript grids of bricks and mortar, a swooning reminder of what he had given up. And, at their juncture, at the intersection of encroaching humanity and adamant wilderness, stood a "media mogul" headed toward decline, but an environmentalist in his ascent.

CHAPTER TWO

Survival

"My dear son,
I am appalled, even horrified, that you have adopted Classics as a
major. As a matter of fact, I almost puked on the way home today . . . I
think you are rapidly becoming a jackass, and the sooner you get out of
that filthy atmosphere, the better it will suit me. You go ahead and go
with the world, and I'll go it alone."
—Ed Turner, in a letter to his son, Ted Turner, shortly
before he made him withdraw from Brown University

"I don't like to admit it, but I'm getting old . . . Though not 'old' in
the way we remember old people being when we were young."

The year is 2005. Ted Turner sits at a breakfast table in Patagonia, in
the middle of one of the three ranches he owns in southern Argentina.
I am across from him. Estancia Collon Cura was named after a river
revered for its trout fishing. Outside the window, he watches a flock of
ravenous parrots squabble in the fruit trees, boisterously consuming pears.
The colorful birds are fueling up for an autumn journey northward into
the tropical jungles of the Amazon.

He says he needs to get a few things off his chest. He's been pondering his own mortality—the snatches of time he has left—and he starts
in by speaking cathartically of a night when he was alone in Montana. "I

thought about it. I had reached the loneliest point in my life and I wondered what I had to live for."

I had been told that it was highly unlikely Turner would broach the subject and when he did I was startled and then surprised. He had given me an opening to go far deeper in our conversations than ever before. I took it.

He does not like to mention the word "suicide." But in autumn 2001, Turner did not have a plan for probably the first time in his life. The twentieth century had come to a crescendo while he consented to the biggest blockbuster business deal ever hatched. The largest presiding shareholder, he gave his blessing to the megamerger between the Internet company AOL and Time Warner, the latter a parent to companies he founded and were synonymous with his name. Turner's net worth had swelled from $2 billion to upwards of $11 billion.

One might assume, therefore, that he had reason to be running a fin de siècle victory lap, taking a bow as one of the richest men in America. Unfortunately, the high of the previous year had not lasted.

In the autumn of 2001, the stock price of AOL Time Warner tumbled, and Turner suffered one of the most precipitous declines of personal net worth in history, equating to losing $10 million a day, every day, for two years running. But the worst, he said, wasn't losing a colossal amount of money. "I had money. A lot of money. I made it. I lost it," he says wistfully. "But I can tell you, there's more to life than having money. You can always make more. That part's been relatively easy for me."

On the night he considered killing himself, Turner wasn't thinking about his financial decline. He was thinking about his father, Robert Edward Turner II, better known as Ed, who had committed suicide.

Their fractured relationship has been the topic of much speculation. One of Turner's closest friends says, "If you want to unlock Ted Turner, get him to open up about his father . . . Ted had the kind of traumatic childhood that would destroy many of us."

In 2001, Turner the son had already surpassed his father's terminal age. And, as he does in autumn, he had repaired to the Flying D to fly fish, ride horses, and inspect his bison herd. But as opposed to other autumns on The D, he felt little pleasure in the trip.

It was no secret that during Turner's career, he had found himself in deep mood troughs, swings in which he would retreat into himself and escape to his properties for long walks. Personal physicians attributed those low periods to stress overload, not, as some observers have speculated, to clinical depression. Despite what some unauthorized biographies about him have alleged, he does not take lithium and is not bipolar. He does see a therapist.

During the summer of 2001, the sleeping pills prescribed to help him wrestle with insomnia caused by stress and sleep apnea proved ineffective. And hovering over him, at night, was self-doubt, persuading him that, after decades of staying busy and not confronting his past, he was venturing close to understanding the feelings of imminent doom that had destroyed his father.

On September 11, 2001, he was in Atlanta when he received a telephone call informing him to turn on the television. On the only news channel he watched, CNN, he saw smoke rising from one of the World Trade Center buildings, then he watched, dumbstruck, as a plane flew into the second building. Not long thereafter, he watched both towers fall, killing more than twenty-six hundred people. He was left speechless and helpless and horrified. That quickly, surreal had become the new normal.

The AOL–Time Warner merger had been approved by the Federal Communications Commission on January 11, 2001. The value of Turner's one hundred million shares in the new conglomerate had skyrocketed. By early September 2001, Turner had made huge commitments to charities, not the least of which was a $1 billion gift to the UN, honored through an annual $100 million in the sale of stock. He also had pledged a quarter of a billion in stock to slow nuclear proliferation while funding the Turner

Foundation at $50 million annually. And he was in the midst of launching a new restaurant chain, Ted's Montana Grill, that featured bison on the menu. And he had two million acres of land and hundreds of employees on his payroll to look after. Then the stock plunged.

The tanking of AOL Time Warner caused a panic, and the sadness he felt for the victims of 9/11 was a devastating blow. To confront his own gathering financial crisis, Turner and his advisors hastily drafted a contingency plan in the event that liquid assets had to be sold. No one outside his circle knew how dire it was.

Turner and his inner circle gathered in Montana weeks after 9/11. What some of his friends who were there with him remember is how unusually taciturn he became over dinner at the Flying D. They looked into his face for evidence of his usual feistiness to ease their own worries.

Turner had always been a rhetorical gunslinger known for showing confidence when the odds were stacked against him. He's legendary for being a competitor who does not enjoy losing. He once jokingly opined from the swaggering perspective of middle age: "If I only had a little humility, I'd be perfect."

That indomitable Turner was not present in the room. There were dark circles under his eyes and his skin was ashen. Turner says he was burned out, and all that he could focus on was the thought that he was a personal failure. He did not know if the collapse of AOL Time Warner would extend to his prized possessions, the $500 million worth of ranches.

His duress, amplified by 9/11, was making those at his side anxious about leaving him alone.

━ ⌣ ━

"Was I thinking about my dad that night? Sure I was. I think about him every single day. What son doesn't think about his father?"

Yet why did his domineering patriarch, the man he revered, forsake him twice? Few archetypal relationships are more potent than father and impressionable son. In some families, rules of behavior are handed down to men as dictations from one generation to the next. The Turner clan had its rules. Ted was Ed's only son. And before the boy had even reached kindergarten, he had a lesson imparted to him.

At age four in 1943, Turner commenced a long, protracted exile from normal family life. His father entered military service just after World War II broke out. He sent word that he wanted family members to join him on the base where he was stationed, except for Ted.

Turner remembers the morning he was sent away to what would become a succession of boarding schools. His dad informed him that showing fear or, worse, relying upon other people for emotional comfort, were flaws that must not infect the character of a self-made man. Ed Turner told his adoring son that he needed to wipe away tears and buck up if he ever expected to get ahead in life. Turner tried to cling to the legs of his mother, Florence, who could not look him in the eye. He looked up and pleaded for an explanation. She nudged him away. The boy would hypothesize for many decades afterward that he had done something wrong, something he couldn't remember, something that maybe he needed to apologize for, to warrant banishment.

At the boarding school dormitory, he had nightmares about being abandoned. His room was made of white cinderblocks, devoid of color. A chain-link fence wrapped the premises of the school like a cordon. Turner remembers an overwhelming sense of claustrophobia and a need to flee. His earliest memory is of a kindly marm who occasionally would respond to his nocturnal whimpering, though most of the time no one answered his panicked desire for companionship.

Even today, he's nauseated by the smell of oatmeal, the only food that was served for breakfast. And he still has two primal fears that persist from his early childhood: being left alone and a disdain for fences. "I woke up every morning hoping that my mother would show up and rescue me, take me home," he said. "But she never arrived."

Years later, after Turner's father had taken his own life, his mother told an interviewer something that she had never expressed openly to her son. She said she had been intimidated by and stood powerless before Turner's father. She was ashamed for not marshaling the courage to intervene on the boy's behalf when Ed Turner insisted that Ted be enrolled in boarding and military schools "to toughen him up."

"I cried. It did no good," Florence said. "Ed told me he had the purse strings. I had to do what he said. Ed always insisted on sending Ted away to school because he was jealous of my love for the boy."

When, much later in his life, Turner learned of what his mother had said, he sobbed, not out of sorrow but relief. It wasn't anything he did, after all, he realized. It was about them. But it still didn't fill up the hole of insecurity. He says, "I don't think that with age you ever outgrow those feelings that go back to your childhood."

<hr/>

During the Roaring Twenties, novelist F. Scott Fitzgerald wrote, "Let me tell you about the very rich. They are different from you and me."

Hard work and luck had enabled him to assemble an incredible portfolio of land, Turner says, but he's never claimed that material wealth immunizes or insulates a person from suffering. Yes, there's irony in the Fitzgerald quote and Turner would seem to contradict it. Despite decades of soaring forward at warp speed and never allowing himself to slow down, his greatest epiphany is this: "No matter what you do, you cannot outrun your past, or forget the effect it has on you, nor should you because, for better or worse, it is who you are."

Of all expressions of human emotion, the one Turner regards as most pathetic is self-pity. It was Ed Turner, in fact, who first taught him that feeling sorry for oneself is a cardinal sin. But that day in September saw a convergence of calamities that made self-pity almost impossible to avoid.

In addition to his financial dissolution, his ten-year marriage to Jane Fonda had formally ended in the spring of 2001, following a separation that started on January 1, 2000. After the divorce became final, Turner lay on the floor of their bedroom, crawled into the fetal position, and cried.

Turner's friends did not wish to offend him by voicing a suspicion about his emotional fragility. His associates were not the only ones who worried about him. His youngest son, Beau, the child with whom he has the strongest rapport, was bothered by his father's melancholy. Beau pulled him aside.

"I told him, 'Dad, don't be like your dad. Don't take your own life.' He smiled at me and said, 'You don't have to worry about me doing something that extreme, son,'" Beau says. Of course, Ed Turner had said the same thing to Ted.

Beau Turner wasn't comforted. He watched his father in subsequent weeks withdraw steadily into himself. On that night in autumn 2001, Turner excused himself early from the long rectangular supper table just as the sun was dipping behind the mountains. He bid his friends good evening and disappeared in his bedroom.

Hours later, he was awake and alone. He had not brought along one of his female friends on this trip to Montana. He had become the owner of more private property than any individual citizen in America, but he was isolated. He had suicide on the mind—his father's and the prospect of his own. The easiest means would be a gun—a hunting rifle or a .12-gauge; it would fit with Turner's identification as a man's man. If he had an intricate plan, he doesn't share it now as he thinks about the intense feelings he had that night.

Rubbing his eyes, he swung open a bedroom door to stand on the outside deck. Black silhouettes of the Spanish Peaks reminded him how insignificant he was. Turner shivered in the cold air.

He began practicing an old ritual from his sailing days on the open ocean. He looked into the sky and started connecting the dots of stars—a game taught to him when he was a Boy Scout.

Ed Turner had stoically drilled into his son a mantra that only fools allow themselves to be afraid. Sixty years after the advice was imparted, the son felt petrified.

In the immediate foreground, there was a pond that he had designed from scratch to share with Fonda as a wedding gift. Fonda had ventured nearest to the point of understanding and forgiving his complicated personality, he says. From the picture window designed for grand views of the property to the fieldstone in the fireplace hearth she had chosen, down to the trees planted in the yard that formed a sheltering grove where Turner's visiting grandchildren climbed and played, he was surrounded by reminders of their life together. The marriage had become strained, and ended, by his own admission, without him putting up a heroic fight to save it.

All his life he had difficulty in totally embracing intimate relationships with women, beginning with his mother and including his daughters and wives. He had heard the observations made of what a contradiction it was, that a man who had helped revolutionize modern mass media could flounder at bonding with those from whom he seeks the tightest connections.

During the summer of 2001, Turner's young granddaughter, the child of his daughter, Jennie Turner Garlington, and son-in-law, Peak, died. After he attended the funeral in Kentucky, he reflected on the girl's grief-stricken parents. He wanted his daughter to know that he could understand her hurt. As a teenage boy, his kid sister, Mary Jane, had died after a drawn-out illness. On his rare visits home from boarding school, Turner says, she had beamed in his presence. As a big brother, he was protective of her, and she sought out his companionship, ruing that their father had sent him away to military schools. At night during those interludes at his parents' house, he would listen to Mary Jane shriek from pain associated with advanced stage terminal lupus. When it became unbearable, he says, she lost her will to survive. She pleaded from her room, behind the walls, believing no one else could hear. "She said, 'Please, make the pain go away. Please, God, let me die.'"

If he could have, he says in reflection, he would have switched places with Mary Jane and allowed her to have his life. When Turner tried to seek consoling from his parents, he was told to pray.

Being a Christian, he asked God to stop his sister's suffering. But three more years passed before Mary Jane succumbed. His parents, after her death, pulled further away from each other until they divorced. Ed Turner had always had several girlfriends and made no attempt to hide them. Adrift, Turner lost confidence in the ability of organized religion to offer an explanation or a purpose for his familial disintegration.

God, he figured, should not be elusive to the people who need him most—especially those in the world who most deserve human compassion.

As Turner assessed his mistakes in 2001, he realized that his last refuge —work, where he could always escape as a workaholic and find a mission —had also vanished. September 11 had given him a stinging reminder that he could not go back to his old professional origin ever again. His companies had given him a sense of purpose and a means to heal his wounded self-esteem after his father died. But just as abruptly as Ed Turner departed leaving him cold, he had a similar feeling being stripped of control over the Turner Broadcasting System. He never imagined it could happen.

From his penthouse suite atop the CNN Building in Atlanta, Turner followed a routine. Rise well before 6:00, duck down to the street for a brisk stroll around Centennial Park with his Labrador, Blackie. Eat a light breakfast set out by a maid. He'd peruse the morning papers— the *Wall Street Journal*, *New York Times*, and the hometown *Atlanta Journal-Constitution*, though mostly his attention would be pegged to CNN and Headline News. Turner doesn't own a computer, never has; he doesn't know how to log on. He doesn't carry a cell phone, or any other kind of electronic gadget, save the clicker lock for his hybrid vehicle. For years, he'd walk down the stairs from his apartment to the nerve center of TBS and excitedly he'd visit with the editors and newsreaders congealing the line-up for its best-known asset, CNN. Famously, he had barred the word "foreign" from the newsroom lexicon and ordered that everyone use "international" instead. He found "foreign" to be derogatory.

Turner had earned stature in the news business the hard way. He already had been proclaimed "the newsman of the future," had been *Time* magazine's "Man of the Year," had been given an award named in honor of Edward R. Murrow, and commanded the respect of, among others, CBS News veterans Walter Cronkite and Charlie Rose and his close friend at NBC, Tom Brokaw.

And on the morning of 9/11, within minutes of CNN breaking in with views of a burning World Trade Center, Turner hustled downstairs from his apartment to be part of the action. He had instincts as to how to cover the biggest breaking news story since Pearl Harbor. He suggested that Headline News keep its cameras trained on the trade center's twin towers, and his shrewd advice was heeded. For a moment, Turner said it seemed like the old days.

But he felt a downcast vibe, he says, and it emanated from the attitude of his former subordinates. After the AOL Time Warner deal happened, Turner's direct influence over CNN had shifted in a reorganization of job titles that he didn't expect. No one had to tell him that the heads of the new company, Gerald Levin and Steve Case, had rendered him persona non grata. It was written in the body language of veteran reporters he had had a hand in hiring. "Getting the cold shoulder hurt," he says.

In 1995, the collection of cable channels, movie studios, entertainment content, and sports teams Turner had assiduously assembled under Turner Broadcasting System was consolidated as part of a strategic merger with media company Time Warner. The creation of Time Warner Turner proved fruitful for his brands and for shareholders, of which Turner was the largest.

Five years later, Time Warner Turner was targeted and then subsumed. The $147 billion reverse-leverage takeover by AOL became the biggest deal of its kind. Turner's agreement was critical. On the advice of Gerald Levin, a trusted friend and Time Warner Turner colleague, Turner consented, albeit with suspicions.

Levin had risen to prominence most notably for his leadership at HBO and in putting the merger with Time Warner together. "We've known each other a long time, Ted," Turner says Levin told him. "You got to trust me."

Levin had publicly referred to Turner as "one of his best friends" and Turner, who does not take such compliments lightly, returned it in manifold ways. The AOL Time Warner merger resulted in Turner being given the title of executive vice president by Levin and Case, but with it came no power or responsibility, Turner says.

As part of his cajoling, Turner says Levin had promised that his valuable insight, experience, and leadership charisma would be called upon, after reorganization, to bring news and entertainment into a bold new era. Turner admits that the wooing worked. Sitting alone in Montana in autumn 2001, he was ashamed that he'd allowed himself to be hoodwinked. He could only imagine the berating disapproval it would have attracted from his father. "They paid me a $1 million salary basically to do nothing," Turner says. "For that amount of money, I think they believed that, I would be grateful and attend board meetings and politely keep my mouth shut— and not ask questions. But I've never been a lapdog to anyone."

In fact, Turner was insulted by the callousness of their attempt to buy him off. Behind the scenes, he heard that some executives of the new company fed the perception that he was a relic, too controversial of a figure because he refused to speak in choreographed sound bites. He always said what was on his mind.

When Turner sat in board meetings, he did keep quiet—in the beginning. But he began to become increasingly bothered by what he was hearing. Even as AOL Time Warner's stock price plummeted, he incredulously listened as the executive team spoke of bonuses and perks.

"When revenue targets weren't being met, they were talking raises even as the so-called peons of the company were being fired," Turner says. Some of the companies in Atlanta that he had bootstrapped into profitability and respect were having their staff rolls gutted. Turner found the attitude of his peers, seemingly focused on personal enrichment and not the values of running quality companies, to be surreal. At one point, he piped in: "So, let's get this straight, while we're laying off $30,000-a-year employees in Atlanta, we have million-dollar oil paintings hanging on the walls of our offices in New York?"

Eventually, the paintings were taken down and sold, but his dissent didn't sit well. His colleagues wanted to hear nothing of his criticism. But Turner had been through a convergence before. This was a man, after all, who, when Turner merged TBS with Time Warner in 1995, had allowed his own son, Teddy, to lose his job as a cost-saving measure. He did it to demonstrate fairness.

Turner sensed trouble was brewing for a long while. The suspicion was confirmed by his dear friend, the cable TV magnate and fellow major shareholder in Time Warner Turner, John Malone. Malone told me he had warned Turner to be wary.

"I told Ted that if he wasn't careful he was gonna get screwed," Malone says. "The financial parts of a deal are one thing. Machinations that steal your identity are another."

Turner had become a titan without any say in his eponymous company.

✦

That night in Montana, Turner says he felt like a fool. "How could I have been so stupid. Jerry [Levin] said that I should trust him, and I did. How could I put any faith in a friendship when he never even had me over for dinner the whole time I had known him?"

This slight proved only to be the tip of the iceberg. For Turner, it would become a reminder of how cutthroat a few of his associates were, and how Machiavellian those on Wall Street orchestrating megamergers had become.

On paper, the merger made Turner an astoundingly wealthy man. His worth, in the first few months of the deal, elevated him to twenty-fifth richest in the world. What he didn't have, however, was a decision-making role at the top of the new company. Levin told him he needed to be patient, to focus on the stock value as a monster consolation prize.

If Turner couldn't have his companies, he rationalized, he could at least adhere to the admonishment he made in 1997 when he gave $1 billion to the United Nations, and challenged fellow billionaires to do more for society.

Counting on the value of his AOL Time Warner shares holding up, he summoned the heads of his major foundations and started crafting an action plan to dispense the windfall. "I knew the impact that $1 billion could have in aiding the mission of the UN. I had started thinking about what you could do with $4 billion or $6 billion or $8 billion. You could literally change the world and fix some real problems. I figured that I'd kick in my share and then lean on my wealthy friends. We wouldn't have to wait for governments to take action. We could show that the private sector is capable of doing things faster, better, cheaper."

Among Turner's priorities, adopted over two decades of involvement with global media and a number of international organizations, including the United Nations, and friendships with people ranging from Jimmy Carter to Mikhail Gorbachev: getting malaria nets into the homes of every family in Africa, assisting Rotary Club International in its noble attempt to eradicate polio from the world, and working with governments to reduce nuclear dangers around the world. On the environmental front, he would pump hundreds of millions of dollars into getting imperiled species out of biological triage, including the critically endangered California condor that he hoped to reintroduce to a ranch he owned in the desert Southwest.

He also wanted to help launch clean water projects, eradicate poverty by supporting micro-businesses in the developing world, and support women's rights. Out West, he was growing the largest bison herd in existence, and wanted to show how the animals could be used to restore the environment and help people eat healthier. There was talk that Nelson Mandela had him in mind for a special assignment to try and bring reconciliation of the two Koreas.

Yet always in the back of Turner's mind, there was the possibility of making another attempt to buy one of the big three American television networks that had evaded him. Were he ever to prevail with that dream, he had aspirations of expanding the influence of television to dimensions that surpassed CNN. As he did when assembling an ace pitching rotation for the Atlanta Braves, Turner would have marshaled the resources to recruit the best talent money could buy.

Imagine, he mused, if he could bring the following talent pool to one channel: Cronkite, Rose and Brokaw, Peter Jennings, Ted Koppel, Bill Moyers, Jim Lehrer, Diane Sawyer, Judy Woodruff and Al Hunt, Oprah Winfrey, Catherine Crier, the entire team at *60 Minutes,* and, of course, former colleagues from CNN and retired objective statesmen such as politicians and judges. As moderators, they could deliver insightful, intelligent examination of presidential candidates, discuss the risks posed by nuclear weapons, the important role of the UN, solutions for addressing climate change, solving the Social Security and health care crises, having real conversations about population, and approaching alternative energy as both an environmental and national defense issue.

"It would have been the antithesis of FOX News," he says. "Imagine applying that kind of human capital and the might of television to uniting America in the spirit of cooperation and sacrifice that existed during World War II rather than dividing the country for ratings' sake or using TV as a propaganda arm of a political party? I would deploy TV as a tool for bringing the world together and leveraging peace."

Things did not go according to plan.

Financial pundits have since wondered why Turner didn't diversify his holdings of AOL Time Warner and, after the merger, immediately stagger out substantial withdrawals of his stake in the company.

To this there is an answer. As he reassessed the moves he did and didn't make, Turner confesses that Levin did a masterful job of captivating his ego. Confidants at AOL Time Warner had convinced Turner to hold onto his securities in the company—even as some of those same people, it later turned out, divested themselves of the stock. Turner remained a loyal shareholder because that's what he'd done as he'd put together the Turner Broadcasting System. If he didn't demonstrate his faith in the new company, he figured, why should shareholders be expected to have confidence? But he discovered, keenly, that such idealism was naïve.

Implicit in the conceit dangled before him by Levin was the possibility, implied, that if things did not pan out with new management, and if Turner had maintained his stake as largest shareholder, that he might be summoned to mount a heroic rescue of the company.

Turner was ready to receive that solicitation from Levin and Case. It never came.

In the autumn of 2001, $8 billion of his personal fortune was swiftly evaporating, endangering the environmental and humanitarian projects that had given him more personal meaning than anything he had done in media. To keep his bison ranches, newly launched restaurant chain, and other investments solvent, he had to prepare himself for a possible liquidation of assets.

—~—

On the deck of his house, under the clear autumn night sky in the Rockies, Turner felt as though he could touch the desolation that had swal-
lowed up his father. More accomplished than Ed Turner could ever have
dreamed, and now flirting with a reversal of fortune equally unimaginable, he struggled to resist an impulse that he knew was in his bloodline.

Were detractors here to judge Turner with schadenfreude, one might
be tempted to draw an analogy between him and the fictional media
tycoon Charles Foster Kane, portrayed by Orson Welles in the movie
Citizen Kane. (Besides being one of Turner's favorites, it was a film that he
came to own when he shrewdly acquired the MGM film library.) Kane,
of course, was the unhappy, despondent magnate who discovered, in the
end, that money and power couldn't buy contentment.

"You know," Turner said, "I've always prayed that my own end
wouldn't resemble Charles Foster Kane's. I've never forgotten the last
scenes in the movie."

Kane dies in self-imposed exile from other people. He dwells in a
mansion, Xanadu, erected behind a gated mass estate in Florida named
after the ancient mythical Mongolian city. The narrator says:

*One hundred thousand trees, twenty thousand tons of marble are
the ingredients of Xanadu's mountain. Contents of Xanadu's palace:
paintings, pictures, statues, the very stones of many other palaces
—a collection of everything so big it can never be catalogued or
appraised; enough for ten museums; the loot of the world. Xanadu's
livestock: the fowl of the air, the fish of the sea, the beast of the field
and jungle. Two of each; the biggest private zoo since Noah. Like the
Pharaohs, Xanadu's landlord leaves many stones to mark his grave.
Since the pyramids, Xanadu is the costliest monument a man has
built to himself.*

In the film's final moments, administrators of Kane's estate attempt to decipher the secret meaning of the last word the tycoon muttered before he died: "Rosebud." It was, of course, the name that Kane, as a boy, had bestowed on his trusty snow sled before he was sent away to boarding schools. The sled has two symbolic meanings: the forsaken love of Kane's parents who gave up their son so that he would have money over a relationship with them, and secondly, a broken connection to pure innocent bliss that he had known in the outdoors as a child.

"Mr. Kane was a man who got everything he wanted and then lost it," the narrator says as an epitaph. "Maybe Rosebud was something he couldn't get or something he lost. Anyway, it wouldn't have explained anything. I don't think any word can explain a man's life. I guess Rosebud is just a piece in a jigsaw puzzle—a missing piece."

The message of the film was never lost on Turner. "The movie gave me chills. Seeing the emotion drained out of Kane when he dies an old man with an empty heart and surrounded only by stuff, nothing really of substance. That was it. The end. No big speech. Lights out."

A man of wealth and means, one moment here, the next gone. "No one cared. Nothing to show for all the potential he had to try and do good," Turner says. "It was as if he had never existed. He had no one close to him at his side. Those who claimed they cared for him but only wanted a piece of his money, were gone. He left the world feeling completely alone."

Out of silence, he adds, "I can't think of anything being more sad."

⌁

In Ed Turner's final months, Ted and his father had a fateful telephone conversation. It was the first time that Ted Turner ever forcefully stood up to him, and it would be the last time they ever spoke to each other.

Turner explains that his father had made a move to expand the family's outdoor advertising business, but had then panicked with second thoughts and lack of pluck. Turner, who was being groomed to take over the company, was twenty-four when he heard, secondhand, that his father was planning to sell the company. "Dad, all my life you've taught me to work hard and not be a quitter and now you're the one who's quitting!" he said. "What's happened to you? How could you do this?"

His father refused to give his son a sound explanation.

"We had a falling out. I stood my ground," Turner says.

Not long after the exchange, Ed Turner, suffering from smoking-related emphysema and bad health caused by alcoholism, ate breakfast at his southern plantation, calmly read the newspaper, had a cigarette, then went upstairs to the bathroom. He put a handgun to his head, and pulled the trigger.

Ted Turner, who once blamed himself for being sent away from home as a four-year-old, shouldered new guilt.

Decades after the suicide and doubting his ability to mount a comeback from the AOL Time Warner debacle, Turner thought of how taking his life would be done, and what rational justification would be used as an explanation to his children and grandchildren.

He thought of Jane Fonda. The truth is that among their intimate conversations as a married couple, Turner and Fonda had had heartfelt discussions about suicide and its lingering effects. Fonda's mother had taken her own life. He and his wife related to one another in a way that could not be explained to others. It's well known that surviving children of parental suicides keep track of the days and years until they reach the chronological age when a mother or father died at their own hands. Once they surpass it, they are supposed to feel liberated.

But that's not how it happens, both Turner and Fonda say.

"You never stop thinking about it," Fonda says. "Never."

Ed Turner was fifty-one at the time of his death. Ted Turner in 2001 was nearing his sixty-third birthday.

Before his final act, Turner's father confessed that the goals he had set, those that represented to him the epitome of success, were all material. Having $1 million in the bank, owning both a plantation and a yacht. . . . "Son," he said, "you be sure to set your goals so high that you can't possibly accomplish them in one lifetime. That way you'll always have something ahead of you. I made the mistake of setting my goals too low and now I'm having a hard time coming up with new ones."

"My dad had achieved those things and he wasn't happy," Turner says. "He didn't know why. Basing his contentment on material possessions, he could not find a reason to live."

The surviving son had indeed accumulated a notable collection of high honors. "I realized those are the kinds of things that start people's obituaries, but they are backward looking, not forward," he says. "But what do they matter?"

Occasionally, though he tried to forget, Turner would think about the handgun his father had used to take his own life, and it left him feeling dulled inside. He never knew what happened to the weapon.

But he reflected on it again in 2001. In Montana, he had shotguns and rifles in cases at the Flying D Ranch. If he had to, he could, he figured, go out like Ernest Hemingway.

There was a complication. When he was an unknown twenty-something and left to grieve largely alone, his father's death had caused him to promise that, no matter how bad his life ever got, he wouldn't copy Ed Turner. Suicide had made his father's life irredeemable. "I honestly think if he had given me a chance, I could have helped him."

In the bedroom at the Flying D, Turner closed his eyes. He searched for mental photographs of his offspring. One by one, they surfaced. He says he flashed through them, and then added pictures of his grandchildren. Hours passed until a muted glow of color began seeping in the window. He grew tired and his mind calmed. Slowly, his desperation winnowed. At dawn, he felt ashamed, not triumphant.

He had never shared the details with his family and closest friends. He didn't want them to think less of him.

"Ted didn't get the love he needed or deserved early in his life, at the time when it is supposed to be hardwired," Jane Fonda says. "But the miracle is that he felt compassion for living things by submersing himself in nature. It saved him. All his life he's had to relearn how to love and be loved the hard way and what I've noticed is that communing with him in nature is the way that he accelerates the bonds of love and friendship."

Often, he meditates on the things he has done and might still do that will outlast him. True power isn't in the making of money; it's how that money is channeled, he says.

In the early 1980s, he was aboard the deck of a ship, a cocky, much younger man. He was so full of pride and had no idea of how little he knew. He was in the company of an influential elder, Jacques-Yves Cousteau, a mentor and father figure. They were anchored up the Amazon River. Turner says he can still hear the inflection in Cousteau's voice when he suggested that the environmental problems facing the world—nuclear catastrophe, resource depletion and scarcity linked to consumption, and exploding population growth—might be insurmountable.

"But Ted, we cannot afford to get discouraged," Cousteau said. "Even if we know the end of our world is coming for certain, which we do not, what can men of good conscience do but keep trying to do the right thing until the very end?"

Turner had no idea that it would become an admonishment of self-preservation. Had he capitulated decades later in pulling the real and proverbial trigger, any and all of his previous accomplishments would have been tainted by the flaw of a final impetuous act. Anything yet to come afterward, involving ideas that took shape earlier and blossomed only in the ensuing years, would not exist. There certainly would be no reason for a book to document them now. In hindsight, people today would be looking at Turner and wondering: Was he really a shrewd thinker, ahead of his time, albeit crazy as a fox and eccentric, or was he just crazy?

At some deep level, Turner grasped this reality and he reeled. He did not want to represent the personification of squandered opportunity. As romantic as tragic figures are, in serving as muses for classical rhyme and verse, he did not want to become one. And yet, he thought of Publius Horatius Cocles, immortalized by Thomas Babington Macaulay (Turner's favorite bit of heroic prose) and he thought of Cousteau and, lastly, he thought of Robert Edward Turner Jr.

He realized that he could still love his father without having to suffer shame and guilt by refusing to emulate him. Alone, haggard from his all-nighter, but not paralyzed by a fear of loneliness, Turner walked through his ranch house past the room where the guns are kept. The Sirens' call was gone. For the first time. More than a decade has passed since he thought of ending it all, a span that in measuring Turner's life, has become in a way, a personal triumph and capstone. His financial fortune would reverse and he would become an emblem for how to give money away. His bison herds would grow; his rally in defense of the United Nations would become ever more voluble, and he's declared: "I'm still here. Nobody's going to shut me up until I'm dead and gone." And, even then, he has the satisfaction of knowing that the initiatives he's established—a way of thinking about the human relationship toward the land and among people toward each other—will continue.

At the end of many days, he still wonders what Ed Turner would be thinking of how he sold his boy short. Perhaps the biggest triumph in Ted Turner's life is that he did not become his father.

The difference between projecting a mask of blind stoic fearlessness and possessing real courage and wisdom, Turner says, is knowing what you throw away if you choose to give up on the things you love—and those who love you.

CHAPTER THREE

My Captain Was Aquaman

"Ted said that one of the best lines he knows about honour was written by Shakespeare in Richard II, and he went on to quote it word for word: 'Mine honour is my life; both grow in one: Take honour from me, and my life is done: Then, dear my liege, mine honour let me try; in that I live and for that will I die.'"

—Sir Richard Branson, businessman, Turner friend and
fellow eco-humanitarian

When a father dies by his own hands, who is left to guide the abandoned son forward not to avenge a loss but to help rectify the hole that's been created? Who becomes the next role model? Who fills the *void*? In hundreds of speeches and interviews given over the years, Ted Turner has paid homage, without elaborating, to one of the most widely recognized scientists on the planet, a man whose medium covers most of Earth's surface and sets it apart from the other, lifeless planets in our solar system: a man who was a crucial catalyst for Turner's budding identity as an environmentalist.

"I can't remember when I first heard his name," Turner says. "It might have been when I arrived at college in my years at Brown, before I had to leave. Those of us who spent time around the ocean liked to talk. Here was this guy, this Frenchman, who seemed to be pulling back a veil on the world beneath the waves."

People come into your life at certain moments—people who play the role of guru, Turner says, and you're either ready to receive their wisdom, or you're not. They cause course corrections in thinking.

Enter Jacques-Yves Cousteau. During Turner's halcyon days as a competitive sailor when he covered sixty thousand miles on the water, and subsequently during his pioneering launch of TBS and CNN, bronze busts of Alexander the Great and British Navy admiral Horatio Nelson adorned his desk in Atlanta. By design, he admits, they were props that journalists often referenced. They were chosen to help illustrate his competitive mettle and desire to someday have a place in history.

Those men were warriors, and they helped to secure Turner's mystique as a modern David taking on Goliaths. Yet in fact the paladin he came to rely upon for grounding was an unlikely living man. Cousteau was diminutive, had a big nose, smoked a pipe like a college professor, spoke with a continental accent, and had served as an inventor of the aqualung and scuba diving. And though they were a generation apart, Turner and Cousteau had both experienced similar epiphanies precipitated, ironically, by periods of estrangement.

"Sometimes we are lucky enough to know that our lives have been changed, to discard the old, embrace the new, and run headlong down an immutable course," Cousteau had famously written in his book, *The Silent World*. "It happened to me on that summer's day, when my eyes were opened to the sea."

Cousteau also opened Turner's eyes, baptizing him into a life of environmental activism and, Turner says, he became something of a surrogate father.

Hindus and Buddhists look upon the selection of *calling* as Dharma. Turner the agnostic—who is open to being convinced of an all-uniting divinity—does not think of his own stirring of consciousness in religious terms; he does, however, explain it as an act of pure faith.

━━━◦━━━

Turner has vague recollection of a film, *Le Monde du Silence* (in English, *The Silent World*) showing in art house cinemas toward the end of his teenage years. Under the instruction of Jimmy Brown, a black Gullah caretaker who had been hired by Ed Turner to help raise Ted, Turner had been racing small sailboats to victory in regattas off the coast of Charleston, Savannah, and other Atlantic port towns. And *The Silent World: A Story of Undersea Discovery and Adventure*, a documentary that won an Academy Award in 1956, showed him a new world under the rudders of his boats. But it would be a long while before Cousteau had any bearing on Turner's life.

Upon graduation from McCallie Prep in Chattanooga, Tennessee, where he was a champion in speech and debate, Turner enrolled in Brown. There, he became a leader on the forensics team and was captain of the sailing club. He also got suspended after he became rowdy and threw chairs out of a dormitory. After a year he was reinstated, but in the interim, he enlisted in the US Coast Guard Reserve at Cape May, New Jersey. Just as he had done on the Brown sailing and debate teams, he demonstrated leadership abilities on and off the water.

During his third year, he was forced to withdraw from the Ivy League institution after Ed Turner pulled financial support for his son's tuition. Penning perhaps one of the most poignant father-to-son missives ever, the elder Turner chided his son for pursuing an undergraduate degree in classics, studying the works of ancient philosophers, and learning to speak Latin. Why does Turner relate to the stories of the ancients and maintain an interest in quoting Shakespeare? It goes back to those days.

Ed Turner, however, was irate that Ted wasn't majoring in something practical, like business. And he had no interest in investing his money into a college education that he believed his son couldn't use to succeed.

"My dear son," Ed's letter to Ted began. "I am appalled, even horrified, that you have adopted Classics as a major. As a matter of fact, I almost puked on the way home today. I suppose that I am old-fashioned enough to believe that the purpose of an education is to enable one to develop a community of interest with his fellow men, to learn to know them, and to learn how to get along with them . . . These subjects might give you a community of interest with an isolated few impractical dreamers . . . and a select group of college professors. God forbid! . . . There is no question but this type of useless information will distinguish you, set you apart from the doers of the world. If I leave you enough money, you can retire to an ivory tower, and contemplate for the rest of your days the influence that the hieroglyphics of prehistoric man had upon the writings of William Faulkner. Incidentally, he [Faulkner] was a contemporary of mine in Mississippi. We speak the same language—whores, sluts, strong words and strong deeds. . . . I just wish I could feel that the influence of those oddball professors and the ivory towers were developing you into the kind of a man we can both be proud of . . . I think you are rapidly becoming a jackass, and the sooner you get out of that filthy atmosphere, the better it will suit me . . . You go ahead and go with the world, and I'll go it alone. I hope I am right. You are in the hands of the Philistines, and dammit, I sent you there. I am sorry."

Turner the younger was stunned, and then amused, and finally incredulous. He didn't believe his father would follow through on his implicit threat. He allowed Brown's student newspaper to publish the letter verbatim. It became the talk of the campus, but left Ed Turner furious, and vowing to teach his son a lesson in one-upmanship. He was paying the tuition, he knew that Ted knew it, and he could take away what his son valued if he didn't play by Ed's rules. An alcoholic and chain smoker who developed emphysema, Ed had set a strange example for his son. He told Ted that men are by their nature promiscuous and that "real men run around."

He once boasted to Ted of having slept with over three hundred women—in addition to Ted's mother—by the time he turned thirty. Obviously unhappy and, according to Ted, suffering from chronic depression, he also had a mean streak when he was drinking and had paddled Turner or slapped him if, as a boy, he got crosswise. The razor strop was a favored implement. Once, when he was convinced that his corporal discipline wasn't having the desired impact, he resorted to reverse psychology. He handed his son a wire hanger and told Ted to beat *him*, saying, "this is gonna hurt you more than it is hurting me." When Turner refused, he was verbally browbeaten, derided as a weakling, and taunted until he complied.

The oft-repeated explanation of why Turner left Brown, publicized in several unauthorized biographies, is that Ted was tossed out for fraternizing with females in his dormitory room. Indeed, that was a contributing factor to his departure; he has always had a fondness for women, following in the footsteps of his father. But the truth is Ted couldn't stay in Providence, even though he wanted to. His father cut him off and, having no resources, his college career ended. It was a lesson in emasculation and a scarring episode that, ultimately, has made him more sympathetic to issues involving empowerment of the have-nots.

Heading back to Georgia, Turner went to work in the family outdoor advertising business, subject to his father's whims. Ed informed him that he needed to prove himself worthy of moving up in the family company. One day, if he worked hard, his father said, he would become a full-fledged partner. He also tried to manipulate many aspects of his life, including telling him where to live, demanding to know whom he was dating, and how he was spending his time away from the office.

At twenty-one, Turner married for the first time—a woman from Chicago named Judy Nye whom he had met while sailing. The courtship, he said, happened too fast and the wedding should have been called off. Needing to provide for his young family, he took over an outdoor advertising venture for his father in Macon, Georgia. He became the youngest member of the local Rotary Club (and a lifelong devotee to the worldwide organization), served on the board of the Red Cross, and assisted with publicity for The United Way. Handed a junior management position in the billboard company, he recalls a personal on-site inspection made by Ed Turner to assess his progress. Afterward, he received a rare note of commendation. It contained a few complimentary lines that left him beaming.

"My father was usually very sparing with his praise, and nothing he did before or after that day ever made me feel so good," Turner noted in his memoir *Call Me Ted*. "I had no way of knowing at the time just how special and precious our days together then would later prove to be."

Nothing, of course, is ever black and white. Ed Turner *did* show flashes of love. His son pined for them.

~ ~

When his father committed suicide just shy of Ted's twenty-fifth birthday, Turner by then was a young parent of two children—Laura and Teddy Jr.— and newly divorced from Judy Nye. He says they were not compatible. Judy Nye agreed, pointing to his incorrigible infidelity as one reason for their split. Turner met Jane Smith, an airline flight attendant from Alabama, at a young Republican social mixer, married her, and became the father of a third child, Rhett. Turner was scrambling to hold the billboard business together even while gaining a name as a competitive yachtsman. And he repeated the example of his father insofar as he again did not adhere to the strict discipline of monogamy. He does not make excuses; to this day, when interacting with his closest friends who have enjoyed happily married lives to the same person, he expresses admiration of them, and personal regret.

Just as there was no indication of his converging path toward Cousteau and environmentalism, his political ideology in this period was further to the right than one might think, given his support of progressive causes in recent decades. He was a Goldwater conservative, in emulation of his father. Indeed, Turner's first bold independent public statement came after Ed Turner's death.

To make a statement, he covered several of his billboards across the Southeast with the famous opening line to Ayn Rand's objectivist Libertarian manifesto *Atlas Shrugged*: "Who is John Galt?"

The wounds of his sister's and father's deaths, and his fading confidence in organized religion, made Rand's promotion of hedonistic materialism, small government, and no regulation appealing to Ted. And while eventually he would reject Rand's cardinal tenet that self-interest takes precedence over one's duty to others and the common good, he was then, and remains now, a devotee of the notion that the free market can be a positive agent of raising social consciousness and expanding prosperity in the world. Again, his refrain is that capitalism isn't the problem but how it is being applied.

During these same years, Cousteau won another Academy Award for a documentary, and was featured in the television series *The Undersea World of Jacques Cousteau*. It ran from 1966 to 1976, and showed in millions of American living rooms on television sets with rabbit ear antennas.

"By being the first subject of environmental programming on TV," Turner says, "the Captain was the first champion of science for common people. You didn't need a degree to understand the message. The beauty of the ocean gave people a reason to take notice, and his narration offered them a reason to care. He led tired, working class people on escapes to places they would not otherwise think about, and he told them why the ocean had a connection to their lives."

Until then, American heroes were largely war veterans, astronauts, politicians, sports figures, and movie stars. "Cousteau gave us a new category," Turner says. "If Rachel Carson is credited with being the mother of the modern environmental movement, then the Captain should rightfully be considered the movement's father."

It was a reference that, upon Cousteau's death, would tie Turner and Cousteau together. Turner's assessment was cited in obituaries around the globe. Without television and the feature stories in *National Geographic* magazine, Turner says, the appeal of Cousteau's scientific endeavors might never have broken from obscurity, nor might the environment have been a coming-of-age interest for those baby boomers who went on to devote themselves to environmental causes. "In one form or another, we are his offspring," he says.

The same kind of impact Turner credits to Cousteau, he also extends to chimpanzee researcher Jane Goodall; the twin brothers, John and Frank Craighead, who studied Yellowstone grizzly bears; American wolf man L. David Mech; and late gorilla researcher Dian Fossey.

In 1970, Turner bought an obscure VHF television station in Atlanta and ingeniously linked it to satellites, creating the SuperStation, earning accolades as an important technology disruptor of the modern age. During the first half of the 1970s, as sailing took precedence over media, he walked a thin line of financial solvency. Not until the end of the decade, after he had triumphed as a consummate underdog in the 1977 America's Cup, was Turner ready to enter his second phase, this time as a businessman, free of recreational distraction.

Turner's antics as a self-promoter and marketer extraordinaire are legendary. The lengths he went to try and generate public interest in his media properties and put fans in the stands to watch the Atlanta Braves and Hawks were innovative and embarrassing. Many people who never forgot that side of Turner would be understandably hard pressed to believe that a different self-effacing, disciplined, magnanimous version could exist. The dual Turner is not a diametric pole in a Jekyll and Hyde character; it is the inner person he aspires to be when he is free of the anxiety that besets him when he feels overwhelmed. My observation: Turner the extrovert is a role he plays; I believe he is, at heart, an introvert who does a lot of living in his head. Empathizing with the causes of environmentalism and humanitarianism isn't something he learned; the paradox is that he knew he could only save himself by helping others. He sees his own desperate self in others' plight.

Photojournalist Barbara Pyle met Turner at Bannister's Wharf along the waterfront of Newport, Rhode Island, in 1980. She was then working for *Time* magazine, covering the anticipated showdown between reigning America's Cup champion—Turner—and his former shipmate-turned-archrival, Dennis Conner.

Running into Turner on the docks as preparations were being made for *Courageous*'s defense against Conner's state-of-the-art *Freedom*, Pyle thought it odd that Turner deflected her inquiries about racing and instead bombarded her with questions about the protocol of news gathering at NBC, where she had worked briefly in the news division.

The reason soon became clear: On June 1, 1980—as the America's Cup challenge races were playing out in Newport, a Turner invention, his second noted expression of technology disruption, the Cable News Network [CNN] went live in Atlanta.

"In the mornings at Bannister's Wharf, Ted was on the phone with his business partner Robert Wussler, right up to the minute that he had to launch the boat. Then he sailed the race, but without his trademark intensity. At the time, he was considered the best sailor in the world but his head was someplace else," Pyle told me.

Even before *Courageous* lost its bid to repeat, Turner revealed to Pyle that he planned to retire from sailing. She was puzzled; this was supposed to be his glorious prime. But his focus in the future was going to be on taking the continental reach of TBS and extending it to CNN.

Turner says he had always thought that sailing at the highest level would leave him fulfilled. But a year earlier, he and his crew on board another craft, *Tenacious* (a crew that included his son Teddy), had prevailed in the 605-mile Fastnet race off the British coast. A victory for Turner, yes, but this 1979 competition is remembered today as a notorious disaster. Fifteen competing sailors perished when the equivalent of a hurricane swept across the North Atlantic. Sixty-nine boats did not finish. What should have been a nautical triumph for Turner was overshadowed by a pall of mourning. I asked him about it, particularly the fact that the fate greeting his competitors could easily have happened to him. Some had accused him of being reckless and he seemed willing to risk the potential demise of his own son.

As a younger man, he was deceived by his own hubris, he says. That is not a man that he still relates to. It's tough for him to confront those parts of his life that happened and cannot be changed. When I asked him if he was trying to deflect questions away from painful episodes, he says that's not it. Just because he doesn't wish to analyze them publicly in print doesn't mean he doesn't think about them. He regards Fastnet as a race when he let go of his adolescence to seek other kinds of meaning, including deciding how he could be a different father from the mold handed to him.

"It was a humbling moment. The seas were rough. I had been driving pretty hard. I was going for the trophy and the glory but, given the conditions, the biggest prize in hindsight was that something bad didn't happen to the crew, which included my own son."

Critics of Turner have accused him of being unable to engage in introspection. It's true that he doesn't dwell on how things might have been different in the past, though his sometimes strained relationships with his children and loved ones have, in these later years, caused him to reflect. In hindsight, and to appropriate a sailing metaphor, Turner's life is defined by a series of sharp tacks turned against heavy seas, each new angle punctuated by epiphanies that take time to become fully illuminated.

Twenty-four hour news was never, for Turner, a gimmick, but looking back he says the concept was so obvious as to be inevitable. He thought it could make people smarter, less insular in how they conceptualized the world. He believed that news delivered in half-hour increments at dinnertime was too anemic. But his initial efforts, CNN's inaugural days in

Atlanta, were (to put it mildly) fitful, laughed off as amateurish by the three major network giants. His beloved CNN was lampooned as "the Chicken Noodle Network." Nevertheless, launched with a shoestring budget of $30 million (one-tenth the amount that major networks spent on news gathering), CNN managed to generate ten times the volume of programming. And it would eventually net a lot of money.

At the same time, Turner was continuing to expand the breadth of his TBS SuperStation. And he realized that while expensive to generate, original content (combined with quality reruns of old television shows) was critical if he were to attract ad dollars and stay afloat. "He hustled his ass off," remembers John Malone, the CEO of Liberty Media who worked tirelessly with Turner to elevate the credibility of cable TV and eventually would surpass Turner as America's largest landowner, admitting that it was Turner who inspired him. In the early 1980s, Turner was living out of a suitcase. He flew economy class, rented subcompact cars, stayed in budget motels, and had his family at home on a tight regimen of turning off lights, using fans instead of an air conditioner in the hot southern summers, and putting on sweaters inside during the winter. He leveraged everything he owned.

Meantime, to maintain his sanity against the pressure of meeting payroll and staying on the air, he had squirreled away enough cash and credit to purchase Hope Plantation south of Charleston, South Carolina, and St. Phillips, a barrier island north of Hilton Head. Today, Turner is mindful of the mixed message and the contradictions. He was unconsciously still adhering to the imprint of his tough-love father, unaware of how it was affecting his own children. "Was I hard on my kids? I'm aware. They've made me aware."

Whatever money he saved through his austerity measures he was funneling back into keeping his companies viable and making investments in what he still believes are the most conservative and self-rewarding assets: land. Successful people have land, though Turner never saw his initial purchases of Hope Plantation or St. Phillips Island as real estate plays. He put some of the first conservation easements in the country on each piece.

The late Robert Wussler, a key figure in the world of broadcasting, had been wooed to Atlanta after being the youngest executive at CBS and having transformed CBS Sports into a powerhouse brand. About the early days of CNN, Wussler said in a phone interview, "Those were scary and exhilarating times. It was touch and go. I won't kid you, I had doubts sometimes with whether we'd be able to pull off CNN, and Ted was trying to acquire content to put on the channels. For Ted, thank God, he had those properties to get away to. I always thought that if Ted hadn't been involved in media, he might have been a scientist or an explorer. It made perfect sense to me when he became fast friends with Jacques Cousteau, who, of course, had more star power than anything else we could put on the air."

⌒ ⌒

While Turner's progression as a media executive adheres to a linear chronology, his evolution as an eco-capitalist does not conform to an exact timeline, but rather a convergence of different stimuli, people entering his life, and a burgeoning world view. As Turner was in Newport preparing to defend his America's Cup crown, and even as he was dealing with the logistics of launching the world's first twenty-four-hour news channel, he had in his possession a lengthy document called *The Global 2000 Report to the President*.

"When the president of the United States gives you a document and says you should read it, most people would be honored," Turner says. "I was."

Commissioned by President Jimmy Carter in May of 1977, and released by the US State Department and the Council on Environmental Quality, this was a document that connected the dots between rising human population, expanding poverty, famine and depleted natural resources, loss of biological diversity, and lack of regulation and serious impacts on environmental and human health.

The report stated unequivocally: "The available evidence leaves no doubt that the world—including this nation—faces enormous, urgent, and complex problems in the decades immediately ahead. Prompt and vigorous changes in public policy around the world are needed to avoid or minimize these problems before they become unmanageable. Long lead times are required for effective action. If decisions are delayed until the problems become worse, options for effective action will be severely reduced."

Turner felt chastened as he read the litany of serious converging challenges. "I think it drove home the point to me, for the first time in my life, that, as a business person, the decisions I make can either contribute to making problems for the Earth worse, or they can help advance a solution," he says.

Reflecting on his former devotion to Ayn Rand and the way she equated avarice with moral goodness, he had an awakening: "This is where Ayn Rand was wrong. If pursuing self-interest means that you are unfairly foisting the cost of doing business on other people, including taxpayers and future generations, then you're not thinking about the betterment of society. You're no better than a *robber baron*."

Turner handed Barbara Pyle a copy of the Global 2000 Report. Her impression of Turner had been shaped by his reputation for being adolescently fun-loving, impolitic, and everything that led to the moniker "Captain Outrageous." She saw another side.

"You take this stuff pretty seriously, don't you, Ted?" Pyle said.

"Don't you think it is important?"

"It's too bad a person can't make a living trying to fix the problems," she said.

Whimsically, Turner invited Pyle to come work for the fledgling CNN in Atlanta. Her new job would be overseeing the station's first environmental news division comprised of a staff of one: her. Her assignment? Telling personal stories of people affected by the issues raised in the Global 2000 document.

A decade after the first Earth Day in 1970, it was Turner who began giving the environment regular media coverage. Pyle's nascent environmental bureau would grow to become the largest in television.

⌣⌣

Turner and Jimmy Carter were friends, even though Turner identified as a Republican verging upon aligning himself as an Independent. He had gotten to know Carter when he served as governor of Georgia, and then marveled at Carter's ability to mount a folksy, populist campaign for the White House in 1976. Turner backed him.

Almost forty years later, Turner is still unrestrained in his admiration of Carter. He does not stand behind people based upon whether they are popular. For advocating conservation and alternative energy to shake US dependence on Middle Eastern oil, for his courage, for being decades ahead in his thinking, Turner says that Carter deserves praise. "I don't care what people say about President Carter, he was right about a lot of things . . . he spoke his mind honestly . . . he called for more private and public sector investments in solar, synthetic fuel, conservation and energy efficiency in cars and homes, as well as wisely using the resources we have at home. He had the guts to say what citizens *needed* to hear, but didn't *want* to hear. He got beaten up for it and it probably caused him to lose his reelection."

Within the larger landscape of Turner's evolving sensibility as an environmentalist, second perhaps only to Cousteau in influence is Carter. And when Carter delivered his so-called Malaise Speech, it had enough of an impact on Turner that he remembers certain resonant pullouts. "Human identity is no longer defined by what one does, but by what one owns," Carter said. "But we've discovered that owning things and consuming things does not satisfy our longing for meaning. We've learned that piling up material goods cannot fill the emptiness of lives which have no confidence or purpose."

Carter presciently added on that night: "Energy will be the immediate test of our ability to unite this Nation, and it can also be the standard around which we rally. On the battlefield of energy we can win for our nation a new confidence, and we can seize control again of our common destiny. In little more than two decades we've gone from a position of energy independence to one in which almost half the oil we use comes from foreign countries, at prices that are going through the roof . . . This intolerable dependence on foreign oil threatens our economic independence and the very security of our nation."

"By not listening to what Jimmy Carter said, by behaving like children who do not want to have discipline, either imposed upon them or embraced voluntarily, we fell behind when we could have been ahead," Turner says.

"Unfortunately, we live in a world that punishes people who are ahead of their time. It happened with Galileo, with Abraham Lincoln, Martin Luther King, and with President Carter. He wanted us to take a long hard look at ourselves in the mirror, *as a nation*. It was tough medicine. He had as his model the kind of shared sacrifice that brought us together and made America stronger during the Depression and World War II. The words conservation and conservative originate in the same place."

Carter impressed Turner more as a conservationist cut from the cloth of Republican Theodore Roosevelt. Under his tenure, Carter signed the Alaska National Interest Lands Conservation Act into law, bringing more public real estate—79.5 million acres—into strict natural resource protection than under any previous administration. Yet it was another achievement, less recognized, that became a mile marker in Turner's environmental thinking. This was the document Turner later handed to Barbara Pyle.

"Read this," Carter had told Turner then, smiling, "you might learn something."

And, in 2008, Carter told me, "It surprised me a little how receptive to it Ted was. But Ted's entire career has been about surprising a lot of people."

Another surprise is Turner's knack for foreshadowing. On the first of June in 1980 when he formally inaugurated CNN, Turner stood in front of its small digs in Atlanta—a renovated golf course clubhouse—and declared playfully (unaware of how ominous his words would sound decades later): "We won't be signing off until the world ends. We'll be on, and we will cover the end of the world, live, and that will be our last event. When the end of the world comes, we'll play 'Nearer, My God, To Thee' before we sign off."

Except for the fact that the names of their aquatic vessels, *Calypso* and *Courageous*, had become emblems, Captains Cousteau and Turner seemed like an odd pairing.

Cousteau would often invite friends to hang out on *Calypso*, the mothballed World War II minesweeper used by the British Navy that he had converted into a research ship. One of the regular guests was John Denver, the folk singer who had composed a song about Cousteau's boat and dedicated the profits to advancing ocean conservation.

Denver and Turner, as they eventually found out, were mutual admirers. Turner enjoyed Denver's down-home ballads and played his albums on 8-track tape players in the yachts he raced. The singer's burgeoning activities as an eco-philanthropist left Turner intrigued. Denver had formed the Windstar Foundation to aid fledgling conservation efforts, including the launching of Project Lighthawk, which provided free aerial flyovers to give activists, policy makers, and journalists a bird's-eye view of threatened landscapes.

"I held John in high esteem. Like Bob Redford and Paul Newman and a short list of others, he was out there promoting environmental protection without worrying about the consequences it might have on his career," Turner says. "It was gutsy. He did it because it was right. I've always felt the same way. If you let intimidation and fear of retaliation stop you, you're destined to be silent. And then what good are you?"

Cousteau became a point of triangulation. Widely beloved, his mercurial moods, insecurities, and large ego could also make him a difficult personality to manage. It alienated him from some of the decision-makers in television. He had pitched ideas for new series, but none of them were green-lighted. His oldest son, Jean-Michel, remembers the frustration of rejection, and how John Denver provided their next step. "John said to my father, 'Captain, maybe you should contact Ted Turner.' And my dad asked, 'Ted Turner. Who iz zis man?'"

Denver described him as the fellow who had won the America's Cup and just founded CNN.

"Then the light went on in my dad's head," Jean-Michel explains. "And he said, 'Oh *heem*, zat guy who started the *Suuper* Station, ze American with ze loud personality?'"

Jean-Michel asked Denver: "But how do you know he will see us or have any interest in our proposal?" They wanted to start a new series on the threats facing marine ecosystems.

"Because Ted has committed to make a documentary about me, and I'm sure he would love to meet you and your dad. He's a bit of a character, I should warn you, his behavior is kind of unusual, and they call him 'Captain Outrageous,' but he's got a good heart."

Turner was flattered that Cousteau wanted an audience with him. Not long before, he had begun a friendship with cosmologist Carl Sagan and conducted a memorable interview of him on CNN. There was already precedent on Turner's stations for a serious treatment of science.

But Jean-Michel and Jacques knew that they would only have seconds to make their case.

Sitting down with Turner, the Cousteaus expressed their concern about troubling problems taking hold in the world's oceans, the stories that needed to be told, and how the only lever to force change was educating the masses so that citizens might lean on elected officials to take action.

"How much would it cost to put a new series on the air?" Turner asked.

"Ted has always been direct," Jean-Michel says. "He doesn't beat around the bush. If he has a thought in his head, more than likely he will share it with you. At least in those days, he didn't do much self-editing."

The Cousteaus asked for $5 million spread over five years—a sum that in the early 1980s could have paid for a significant part of Turner's Atlanta Braves professional baseball roster.

Turner rocked back in his chair, arms butterflied behind his head. He studied Cousteau, and then Jean-Michel. Thinking of what happened in his own family, he was touched that a son was beside his father for support. And here was the real Jacques Cousteau in the flesh. Turner had an opportunity to collaborate with a living legend.

Cousteau, he reasoned, could help elevate the credibility of his cable channels. Turner quickly calculated how the costs of creating original content could be amortized through subsequent syndication and be a boon for generating advertising. If the right deal was struck, he might also gain access to Cousteau's earlier work, which would be an improvement over twenty-year-old reruns of the *Andy Griffith Show* and *Leave It to Beaver*.

"He apparently liked what we proposed because, on the spot, without any lawyers present, he said he would support us and we were to work out the arrangements with Bob Wussler. No contracts, nothing," Jean-Michel says. "Just a handshake. His commitment was based solely on the authority of his word."

Wussler was, in fact, shocked at the deal Turner had struck, but Turner was insistent.

Cousteau didn't let on, Jean-Michel says, but his father felt an affinity for Turner the instant they met. The mutual fondness was solidified in subsequent years as they learned of each other's painful pasts. They had each had tempestuous and distant relationships with their fathers, both sent to the equivalents of military school, and both endured lonely, uncertain childhoods. A short while before their meeting, Cousteau had lost his younger son, Philippe, to a seaplane accident. Turner had experienced the loss of both sister and father. They each had learned to persevere, to count only on oneself, seeking out nature as a refuge.

"I know that Ted saw my dad as a second father and that my dad viewed him like he would a son," Jean-Michel says. "Sometimes it's easier when you are not connected by blood line because there isn't so much personal history and baggage."

"He took me seriously," Turner says. "He believed in me. He didn't have to, but he did. I needed that. Every man does."

The collaboration with Cousteau occurred even as Turner was entering into a separate agreement with filmmaker Chris Palmer and the National Audubon Society and other entities to turn out wildlife documentaries featuring narration by Redford and Newman.

———— ~ ————

Jean-Michel Cousteau says the pitch they made to Turner did not involve full disclosure. In June 1979, when Cousteau's son and Jean-Michel's younger brother, Philippe, died in a plane crash on the Tagus River near Lisbon, Portugal, the Cousteau brand almost died with him.

Philippe had gone to film school in Paris and served as his father's right-hand man with the nonprofit Cousteau Society. Jean-Michel, who had pursued other interests, was with Jacques-Yves when they buried Philippe at sea. "My father was completely devastated with grief, and I mean completely. He turned to me and said, 'I need your help, son, to keep the Cousteau Society running. If you don't do it, then I will probably stop.'"

"What can you do when your father says he needs you?" Jean-Michel asks. "It was simple. I dropped my plans and went to work for him."

Soon after he began putting the Cousteau Society's books in order, Jean-Michel discovered that the organization was $5.1 million in debt and nearly bankrupt. Costs of keeping *Calypso* shipshape were expensive, the inability to land another series hampered their cash flow, and while his father and brother were charismatic people, they weren't accountants.

"I thought, 'Oh shit, what am I going to do now?'" Jean-Michel explained.

The society was told that it might be forced to liquidate assets, including *Calypso*. Jean-Michel said his father had been largely unaware of the magnitude of the financial challenges, and selling the boat would have brought him shame and embarrassment in the twilight of his life.

John Denver had been briefed by Jean-Michel, and his eponymous song about the research vessel was written so that royalties would keep the boat afloat. The meeting with Turner was essentially a desperate Hail Mary pass. "Ted didn't know at the time that he was really our last hope," Jean-Michel says.

Fortunately, based on their proposal, the $5 million deal that Turner and Wussler negotiated called for the Cousteaus to shoot and produce new shows. It also gave TBS rights for twenty-five years to air twelve hours of a series called *Cousteau Odyssey* that had originally premiered on PBS. The money enabled the Cousteau Society to clear debt from its books without double-mortgaging *Calypso*.

"You want to know the truth? Ted Turner bailed us out," Jean-Michel said. "Without a clue of what he was doing, he helped save my dad's reputation and breathed new life and excitement into him. My dad lived to make more documentaries, and Ted gave him the chance."

And for his part, Turner was proud that he could now add the title "nature expedition underwriter" to his resume. Like Thomas Jefferson meeting with Meriwether Lewis and William Clark in 1803, he and the Cousteaus charted a route through their storyboards. Their upcoming collaboration would probe the watery conduits of the Amazon River, recording the links between the heart of the South American rainforest and the Atlantic Ocean, a connection that scientists have come to recognize as a hotbed for biodiversity and an important thermostat in regulating Earth's climate.

Nothing like it had ever been done. In recent years, copies of the series used in college and high school classrooms for environmental studies have been used to illustrate the vital role of that rainforest and what has been lost to logging, pollution, and climate change. Much of its function as a pump for freshwater and a sink for carbon is now being threatened as desert expands across the basin.

At first, Turner agreed to produce four hours, edited down from hundreds of hours of proposed filming. Then the series was expanded to six hours. Based on his blind faith in the Cousteaus, Turner opened up his checkbook to augment the original deal. Then he saw them off.

"I know it doesn't seem like that along ago, but when we started up the river in 1981, there was no cell phone contact, no sophisticated SAT phones and certainly no Internet—just shortwave radio. We kind of felt like we were characters in a South American version of Joseph Conrad's *Heart of Darkness*," Jean-Michel says.

Turner and Wussler had many discussions about projects Turner wanted to underwrite, some of which Wussler believed were wastes of money. "What I didn't fully appreciate until recently was that Ted was hustling to pay the bills for TBS and CNN. He had mortgaged his house and everything he owned to meet payroll for his employees in Atlanta. He was under a lot of stress. It would have been a reasonable, perfectly understandable thing for him to say no to us. But he doesn't back out of commitments he makes," Jean-Michel explains.

"He always follows through. To be honest, though, I think his involvement was also giving him a vicarious thrill."

A few years later, Turner, Pyle, and colleagues put *Captain Planet and the Planeteers* on television, the first-ever Saturday morning children's cartoon series with an environmental theme. Its purpose was entertaining and educating the next generation about the importance of saving things in nature crucial to human quality of life. Turner figured that in order to make his green programming work, he would just have to toil harder and log more hours. And that's what he did, staying late at the office and rising early. Finally he had a pullout bed installed at work. He would sometimes say goodnight to his staff with his pajamas on and a nightcap in hand, then greet them with the same attire on in the morning clutching a cup of coffee.

~ ~

The making of the Amazon documentaries is its own saga. Far up the narrowing channels of the Amazon, *Calypso* searched to find the innermost reaches of the river's main stem and its tributaries, extending into Colombia, Ecuador, Bolivia, and Peru. The crew met not just native river people in dugout canoes, but cocaine runners in speedboats, toting machine guns. "We were approached by people who said we could make a lot of money if we 'volunteered' to use *Calypso* for transporting coca paste and carrying it out to boats at sea," Jean-Michel says. "They made it sound like we didn't have much of a choice and we declined at our own peril."

Rainforests were being toppled to create clandestine coca plantations even as massive open pit mines and oil development were stabbing into the isolated wilderness. The more Jean-Michel and his father thought about it, the more they realized a connection between environmental conditions and the desperate things people do to survive.

"The viewers of our shows in North America and Europe had no sense of the consequences of drug consumption in the North or the way that multinational companies were exploiting resources in Third World countries. The drugs and minerals and oil that we use connect us to the most sensitive places on Earth," Jean-Michel says. "It was a dangerous time for outsiders to be there poking around, especially film crews. The drug cartels are ruthless. This was bigger than an ecology story. I told my dad that we needed to make another call to Atlanta."

They docked at the edge of a remote outpost and patched in a telephone call via shortwave radio. But they weren't radioing Turner to say they wanted to pack up and leave. They wanted to push further. "I said to Ted that I thought we really needed to produce a seventh hour of the series that focused on the drug trade because its impact on humans was as important as the effects of deforestation and mining and all three are linked to destruction of the environment," Jean-Michel says.

For whatever reason, Turner thought he needed to shout over the phone, Jean-Michel remembers. "Drugs?" he asked Jean-Michel loudly. "You want to make a show about drugs? I thought we are making films about *the environment*."

Cousteau laughs recounting the conversation. "We actually didn't have a very good radio hook-up and you could tell that Ted was multitasking. I held the radio up away from my ear and you could hear him yelling questions to us and talking to other people wherever he was. He was in downtown Atlanta and I was in the middle of the equatorial jungle trying to impress upon him what was happening."

Turner cut to the chase: "Awww, Jean-Michel, are you telling me you *need more money?*"

Cousteau, who said he felt meek in hearing Turner's formidable voice, answered, "Yes, Ted, that's what I'm asking. To do this right we need more."

"Well, how much more do you want?" Turner inquired.

"Maybe half a million dollars" [equal to at least $3 million today].

"Do you know how many good pitchers I can sign for the Braves with half a million dollars?" he asked.

There was silence.

"Ted?" Jean-Michel queried.

"Ted, are you still there. Over?"

Silence.

Cousteau thought maybe the line had gone dead or Turner had hung up.

Hearing no answer, he began to regret making the request.

But Turner was toying with him. "You don't need to apologize. You got it, pal. I'll find a way to get you the money. Just make sure that you and your father stay out of trouble and give us something we will be proud of."

Turner says the project made vivid for him the truth that most humanitarian challenges have an environmental element. They have multiple dimensions and tentacles. It was a realization that would ultimately influence his thoughts about the United Nations.

He told his reporters at CNN that the environment wasn't a fringe topic that should be treated like the weather report, Hollywood gossip, or reading sports scores. During the 1980s, Pyle, Pat Mitchell (today head of the Paley Center), the late former Delaware governor Russ Peterson (who was head of the National Audubon Society), and Turner recognized the power that documentaries could have not only in serving as entertainment but in helping to educate the masses as well. They evolved the art form to a level that went beyond Mutual of Omaha's *Wild Kingdom* and the specials produced by PBS, BBC, and National Geographic.

Palmer, recently the author of *Shooting in the Wild: An Insider's Account of Making Movies in the Animal Kingdom*, cites the source of the breakthrough in thinking. "It was our deteriorating environment that led me to believe, like Ted, that we needed to use every means at our disposal to persuade the country, and the whole globe, to change course to be more sustainable. Population growth, toxics, acid rain, loss of biological diversity, overfishing, clear-cutting, loss of topsoil, and many other problems led me to view the body politic as heading for disaster, unless something dramatic and major was done. I saw powerful, popular, and dramatic documentaries on prime-time TV as one action that desperately needed to be taken."

Pyle and Pat Mitchell, who spearheaded TBS and CNN's environmental projects, said that Turner caught flack from advertisers because some of the documentaries specifically pinpointed the perpetrators of pollution and wildlife habitat destruction. What set Turner apart is that he, unlike network executives, personally owned the channels where the programs were running, and he refused to kowtow to their threats of pulling advertising.

Palmer says that Turner stood up for the integrity of the narratives. "There was a clear conflict that would have been resolved in favor of the bottom line if Ted had not been in charge. You see in the way some decisions are made by the major networks today—a fear of alienating advertisers, which should cause us to ask, 'Who has the power in our society?' Ted was crucial in the fight to stand up and resist the two boycotts we faced—one over a film with Paul Newman on clear-cutting, and the other on overgrazing rangelands by cattle."

"When you lose a baseball game, the team can get it back tomorrow," Turner says. "You wreck a river or a place like the Amazon or Gulf of Mexico and the damage can last decades to centuries."

He was convinced that environmental stories needed to be aired over and over again until people got the message. He said those conclusions didn't need to be confirmed by market research. Today, Turner asserts that if he were still owner of CNN and TBS he would have investigative reports about the impacts of coal and fossil fuels airing around the clock until Congress became so inundated with letters and phone calls from constituents that it passed legislation to apply a tax on carbon and incentivize private investment in wind, solar, natural gas, carefully controlled nuclear facilities, and ultra-efficient energy grids.

"Ted gambles on people as much as he backs causes," Pyle says. "His faith isn't placed in an unseen deity. It's in the potential that he believes exists in all of us to act on good information if we have access to it. . . ."

For a week in the early 1980s, when the atmosphere around CNN was still chaotic, Turner and his youngest sons, Rhett and Beau, visited Cousteau in the Amazon. The Cousteaus had offered Turner an invitation to see, first-hand, what they were doing over the course of their eighteen months in the field. Turner decided to treat his youngest sons to a weeklong adventure. Today, both recount their foray to the Amazon as jarring but formative.

Jean-Michel was in the States during the time of their visit, doing production work and attending meetings, but he heard plenty about it from Jacques-Yves. "My dad was a quiet man in private who was gregarious when he had to be, and he told me about the Turner visit. Again, how many network executives would do that, check out what they are investing in, and take their sons along? Ted is a very physical, very active person and I think that being stuck on a boat kind of left him impatient. Film work can be mundane and boring. Ted was there to be stimulated. In those days, he couldn't settle down. And he had a short fuse because he was under a lot of pressure. At the time, he was chewing tobacco and had a can that he carried around in his hand, spitting into it, which left the film crew wondering, "Who is this redneck American?"

Jacques-Yves pulled his team aside and whispered, "Zat iz Ted Turner. Be kind and don't judge him. He's one of the few businessmen who are trying to save the planet."

"To be honest, my father was, at first, more amused by Ted because he's such a character," Jean-Michel says. "He saw him as this outwardly boisterous figure who was a different person inside. He defended Ted. And he told me, "Give him time, Jean-Michel. You will see. He is still young, just as you are. He has the capacity of learning and doing great things. I see it in him. I feel it.""

In 1981, months after Turner launched CNN, author Christian Williams penned a rush-to-print biography about Turner titled *Lead, Follow, or Get out of the Way: The Story of Ted Turner.* Turner then was not yet forty-four years old. The book sheds light on a Turner whose ideas were amorphous, perhaps naïve about how the world worked, and he shoots from the hip in expressing himself. At one point in the book, Williams lets the tape recorder run. The following passage captures Turner's frame of mind and it presages Turner's subsequent engagement of world leaders, including a meeting with Cousteau that would qualify as an example of Turner going "guru-to-guru" with big thinkers.

What I've got to do now is broaden myself . . . And I've got a plan. I'm going to hook up a two-way send-and-receive station here, so I don't have to run around so much talking to people. Instead of spending half my life on airplanes, I want to put on a wizard's cap and think. I want to confer with the best and the smartest people there are, and with the send-and-receive station I can do that right here, without burning any fuel. There'll be a little shack down a dirt path from the house, and I can stroll over there and tune in anybody I want. That's the great thing about the satellite—it lets people talk to one another directly. Hey, I'll be like the guru on the mountaintop. It'll be guru-to-guru communication. But I'm also going to make my own pilgrimage, around the world. There's so much I don't know, but I'm going to find it out. I'm going to visit every country that will let me in, in Europe and Asia and Africa, wherever they have a lot of problems. I'm going to meet with the leaders and I'm gonna find out what they're thinking. Reading only gives you so much, but if you actually go there you can figure it out. Boy, are those foreign kings and presidents going to be surprised to see me. It'll be interesting as hell for both of us.

One evening after his sons had gone to bed, Turner and Jacques-Yves sat together on the prow of *Calypso*, listening to the twilight sounds of the jungle and the gurgling river. Fish jumped. Howler monkeys and birds vocalized in the canopy. They could feel the Amazon's power flowing beneath them.

Cousteau mentioned disturbing trends he and his diving crews had observed over the years since his first documentaries were made. Based upon what he witnessed, he began to extrapolate with deadly accuracy today's destruction of coral reefs, the expansion of dead zones caused by pollution in the ocean, humans being poisoned by eating fish contaminated with mercury and PCBs, the decimation of high-end bellwether species like sharks, ocean bottoms being destroyed through commercial trawling, the toll of driftnets and bycatch, and the effects of swift-melting of ice caps on ocean levels.

On land, Cousteau foretold the precipitous decline of amphibians, the widespread effects of freshwater shortages and droughts, increased desertification, and the over-pumping of the Ogallala aquifer on the high plains of the United States. The result of accumulating abuse and neglect, Cousteau warned, will be an ever-expanding crisis, the ecological interconnections no less entwined than the international economy and banking system.

As Cousteau rendered his assessment, Turner was left speechless. He had come to the Amazon to be inspired and pumped up. He was conversant about the Global 2000 Report but Cousteau's authoritative litany jolted him and drove up his pulse rate. Turner said, "Captain, not only am I depressed, but now I'm discouraged."

For Turner, the implication was, "Why bother?"

Cousteau told Turner to look him in the eye. "Ted, we cannot afford to get discouraged," he said. "Even if we know the end is coming for certain, which we do not, what can men of good conscience do but keep trying to do the right thing until the very end?"

If an asteroid were streaking on a collision course and *Homo sapiens* had a few decades to plan ahead, would humanity accept its fate with indifference? The environmental challenge, Cousteau said, is no different.

Turner still returns to that conversation. "I think of those words and I press on," he says. "Failure cannot be an option here. We're talking about the survival of the human race and of all the major life forms on the planet."

Cousteau was effectively handing Turner a challenge to use his influence and place in media to raise awareness about the environment based on his assumption that human society had little time to act. In 1971, Cousteau had calculated that we had a fifty-year window of opportunity. Given the convergence today of human-caused climate change, population, and increasing threats of terrorism in the last few decades, Turner believes we have until the middle of this century to safely take corrective action or risk calamity.

Turner has many quirks. Millions have heard him recite various verses of Thomas Babington Macaulay's famous 1842 poem, "Horatius at the Bridge."

Macaulay's work hails Publius Horatius Cocles, who stood on the Pons Sublicius, a pedestrian span over the Tiber River in what was then the outskirts of ancient Rome.

Against all odds, Horatius held back an Etruscan military invasion launched by King Lars Porsenna. As the Etruscans surged toward them, Horatius's countrymen dropped their weapons and fled in fear, leaving him alone to fight. The message: that spinelessness and complacency based on self-preservation undermines the persistence of society.

In Macaulay's tribute, Horatius "reproached [his fellow citizens] one after another for their cowardice, tried to stop them, appealed to them in heaven's name to stand, declared that it was in vain for them to seek safety in flight whilst leaving the bridge open behind them, there would very soon be more of the enemy in the center of Rome."

Horatius was regaled as a hero for the ages, though the battle would have been easier, and glory shared by all, if his countrymen had stood their ground. Turner memorized the ballad during his prep school days. He fired up his yachting crews with Macaulay's words aboard *Courageous* and *Tenacious* prior to important races. He summoned it in the presence of TBS colleagues in battling the Big Three networks. And he shared it with Cousteau, who hadn't realized Turner was such an ardent student of the classics. Cousteau patted Turner on the back. "Ted, sometimes you surprise me. I am impressed."

Turner admits that it wasn't until he heard the Captain identify the scope of environmental problems that he began equating Macaulay's epic with the cause of human survival.

If humans were only logical beings, the future would be bleak indeed, Cousteau said. But *Homo sapiens* is more than logical. "We are human beings, and we have faith," he told Turner, paraphrasing what he had written elsewhere, "and therefore we have hope."

In the humid mist rising off the Amazon, backlit by a flood lamp on the deck, Cousteau appeared in silhouette. Imprinted upon Turner in that glimpse was the outline of a notion, a vague thought that would later morph into *Captain Planet and the Planeteers*—the first depiction of eco-superheroes.

That Cousteau expressed confidence in Turner left him feeling more validated as a person who wanted to make a contribution to the world. It was as empowering as anything he had known. He'd never had a conversation like this with Ed Turner.

The Turner men expressed themselves with handshakes. But on *Calypso*, Turner and Cousteau embraced and, for the rest of Cousteau's life, the Captain gave Turner a warm hug whenever they greeted one another.

"My dad was gone, and Cousteau filled in something that was missing. 'O Captain, My Captain' is the tribute by Walt Whitman to a fallen Abraham Lincoln to give us purpose. Cousteau was that person for me. I guess you could say my captain was the original aquaman."

Turner arrived back in Atlanta with a twin mission. If he were to carry the mantle of Cousteau's mandate, he was going to be forced into a steep learning curve. He needed to be better read and more learned on issues. He needed to reach more people to make them aware of environmental and humanitarian issues. And, foremost, he knew that he wanted to use his media properties as a stage for education and offering support to green-minded leaders. He met the renowned natural resource economist Lester Brown, who became a close friend and the man that Turner describes as "the statistician for Planet Earth."

"I've learned more about the environment from reading Les Brown's State of the World Reports and subsequent books than from any other individual," Turner says. "Around the world, heads of state and policy makers rely on Les's analysis of problems. I valued them so much that, for years, I sent copies of his major publications to every member of Congress, presidential cabinet member, and ambassador to the UN from nearly two hundred countries around the world."

To generate the funds for expanded environmental programming at CNN, Turner founded the Better World Society, an organization that brought together many of the brightest green visionaries of the last half century. He tapped Jacques-Yves and Jean-Michel Cousteau, Brown, and Russ Peterson, former governor of Delaware, to help lead the organization. Joining the board of trustees soon thereafter were former president Carter and Prime Minister Gro Harlem Brundtland of Norway, Rodrigo Carazo of Costa Rica, Dr. MS. Swaminathan of India, Prince Sadrudding Aga Khan of Pakistan who previously served as United Nations high commissioner for refugees, and Julia Henderson, the former secretary-general of International Planned Parenthood.

Creating original content isn't cheap. Turner's investment in the Cousteaus generated tens of millions in profit through ad sales. His motivations with the Better World Society weren't purely altruistic. With the programming he produced, he could air it as much as he liked and sell advertising. He doesn't make excuses for mixing motivation. "To run a media company you have to make money and it meant selling advertising," he says. "The fact is we couldn't have put so much environmental programming on the air, far more than the three major networks were doing by the way, unless we could pay the bills. You accomplish nothing if you have terrific shows but run yourself out of business."

Because the content called some resource extraction industries on the carpet, he faced threats of advertising boycotts. When confronted with the dilemma of placating advertisers or running the shows, Turner says he almost always sided with the latter, at huge cost to his bottom line. What profit he lost he gained in credibility and respect among world leaders. Moreover, CNN became the network of choice internationally.

"Advertisers wield enormous power," Turner says. "But I'm proud to say that at CNN and in some of the environmental specials we produced, we exposed issues that the Big Three wouldn't touch with a ten-foot pole."

Keeping the Better World Society required constant fund-raising and ultimately it was sunsetted in the early 1990s after failing to become the engine for environmental programming Turner had envisioned. However, now smarter and better connected with people in power, Turner used all of the knowledge he gleaned to think of how he would better organize a foundation committed to eco-humanitarian causes. Soon thereafter, around the time that Time Warner acquired TBS and he became a billionaire based on the value of the new conglomerate, he started the Turner Foundation. In 1997, following a $1 billion gift to the United Nations, he created the UN Foundation. With a network of chiefs of state, the brightest scientific minds, and businesspeople in his immediate circle of friends, it was Turner going "guru-to-guru" writ large.

In reflection, Turner says it meant a lot to him whenever Cousteau expressed praise. When the Captain died in 1997 at age eighty-seven,

Turner paid homage by calling him "the father of the environmental movement," a reference that newspapers around the world cited.

Jean-Michel Cousteau has pondered the meaning of that citation, and the symbolism of Cousteau the elder passing the torch to a handful of protégées. As Jacques-Yves Cousteau aged, Jean-Michel says, he became increasingly despondent, almost bitter about the direction of the world. Overwhelmed by the magnitude of serious problems, he was frustrated by the recalcitrance of governments to take action on ocean protection. Part of him had given up hope that the oceans could ever be saved.

Jean-Michel says the fathers and mothers of movements are products of their own time and can only carry them so far. They need to be constantly reinvigorated with fresh blood. Plus, it's hard to be an activist forever. Some people wear out. Jean-Michel says that he and Turner are of one generation and his father of a different era.

Those closest to Turner remember a rendezvous he had with Cousteau. His mentor was in decline. He was tired, disheartened, and felt forgotten. Turner reached out by inviting him to share in the premiere of the motion picture *Gettysburg* at the National Theatre in Washington, DC. Turner had bankrolled the project, and considered it an achievement of personal importance.

Turner ushered the old oceanographer to his seat and together they watched. On one side of Turner was Cousteau and on the other Turner's daughter and son-in-law, Laura and Rutherford Seydel, and other members of his family. Nearly an hour into the viewing the reel broke and the film needed to be spliced back together. Lights in the theater came on.

People for several seats around pressed closer to hear the conversation playing out between one of the architects of the green age and one of his prized students. Jacques-Yves had become so distressed by the trend lines he was witnessing that he no longer had any fight left in him. Coral reefs were rapidly perishing, pollution was prolific, and carbon dioxide had begun acidifying water chemistry, the great amniotic fluid of creation.

"Ted," Cousteau said that night, "you worry too much. My advice to you is to not let it get to you. Enjoy the time you have, because it is already too late. We've passed the threshold. The beginning of the end has started. Man may, or may not be, part of the plan nature has for the Earth in the future. Life will be reborn, but first the world as we know it now will die."

Those around Cousteau could not believe what they were hearing. They looked to Turner for his response.

"I thought Ted would be crestfallen," Turner's son-in-law, Rutherford Seydel, says.

But Turner remained quiet for a few seconds. Finally, he put his hand down on Cousteau's, defying his reputation for not being touchy-feely. "Captain, you are a great scientist, you've been a friend who was always there for me, but isn't there a possibility, say, even a 3 to 5 percent chance that you are wrong? It may be a long shot, but that's what I am going to focus on. I'll take those odds. You know that I admire you, that I love you, but I can't accept what you are saying."

Turner's family members were touched by the expression of warmth and they waited for the answer.

"I'm sorry, Ted, but I can't agree," Cousteau responded.

To those witnessing the exchange, it was almost as if a transference had occurred. "Ted is ever the eternal optimist because the alternative is part of the personal pain he has carried forward all these years," Seydel says. "If there is an infinitesimal reason to have hope, he will choose to search for it rather than resign himself to the bleak future Captain Cousteau told him was inevitable."

Says Jean-Michel Cousteau: "My dad told Ted in the beginning to never give up. For Ted, I know that my father represented a role model whom he did not want to let down. And he has managed his life in a way to make certain it never happens. But what I don't think Ted realizes is that he is doing what my dad did not possess the strength and endurance to do, which is maintain optimism to the end."

His father became cynical. Turner kept going, even accelerating his work as an environmentalist. "He has fulfilled the challenge my father placed upon him," Jean-Michel says, "and succeeded in a way my father himself never could . . . Ted started as a follower and he has become a leader of the pack. My dad used to tell me that the American dream isn't about money. It is about the possibility of exceeding a person's own expectations of himself."

Turner remembers Jacques Cousteau only with deference and humility. "He was my first hero and I'm grateful for having known him. The legacy of activism that exists in Jean-Michel and all of the Cousteau grandchildren is inspiring."

Turner wonders how Cousteau would be responding to the debate over climate change. He would not be marveling at the prospect of a new commercial shipping lane opening through Arctic waters. He would be in a wetsuit with camera, accompanying desperate polar bears that literally are having their footing melt away beneath their paws and, as a consequence must swim hundreds of miles further to find seals and walruses—their sustenance—on waning pack ice.

The epic challenge, which he credits Cousteau with recognizing, is making the environmental crisis real and tangible for average people before it is too late.

"When you lose hope, you become a pessimist," Jean-Michel says. "Instead of believing in brighter possibilities, you accept the things that are wrong and surrender to them. Rather than working to change them, you pray they don't become worse or impact you personally even as they harm other people. I think that's why Ted feels drawn to the parable of Horatius."

Jean-Michel says he and his father would argue in the years before he died. "When he told me he didn't believe that we could win the battle, I told him that, of all people, it was an unacceptable conclusion coming from him."

All hope, however, was not lost for Jacques-Yves Cousteau. Jean-Michel shares a conversation that his father had, while on his deathbed, with Jean-Pierre Cousteau, the attending physician (and Jean-Michel's first cousin). The world's most famous aquaman looked into the approaching twilight and had a final statement of conviction. He didn't say, "I don't want to die, I want to live," Jean-Michel notes, but rather, "I haven't finished my work."

The surviving Cousteau regards Turner as one of the new silver-haired elders.

"Every time that I get depressed I look into the eyes of a child and I think to myself, 'We can't let you down.' Ted has the same set of values with his grandchildren and all young people he meets. That's why young people like him. He doesn't sell them short. He is telling them to go out and change the world. There is no time to think about 'what ifs' as in 'What if we do nothing?' With the limited time we have, we can only be thinking about brave solutions."

CHAPTER FOUR

The Songs of the Cranes

"He lives a lot in his head. Sometimes Ted will disappear into himself. It's the only safe place he has ever known. But he doesn't allow others to go in there with him."

—JANE FONDA

A NOTORIOUSLY LIGHT SLEEPER, TURNER SAT STRAIGHT UP, CAUSING Jane Fonda to jump.

He caressed her shoulder to calm her. "Honey, did you hear it?"

Fonda had been startled by the noise. They pulled each other closer, listening. After a moment, according to Fonda, Turner chortled. "I think a baby just hatched on the nest."

Moments later, a melodic cooing floated through the open window of their bedroom. Fonda recognized the "unison calling" described in their *Birds Of North America Field Guide*. For sandhill cranes, the song is an expression of gladness between mated pairs, commonly emitted when chicks hatch on the nest. Jane Fonda and Ted Turner had become avian godparents.

Turner and Fonda, Ted and Jane. They were called America's ultimate power couple by the tabloid press. "Of all the relationships I've had in the past," Turner says, "my marriage to Jane was the most intense and fulfilling. Do I have any regrets that we came into each other's lives? None. Do I still think about her? I would be lying if I didn't say yes."

Together for more than a decade, Fonda forced Turner to look inward and try to confront pain that had emotionally hobbled him since childhood. She also inspired him to be a committed feminist, advocating to empower women, half of whom worldwide, around two billion, don't have the same rights or level of respect as men. For her part, she says, it was Turner who inspired her to better appreciate the role that environment plays in shaping human civilization and quality of life.

Any book about Turner would be remiss if it didn't include a deeper look at his relationship with Fonda. Several books have mentioned it superficially, but the impact on both of them was not superficial. The magnetism of their bond had little to do with money or fame, they say. It involved instead a willingness to feel the pull of nature and, at their most vulnerable level of insecurity, allow it to be a platform for healing.

America's fascination with her runs as deep as it does with him. Lady Jayne Seymour Fonda: American actress, fitness queen, liberal activist, spiritual seeker. On her fifty-first birthday, Fonda's second husband, the California legislator and civil rights activist, Tom Hayden, informed her that he was in love with another woman. The news left Fonda devastated. Around the same time, Turner's second marriage to Jane Smith, the mother of his three youngest children, Rhett, Beau, and Jennie, was ending after two decades.

In an interview with Lesley Stahl on *60 Minutes*, which coincided with the 2005 release of her memoir, *My Life So Far*, Fonda recalled Ted's wooing. "The phone rings, and it's this booming southern accent. And the first words out of his mouth were, 'Is it true?'"

"Is what true?" Fonda said, thinking it was a strange way to start a conversation.

"And he said, 'Are you and Hayden getting a divorce?' Now, I mean, I'm in the middle of a nervous breakdown, right? I can't talk above a whisper."

Turner told his executive assistant Dee Woods to keep calling Fonda to see if her schedule would allow for a date. Fonda said she needed a year to get over her divorce. Woods called on day 366.

About their first date, in Los Angeles, Turner wrote this in his 2008 memoir, *Call Me Ted:* "From meeting her before and watching her in the movies I knew she was attractive, but as we talked through our dinner date I was surprised by the strength of our connection. Knowing that a lot of people assumed I was a male chauvinist and a greedy capitalist, I was up front with her. I let her know that my dad had raised me without a lot of respect for women and that this was something I'd been working hard to change. And knowing of Jane's political leanings, I even bragged to her about how many friends I had who were communists, including Castro and Gorbachev. I always tend to talk a lot when I'm excited or nervous and that night I was really excited."

The evening ended with a hug. Fonda told Turner she wasn't ready for a serious relationship. Still, Turner continued the charm offensive and refused to relent. There was something about him, she told me, that was undeniable.

"He pursued me and sometimes would drop to one knee and recite poetry that he composed himself or recite long verse that he'd learned in high school," Fonda said. "I mean, it was irresistible." Following months of relentless courting, they became a steady couple. On *60 Minutes*, Stahl asked Fonda if she was repeating a pattern of allowing herself to be sculpted by a powerful man.

"In a positive way, yeah. I mean, I know I'm a chameleon in some ways. I mean, you know, I was going to all these receptions. Ted goes from one thing to another. A lot of tuxedos, a lot of gowns, on the arm of a corporate executive . . . What was really going on though was very, very different. What was going on was he gave me confidence. Ted Turner would wake up every morning and say, 'I love you so much. You are so beautiful.' And I would think, 'Well, he's no dummy. Gee whiz.'"

～・～

Very early in their courtship, Turner invited Fonda to join him at the Bar None Ranch, the first property he'd purchased in Montana. The buy had come at his son Beau's suggestion, and it had been intended as a fishing and hunting getaway. Many say it was bison that brought Turner west. In fact, it was him stepping into a stream at the Bar None and becoming hooked, at his own half century mark, on fly fishing. He quickly mastered the sport, and enthusiastically introduced it to Fonda. It's a passion she still practices to this day.

Fonda had been to Montana. Her actor brother, Peter, lived in the next dale over, Paradise Valley.

"He was a true southern gentleman," Fonda says of the first weekend she spent with Turner at the ranch. Arriving late in the day and spending the night, Fonda says that Turner greeted her out front the next morning with the door to his Land Rover open. He had outfitted them with binoculars, fishing rods, and lunches.

"I don't think the grin left his face the entire day," she remembers. "He was different from his reputation in the press. He was softer, gentler."

"I wanted to show Jane around the country," he says. Turner had always fancied himself a naturalist.

In his four-wheel-drive vehicle, he set out east from the historic homestead along Sixteen Mile Creek, pointing out stream banks he was restoring after decades of overgrazing by cattle. He directed Fonda's attention toward an osprey carrying a fish back to its nest. They watched red-tailed hawks and mule deer, walked along elk trails in aspen stands, and exchanged stories about their grown kids.

"We were driving along and Ted tilted his head out the window to look into the sky. I asked him what he was doing. He pointed to something.

You could hardly see anything with the naked eye. He recognized this speck high above us as a golden eagle based on the way it was flying."

Turner stopped the car and they tracked the bird with binoculars, his arm around her. They leaned against the vehicle and continued to chat. Fonda, like Turner, doesn't believe in making small talk. She bluntly asked him honest questions, such as his reputation as a playboy. Turner says he wasn't put off, but impressed by her directness.

Turner's sensitivity for nature and fluency in talking about it moved her. "I have met a range of enormously successful, talented, driven men in my life, but never one who could identify a bird in silhouette and find such happiness in doing it. Other people look past such things. It's so simple, but it's so wonderful. So many of us take so much for granted. Ted doesn't where nature is concerned. I said to myself, 'I think I can love this man,' and my heart started to open."

When Fonda looked at him, he felt like she could see his soul. He trusted her. The following year, he purchased the Flying D Ranch. He was making plans to build a home and he walked the home site with her. She was impressed that his instincts were not tiered toward making a grand architectural statement on the land, but blending in with the surroundings. It was an expression of values different from how the rich live in Hollywood.

A year later, Turner proposed. The couple, because of their diverse interests and demand as public speakers, were constantly in motion, attending environmental conferences and galas in Los Angeles, New York, and back in Atlanta where they maintained a tiny nine-hundred-square-foot penthouse on the top of the CNN office building.

Everywhere they went, their presence electrified the room. She was undaunted by and uninterested in the size of his bank account, and had evaded the curse of getting lost in her own celebrity. In fact, at Turner's request, she gave up acting, and collaborated with him on philanthropic endeavors and ultimately setting up homes on a dozen ranches he acquired to grow his bison herd.

The mutual unspoken truth was that they didn't need to explain to each other the importance of staying real in a world full of artifice, sycophants, and deception. One liberating the other, they could simply be themselves, Fonda says, weaknesses and all.

When they sought solace, it was in the West. Whether with guests or alone, Fonda says that she and Turner would cuddle in front of a television at night with a bowl of popcorn. After active days, they would watch nature documentaries underwritten and aired by TBS. She met Cousteau and had conversations with Barbara Pyle about scripts for *Captain Planet and the Planeteers* that Turner was green-lighting.

"Ted has this emotive attachment to animals. Some of those films, for Ted, were real tearjerkers. And it didn't matter how many times he watched them, he would cry at the parts when an animal died, or it had its home taken away by habitat loss, or when young were turned out into the world by their parents."

Some of the films were narrated by actor friends turned environmental activists such as Robert Redford, Paul Newman, and Ted Danson. In fact, when Redford was shooting his movie adaptation of Norman Maclean's novella, *A River Runs Through It*, in Montana, the couple had him over for dinner. Redford and Turner could relate to one another. For years, Redford had been pouring much of the money he made from movies into expanding the size of his Sundance Ranch in Utah. He operated the site not only as the administrative headquarters for the independent film festival he founded, but he would also routinely invite prominent environmental experts to help inform his thinking about conservation.

"Jane, Bob Redford, and those other actors have a lot of guts," Turner says. "I have a lot of respect and admiration for them. They don't speak out for the environment because it's fashionable or because they think it will increase their celebrity. In fact, probably the opposite is true because anytime you are outspoken on something, people will disagree with you.

That's okay. What matters is standing up. Captain Cousteau told me that. Through Jane, I met a lot of great people—folks who were kind of dismissed by people I knew because of their liberal reputations. What they forget is that conservation is one of the most basic parts of being a conservative. And whether a person wants to call himself an environmentalist or not, people like Bob Redford always do their homework. He knows what he's talking about."

Far from being a strange pair, their friends say the combination of Turner and Fonda created a symmetry, with passions that seemed to feed on each other.

"They had a dynamism," says renowned economist Lester Brown, who has advised Turner on environmental and humanitarian issues over the years.

Brown, who heads the Earth Policy Institute in Washington, DC, and earlier founded the influential Worldwatch Institute, is not the sort of gentleman who regularly ponders the caprices of pop culture. He is a bow tie–wearing, bicycle-to-work, former-tomato-farmer wonk. His yen is assessing how natural resource consumption and environmental challenges threaten the human race. He often joined Turner and Fonda as they attended international environmental conferences, and he served on the board of Turner's first foundation, the Better World Society.

At his modest office along Connecticut Avenue near Dupont Circle, Brown recalls a black tie party at the British Embassy. Queen Elizabeth and Prince Philip were visiting America. A high-grade mixture of politicians, businesspeople, and entertainment icons had been invited.

Brown and his sister sat next to Turner and Fonda as their guests. As people mixed, a crowd, larger than the one flanking the Queen and Prince, gathered around Ted and Jane. "It was kind of fun just watching the scene unfold. British royalty is fascinating, I admit, but the kind of interaction with them is formal and distancing. With Ted and Jane, it was different. People related to them as real and approachable giants. Democrat and Republican friends of theirs—governors, senators, and ambassadors—came up and wanted to have their pictures taken with them. Ted has testified on Capitol Hill as a TV executive. It's amazing to see him in action when he's 'on.' He has a public persona that is different from his more quiet and serious side that he shares only with his friends. The fact is that everybody of importance in this country seems to know him, and if they don't, they still have an urge to want to talk with him or form an opinion about him. I've watched it happen with heads of state from other countries, too. He's sort of a man's man to men and a curiosity to women."

Brown thinks for a second and goes on. "Jane has her own way of disarming people and she does it with grace and genuine sincerity. In person, she's really not anything like the negative stereotype that has been crafted by the political right seeking to demonize her. In fact, I think she is rather self-effacing. If you think about it, because of all the media exposure they've received, either of them would be considered a major headliner. And yet when Jane and Ted were together, the sum was greater than the individual parts, which isn't often the case with charismatic figures. They had, I guess you would call it, gravitas, and it didn't matter if they were at a red carpet event or a baseball game with fans hollering at them. I was impressed by their poise."

When they traveled, there was no entourage. Turner dislikes the paparazzi but with his masculine energy he could charm them into staying away. Around Atlanta, Turner likes to drive to some social events in his compact economy car (later they would buy hybrids for themselves and all of their kids). They took walks around Centennial Park with their dogs, carrying a plastic bag to pick up poop left behind by the canines. And always, if he found others' discarded trash on the sidewalk, Turner would carry it himself to a trash can. Matter-of-factly, he says, "Jane and I just wanted to be responsible citizens."

~ · ~

In December 1991, the couple married before family at Turner's Avalon Plantation near Tallahassee.

The Flying D, however, was their main base camp. A focal point in front of the main house is a pond reflecting the Spanish Peaks.

"This was our Golden Pond," Fonda says, alluding to the title of a film she starred in with her father, Henry Fonda. A movie about healing and redemption between parents and children, it provided an impetus for Fonda to begin forgiving her father for his absence in her life.

Turner kept adding to his real estate portfolio. A few acquisitions lay in the very heart of what had been the historic vortex of the great bison herds. The Sandhills of Nebraska were also home to a namesake staging area for the cranes that appeared in Montana at their back doorstep.

~ · ~

Before he became the assistant general manager of Turner's ranches in the West, John Hansen and his wife, Jaynee, oversaw Turner's bison operations in Nebraska. Back then, Hansen was based at the Spike Box Ranch between Valentine and the tiny outpost of Mullen.

"Ted, unlike many businesspeople who buy up ranches, does not believe in being an absentee landowner. He and Jane would come out and visit for stretches of time and they would stay with Jaynee and me. We'd cook dinner together and all ride around the back sections of the ranches in a pickup truck. And it was just like being together with family."

Hansen said part of the couple's routine centered on walks. Fonda acquainted herself with the diversity of wildflowers. Turner liked to scavenge for Indian arrowheads because he knew there had been aboriginal encampments there. For both of them, unwinding meant losing track of time, getting lost in the moment, forgetting that they had lived their lives on hamster wheels. For a spell, Fonda says, Turner slowed down.

"You could kind of tell that Ted hadn't, probably ever, spent down time like this where he could just be himself," Hansen said. "He didn't have to rush off and tend to a crisis. His companies were running smoothly. It took him a while to settle in but when he did, he wasn't thinking about the office in Atlanta."

Fonda and Turner were surprisingly easygoing, Hansen says, and they took a liking to Nebraska and the people. When they would drive down the road and stop to talk to passersby in their pickups, as is the local cultural custom, Hansen said there would be a startled expression on the faces of neighbors when they saw that the passengers in the other vehicle were Turner and Fonda.

"Neighbors did double takes. I have fond memories of those days," Hansen says. "Ted and Jane truly loved each other's company and they were absorbing all they could about the history of the Great Plains and sympathized with the human struggles to stay on the land, from the Indians to the sodbusters into challenges of the twentieth century."

Turner jokes that when he first dispatched Hansen to Nebraska, he sent him a copy of *The Wind*, a 1928 black and white film that portrays homesteaders in Texas fighting a perpetual battle against wind and sand.

"He thought it was funny and in hindsight, it was," Hansen says. "Ted respects the Sandhillers because they are a tough, tough lot. They had cattle. Ted's brought back bison, but he admires the people who pursued their dream there. To stay on the land you have to find a way to make your tenure economically and ecologically sustainable. There's no fooling around. That's reality."

For her part, Fonda enjoyed reading Willa Cather, a Nebraska novelist who, in *O Pioneers!*, wrote, "She had never known before how much the country meant to her. The chirping of the insects in the long grass had been like the sweetest music. She had felt as if her heart were hiding down there, somewhere, with the quail and the plover and all the little wild things that crooned or buzzed in the sun. Under the long shaggy ridges, she felt the future stirring."

———

"Through Jane, I became much more knowledgeable about the plight of women, especially in the developing world. So many issues of poverty relate directly to how women are treated by men," Turner says. "You can't have a healthy society unless men embrace women as equal partners."

In turn, Fonda says she gained an appreciation for the impulses of sportsmen. Turner and his son, Beau, and all of the ranch crews, took her under their collective wings. With Turner, she learned how to fly fish, and was gently introduced to firearms safety and how to shoot and clean a gun. She went afield and honed her aim on clay pigeons and shooting rifles at targets.

Turner joined his wife on her first hunt at the Flying D. She shot a white-tailed deer, assisted in field dressing it, and brought it back to the ranch house where she joined chef Karen Averitt in fixing venison steaks for dinner.

"I have infinitely more respect for hunters today than I ever had before I met Ted," she says. "I had been intimidated being around guns, but I'm not afraid of them anymore. And I understand why sportsmen and sportswomen are so dedicated to defending the Second Amendment."

"Jane is far more fearless than her critics give her credit for," Turner says. On a corner of the Flying D, there is a rock effigy hundreds, if not thousands, of years old. Archaeologists say it served as a marker for native peoples stalking bison and wandering up and down the Rockies between the Far North and the southwestern deserts.

During one gathering there with Native American tribal elders, a bison was offered by Turner and Fonda for harvest. After it was killed, one of the traditionalists cut out its liver and dipped it in the bile sac of the beast—a ritual practiced over generations by Indians in celebration of the animal's bounty. Turner and Fonda were invited to partake. Without hesitation, Fonda stepped forward. She never winced, Turner said. The men around her were impressed. He beamed.

"Jane is a warrior in a lot of respects," Turner says. "She did things that could leave you surprised."

Fonda says she came to realize why her husband could become so stir crazy in cities and had to get his regular fix of the outdoors. "It was the one thing that didn't change. Because his childhood was so crazy and dysfunctional, the way he found solace was by going out in the woods and being alone and paying attention to whatever was around him, I think even having a conversation with it. Mostly, he went to find and watch animals. I learned from him that some of the most ardent environmentalists are hunters."

Another first that Turner encountered in Fonda is that she called him out on things that other women in his life might have allowed to pass or would have been afraid to confront, including his occasional bouts of yelling, or speaking brashly. His own mother had been meek and submissive.

"There is a side of Ted that is totally unconscious—the projection of his father," she says. "It rises out of him and he isn't aware of why it exists or how it comes across."

—◆—

"I had known Jane Fonda from earlier years, so we were happy to see each other again after she had gotten together with Ted," says former US senator Timothy Wirth, who oversees the UN Foundation. "I asked her how it was going, and she responded with her characteristic big smile and humorous comment: 'You know, he's the only person who has apologized more than I have.'"

Fonda caught her first flash of Turner's combustible personality in 1991 when the Goodwill Games were being held in Seattle. Turner's longtime executive assistant Dee Woods had made a rare faux pas in Turner's ordinarily precise calendar.

"Ted doesn't like being caught off guard with multiple surprises," Fonda says. "He panicked when he discovered he was supposed to be in a couple of different venues at the same time. For a man known for speaking off the cuff, he is actually very rigid in his demand for organization."

Stressed, Turner charged into a trailer at the Goodwill Games and snapped. He berated Woods in a way that Fonda hadn't witnessed in him before. The rigid scheduling that he used to maintain stability in his fast-paced life had failed. He didn't cope well in the absence of structure. And he blamed Woods, who had otherwise done an admirable job of arranging his nonstop life for years. "She was a sweet woman who looked out for him, and didn't deserve to be treated that way," Fonda says.

Other women in Turner's life had observed similar outbursts. His forceful personality and his ability to deliver insulting put-downs to antagonists has intimidated many. Fonda found it to be juvenile and she wouldn't let it pass. She pulled Turner aside and said sternly, "If this is who you are, then I don't want to be around that person."

No man is so high and mighty that he can justify such behavior. Turner told her that sometimes he just loses it, that it dates to frustration he coped with early in his life. Fonda informed Turner it was no excuse. "I said, 'Ted, you don't have to be this way,'" she explained to me. "'You can control it if you want. No one is making you behave like a jerk.'"

Turner looks back on the incident and says Fonda was right to give him a dose of tough love. He knows that she did it because she genuinely cared for him. And he realizes she wasn't trying to control him; she wanted to help him find solace. Like the Fastnet race when his son, Teddy, was placed in peril by his judgment, Turner is abashed.

"Jane toned Dad down," notes Laura Turner Seydel, Turner's eldest daughter. "He can be kind of high strung, but she made it clear that the way he behaved was a choice he made. He needed to think, in advance, about how the words that came out his mouth would be interpreted by others."

Turner Seydel said nature was a balm for her father and Fonda. "Dad started to become a different person, a guy more fun to be around and less intense. We kids saw it happen. That's why we all love Jane so much. She had a powerful effect on him."

~~~

About Turner's childhood, and how it shaped the man she married, Fonda has this to say: "Ed Turner believed that withholding love and affection was a way to induce hunger for achievement, a way to toughen Ted up, to make sure he never depended on other people. Tragically . . . Ed Turner was right."

In retrospect, Fonda admits she made a tactical miscalculation. She believed during the middle of the marriage that she could change Turner or at least, through discussions and therapy, have Turner explore the cause of his inner pain, convince him that he could prevail over it, and move on.

"People say you can make peace with your past, but with Ted it's not true. It is so hardwired into him that it's part of his psyche. His ability to be heroically generous is an expression of his own need to feel loved."

Fonda kept pushing Turner to accept that he was not responsible for the things his father had done to him. He needed to reject the curse of self-loathing that was imprinted upon him. He was not bound by any code of honor or faithfulness that required him to make excuses for Ed Turner's behavior. The flaws in his father did not have to be his own.

"Given everything that happened to Ted when he was a child—the beatings, the psychological manipulations—like his father asking him to beat him, his mother screaming outside the door, the trauma of his sister's slow painful death, his father coming home drunk at night and telling Ted stories about women he had slept with who were not Ted's mother, and Ed Turner's suicide, which was a violent act committed against Ted—there was complete toxicity," Fonda says. "Ted views it as a betrayal of his father to talk unkindly about him. He can't bring himself to do it. He couldn't in his own memoir. What he must acknowledge is that his father betrayed him—and it wasn't his fault. He's stuffed that psychic energy all these years. He needs to let it go."

When Turner and Fonda became acquainted, she knew of his reputation for carousing. She told him that if they were going to continue dating, he needed to reveal himself, open himself up emotionally, and refrain from repelling any questions she had.

Turner admits that the more that Fonda pressed him, he may not have liked it, but he realized it was necessary. One of the few regrets he has is that he didn't understand the importance of their exchange while the couple was still married.

Fonda knew from the sometimes-detached behavior of her own father and the suicide of her mother how cruel treatment from a patriarch or matriarch—a person one loves, idolizes, and craves affirmation from—can be devastating. One evening in Montana, everything about Turner's grief spilled out.

Turner shared the story of his childhood in ways he hadn't with other women. How he was sent away to boarding school, never developed a bond with his mother while his dad was cold and emotionally abusive, watching his sister die, and enduring years of demeaning commentary from his father, a man who told Turner he would never amount to anything. Fonda says she began to weep, yet she vividly remembers Turner not allowing himself to grieve for the absence of a loving, nurturing environment as a boy.

"Ted has a profound external capacity, a sense of compassion, for the pain and suffering of others, but he has no empathy for himself,"

Fonda says. "His father drilled it into him that he should never feel sorry for himself—that he should feel ashamed to even think about doing it. He has not made peace with what happened between him and his father because he will not allow himself to go to that internal place. It's not that he's stubborn. He is *afraid* to go there for fear he will be branded weak."

Men of his generation were told to be stoic, to reject the psychological probing that goes with therapy as a sign of weakness. The negative consequences for sons and daughters still reverberate. Turner does not deny that analysis and he discusses it today with his therapist.

On the morning when research for this book began at Turner's Collon Curá Estancia in Argentina, Turner went into detail with me about how devastated he was on the day when he received the telephone call from Jimmy Brown, the black man hired by Ed Turner to help raise him as a boy, that his father had killed himself.

Biographers have speculated that Turner is "haunted by the ghost of his father." Fonda believes it. Turner has a different explanation.

"Do I wonder what he would make of me now?" he asks. "Or how he might have enjoyed being out on a ranch with me, the two of us, surrounded by friends? Or having sat in the stands together at Braves games? Or seeing what happened with the SuperStation and CNN, or the issues that I am working on with some of the most brilliant minds on Earth?"

How much confidence would Ed Turner have had in his son to succeed? "That," Fonda says, "is the open-ended question that haunts Ted."

Turner acknowledges that his father's lack of support drove him to be consumed by his work. Always, he has been apprehensive about the notion of "resting" because for him it means that if he slows down and looks over his shoulder, failure might be gaining on him.

"That's what drives him to try and stay ahead," Fonda says. "People who come from tough childhoods, who have big egos and distinguish themselves by their genius can go in two different directions. They can cause enormous harm or they can devote themselves, driven by something within, to being forces for good."

~

Recently, a group of three dozen billionaires pledged to give away half of their wealth. It didn't surprise Fonda. Turner, who was among them, personally had fulfilled the promise more than a decade earlier.

On a night in 1997, Turner announced that he was gifting $1 billion to support the mission of the United Nations. Fonda was on the other side of the country attending a different social engagement. But she had been the first person that Turner informed after he made the decision, even before he had consulted his chief financial advisor Taylor Glover on how to give away what was approaching half of his net worth. Glover was stunned but not surprised.

Fonda says, "Giving away money and getting involved in human survival issues doesn't leave him feeling depleted of time or money. It may make him exhausted, but this is how his conscience operates. Nothing he does gives him greater satisfaction. When he told me what he planned with the UN, I cried. Why? Because I knew how selfless it was. Ted had no idea of its significance, or the impact it would have."

~

Fonda and Turner were never happier together than when they spent time in the West. While each has differing versions of certain episodes in their marriage, their memories about one important event of natural history coincide exactly: the day when cranes set up a home in the pond behind their home at the Flying D and the morning when they gave lift to the first generation of native, Flying-D-hatched offspring.

They were still in their honeymoon phase, carrying on a travel schedule that seldom allowed them to be in the same place for more than a week. They had made a stopover at the Flying D and they were dozing before dawn. The yaks of magpies and the warbles of mountain bluebirds drifted in over them. Then the dim peace of dawn was interrupted by a loud squawk from the marsh just outside their window.

The sandhill pair had arrived weeks earlier, Turner says, in a wobbly glide, more like massive transport planes than fighter jets. They flew in tandem, necks extended forward, legs pointed behind. And they hung around, making it clear they were not moving on, engaging in a courtship dance and gravitating toward an island mound. The water around them served as protection. Then they made a nest.

Turner and Fonda pored over birding and natural history books, reading information to one another out loud. They delighted in knowing that these summering birds were likely spending their winters at Bosque del Apache National Wildlife Refuge along the Rio Grande River in New Mexico. The refuge happens to be at the northern end of a ranch Turner would soon acquire, the massive Armendaris. The information gave the couple and the birds a connection at both ends of the flyway, and to the crane stopovers in Nebraska.

Turner and Fonda pondered the dimensions of the journey, becoming acutely aware of the remarkable spectacle of the great north to south migrations involving billions of avians across the continent.

The cranes built a nest bed from dried wild grass, pieces of plumage, twigs, and mud. The couple was riveted by the process. Dinner guests were regaled with details of avian minutiae, and would take turns peering into the spotting scope as Turner and Fonda offered naturalist descriptions of what they were observing. Some jokingly referred to it as another episode of "Ted and Jane's wild adventure."

One evening recently in his living room at the Flying D surrounded by guests, Turner waxed for an extended period on the life cycle of cranes, describing the patterns of migration involving lesser and greater sandhills.

"I know enough that I could write a book about cranes," he says of visits he's made to Bosque del Apache and to the Platte River where the largest migratory concentration of cranes occurs. "I've studied them. I understand their behavior. They're one of my favorite birds."

When the first crane chick hatched, Turner was ecstatic because it proved to him that if he protected or enhanced habitat through a manufactured waterhole, wildlife would somehow find it.

Cranes are famously attentive parents. The mother or father is always there to keep the eggs warmed and covered against the elements while the other goes foraging and stands at the ready to engage intruders. From a distance, the human onlookers had a front row seat, concerned about predators and aerial scavengers, threats that included ravens, golden eagles, black birds, and prowling the shore, coyotes, foxes, raccoons, weasels, and skunks. The mother and father cranes, aware of the menaces, stood vigilant guard for weeks.

Then on that day in June, Turner and Fonda were awakened. After the single crack of motherly astonishment, they remember the primordial cooing, the "unison calling."

With the sun climbing over hills, the first beams hit the wings of the birds and cast them in a bright pearlescent glow. Fonda says she looked at her husband and he had tears in his eyes. Seeing that, she cried, too. They held each other for a long moment, saying nothing.

"That's the soft, sweet spot of Ted Turner," she explains.

"I never felt like I had to hold it in," Turner says of sharing the moment with Fonda.

Not long after the first sandhill hatched, the other egg was pushed out of the nest unhatched. Not uncommon behavior for adult cranes, given the challenges of raising young. The chick fledged the nest and grew under the watch of its guardians before it was forced to fend for itself. In the fall, all three birds departed.

~~·~~

Except for a few seasons, cranes have continued to nest at the pond. Yet in the late 1990s, and before they separated as a couple, Turner and Fonda remember a lone crane returning. It appeared to be searching.

Turner isn't trying to be melodramatic or sappy. He's not trying to make too much out of it. But when he thinks about his marriage, the cranes sometime come to mind. "Only half of the pair came back in the spring," he says. "Somehow one crane had gotten separated from its mate and came back to the pond to rendezvous. But the other sandhill never showed up."

The survivor looked around and called out and sat on the old nest site. And then it left alone. It would pass through solo for a couple of seasons afterward.

Turner honestly believed that his union with Fonda would last. "Jane helped me learn some things about myself and opened me up more than I had been. But you can't go back. You can only move on. If you dwell on what might have been, you can drive yourself crazy."

Fonda wrote in her memoir that she believed Turner felt threatened by her adoption of Christianity, the seeds of which were planted when she was in Atlanta. She spent time with black ministers in neighborhoods once frequented by Martin Luther King, and she got together regularly with former president Jimmy Carter and wife, Rosalyn, both born-again Christians. Her conversion happened when Fonda and Turner were apart.

"Of the three men I've been married to, Ted is my favorite husband. I still love Ted. Very much. But I'm not *in* love with him anymore. What I need is to have absolute intimacy with a man, where emotional vulnerabilities can become strengths in a relationship. It is about knowing another person at the deepest level. I had wanted to accompany Ted on the journey to reach that place, but we couldn't get there."

Turner says he was never dismissive of Fonda for finding religion. "I'm happy for her, but it's not my way. And I guess I was surprised because I didn't see it coming, and I probably should have."

"I found a place that works for me," Fonda says. "I don't think the inability to reconcile the difference between physical intimacy, emotional intimacy, and spiritual intimacy is unique to Ted. A lot of men who grew up during the time Ted did had distant relationships with their fathers, and they had mothers who wilted in the presence of their domineering husbands. It's a pain not only of sons, but wives and daughters."

She adds, "The spiritual journey is an individual one. Ted may not be profoundly introspective about himself, but his soul is attached to nature in a very interesting way. He has been skeptical of Christianity because he didn't feel it was there for him in his struggles as a child. And people therefore say it means he's not a spiritual person. But he is. For him, he finds meaning in nature. I don't know—I doubt it—if organized religion will ever fit back in his life. Each of us needs to realize that it's okay to search. That's really the point, isn't it?"

In an interview with writer Ken Auletta in the *New Yorker*, Fonda said, "For some reason, he has a guilty conscience. He went much further than his father thought he would. So what's left? To be a good guy. He knows he will go down in history. He won't go down as a greedy corporate mogul. Although he claims to be an atheist, at the end of every speech he says, 'God bless you.' He wants to get into heaven."

Since his divorce from Fonda, Turner has enjoyed the company of a few different girlfriends, all of whom know and are aware of the others. He makes it clear that he probably will never marry again. The arrangement seems to work because he is open about his dating and his companions are free to accept it, or not. Some have not. Those who do are not threatened by the reality that he doesn't hide his continuing affection for Fonda.

In 2012, while appearing on Piers Morgan's show on CNN, the host asked Turner if he still loved Fonda. He had been somewhat coy in earlier TV interviews, though always smiling and exuding his fondness. This time, he said, unequivocally, "Yes." He didn't make the acknowledgment with a swooning sense of loss. It was a recognition, he noted later, of what she had brought to his life.

—————

Despite what's been written about him, Turner says he doesn't reject mainstream religions but he's not pining to reach the hereafter. He believes in the notion of heaven on Earth and says that too much of humanity lives in hell.

It is a hot summer afternoon in Montana years after Turner's marriage to Fonda ended. Thunder reverberates, shaking the glass in the Flying D ranch house. Turner sits on a couch, staring meditatively out a window. "All that any of us have, that we can control, is now," he says. "And the only thing separating us between today and the future is a series of nows. On the other hand, I can't see how a loving and forgiving God would want to let you into the heaven of an afterlife if you trashed this world and didn't bother to help other people the best you could. This is the message in every holy book that's ever been written. I don't care how much praying and preaching and pointing fingers at other people that goes on by televangelists. I think a person has to demonstrate true religious values through actions. Otherwise, what good is religion?"

He walks to the window and peers into the old spotting scope. A new crane pair has made a nest, and a chick with primary feathers is in view. "A lot of my friends remain active members of established churches and they read the Bible, as I still occasionally do. But you don't have to have organized religion to be a good person. And I don't believe you should pursue charity only if your motivation is that it will get you through the gates. Do good because it's in your heart."

Turner squints through the scope. "Where do I put my faith? In the common sense in all of us, in the courage of other people. We need to stave off Armageddon, not welcome the end time. What kind of religion would want a prophecy fulfilled by destruction?"

PART II:

THE GREEN CAPITALIST AT WORK

CHAPTER FIVE

Ted's Side of the Mountain

(A Tale of Two Modern Barons)

"Ted reminded us all, using CNN, that apart from politics, there are far more inspiring things that unite us. After I stepped down [following the breakup of the Soviet Union] and became a free man, my relationship with Ted blossomed. We found that we were linked by our enormous interest in nature and the environment. At that time, and with time, I came to understand the most important thing about Ted: He is a person who is not seeking personal gain, who is not trying to seek profit at every opportunity."

—MIKHAIL GORBACHEV

JUST INSIDE THE MOUTH OF THE GALLATIN CANYON, MARK KOSSLER, who today is Turner's general manager of all properties west of the Mississippi, climbs into a bush plane. Goosing the throttle, his Cessna rumbles down a bumpy horse pasture on the Flying D. Soon, he is airborne above the Gallatin River, tracing the watercourse north until it enters the Gallatin Valley.

Gaining altitude, Kossler points to the modern sprawl on the outskirts of Bozeman. Metal roofs and windows glint in the sun. A maze of roadways covers former wheat fields. "Not much of this was here thirty years ago," he yells over the sound of the engine, making the point that Turner's arrival in the late 1980s coincided with Bozeman being inundated by a migration of "lifestyle pilgrims." To Indians, the Gallatin was known as "the valley of flowers." Now, thousands of homes have sprouted across what used to be the richest agricultural soil in Montana.

Kossler banks left, leaving subdivisions behind, crossing westward over the outer perimeter of the Flying D. His mission today is surveying the ranch at the peak of green-up and then predicting which vast carpets of grassland will appeal to cow bison and newborn calves in the months ahead.

The heights of the ride soon expose something else: two different kinds of wealth expressed by two different "New West" billionaires—one who held onto his ten-figure fortune, the other who bet and lost on real estate. Both have big egos. Both believed what they were doing was virtuous. One's record is etched indelibly into the landscape; the other's is aimed at achieving an opposite effect. Both are playing out rather spectacularly on different sides of the same mountain range.

Peer at the contrast closer and, no matter where one resides in America, it's a divide that is universally shaping the direction of the world.

—◆—

The Flying D is a blank natural canvas. Ten Manhattan Islands would fit inside the ranch's rectangle. "When I first went to the Flying D and drove into that huge beautiful complex," reflects former US senator Tim Wirth, "I had the feeling that something was missing—something was wrong. Then I realized that there just weren't any fences or telephone poles or wires—no big manifestations of infrastructure. All my life I have driven through land that had the wired stamp of man. This was different—it was the way the land originally looked, and it was so . . . well, striking."

Geographers express amazement that a piece of raw, undeveloped land this size still exists next to a booming small city and between two famous blue ribbon trout streams, the Gallatin and Madison. When Turner's friend in philanthropy, nuclear disarmament, and capitalism, Warren Buffett, shows guests around Omaha, eighteen hundred miles downstream (where Buffett's company, Berkshire-Hathaway, is headquartered), he and Turner share a liquid connection to the latter's stewardship practices high in the basin of the Mighty Missouri. The rain and snow that flows off Turner's ranch is headed in Buffett's direction. The cleaner the water being passed along, the less that it needs to be treated by municipalities before reaching the tap, and thus the safer to drink for tens of millions. Omahans, Kansas Citians, and folk in New Orleans can trace their headwaters *here*.

Kossler is in the cockpit, and today Turner is on the ground riding horseback with friends, showing off a cranny in the ranch interior that he fondly calls "the Enchanted Forest." It's a pocket of massive Douglas firs a couple of hundred years old—their thick columnar trunks coated in jackets of moss that glow neon when struck by falling shafts of sunshine. "I love going there," Turner says. "It reminds me of the woods I would escape to as a boy. Listening to the birds, breathing in the smells of the forest. Maybe seeing an animal. I still get as much of a thrill being in a place like that as I did when I was ten years old."

When Turner first came to the West, his objective was simply to have a few recreational retreats where he could catch some fish, maybe hunt a large wapiti or bird. "But the more that you become familiar with the land at river level, and contemplate all of the things that go into creating a healthy trout stream, your thinking naturally expands. Then it's your choice to act on it, or not."

On foot, the Flying D could take days to cross. Turner has thought of having some of his ashes spread at his favorite haunts. Aldo Leopold writes of the psychological transformation that people go through, reflecting on the places where their bodies might one day be repatriated. It is an impulse to go back to nature. People seek a nourishment they can't find anywhere else. The reasons that a young person goes wandering can be very different from the impulses summoning an adult in midlife. Leopold, as so many others still do, went west as a young man and then retired to a farm in rural Wisconsin; Turner planted stakes in Montana just shy of his fiftieth year, with a different reason for his perambulation.

By any standard, the Flying D is a "trophy property," harboring big game species and scenery to match any national park. In the first few years that Turner owned the ranch, he stalked some of the biggest elk and deer with a gun in his hands. At the edge of the property, his youngest son, Beau, has a log home, its walls covered with the heads of animals, many of them qualifying for inclusion in the Boone & Crockett record books. Turner the elder will always call himself a sportsman, he says, but he no longer harvests anything larger than a pheasant or quail. His time for killing has past.

When Turner arrived in Montana, rumors were rife that he would leverage his purchase of the Flying D into a massive real estate play, keeping the best for himself and carving the rest, lucratively, into forty-acre "ranchettes." But he notes that he never had an interest in coming as a conqueror; in fact, he feels personally insulted that the speculation was even made.

At the Flying D, he has dozens of personal Leopoldian "blank spaces" he seeks out—hideaways like the Enchanted Forest. "The map for reaching them I keep up here," he says, tapping his temple. As a septuagenarian, he still tries to walk and ride as much of his ranches as possible, though he has resigned himself to the fact that he will not cover them all. "I'm leaving the rest for my kids and grandkids to explore."

Kossler eases the plane downward. Wings cast sun shadows over small rivulets, a few waterfalls. Below, trotting in single file between clusters of aspen and pine, are perhaps two hundred elk.

Swooping lower, he follows the wends of Cherry Creek, where Turner, the state of Montana, the US Forest Service, and Trout Unlimited have restored imperiled westslope cutthroat trout in an unprecedented project by first purging the waters of nonnative browns, rainbows, and brook trout. "It's one thing to work to recover native species on publicly owned lands," says Chris Wood, president and CEO of Trout Unlimited. "But when private landowners such as Turner embrace conservation and restoration, that's when we really begin to see watershed-level recovery occurring."

Westslopes swam in the melt of receding Pleistocene glaciers, but pure-strain examples of the species have suffered a precipitous decline caused by water quality impairment in the West and by transplanted, nonnative trout producing a hybridized species. Westslopes represent one of the last pieces in a puzzle of biological completeness Turner has been trying to assemble. Carter Kruse, Turner's nationally acclaimed aquatic resources biologist who chaperoned it, calls the establishment of pure-strain westslope cutthroats a momentous achievement. Overall, it resulted in westslopes gaining sixty new river miles of habitat, among a much larger blueprint for fish restoration across the West Turner is taking on. These efforts have attracted national attention and rank as high in importance to his boss as allowing grizzlies and wolves to share the ranch premises, Kruse says. "Not all of these projects have been perfectly executed, but that's expected. We're doing things that were never attempted before. Ted knows that's how innovation happens."

Over the next thirty minutes, Kossler glides over moose, then a sow grizzly with two cubs. On the other side of the Madison River, he takes note of antelope and bison ambling over hillsides peppered with tepee rings thousands of years old. Then, in a kind of visual crescendo, he passes in front of the Spanish Peaks—the same chiseled summits that are part of the Madison cordillera rising in front of Turner's living room window and extend southward for sixty rock-ribbed miles.

Those mountains are also visible from Main Street in Bozeman twenty miles distant—as are the treeless highlands of the Flying D. Like a giant wave curling on the western horizon, they are part of the visual commons that tens of thousands of denizens savor with their eyes, and they leave a resonant impression on millions of visitors passing through southwest Montana. They shape their experience and Turner owns them with a sense of obligation.

"I had no idea how special the Flying D was to so many other people until I had been here awhile," he explains later.

Today, ecologists say, the Madison Range would be one of the wildest stretches of mountains in the entire, twenty-million-acre Greater Yellowstone region—were it not for scattershot development around the resort of Big Sky. The Spanish Peaks represent a point of demarcation between Ted Turner's influence and that of another wealthy man, a developer and former billionaire named Tim Blixseth.

~◆~

Joe Gutkoski is familiar with the contrast between Blixseth and Turner. He's qualified to assess each man's handiwork. He's roamed the mountains dividing each man's vision for more than half a century. Now in his eighties, Gutkoski was one of the first college-trained landscape architects to work for the Forest Service in the northern Rockies. His academic discipline involves the art and science of how human activities, including logging, ski development, and home building, blend with wildlife habitat and scenery.

Around the greater Yellowstone region—the wildest ecosystem in the Lower 48 states—the tops of many mountains have canisters with logbooks inside them. Gutkoski's name appears in dozens, a testament to how much backcountry he's scoured. A hunter and angler, a resident eco-historian, an oral keeper of battles won and lost, he is revered for his involvement in nearly every significant conservation issue in southwest Montana since the 1960s. He is also an advocate for free-ranging bison restoration on the open plains, and has recruited his own army of activists to make it happen.

"The Flying D, when I arrived in Montana in the 1960s, was focused on cattle production," he said, "but the country south of it was wild. Wilder, I should say. There wasn't much tolerance on the ranch, before Turner got here, for predators such as grizzly bears and mountain lions. Wolves had already been exterminated from the ecosystem. And if a coyote was spotted, it was shot by the ranch hands out of provincial habit.

"If you wanted a taste of wild Montana, you could start at the Spanish Peaks and keep walking southward for a couple of days toward the Yellow Mules and Lone Mountain and you would encounter few structures except for an old broken-down log cabin here or there."

For work and pleasure, Gutkoski traipsed the entire wild gap between the Flying D and Lone Mountain, the centerpiece of the Big Sky resort community. He's traversed it on foot, snowshoes, and backcountry skis, on one-hundred-degree days and in midwinter blizzards, with a hunting rifle in his hands and a backpacker's topo map. He has encountered wolverines in the high alpine cirques, ambled into grizzlies, and harvested elk to fill his freezer. His first circumnavigation, he says, was in 1964.

"It's hard to believe how much has changed," he says.

Two generations ago, the flanks of Lone Peak and the Yellow Mules were summer cattle pastures connected to parcels deeded to the Burlington-Northern Railroad Company. These parcels were, in frontier times, set aside to provide wood for railroad ties. But the steep slopes were also perfectly suited for another purpose in the twentieth century—downhill skiing.

The idea for the Big Sky Resort is credited to a famous figure in American journalism. As a Forest Service landscape architect, Gutkoski was present in a small room when legendary NBC newsman Chet Huntley, a native of Whitehall, Montana, proposed building a ski destination at the base of Lone Mountain.

"I remember those initial meetings when Chet laid out his plans. The emphasis was on having a development that would generate jobs and revenue yet be *compatible* with the surrounding land," Gutkoski says. "I heard him personally say that he wanted to honor the setting, not detract from it. Who could argue with that?"

In those days, ski resorts were purely about the skiing, and had a limited infrastructure at the foot of the slopes. "You thought of them as almost being benign because the bustle of activity occurred in winter when the wildlife had left the high country. When the snow melted, that's when the people went away. Ranchers didn't like grizzlies, but the bears, if they were smart, could avoid conflict," Gutkoski says. In terms of any year-round residents, there was one man, an old hermit, who lived up the valley, and in the summer there would be a few cowboys and maybe a few horseback riders from some of the dude ranches.

Huntley's dream was slow to form. Montana, with limited commercial jet service, was considered out of the way compared to the ski hills in Colorado, Utah, and Idaho. By all accounts, Huntley didn't want to emulate the sprawl that defined those other destinations. But unfortunately, Gutkoski says, Huntley died in 1974 from cancer, and so wasn't there to influence what followed.

"He loved the character of the land at the base of Lone Mountain and he wanted people to experience a sense of awe for nature, not to have human presence be the dominating impression. I think he was kind of dispirited at the end of his life because the idea had not taken off the way he hoped it would."

As the 1980s ensued, developers dusted off Huntley's blueprint and tilted toward something more economically ambitious and lucrative. A network of roads was built and lined with lots. Burlington Northern also started clear-cutting huge swaths of its forested holdings.

The old hermit on the mountain, Gutkoski says, disappeared, and the once quiet valley was replaced by hundreds of homes and condos, presaging thousands more, many owned by out-of-state visitors who only use them as second-home vacation properties a few weeks out of the year. Huntley's sister told a reporter disdainfully: "He always intended it to be a little community."

"It happened so fast, in retrospect, the development and the logging, that it kind of made your head spin," Gutkoski says. "The country I used to know had disappeared. What eventually happened on the flanks of Lone Mountain, I believe, would have Chet Huntley spinning in his grave today. It's not that the people who bought property and live in Big Sky today aren't nice people. Most of them are. Most of them came from somewhere else. It's that they don't know, can't understand, what was here before. And I think Chet would really have chafed at the way subsequent events unfolded."

When Turner was seven years old, his parents moved from Ohio to the Georgia port city of Savannah. The Atlantic coastline of his youth was still largely wild and untouched. During the 1970s and 1980s, however, he saw the low coastal country of Georgia and South Carolina get hit by a hurricane of development. It's one of the reasons that when Turner purchased St. Phillips Island near Hilton Head, he voluntarily attached a conservation easement to the deed so that the land could never be turned into a cookie-cutter golf course resort.

In 1989, Turner correctly ascertained that similar patterns of development would soon be bearing down on Montana. "It didn't take a genius to recognize," he says. "I think a lot of people fantasize about having a place in the mountains. What was surprising was the pace. Nobody in the Southeast thought the southern Carolina coastline would look like Florida, but it happened. In Montana, there was just more to lose."

Not long afterward, the movie *A River Runs Through It*, which presented Montana as a fly-fishing paradise, attracted a wave of lifestyle pilgrims. Phones in real estate offices started ringing off the hook.

"Over and over again, Ted has demonstrated himself as a man who possesses impeccable timing," says Chris Francis, a fish habitat specialist who has helped restore trout streams on a handful of Turner's ranches and today is Turner's full-time fly-fishing guide. "Ted got here before the worst kind of real estate speculators did."

Besides the Flying D and the Bar None, Turner purchased the Snowcrest and Red Rock ranches in western Montana for fishing and bison. Their watersheds had been hammered by bovine hooves. The stream banks were suffering from erosion problems that muddied the water and destroyed trout spawning habitat; the corridors held few trees, and the uplands had been grazed heavily by ranchers compelled to pasture more animals than the conditions could accommodate.

"Eventually, that catches up with you, and the land looks like hell," Francis says. "Ted never sees a property as it is. He envisions what it's going to look like next year, in ten years, one hundred years down the road."

"I didn't want to change the Flying D," Turner says. "I wanted it always to remain whole."

Within months of acquiring it, Turner followed the same strategy as he had with Hope Plantation and St. Phillips in South Carolina. Defying the recommendations of real estate experts, he attached a conservation easement to the property. A conservation easement is a voluntary but binding legal restriction that limits what kind of development can occur. It cannot be undone. Landowners are motivated not only to make sure the property remains undeveloped in perpetuity, but tax incentives better enable land to be passed down from one generation to the next.

His easement on the Flying D, drafted by The Nature Conservancy, made conservation history. It was, at the time, the largest of its kind in the country and left some people, used to the old way of thinking, scratching their heads. Some in the Montana real estate industry told Turner that he was making a mistake by encumbering his ability to develop the Flying D to its "highest and fullest potential"—code for potentially slicing it up into tinier pieces if he needed to generate cash. According to the laws, Turner was entitled to save a few million dollars in taxes for diminishing the value of the Flying D by not developing it. But over the coming decade as he increased his charitable giving, he didn't need those deductions. Some have accused Turner of shrewdly parlaying the easement into a tax advantage, but as his financial advisors point out: If Turner were really that concerned about cutting corners in order to bolster his bank account, it would have been folly to put an easement on the place to begin with. He was motivated, they said, by something other than money.

Soon enough, Montanans would come to understand the accuracy of Turner's fears.

The battle between citizen conservationists and developers is occurring in most every community in America to varying degrees. But the contrast between Turner and Tim Blixseth is regarded by many as paradigmatic.

In considering these two property owners, it's important first to consider how frontier policies from the nineteenth century continue to reverberate. After the Civil War, congressional and presidential priorities were to spur settlement and build an intercontinental railroad. The federal government gave railroad companies forestland as inducement, properties that could be timbered for track ties, lumber, and commercial sale. As a result, in Montana and elsewhere, a checkerboard of railroad lands overlaid huge stretches of national forest.

Imagine this alternating pattern stretching for hundreds of miles, wherever track line was built. One stretch reached from the outskirts of Bozeman up the Gallatin Canyon past the Flying D, paralleling the Gallatin River past Big Sky to the western edge of Yellowstone National Park. The private checkerboard squares were often located inside larger national forest boundaries.

When the twentieth century arrived, the checkerboard pattern became a major impediment to sound, cohesive ecological management. It's difficult to act in the public's interest—protecting wildlife habitat, safeguarding watersheds, and fighting forest fires—on private ground. It's also possible for private ground to be liquidated of its trees right in the middle of important elk range or along a river.

Often the solution, embraced by government agencies and the railroads alike, is to swap land in a way that enables parcels to be consolidated into contiguous blocks. In southwest Montana during the late 1980s, Plum Creek Corporation, the real estate spinoff of Burlington Northern, let it be known that it was open to bargaining. The company had 165,000 acres and a sawmill in Belgrade, Montana. Some of its prime sections were located in the Bridger, Gallatin, and Madison mountain ranges around Bozeman, including terrain that almost abutted the Flying D. Several key sections were located between the Spanish Peaks and Big Sky right in the middle of important corridors for elk, moose, deer, and imperiled species like grizzly bears, wolverines, and lynx.

Turner had a chance to purchase it, his general manager Miller says, but balked, and then later regretted it. "In the moment, none of us knew what would happen on that parcel," Miller says.

Then The Nature Conservancy quietly made an overture and proposed a deal. The man in the middle of negotiations was Brian Kahn, then The Nature Conservancy's state director, who also had worked closely with Turner to write the terms of the conservation easement for the Flying D.

An offer of $24 million was advanced to acquire Plum Creek's holdings—just $3 million less than Turner paid for the entire Flying D. Turner supported the consolidation, and pledged $10 million cash. Innovatively, the plan called for The Nature Conservancy to buy two big parcels and then deed them over to the Gallatin National Forest.

"Ted loves to operate at large landscape levels because he grasps the bigger patterns of what's going on," Kahn says. "My discussions with him were all about the conservation value of blocking up lands under single, consistent ownership, getting rid of all those inholdings that brought with them serious risks to habitat and the integrity of the larger ecosystem, of which his own ranch was a part."

Turner's offer was a magnanimous gesture, Kahn explains. He wasn't out to enrich himself. Buying the tracts and giving them over to the Forest Service—US citizens—would accrue huge public benefits for wildlife, hunters, and recreationists.

"If we had pulled it off," Kahn says in retrospect, "it would have been huge."

But Plum Creek came under pressure from regional interests that wanted to make sure its forestlands, if sold, would contribute logs to feed the mills. It wanted the deal to help support the timber culture. But lines of communication broke down with The Nature Conservancy.

"Ted got impatient with the delays in the negotiations, which was understandable . . . I think he gave thought to stepping in as a negotiator, gathering all of the entities together and taking the lead," Kahn says. According to Turner, Kahn's assessment is accurate.

This was also the early 1990s, and Turner was newly arrived and a controversial figure. He'd made derogatory comments about cattle, and he was married to Jane Fonda, whom political conservatives had branded a traitor for going to Hanoi during the Vietnam War.

"The Nature Conservancy did not want Ted out front and center, as we needed to develop and maintain broad public support to get the deal done," Kahn says. "But as things turned out, had Ted Turner chosen to step in and had we encouraged it, I think the deal would have gotten done. Hindsight is 20-20. It was our mistake not to maximize the skills of Ted. We know how disarming he can actually be. The consequences of that miscalculation are forever."

Plum Creek, in the end, rejected the conservation offer. Eventually several sections of the prime holdings were sold to an outside partnership from Oregon led by Blixseth and two brothers named Mel and Norm McDougal. The final purchase price was $27.5 million. Blixseth had, according to some, established a reputation as a wheeler-dealer with timber lands on the West Coast and had already been caught up in one bankruptcy. Ultimately, Montana would give him a colossal second episode of financial problems, but the plot would take years to play out.

Blixseth and the McDougals reached a final agreement with Plum Creek. They embarked upon a plan that would, in some ways, result in the kind of outcome that Turner, Kahn, and other conservationists had desperately hoped to avoid.

The threesome divided off a twenty-five-thousand-acre chunk in the Jack Creek Drainage just over the mountain from the Flying D and sold it to a group of local developers for $6.5 million. Eventually, the parcel would turn into a high-end gated subdivision called Moonlight Basin. Moonlight now features a downhill ski area, golf course, and a wide scattering of homes. Major parts of that tract had been completely logged over, but ecologists say it represented good potential for future wildlife habitat.

Blixseth next turned around and divested the timber mill to Louisiana Pacific Corp. for $9 million, replete with a guaranteed supply of trees. As for the rest of the land, Blixseth did work with conservationists and the Forest Service to safeguard swaths of the Gallatin Mountains stretching north of Yellowstone National Park. But the reasons he gave were never ones based on profound reverence for wild lands. Indeed, as the deals were coming together, he dismissed environmentalists when they raised concerns that he might cut and run. He talked about the value of private property rights and said that he could do whatever he wanted— do-gooders be damned. To generate more cash, he carried out a series of quick, intensive logging operations.

"He had come to saw logs and make money and wasn't worried about battles with environmentalists," wrote reporter Scott McMillion in a profile he wrote about Blixseth for the *Bozeman Daily Chronicle* (it ran on April 13, 2006). "He referred to the property as a 'tree farm' and once said he was 'tired of people saying clear-cutting is a bad word.'"

McMillion quoted Blixseth as saying: "Maybe someplace in this United States of America, somebody needs to draw a line and protect private property rights [to do whatever one wants with the land]. Maybe I'm the guy and that's the place."

These lands northwest of Yellowstone National Park functioned as vital big game range for elk, deer, and moose. Conservationists wanted them protected. Blixseth dangled ecologically important pieces of terra firma before the potential green suitors—places he knew they desperately wanted. Buy the forests, was the message, or watch them get razed. The implicit threat of logging forced environmentalists and sportsmen like Gutkoski to plead with the Montana congressional delegation to expedite a series of land swaps that would put the land in the hands of the Forest Service.

At one point, Blixseth theatrically parked a bulldozer at the entrance of one old road leading into the Porcupine Creek Drainage, a beloved hunting area and calving grounds for elk in the center of the Gallatin Range. Someone described it as a bald metaphor. "Metaphoric or not," he told reporters. "The best way to get a deal done is to keep everybody's attention on the deal. Everybody paid attention."

Gutkoski watched all of this play out with horror. "Almost everything Blixseth did," he says, "was about leveraging a minimum investment of a few million dollars into getting more valuable assets, but he did it by using fear and threatening the possibility of very undesirable outcomes for his holdings. Some might call that shrewd strong-arming. I thought it was shameless and despicable."

He adds, "The people who later ended up worshipping him forget how crass he was in telling the people to either give him what he wanted or else he'd play the role of robber baron."

In the end, Blixseth and the McDougals had to put up a small amount of actual cash of their own for their acquisition from Burlington Northern. Blixseth leveraged every piece to his advantage, playing parcels like poker chips. By the time he was done with his horse-trading and Congress had ponied up millions to purchase tracts or trade out lands in the Gallatin Range, the threesome had increased their equity position several fold. The McDougals walked away with a multimillion-dollar profit.

Mike Clark, the recently retired executive director of the Greater Yellowstone Coalition, a regional conservation group, reflects on the outcome of those hastily crafted trades. "At the time, it was a victory because we prevented some valleys from being logged and subdivided, but we had no idea what Blixseth planned as his next step. No one did."

Blixseth had become aware of the same socioeconomic trends Turner had recognized years earlier. The Rockies were America's Third Coast in terms of real estate development. Far more money could be made with selling lots in the vicinity of downhill ski resorts. South of Big Sky, he set aside almost fifteen thousand acres of his Plum Creek acquisition for himself.

———

Blixseth was dubbed "Mr. Hustle" by the newspaper in Bozeman, based upon his reputation for buying land low and selling high. Gazing at the land south of Lone Mountain on a spur ridge called Pioneer Mountain, he announced that he would create the most exclusive high-end, invitation-only gated community—a retreat for mega-millionaires seeking seclusion—that had ever existed in the Rocky Mountain West. He would call his brainchild the Yellowstone Club.

"The contrast between a man like Tim Blixseth and Ted Turner isn't insignificant at all," Clark says. "In fact, I think it's a parable. Putting them side-by-side provides a valuable lesson for modern conservation and the larger decisions that face us all in this world. Each man proffered a very different vision for how to use the natural capital they acquired by buying land."

Marketers for the Yellowstone Club billed it as "authentic Montana." It ultimately came replete with armed guards, a private downhill ski area, an eighteen-hole signature golf course, riding facilities, massive guest lodge, a network of roads, and other amenities carved in the habitat where Gutkoski used to hunt elk. The lots alone were sold for millions of dollars, and the cost of constructing homes ranged from around $5 million to $25 million. Among the 350 or so official club members who were on the board or owned lots (one had to be a bona fide millionaire to get in): former US senators Jack Kemp and Bill Frist, former vice president Dan Quayle, former Los Angeles Dodgers owner Frank McCourt, Swedish women's golf professional Annika Sörenstam, American cyclist and Tour de France champion Greg LeMond, and Bill and Melinda Gates. Blixseth believed that, by the time he was finished, he would add another five hundred millionaires to his exclusive enclave.

Turner is a quick study of people. He does not say anything to disparage the Yellowstone Club members. He considers the Gateses his friends and extraordinary people in the world of global philanthropy. He also downhill skis every year at Big Sky. But he was disgusted by what was happening to the land that was nearly saved from bulldozers.

Blixseth took a potshot at Turner, and his comments seemed to imply that the bison baron from Atlanta wasn't getting smarter as he was getting older. Otherwise, if he had the sense of a real entrepreneur, he would emulate Blixseth as a land developer.

"It's *his* land," Turner said of Blixseth privately. "He paid for it fair and square, but we'll see who's still here in a couple of years and who proves to be smarter."

~~~

Across the mountain from the Yellowstone Club, Turner was slowly and discreetly increasing the size of his bison herd even while recovering from the disaster that had been the AOL Time Warner merger.

In addition to his ecological restoration projects and the launch of his Ted's Montana Grill restaurant chain, he was traveling in support of nuclear arms reduction and initiatives such as eradicating polio and reducing malaria in developing nations. He also was making major contributions to environmental organizations like the Greater Yellowstone Coalition, groups devoted to keeping large public landscapes intact. He even served on its board of directors.

He remembers getting word from his ranch hands of how grizzlies were returning to the Flying D. They had been largely absent for half a century.

Veteran wildlife biologist Chuck Schwartz, who recently left his job as director of the Yellowstone Interagency Grizzly Bear Study Team (a research unit within the US Geological Survey), shared an observation: "The critics of Turner said he was way out there on the fringe of reason when he replaced cattle with bison. When you look closer at what he's trying to accomplish, it makes perfect sense. With beef cows and sheep, in an attempt to make them docile, humans have bred certain traits out of those animals to make them easier to grow. But in doing that, those animals have become more vulnerable and less capable of surviving in the Wild West, especially with predators."

Schwartz also referred to the wave of human immigrants flooding to the northern Rockies, drawn to its wildness and natural beauty yet refusing to take responsibility for where they choose to build their dream homes. After decades of suffering declines, Yellowstone-area grizzlies are at last recovering, only because of habitat protection efforts.

But Schwartz says Big Sky, the Yellowstone Club, and other nearby developments have reversed progress for bear conservation in the heart of the Madison Mountains. Essentially, they are constricting the ability of wildlife to move through the landscape. He describes Big Sky as a gauntlet filled with "human minefields" such as ever-increasing numbers of people, garbage, smells emanating from barbecue grills and restaurants, roaming domestic dogs, traffic, homes, and high concentrations of hikers, horseback riders, golfers, mountain bikers, and all-terrain-vehicle enthusiasts. The expanding footprint of development represents a "sinkhole" for bears. If bears and wolves and mountain lions pass through, they have a fairly high probability of getting into trouble with people and having to be destroyed.

"Think about it. All of these temptations and obstacles are presented to grizzlies which, for the most part, want only to avoid people," Schwartz says. However, if a bear chases someone's dog that was hounding the bruin, the bear is blamed. If a mountain biker comes barreling down a trail and meets a grizzly mother with cubs, and the bruin acts defensively, she is labeled a menace. If a golfer on one of the high-elevation links at the Yellowstone Club spots a grizzly crossing a fairway, the bear will most likely be trapped and removed.

Schwartz says that because of changes in management implemented by Turner, the Flying D, as a point for comparison, has yielded a large block of secure habitat, a net gain for grizzlies.

Prior to his coming west a few decades ago and then leading the Greater Yellowstone Coalition, Clark had been a revered community organizer for Greenpeace who helped call attention to "mountain top removal" mining methods in West Virginia and Kentucky.

"Why does private stewardship matter in the contrast between Turner and Blixseth?" he asks. "Well, in the East, I witnessed the death of special places where simple folk lived. Whole valleys and mountains literally gone, ways of life being altered, and not simply in a minor way," he says.

"You have to see it to believe it. The rapacious appetite of coal doesn't only mar viewsheds. Streams and the life forms in them have been eviscerated, people forced from the land, their water contaminated, and wildlife pushed off or destroyed in the process. The impacts of development in the West are different but their impacts are equally as permanent."

Christopher Boyer, a pilot and aerial photographer who helps conservation organizations document the impacts of sprawl, says Clark's analogy is appropriate. He has a series of stunning images taken above Big Sky and the Yellowstone Club and he says the degree of intense landscape fragmentation is similar to industrial open-pit mining.

In essence, ecologists say, the combined tentacles of Big Sky, the Yellowstone Club, and neighboring enclaves are producing a form of "ecological decapitation." When habitat becomes more fragmented and islandized, large-ranging species suffer higher rates of extirpation.

"For animals that run in herds like elk, and for grizzly bears and wolves and even wolverines that seek solitude," Clark says, "a residential subdivision, even though it has green lawns, represents a giant barrier. When you drop a subdivision out of the sky into the middle of a formerly wild setting, the impacts are basically forever. A forest that is clearcut can, over time, grow back. Rows of trophy homes create the suburbs. If you go to Ted's house, you can't even find it unless you know where to look. And it doesn't cry out, 'Look at me, I'm a billionaire.'"

Turner, he says, has in fact dramatically shrunk the size of his ecological footprint at the Flying D by reducing the number of buildings, eliminating most of the haying, which allowed water to be left in streams rather than diverted for irrigation, and generally minimizing intensive activity. His home nestles inconspicuously into a hill, and the pond in front of it is value-added habitat.

"He raised the bar for other landowners in the region," Clark says.

Today, the conservation easement on the Flying D prevents it from ever being subdivided and prescribes how many bison can graze there. In fact, at Turner's own suggestion, it stipulates that the number of elk and other wildlife that find refuge on his ranch are counted against the number of bison he can raise.

When Turner received praise for putting a conservation easement on his property, Blixseth in turn put an easement on the Yellowstone Club. But he did so after he had carved out hundreds of the most valuable pieces for sale as homesites. Turner's easement allows for just five more homes to be built across the entire 113,000 acres, one for each of his children. The Yellowstone Club, one-eighth or 13 percent the size of the Flying D, reportedly recorded $1 billion in real estate sales in less than a decade.

"There's no question that Ted, had he pursued the same path as Blixseth, could have parlayed his investment into twenty, maybe fifty times what he paid for it," Clark says. "But I think a better question is: Would there be a place for thousands of elk, deer, moose, and pronghorn to winter? Would grizzly bears and wolves be tolerated? Would there be bison? Would that part of the Gallatin Valley still be pleasant or would it resemble the suburbs of Denver and Salt Lake City?"

Turner says he never wanted to do anything with his land that would earn him a place in infamy. "I want to have the respect of local people. I value it. I want to be able to hold my head high for doing the right thing when I walk down the street in Bozeman," he says.

～ ～

A few years earlier, on a winter's day, Mike Phillips, who oversees the Turner Endangered Species Fund, sped to the ranch from his home in Bozeman. I sat beside him in the passenger seat.

Phillips had been on his couch watching a college football game with his daughter and sons when the cell phone rang. It was Kossler informing him that a ranch hand had spotted what appeared to be fresh wolf tracks in the snow.

Half a decade before that phone call, Phillips had been on the ground in Yellowstone, carrying some of the first wild wolves back to the Park for release after a sixty-year absence. Phillips went to work for Turner in 1997, and has since maintained close ties with his biologist colleagues in the National Park Service and US Fish and Wildlife Service.

"Having wolves on the Flying D is something Ted always hoped would happen," Phillips said at the time. "He would deposit them there himself if he could, but doing that is illegal and there is no way to contain them. But if wild wolves legally re-established in Yellowstone wander outside the park and find their way to the D, he is all for it."

Preparing for that day to arrive, Phillips said, was always an unspoken part of his job when Turner hired him away from the National Park Service. He notes that given the ways wolves disperse, constantly probing for opportunities to establish new territories, it was inevitable they would reach the Flying D.

He hands me a memo sent to Turner and his son Beau dated January 27, 1999. It begins, "Given your keen interest in wolf conservation I thought you would appreciate knowing that during the last few days wolf tracks were detected just east of Upper Green Hollow by our carnivore survey team. Also, apparently Jim Averitt saw a wolf near that area about the same time . . . This may be the same wolf (or wolves) that friends of mine detected as they were skiing near the Spanish Creek campground just south of the Flying D in late November. They cut the tracks of three wolves. . . . As we discussed several months ago, it remains just a matter of time before wolves settle the ranch."

Turner was left ecstatic by the news. Three years later, I was with Phillips when he drove his pickup truck as far as it would take him into the ranch interior before snowdrifts left the road impassable. With only two hours of daylight left and a cold wind sandblasting the ground with fresh snow, he knew his time to cut tracks was short. In time, he found a single pattern of tracks that were too large to belong to a coyote. Here was more prima facie evidence.

He jotted a few remarks in a pocket notebook and headed back to the truck. He couldn't wait to inform Turner. "Ted is always keenly interested in details about wildlife on his properties. He was overjoyed that wolves were adopting the Flying D as a home."

Eastward from our knoll was the bright glow from Bozeman and its suburbs. "I'll bet most people in this valley don't have a clue how close they are living to wolves," Phillips says. "Most would be excited by it. They might think differently about the landscape around them if they knew."

As with bison and grizzlies, Turner had started to close another broken circle on the "D." Every major mammal known to exist in the Rockies at the time of Leif Ericson's arrival in Canada could now be found on his ranch: grizzlies, wolves, mountain lions, bobcats, lynx, coyotes, foxes (red and gray), bighorn sheep, wolverines, elk, moose, mule deer, whitetails, pronghorn antelope, badgers, and bison. Few other private properties in the Lower 48 can claim the same distinction.

After Phillips delivered his wolf update to Turner, he briefed Ed Bangs, his friend with the Fish and Wildlife Service, who for years was the agency's national wolf recovery coordinator. Bangs notified the Montana Fish, Wildlife and Parks Department. Bangs understands the paradox of how information works and can balloon into hysteria. The peripatetic canids roaming across the Flying D had not killed any household pets or livestock in the neighborhoods around the ranch; and even though no harm had come, Bangs assumed there might be needless panic if he and Turner publicly made a big to-do about a wolf being in the middle of the Gallatin Valley. For now, they would allow wolves to enjoy an invisible presence, albeit keeping government wildlife biologists fully informed.

Turner knew it would take time before male and female wolves had their first litter of pups on the Flying D. In fact, it wouldn't happen for a few more years. He didn't know how long it would take before he would have a chance to have a personal encounter himself.

Meanwhile, the Yellowstone Club had become a showcase of its own—albeit for different reasons.

Dennis Glick, founder of the community conservation organization FutureWest, has worked for forty years as an environmentalist, including stints in Latin America for the World Wildlife Fund where he helped establish a system of national parks. He spent nearly a decade with the Greater Yellowstone Coalition and Sonoran Institute scrutinizing private development. In fact, he was the only conservationist with a land use planning background to testify against the Yellowstone Club at the permitting phase. He knew there would be construction jobs created, but at what cost to the land?

"I asked the local county commissioners to think about the real meaning of sustainability and Montana's competitive advantage in the world. When all of the construction at the Yellowstone Club is over and the Wild West gold rush moves onto another town, what are you going to be left with? At the end of the day, it comes down to us looking ourselves in the mirror and asking, 'What do we really value? What makes Montana Montana?'"

The Yellowstone Club won approval from elected officials, and Blixseth went to work skillfully promoting his project. He loved to wine and dine impressionable journalists, who almost never wrote probing newspaper or magazine stories mentioning environmental impacts or questioning the glam of material excess Blixseth was pitching.

In the wake of the bursting dot.com bubble and following the domestic terrorism attacks of September 11, 2001, real estate in Montana defied the cooling down that occurred nationally. The Yellowstone Club actually seemed to pick up momentum. By the middle of the first decade of the new century, Blixseth's net worth had skyrocketed. In 2006, McMillion with the *Bozeman Daily Chronicle* wrote: "Today, *Forbes Magazine* estimates his net worth at $1.2 billion, and most of that was made in Montana. For him, it started with about $3 million in cash."

Blixseth, in fact, decided to take The Yellowstone Club concept to still another level. Receiving a $375 million credit line from Credit Suisse, he and his wife, Edra, bought European castles, chateaus, ranches, a tropical island, and a golf course in Scotland, among others. "Yellowstone Club World," his new creation, would cater to a higher layer of über-affluent, and promised to give members basically time-share vacations to live out their lavish fantasies. The couple even bought an antique throne made of carved mahogany.

This was the man who had once said, "I don't like most rich people. They can be arrogant."

Blixseth planned to build a spec home on 160 acres at the Yellowstone Club that would, he said, be one of the most expensive personal residences ever sold in the United States. Called "The Pinnacle," the log home would top out at fifty-three thousand square feet of living space. The asking price would be $155 million, or almost eight times what Turner had paid for the entire Flying D.

Scott Bosse, a conservationist with the group American Rivers, wrote a terse commentary on a blogging site: "Tim Blixseth may have an address in Montana, but he will never be accepted by Montanans as a fellow citizen. Flaunting one's wealth and wasting valuable natural resources are the most un-Montana-like values I can think of. How many century-old trees will be cut down to build Mr. Blixseth's shrine to the human ego? How many more gas wells will have to be drilled on the west's public lands to heat this monstrosity?"

Bosse rejects the vision of the "New West" that Blixseth was aggressively selling to the rest of the world. "While more and more of the wealthiest people on Earth—think Bill Gates, Warren Buffett, and Ted Turner—are learning that the best way to leave a lasting legacy is to donate their money to build schools, cure diseases, and take on the issue of global warming, Mr. Blixseth's idea of a legacy is to build a $155 million playhouse so a fellow billionaire can move into his private neighborhood. How sad."

"This was craziness. People were rolling their eyes," says Dennis Glick of FutureWest. "I don't know what the poster child of delirium is, but there were a lot of people pointing to the Yellowstone Club and shaking their heads in disgust."

Old Joe Gutkoski, who was once turned away as he tried to cross-country ski across one of his old haunts acquired by the Yellowstone Club, said it was Ayn Rand's material objectivism writ large. "Blixseth's message seems to be: It's all about me, me, me in my overstuffed McMansion, driving golf balls down the fairway as elk scramble for cover, sitting on my throne, drinking overpriced port by the glass and looking down on other people. Is this what our country has become, that these are the kind of people we aspire to emulate?"

Along the way, trouble began to brew. First, Blixseth came under scrutiny from state environmental regulators when his workers, in their haste to rapidly punch in a grid of roads and lots, had front-end loaders blaze a path right through a tributary steam leading ultimately into the blue-ribbon Gallatin River. He had to pay a seven-figure fine. Meanwhile, some real estate agents warned that the Yellowstone Club property was hyper-inflated and that the club had overpromised what it was able to deliver to members of the gated community.

Prominent Yellowstone Club members, including former Tour de France bicycling champion Greg LeMond, turned on Blixseth, accusing him of failing to honor the rising value of an equity stake LeMond had made before leveraged land values soared through the roof. LeMond's attorney James Goetz said: "Mr. Blixseth thinks he's king up there and can do what he wants."

As the real estate market started to crumble nationwide in advance of the financial market earthquake in 2008, Tim and Edra Blixseth announced they were splitting up. Within months, creditors started calling, and each of the Blixseths, freshly divorced, lawyered up, trying to pin liabilities on the other. Where were the hundreds of millions of dollars, people asked, that Blixseth had borrowed from Credit Suisse, and millions more he made through real estate speculation? It was later revealed that Mr. Blixseth, discreetly and without the knowledge of many of his Yellowstone Club members, had wired a few hundred million dollars into a personal holding company in California.

His growing woes were compounded by the events in autumn 2008 when the implosion of Lehman Brothers caused many financial services companies to call their loans due. When Credit Suisse wanted its money, Blixseth said he didn't have it, and pointed a finger at his ex-wife.

Plans for "the Pinnacle," his once-great monument to luxury, were abruptly abandoned, and the land where it was to be built sold. Blixseth also had to renege on delivering the amenity benefits he had promised to Yellowstone Club members. Cementing the downward spiral, Yellowstone Club World was cancelled for lack of interest. The castles, chateaus, and other high-flying holdings were scheduled for sale.

The Yellowstone Club filed for bankruptcy, the second in Blixseth's career. This time, a judge ordered the now-divorced couple to liquidate their assets. Property and home furnishings were seized, including the carved mahogany throne. Once upon a time, when the tempest of Montana real estate was spinning in cyclonic gyration, a bank president had said: "I think the whole expansion of the economy you could lay at the foot of the Yellowstone Club. They've done more to bring prosperity than any other entity. It's created, I honestly believe, thousands of jobs."

Even with the sale of assets, it still didn't cover millions of dollars in unpaid bills the Blixseths owed to laid-off employees and the local businesses who had provided goods and rendered services. New owners of the Yellowstone Club had to make them whole.

Turner did not gloat. But he did reflect in an interview with reporter Gail Schontzler of the *Bozeman Daily Chronicle:* "I don't really like to be mentioned in the same breath with him. We had a totally different attitude about life. I looked at the land as something to revere, to love and to care for. And he looked at it as something to make as much money as he possibly could. In Spanish, there's a phrase, 'Peso rapido.' That's a fast buck." He added in a separate conversation: "As I've said before, the problem isn't capitalism. The problem is how we practice capitalism."

Consider two data points to chew on: Once, the Montana Department of Commerce offered an estimate that construction in Big Sky, fueled by the Yellowstone Club, created 7,431 jobs. Yet a huge percentage of that workforce vanished with the arrival of the Great Recession and many say it wasn't sustainable anyway—that it was no different than the copper mines of Butte. Hundreds of millions of dollars, on paper anyway, cycled through the Yellowstone Club and where has it gone?

Here is another stat: In 1970, the year that he acquired his first cable television station in Atlanta, Turner had thirty-five employees on the payroll and generated $600,000 in business. A quarter century later, at the time of his merger with Time Warner, he had twelve thousand employees and generated $2.5 billion in income. Today, Turner Enterprises employs hundreds of people in locations across the country. He took his personal income and flowed it into buying land and growing bison, producing clean water, open space, and he's investing in alternative energy. "I'm still here," he says.

These days, Blixseth has bailed out of Montana. In 2010, a federal court judge wrote a 135-page ruling for one case in which he excoriated

Blixseth for committing "self-dealing" and "deception." A new investor, CrossHarbor Capital Partners, has picked up the pieces of Blixseth's empire, though in ongoing court proceedings Blixseth has appeared to blame anyone but himself. The Yellowstone Club, even with good people living in it, continues to be a sinkhole for wildlife.

Kossler's time in the sky has come to a close. He carves one more turn around the center of the Flying D. A former cowboy, he and Turner's other ranch managers call themselves "bisonmen." Kossler never imagined when he took classes in ranch management that his career trajectory would lead to this. "Not in a million years could I have predicted the Flying D would ever become what it has," he says. "Ted shook a lot of people and a lot of things up."

Far below him, Ted Turner has stabled his horses and climbed instead behind the wheel of a white Land Rover. He and one of his guests drive down the public county road that wends through the Flying D.

They stop next to a minivan from Iowa pulled over on the side of the road, a family with children who are watching a group of bison bulls sparring in rut. The bellows sound like roaring lions.

Turner enjoys the expressions on the kids' faces. "Pretty exciting, isn't it? What do you think?"

"This is sooo cool," a preteen girl says. "Who owns these bison?"

"Oh, they belong to Ted Turner," the girl's mother says, absorbed in the scene.

She hasn't made eye contact with the onlooker in the white Land Rover. She calls back without looking, "We ate lunch at the restaurant Turner owns in Bozeman. The waitress said Ted spends a lot of time out here in the summer. Do you ever see him?"

"Yes, I know a little about him. He likes to spend time out here as much as he can," Turner says in his familiar nasally voice. "I know that guy, Turner, because I am he."

The woman looks up, stunned.

For five minutes, Turner shares a few of the nuances of bison behavior, explaining why bison wallow in the dirt, how the bulls jostle for the right to mate and how, next year in the spring, there will be a new crop of bison calves in the very same meadow. "Well, you folks enjoy the rest of the day. I know I will," Turner says.

Then he is gone.

He doesn't hear the young girl's brother say this day has been the best part of their trip. Earlier, the clan had stayed in Yellowstone, their mother explains.

"This is better than Yellowstone," the boy declares. "You don't have all the people."

In the summer of 2012, Turner instructed his ranch manager Danny Johnson to put a few dozen bison on the lower pastures of the Flying D along US Highway 191 near where it enters the Gallatin Canyon en route toward the Yellowstone Club. He wasn't thinking of Blixseth when he made the decision.

"People love bison. They equate bison with real Montana, the real Wild West," he said "I want to give them something they'll remember."

～～

Joe Gutkoski made what could be his final ski not long ago up the backbone of the Madison Range. He went to the place where he shot his first elk in southwest Montana, and had once followed the tracks of a mountain lion, and stood on the crest of the Spanish Peaks spying a shoulder of snow above treeline where he found a wolverine den. He can't make it up there anymore, and even if he could, he wouldn't return to some hideaways because the transformation would be too difficult to take. "My favorite place anymore," he says, "is seeing Ted's side of the mountain."

CHAPTER SIX

Save the Humans

" . . . *Ted realized that someone, an American from outside government, needed to step up and validate the importance of the UN, to put the critics in check. He understood the value of the UN because his international bureaus at CNN had exposed him to its work. It was tangible and it touched him. He had standing because he was an emblem of the modern, successful entrepreneur and an avowed free market capitalist, reflecting the values of Theodore Roosevelt.*"
—THE LATE AMERICAN DIPLOMAT RICHARD HOLBROOKE

WHAT DOES IT MEAN TO BE REGARDED AS A PERSON OF GOOD CONSCIENCE? In retrospect, aspects of Ted Turner's life and personality are explainable. Charted along a linear course with hindsight, they make perfect sense when traced backward from the present into his past. Turner fits the psychological profile of the stereotypical overachiever who seeks to overcome a shortage of self-esteem and prove his worth. But what has defined him more as a conscionable human being is his defiance of expectations by people who underestimate him.

Who could have predicted—that this conservative son of an alcoholic, depressive father who took his own life; a young man who once embraced the me-first objectivist ideology of Ayn Rand; and a kid forced to withdraw from Brown—would become one of the fiercest defenders of an organization that gives right wingers fits: the United Nations.

Today, Turner's name is closely associated with the UN, owing to a record-setting gift he made to the international organization. The affiliation still leaves people scratching their heads. Why did he do it?

If civilization is going to remain intact another one hundred or one thousand years, Turner steadfastly believes, there is nothing that can replace the vital, galvanizing role of the UN. Indeed, as he travels, he often hears antagonists daydreaming about facilitating the UN's demise or having the United States pull out of its 193-nation assembly.

Turner finds the notion to be utterly absurd, repugnant even, and when he is asked for a response, he becomes cantankerous.

"What would the world be like if the UN did not exist?" he asks. "Look at what happened when the League of Nations fell apart after World War I. We suffered through the worst outbreak of violence and destruction in human history. Thank God, there wasn't a widespread proliferation of nukes. Without the UN, we would have already fought World War III by now and we would be no more. I'm convinced that the world would be lost if the UN did not exist."

Turner says the United States and Soviet Union would not have navigated the Cold War without conflict erupting and warheads being exchanged. "Civilization as we know it would've been set back to the Stone Age. I know there are certain kinds of religious fanatics who fantasize about the end of the world coming, but I'm not one of them."

The late Richard Holbrooke, who served as President Barack Obama's special envoy to Afghanistan and Pakistan, told me just a few months before he died in 2010 that he credits "Ted the global citizen" with standing up for the UN at a crucial time when few others would. "I'm smiling when I think back on it, and what the dividends of it continue to be. I'm chuckling," Holbrooke said, "because I don't really believe that Ted understood what his actions meant. I know that citizens of this country don't."

Turner adored his younger sister, Mary Jean, and he began to question his belief in God following her agonizing death from lupus while only a teenager.

Ed Turner had many virtues, but his cold, emotionally abusive behavior—and eventual suicide—affected Ted in profound ways.

Like many impressionable sons, Turner idolized his father, Ed Turner, a hard-driving entrepreneur who taught him the value of the hard work ethic.

Turner has fond recollections of his mother, Florence, who always regretted that she did not stand up to Ed Turner when he insisted that Ted be sent away to boarding schools.

Mary Jean Turner revered her big brother, Ted. "I loved her deeply," Ted says. "When I was young, I prayed to God, asking that she be spared from more suffering."

"The greatest gift I can give my kids and grandkids isn't money. It's the vote of confidence that we have faith in them—and all young people—to step up and work together to save the world," Turner says. Along with their father, all the Turner children are trustees in the Turner Foundation. Pictured left to right: Jennie Turner Garlington, Teddy, Ted, Laura Turner Seydel, Beau, and Rhett.

After he was forced to withdraw from Brown University, Turner enlisted in the US Coast Guard. "Patriotism comes in many forms," he says. "Citizens, no matter where they are from, serve their countries not only in uniform, but by caring for others who need help, protecting the environment, and being willing to sacrifice to achieve a greater good."

Ironically, Turner subscribed to both the ideals of Ayn Rand and the Rotary Club as a young man, but eventually rejected Rand's "greed is good" mantra. "Capitalism isn't the problem," he says. "It's how we practice capitalism that has created many of the challenges now facing humanity."

Sailing taught Turner how Mother Nature can be harnessed as a powerful force and that, when approached with respect and care, she is always there to provide inspiration.

The image of Turner as a swashbuckling underdog, intrepid competitor, and say-anything personality, was cemented after he skippered *Courageous* to unlikely victory in the America's Cup in 1977.

Following his father's suicide, Turner and his colleagues transformed the family's billboard business, based in Atlanta, into a global multimedia empire.

Turner made modern history on June 1, 1980, when he launched the first twenty-four-hour news channel, CNN, and went into battle with the major TV networks. "We won't be signing off until the world ends," he said.

Jacques-Yves Cousteau was more than a mentor for Turner; he was a father figure. For both, their commitment to saving the planet started with their love for the sea.

Turner had meetings with Mikhail Gorbachev in the 1980s to discuss the Goodwill Games and opening a CNN bureau in Moscow. Today, the men are dear friends. This 1986 photo shows Gorbachev and Turner along with Georgi Arbatov and Turner's valued media executive Robert Wussler.

It wasn't fame, fortune, and a propensity for being outspoken that drew Turner and actress Jane Fonda together, but a major influence was their mutual love of nature. Turner says his ten-year marriage to Fonda prompted him to become more introspective. "She also opened my eyes to the serious issues affecting women around the world," he says.

Turner greatly admires British businessman, adventurer, and fellow eco-philanthropist Richard Branson for using his fortune to help make the world better. One of Branson's fondest memories of Turner is joining him at the Flying D Ranch in Montana and howling back and forth with wild wolves.

One of Turner's closest friends is President Jimmy Carter. A Nobel Peace Prize recipient, international negotiator, and participant in Habitat For Humanity, Carter also shares Turner's passion for fly fishing. Here, Turner interviews Carter for CNN.

Turner counts his $1 billion pledge to help enhance the peacemaking and humanitarian missions of the United Nations as "one of the most satisfying things I've ever done. The world would be in much deeper trouble were it not for the UN." Here, Turner joins Jens Stoltenberg, prime minister of Norway, UN secretary-general Ban Ki-moon, and former US senator Timothy E. Wirth, who oversees the influential UN Foundation created with Turner's gift.

"The possibility of an accidental or deliberate exchange of nuclear weapons, and the ever-present danger of nuclear weapons falling into the hands of terrorists, are among the gravest threats facing humanity," Turner says. Together with former US senator Sam Nunn, he created the Nuclear Threat Initiative, respected around the world, by both Democrats and Republicans, for helping to confront the looming menace of nuclear catastrophe.

A potent quartet of problem-solvers: former US senator Timothy E. Wirth, who heads the UN Foundation; Turner; Michael Finley, who oversees the Turner Foundation; and former US senator Sam Nunn, cofounder of the Nuclear Threat Initiative.

Politicians who advocate for the United States pulling out of the UN, withholding its membership dues and going alone in the world "are idiots" in Turner's mind. "That would be one of the dumbest things this country ever did," he says. "As leaders of the free world, we need to stop contemplating how many dumb moves we can make and focus on being smarter. I think we should start a 'Smart Movement' and the top priority would be helping the UN be all that it can be—as those who crafted its mission at the end of World War II originally envisioned."

All the talk about the UN robbing the US of its sovereignty and power and influence in the world "is just moronic and it's not true," he says. "When I hear people like Sarah Palin and Michelle Bachmann holding forth on international policy, you have to laugh. For what the US invests in the UN as its largest supporter, let me tell you something: It's a bargain. Few US citizens understand what we get in return. And how do you put a value on having a stable world?"

In 1997, Turner announced his $1 billion gift in support of the UN and UN causes around the world. "It was historic," Holbrooke said. Turner's reasoning was twofold: Besides wanting to do something outlandish that would get the power elites of the world to pay attention, Turner says, "I did it because, at the time, the UN was in trouble and some people were saying they'd prefer that it disband and just go away. The other reason is that I wanted to put other people on notice, that making money is fun and good, but being motivated by greed is not. Hoarding money as a miser instead of using it to help billions of people in need and protect the environment is shameful."

~~~

Turner is a man whom his critics at his one-time rival cable TV channel, FOX, portray as being erratic and scatterbrained. But Turner shrugs off the criticism. He has a game he sometimes enjoys playing. Like a television quiz show host, he administers a test to some of the brighter minds he meets on the lecture circuit. Occasionally, he directs the same questions toward unsuspecting dinner guests who dare to rail against the UN.

Politely, he will say, "Your opinions about the UN are fascinating. Could you please elaborate a little, maybe rattle off for us the top ten things the UN does and then explain in a sentence or two which ones you believe should be eliminated?"

Turner derives particular enjoyment in engaging adults, self-confident college students, and journalists who disparage the UN and correspondingly suggest the United States should reject globalism or, conversely, pursue an aggressive doctrine of military-led interventionism by stationing troops around the world as a perpetual exercise in nation-building.

"We could behave like England did during the height of the British Empire. That's certainly an option. And we could behave like we did between World War I and World War II," he says. Of course, he believes that neither option secures the United States a respected place in the world, and both leave America financially, intellectually, and strategically bankrupt—if not weaker and more vulnerable to terrorism. "This doesn't even include the huge sacrifice that we ask Americans to make with their lives or coming home so traumatized they'll never be the same," he says.

"Most people like to think they are pretty well-informed on world affairs, enough, at least, to feel comfortable expressing strong opinions, but I can't tell you how often they are stumped whenever they are asked to explain the function of the UN in the twenty-first century. They read about the UN in their high school civics classes or hear about it on FOX, more often with negative connotations attached, but they have difficulty explaining what the UN does. Europeans can do it with ease but many Americans struggle. Hell, what do you expect? We have citizens who don't even know what the state capital is in their own state."

So tonight, Turner is holding court over dinner at the Ladder Ranch in New Mexico. He begins by saying few Americans younger than seventy realize the UN charter was completed on American soil, in San Francisco, on October 24, 1945. It was born with the blessing of President Harry S Truman who said, "If we should pay merely lip service to inspiring ideals, and later do violence to simple justice, we would draw down upon us the bitter wrath of generations yet unborn."

Turner next quickly ticks off the entities and agreements that have grown out of the UN and its confederation of nations that today has 193 country members. He mentions the UN Peacekeeping force, the UN Environment Programme, the UN Fund for Family Planning; the Security Council, the World Health Organization, the World Court, the World Bank, the International Monetary Fund, the International Atomic Energy Agency, the Food and Agriculture Organization, the United Nations Educational, Scientific and Cultural Organization (UNESCO), the Human Rights Council, the World Food Programme, the Office of the High Commissioner on Refugees, and the UN Development Programme (UNDP), among others.

He goes on and translates what the existence of those entities actually means for Americans. Every time a commercial jet airliner makes an international flight, it is the underpinnings of UN-brokered agreements that provide a foundation for air safety and efficient travel times. When deadly diseases such as Ebola or influenza break out, the UN plays an important role in containment to prevent them from becoming a pandemic. When rogue nations are suspected of amassing nuclear arsenals and weapons of mass destruction, it is the UN that helps rally the world to intervene, demand inspections, and help enforce them.

The UN gives the United States and allies in the international community a means for confronting genocide, promoting food safety, responding to humanitarian crises caused by natural disasters, establishing ground rules for fair and open trade for US companies, and holding together a reliable, cohesive structure for banking, mail delivery, shipping, use of the high seas, and food production, he says. It also helps tighten a gauntlet around the trafficking of drugs, blood diamonds, child slaves, and endangered species.

Although the World Bank and International Monetary Fund, outgrowths of the UN, have come under withering criticism from groups on the left for their loan-making policies to poor developing nations in the past—and which in some cases, hastened resource extraction that caused environment destruction—reforms have helped make both of those entities instruments for positive change. "Targeted investment is helping to lift billions out of poverty which, in turn, lessens the need for aid and improves environmental conditions," he says.

I remind Turner that the prevailing perception of the UN, in the eyes of millions, whether accurate or not, is of an organization in disarray, an entity that has no backbone or real might to take on and stop aggressive regimes, and a bureaucracy that is *the* poster child for incompetence. Critics regard Turner's belief in the UN as being naïve and rooted in feel-good ideology.

"Well, what's the alternative?" he asks, his voice assuming intensity. "No, really, what *is* it? The critics have never been able to advance one. And the reason they can't is they know that what the UN does for today's world could not be replicated if we had to start over from scratch. They are the same people who ask us to put blind faith in free markets and then wash their hands of responsibility when things go wrong. They're the same people who sent us into Iraq on the premise that there were weapons of mass destruction. I see the UN as a 'the-glass-is-half-full' proposition. We can make it better. We can help it achieve all that it's capable of achieving. What the critics don't want to admit is that treating people with more dignity and respect now will save the US lots of money down the road, especially with military intervention. If people want to have a debate about the UN, let's bring it on."

With regard to the UN's blue-helmeted peacekeeping force, a frequent target of US conservatives and a popular muse for paranoid "black helicopter" conspiracy theorists, it has been dispatched to myriad venues over the course of the organization's history, the majority of the time exerting a calming influence and alleviating the necessity for individual countries to mount costly interventions, he says.

Peacekeepers, Turner notes, not only protect the most vulnerable people from abuse and exploitation, but their role, as witnesses against oppressive regimes, gives greater comfort to companies doing business in the developing world that otherwise might not make economic investments.

"Ted always notes that international peacekeepers are sent to the toughest places in the world, usually when other forms of diplomacy and remedies have failed," says former US senator Timothy E. Wirth, the UN Foundation president handpicked by Turner. "They are dispatched into the most inhospitable settings and do their work for a tenth of the cost of the mission were it carried out by the US military. UN peacekeeping is a value proposition for the US taxpayer concerned about overextension of our military."

Despite the constant browbeating the UN takes, Turner cites a research study prepared by the conservative RAND Corp. that found this somewhat startling reality—startling in the sense that it defies the image projected by its critics. Whenever the UN was involved in nation-building efforts following war and the subsequent holding of democratic elections that the UN helped monitor, peace continued in seven out of eight cases. Meanwhile, he notes, when the United States itself attempted on its own to set up governments in other countries, lasting peace was achieved in four out of eight examples, or half the rate of success. And it's a costly undertaking for a US government sinking deeper into debt. "Every non-American peacekeeper means there's a US soldier who does not have to be deployed," Turner says. "I'd call that a good deal."

"It's extraordinary how much Ted knows about the UN," says the environmental economist Lester Brown. "Ted gets invited to appear on the David Letterman show and what does he want to bring up? The UN. You can't *buy* that kind of publicity."

❦

Kofi Annan has seen the mischievous look Turner gets when he wins over more advocates for the UN, when he sees the light bulb going off in people's minds. The former UN secretary-general from Africa has been at Turner's side when the pop quiz has been given. He is familiar with Nelson Mandela reaching out to Turner and asking him to help champion the establishment of a green peace park along the tense boundary dividing North and South Korea.

"When he wants to be, Ted, like Mr. Mandela, can be, shall we say, disarming and persuasive, charmingly so," Annan explains.

A Ghana national, Annan was the first career UN employee to become secretary-general. He attended Macalester College in St. Paul, Minnesota, and then rose up the UN ranks from the bottom. He attained the top job after spending thirty-five years on various tours of duty. He says Turner's backing of the UN proved pivotal. "1938 was a very good year," he tells me. "Ted and I were both born into it."

Annan's tenure as secretary-general commenced at a time when former New Mexico governor Bill Richardson was UN ambassador for the Clinton Administration. Holbrooke, who succeeded Richardson, said it was a tenuous era in US-UN relations not because the White House wasn't sympathetic, but because of the blatant hostility fulminating in Congress.

For Turner, history provides lessons that some lawmakers in Congress should heed. Following World War I, Woodrow Wilson was instrumental in creating the League of Nations. But it lost support in the United States amid calls from some conservatives for isolationism.

In Europe, without the League of Nations possessing any real teeth and in the absence of the United States, there was nothing to check the ambitions of Adolf Hitler and the rise of military fascism in Germany.

The lack of a strong centrifugal force left European nations hesitant to stand up to the rise of Nazism. Had the UN existed and the United States been engaged with England and France in those days, Turner believes circumstances would have been different and possibly tens of millions of lives could have been saved.

The UN, Turner says, is far better than the League of Nations ever could have been. "Rather than the UN being something that is fatally flawed, I think it has a solid footing that can be continually improved upon and reformed to confront the emerging challenges in this century."

"Ted has an instinctive feel about people. I can't explain it," Annan says, noting that he has accompanied Turner on UN-related field trips and watched him carry on conversations with rural agrarians or leaders from developing countries. "His empathy comes through when he says to them, 'Hi my name is Ted. What do you do?'"

"And when he hears that they are farmers he says, 'That's great cause I'm a farmer too. I do a little bison ranching.'"

Annan goes on. "Ted really is a farmer—he's a farmer of ideas. Farmers realize instinctively that if you take something from the earth today, you have to put something back to have for tomorrow. Sometimes, when we move into the city and leave the countryside, as more people than ever are doing, we get disconnected from that lesson. Sometimes, when I introduce him to other heads of state, I say, 'Meet Farmer Ted.'"

No economist has influenced Turner more than Lester Brown, renowned for his ability to make sense of diverse data points pertaining to environmental degradation, human population growth, food production, weather, and living conditions. "What Jared Diamond did with his book *Collapse*, analyzing why civilizations failed or succeeded historically, Lester does every day in the way he thinks about our modern world," Turner says. "I consider him to be the resource statistician for planet Earth."

Brown says that because of the multiple fronts in which Turner operates—humanitarian, nuclear issues, agriculture, alternative energy, running restaurants—and given his record as a businessman, few others have better insight into why it's not capitalism that is the problem, but the way that capitalism is promoted and practiced—as a proposition that runs on resource depletion. "Ted doesn't have airs," Brown says. "I think his lack of pretension has an effect on people."

Once, while Brown was at a meeting in Oslo, the prime minister of Norway shared details of meetings he had with a number of world leaders at the World Economic Forum in Davos, Switzerland. Turner's name came up.

The limousine assigned to ferry Turner had become stuck in a snow bank, the prime minister said, and the chauffeur could do nothing to get it out. Turner learned forward and told the driver not to worry, that he would get some people together and push. To the driver's amazement, Turner exited the vehicle and called out to a group of presidents, including the Norwegian prime minister and prominent businesspeople in suits waiting for their own rides. "Hey, I need your help. We need you to push," Turner said. "We're kind of stuck and if we work together we can get the car out of the rut."

"If it had been anyone else, those world leaders might have been horrified to be asked to push, or they might have asked their assistants do it, but because it was Ted, and he was leading the charge and wasn't really giving them a choice, they pitched in," Brown says.

They grunted, and rocked the vehicle forward until it was free, and had a good belly laugh. The experience reminded them that no one is too high or mighty to be asked to do some heavy lifting, Brown says. "The lingering question is whether the vehicle was actually stuck or Ted used it as an opportunity to make a point!"

"Ted has a conscience that is wired to a free spirit," Annan says. "And when you have a combination like that, you have a man who isn't interested in formalities. He cuts right to the chase in sometimes awkward ways that leave people feeling uncomfortable."

At another meeting in Davos during a different year, Annan says, there were intense anti-global demonstrations. The police were dispatched with shields and clubs, standing at the ready with tear gas. World business leaders, the so-called plutocrats, were gathered at windows overlooking a street where thousands of protestors had massed. Some of Annan's colleagues proposed that the meeting be moved to a safer interior location. Annan encouraged Turner to pull back because of the possible danger posed from rock-throwing anarchists.

"Ted walked to the window and said, seemingly naively, 'No one is going to throw a stone,' and I said, 'Look at the facial expressions on the police. They are concerned. They are ready for a violent confrontation.' But Ted seemed baffled—and I mean baffled—by my suggestion. He wanted to be in the middle of the action. He tried to imagine himself as one of the protestors to determine why they would be down there. He wanted to know what they were protesting about so he could better understand. He said the protestors don't want to destroy things. They just want to be heard. They want to feel valued. So, in the end, at Ted's insistence, we didn't move our meeting and, you know what? No windows were smashed. His action reminded those around him that if you must retreat, it gives the impression that you are doing something wrong."

America is, per capita, the most charity-minded nation in the world. For whatever reason, and for as much as her citizens spend domestically, often taking on huge amounts of personal debt per capita, they also voluntarily part with more money, per citizen, in support of charitable causes. This fact wasn't lost on Turner when he created the Turner Foundation to get his children involved with philanthropy.

Turner says there's a folklore associated with his $1 billion donation to the UN. Even some of his friends are under the impression that it was something he spontaneously concocted. It has been joked about that perhaps Turner had been medicated, and had temporarily lost his mind.

During the hours leading up to the moment he took the podium at the UN event in 1997, he shared his intentions with a close inner circle. His friend and chief financial advisor Taylor Glover got a call in the very early morning hours. "When Ted phones and has an idea, sharing it at first light, he's usually excited," Glover says. "Let me just say that I've worked with Ted on some ambitious things over the years, but giving away $1 billion . . . You kind of roll back on the pillow and ask your wife, 'Did he just say one *billion* dollars?'"

Barbara Pyle, Turner's one-time head of environmental programming at CNN, says she paused when Turner reached her on the phone. "Ted, do you know what you are doing?" Pyle worried that the money would disappear into the UN's bureaucracy and be squandered.

When Turner told Fonda what he had planned, she wept. Turner and Fonda carried on a never-ending conversation about the failures of traditional philanthropy and how the prevailing blueprint was often aimed at building new edifices rather than platforms for new ideas. "Ted actually had been talking about doing something like this for a while. But given the tone in Congress, he realized that support for the UN was slipping. The number of challenges in the world are many, and it is difficult to target charitable giving in a way that touches upon as many of those challenges as possible, even though the problems are interrelated," Fonda says.

"I didn't know that Ted was thinking $1 billion, but it didn't surprise me, nor that he selected the UN as the recipient. He saw it as a nexus for addressing global concerns that affect us all, and he wanted to make a splash."

Turner had a number of objectives that explain the timing. Because he was being honored, he had the podium and he didn't want to waste an opportunity. "Nobody's gonna yank you off the stage," he says.

The UN was approaching its fiftieth anniversary and Annan was just coming on board as the new secretary-general. Some members of Congress refused to authorize US payment of its UN membership dues. America was $1 billion in arrears, and it was severely hamstringing the UN's ability to function. "I thought it was shameful and an embarrassment," Turner says. "If you are the most powerful member and you are enjoying the benefits, you don't leave the organization in the lurch by being a scofflaw. You follow through. If you don't like something, you work constructively to change it. That's how adults and mature countries behave. I thought our behavior was childish and petty—not unlike how Congress behaved during the first term of the Obama Administration."

Turner knew that the UN needed to be reformed, and that Annan's arrival represented a chance to move reforms forward, but that without resolving the US debt, Annan didn't stand a chance of success. Initially, Turner thought of outlandishly trying to "buy" the US debt and then hold his country accountable for it by filing a grievance in the World Court. But he rejected that tactic. He also entertained giving $1 billion to the UN to use as it saw fit, but that was prevented by charter.

He finally decided to structure the donation in a way that a new entity, the UN Foundation, would serve as both advocate and watchdog, promoting reforms, helping to elevate the organization's profile, and serving as a conduit between the UN and the business community.

"Do you know that the UN has no mechanism for marketing itself or defending itself publicly against criticism?" he says. "It was just sitting there, taking bad PR body blows day after day without responding. I know from being in the advertising business that you have to be able to push back against attacks from Neanderthals."

That's why, in addition to the UN Foundation, he created the Better World Fund, an organization that can take out pro-UN ads in newspapers and mount a counteroffensive. "When a member of Congress goes on the attack, the Better World Fund can point out that by voting against the UN, that elected official is undermining things in the world that are important to US citizens. And you know what—since some members of Congress have realized they no longer have a free pass to batter the UN at will, without stating facts, they have backed off."

Annan remembers when Turner arrived in New York City the day before the awards banquet and met him at the UN headquarters. Turner mentioned what he planned to do.

"I thought it was a joke, that he was being mischievous—until I saw the expression on his face and realized he was serious," Annan said.

Annan consulted with a colleague, who had been chairman of Price Waterhouse, and was told that "no one gives away one billion dollars just like that."

"How do you respond to such a gesture that is so far outside the boundary of the norm? I had to tell the person that Ted wasn't trying to enrich himself. He had no secret agenda," Annan says. "We all complain about things. It is human nature to criticize, but so few of us take steps to make it better. Whining about things isn't Ted. Taking action is part of his unique focus."

Still somewhat incredulous, Annan put his arm around Turner and told him it was not too late to reconsider.

"No, I've made up my mind and, with your permission, I would like to announce it tonight."

Holbrooke was in the audience as US ambassador to the UN the night that Turner made his announcement. He said, "I think Ted realized that someone, an American from outside government, needed to step up and validate the importance of the UN, to sort of put the critics in check. He understood its value because his international bureaus at CNN had exposed him to the work of the UN. It was tangible and it touched him. He had standing because he was an emblem of the modern successful entrepreneur and an avowed free market capitalist, kind of reflecting the values of Theodore Roosevelt."

It was an evening of fireworks. "Ted not only gave a billion to the UN, but he also challenged others in the philanthropic community. He spared no one," Wirth says. "He made a game-changing move with philanthropy that night, and he focused on the one organization with the highest international profile. On the face of it, it was pure genius. He has been a remarkable leader in philanthropy, not necessarily giving to libraries and hospitals and schools, though he has done his share, but focusing on the great causes that he believes must be championed—environment, population, nuclear arms, climate change."

Turner strolled to the dais not only to unveil the UN-related gift, he climbed to the bully pulpit to shine a beam of guilt on other tycoons. Instead of hoarding wealth to earn themselves higher spots on the prestigious *Forbes* magazine richest persons list, he said, peering down upon some of the most privileged and powerful families in the world, people with wealth ought to give back.

Turner admits he made the admonishment hoping to make people with money, especially those making huge fortunes on Wall Street, squirm. Not long afterward, he challenged *Forbes* to devise a list that tallies not only the richest but honors the most magnanimous as well. A year earlier, he had gone on a rant with *New York Times* columnist Maureen Dowd, who wrote a piece titled "Ted's Excellent Idea" in which he said of the annual *Forbes* hubris-stroking tabulation: "That list is destroying our country! These new super-rich won't loosen up their wads because they're afraid they'll reduce their net worth and go down on the list. [Making the *Forbes* list is] their Super Bowl."

In response, the website Slate.com praised Turner, and ever since has published an annual list online that it calls the "Slate 60" to celebrate the generosity of plutocrats. *Fortune* magazine followed with something similar. And in recent years, consumer protection advocate Ralph Nader wrote a novel about how the world is saved from destruction by billionaires rallying together to change society.

Those who know Bill and Melinda Gates, Warren Buffett, and Oprah Winfrey—four mentioned in Nader's book—say Turner's challenge represented a catalyst for other tycoons to reflect, and that reflection inspired the Gateses and Buffett to make an unprecedented stake in promoting humanitarian causes, including those championed by the UN Foundation. Subsequently, it also led to the recent billionaires' pledge, drafted by Gates and Buffett in 2009 and embraced by other plutocrats. The inaugural group included Turner, the Gateses, Buffett, Oprah, Patty Stonesifer, David Rockefeller Jr., Michael Bloomberg, Pete Peterson, Julian Robertson, George Soros, Charles "Chuck" Feeney, Eli and Edythe Broad, and John and Tashia Morgridge. The gesture inspired a writer at *Forbes* Magazine in 2012 to suggest that no one deserves to be called a billionaire if they behave "Scroogelike" with their money.

Annan says "environmental humanitarianism" is a new category of giving largely invented by Turner. In the past, environmental projects were regarded as secondary or supplemental, but they now figure centrally into private philanthropy strategies. "I have no doubt that it was Ted Turner who set that trend in motion. I know that people he called out did not like to hear it. He said from the podium in New York: 'You billionaires out there, watch out, because I'm coming after you.'"

Turner was unconcerned that he might be committing a faux pas. He even mentioned the Sultan of Brunei by name, Annan adds. Brunei Darussalam, a former colony of Britain, is a Muslim country on the island of Borneo. The current sultan, Hassanal Bolkiah, owns a royal title that has been handed down through twenty-nine heirs since the fifteenth century. With much of his wealth acquired from oil drilling, Bolkiah has flaunted his opulence in ways that have largely gone out of style. He boasts of owning an auto collection encompassing thousands of vehicles worth billions of dollars. The *Guinness Book of World Records* documents him as having five hundred Rolls-Royces alone.

A few months after Turner's challenge was issued, Annan was in Kuala Lumpur, Malaysia, on UN businesses and he chatted with Bolkiah at a lavish social event. "Did you hear about what Ted Turner said?" he asked playfully. "He cited you as a rich man who might be able to do something for the UN and I hope he is right."

The sultan, Annan notes, smiled, but quickly changed the topic of conversation and made no commitments. Borneo has rich species diversity and low-lying coastal human populations that will be impacted by rising seas through climate change. The sultan's fortune is derived from producing fossil fuels that exacerbate climate change. The reign of his heirs could be threatened by social unrest linked to severe weather, high water, and shortages in food. Many wealthy people, Annan says, deliberately try to rationally minimize their moral obligation to help, believing naively that they can escape having to confront the consequences of human misery.

"In fact, he [the Sultan of Brunei] didn't do anything substantive for the UN mission. I've been disappointed in him, but others have stepped up. Ted really woke up the world to the possibility and benefits of mega-giving."

"Ted can be audacious in ways that others cannot ignore . . . That night in New York when he spoke, we heard his words but his actions were expressed loudest. And his actions were not just a token gesture," Annan explained.

Turner continues to make his contemporaries uneasy. At a speech on the University of Colorado campus in Boulder, he chastised high-tech executive Larry Ellison, the chieftain of Oracle, for not being more generous with his wealth. Instead of pouring his multibillion-dollar fortune into a new five-hundred-foot yacht, upgrading from a massive two-hundred-foot boat, he should have been magnanimous. "He'd be happier if he'd spent that money on other people instead of himself," Turner said.

Because the UN charter does not allow individual citizens to make direct contributions, Turner decided to create an entity that works in support of the UN mission. With Annan's blessing, the UN Foundation was created and initially underwritten by ten annual contributions of $100 million. The all-important question was: Who would run it?

A single name rose to the top of candidates, Turner says: Timothy Wirth, the former US senator from Colorado and outgoing undersecretary of state during the Clinton Administration. The brotherly bond between Turner and Wirth is based on mutual affection for the West. Wirth spent twenty years on Capitol Hill as a congressman and senator from Colorado. His work in the House was defined by his grasp of emerging telecommunications issues, including the rise of cable television.

On the Senate side, Wirth was known as a reform-minded political leader heavily involved in formulating budget and environmental policy. Wirth decided not to seek reelection, disillusioned by the corruptive influence of money in politics. Today, he is considered one of the most well-versed and articulate statesmen in the world on the topic of climate change. He considers the recent blitzkrieg of money marshaled by the coal and oil and gas industries aimed at discrediting the science of climate change to be shameful and scandalous.

Turner had gotten to know Wirth when he testified before Wirth's telecommunications subcommittee in the 1970s. Turner wanted cable operators to be able to compete on an even playing field with the major TV networks. Wirth agreed and over the course of their conversations they discussed their mutual concern for the planet. The lanky legislator was known for being a popular, ardent environmentalist. Turner was deeply impressed with Wirth's in-depth understanding "that one of the biggest elephants in the room, environmentally, is the issue of global population and unsustainable consumption of finite resources," Turner says.

Wirth and his wife, Wren Wirth, are close friends with population guru Paul Ehrlich and the late climate scientist Stephen H. Schneider, both distinguished professors at Stanford University who had spent time in the Rockies earlier in their careers.

As a newly elected congressman in 1975, Wirth organized what became known as the "Freshman Revolt," dislodging several older, deeply entrenched colleagues (including Democrats) from committee chairmanships. And he was known for forging a bipartisan bill with fellow westerner, Republican senator Alan Simpson of Wyoming, to address global population.

During the 1960s, the Wirths say they had been inspired by the words of Robert F. Kennedy, who called for serving one's country. Then they were rocked by the assassinations of Kennedy and Martin Luther King Jr. in 1968. A year younger than Turner, Wirth was at Harvard at the time Turner was enrolled at Brown. After being a White House fellow during the Johnson Administration and then serving in the Nixon Administration, Wirth returned to Colorado with Wren in 1970.

"When we moved back to the West, Wren and I talked about why we were doing this. We decided to write down separately what we believed the most important issues were and then try to address them. We both came back with exactly the same answers. One was the threat of blowing ourselves off the face of the globe and the second was overpopulating ourselves off the face of the globe," he says. "These two issues have remained the salient thrust of everything we've done. At that time, we obviously knew nothing about climate change, but not for long."

In 1988, Wirth convened the now famous congressional hearing on climate change at which a respected NASA scientist, Dr. James Hansen, testified for the first time that observed climatic changes were occurring outside the range of natural variability—putting a human fingerprint on the problem of global warming. Hansen spoke presciently on what would happen if human civilization didn't take steps to reduce its carbon emissions. For effect, Wirth opened the windows of the Senate chamber where the hearings were held to let in the humidity of a Washington, DC summer. In the years since, Wirth has been involved with nearly every major discussion of climate and he rues how lobbyists for the fossil fuel industry have consistently blockaded any legislative action and tried to undermine the science.

After leaving the Senate, Wirth was a co-chair of the Clinton-Gore campaign, and then joined the Clinton Administration in the newly created post of undersecretary for global affairs in the US State Department. As Turner asked around in the wake of his UN gift, Wirth received recommendations from then secretary of state Madeline Albright, Vice President Al Gore, Holbrooke, and a cast of others from both sides of the political aisle.

Two years after he accepted the offer to be chief executive officer of the UN Foundation, Wirth recruited Charles Curtis to join him. Charlie Curtis had been an undersecretary and then deputy secretary of energy in the Clinton Administration and was revered as a longtime Washington-based energy expert. It's unclear whether Turner has a better knack for finding extremely competent people or extremely competent people feel drawn to projects initiated by Turner.

One thing is certain: Wirth relates to Turner's need to clear his mind by perambulating in nature. When then-Congressman Wirth was running for office and eyeing a Senate seat, he and Wren led expeditions into the wilderness of Colorado. Over time, they visited on foot and horseback every major wildland being proposed for federal wilderness designation in the state.

During those trips, Wirth spoke with people in logging and ranching communities, old-guard Latino enclaves dating back to the conquistadors, Indian reservations, burgeoning resort towns, and the urban Front Range from Fort Collins to Colorado Springs and Pueblo. Wirth says the experience not only made him a better listener, but it prepped him for his post with the UN Foundation.

"It's no coincidence that if you look at the group of individuals who have been involved with every major environmental issue globally over the last few decades, that Ted and Tim [Wirth] have been part of the mix," Annan says. "They operate from the same roadmap."

Under Wirth's command, the UN Foundation has operated with 93 percent of its funds going directly into programs; for every dollar the foundation spends, it leverages another $1.50 from its partners.

Muhammad Yunus, the economist who founded the Grameen Bank in Bangladesh, sits on the UN Foundation board. He has been a pioneering force in the micro-lending movement taking hold in the developing world. In 2006, he won a Nobel Peace Prize for his innovative approach to grassroots financing. He has demonstrated that just as trickle-down economics works in some countries, micro-lending can create a "trickle-up" effect, mirrored in some of the investments made by the UN Foundation. He knows how a little can go a long way and how a lot, when everyone pitches in what they can, can literally change the world.

The announcement that Yunus had won the Nobel coincided with Ted's birthday. The UN Foundation threw a party for both men at the Willard Hotel in Washington. Turner looked out at the audience, which included former president Bill and then US senator Hillary Clinton, Tim and Wren Wirth, capitalist George Soros, and a wide range of Democrats and Republicans, including Carla Hills, who had served as a trade envoy for President George Herbert Walker Bush.

Turner said it was startling "to have assembled so many do-gooders in one room—people whose stated ambition is to do no harm while attempting to help the weak."

Steve Clemons, director of the American Strategy Program at the New America Foundation and author of the blog The Washington Note, was inspired by the night to write an essay for the *Huffington Post*. "Yunus and the Grameen Bank are what transformational diplomacy ought to look like—and Soros, Yunus, Turner, Carla Hills, Tim Wirth and others there last night are the world's real transformational diplomats," he wrote.

Kijong-dong and Tae Sung Dong would be hamlets of marginal consequence but for the fact that they straddle a narrow green ribbon two and a half miles across at its widest margin, severing a once-united country.

The Korean Peninsula thrusts like a bull's hoof out of mainland China, a mountainous neck of land lapped on the east by the Sea of Japan and on the west by the Yellow Sea. Notoriously, the demilitarized zone dividing one outpost from the other is both a buffer and line of bifurcation.

The corridor in Korea that forms the DMZ along the 38th parallel is part of hallowed ground. Three generations ago, this peninsula about the size of an overpopulated Italy (South Korea now has 48.5 million residents while North Korea has around 24 million) is where nearly thirty-five thousand Americans and millions of Koreans lost their lives. It was here that the newly formed UN mobilized to halt the spread of Communist forces armed by Russia and China. And today the DMZ remains a potential flashpoint for a modern nuclear war and, paradoxically, a focal point for possible reunification.

And now it's the site for one of Ted Turner's more audacious causes: a proposed "peace park" that would simultaneously make a political point as well as create an ecological preserve. A stretch of land that is roughly two miles wide and 155 miles long, and one quarter the area of Yellowstone Park, the DMZ, according to his vision, would ideally be a world heritage site—an ecological preserve—as well as a preserve for peace.

Turner was fourteen years old in 1953 when the Korean armistice was reached and UN peacekeepers were put in action. Half a century later, he passed beneath razor wire strung between Kijong-dong and Tae Sung Dong—the former being a false-fronted "Potemkin" town on the North Korean front; the other a tiny village in South Korea under perpetual protective guard.

Turner knew he was entering an eerie no-man's land. Driving under North Korean escort with his colleague Mike Finley, they pierced the most militarized border in the world, fortified by land mines, tanks, and hundreds of thousands of troops.

No major human population or army is present inside the DMZ. And since the cease fire was brokered by the UN, a strange miracle has occurred. The zone has become, quite by accident, a quiet oasis for some of the rarest wild creatures in crowded East Asia.

Every day in this corner of the planet where more than a quarter of humanity's seven billion–plus people reside, wildlife researchers believe at least seventy species of mammals pass through the DMZ's lush botanic understory that, in turn, harbors twenty-nine hundred different species of plants (encompassing a huge percentage of total plant life found on the entire Korean peninsula).

There are also migratory red-crowned and white-naped cranes, species rooted deep in Asian mythology. These imperiled avians are among 320 different species of birds that nest, breed, and layover in the DMZ. Even greater mystique, however, surrounds rumors of megafauna. Sporadic reports have been made of rare Amur leopards, Asiatic black bears, and Korean tigers.

Organized by the Turner Foundation, Turner and colleagues have met representatives from both Koreas, whom Turner says are proud that inside this front line of potential war dwell animals of concern to the entire world. When he and Finley made their first trip together to Korea, the threat and the opportunity gave Turner goosebumps.

"It is surreal," Turner says. "The DMZ's not a zoo nor is it some obscure wilderness at the edge of the world. It's on the front lines of a potential war. It's kind of bizarre to stand at the edge of a strip you could practically whistle across and to know there are these rare animals inside, and that, at the drop of a hat, they could all be destroyed over nothing."

Finley, who oversees the Turner Foundation, earlier built a distinguished career in US civil service. He was the chief steward of Yosemite, Everglades, and Yellowstone National Parks.

Holbrooke lauded the concept of the DMZ's conversion into a peace park, and believes it has merit. The plan, he says, is "nonconfrontational, asymmetrical, counterintuitive, multilateral, and, I might add, a classic sideways maneuver that you would expect to come from Ted Turner."

Referring to the people leading Turner's foundations—Wirth, Sam Nunn, Charlie Curtis, Joan Rohlfing, and Mike Finley—Holbrooke said that if Turner were a president, he would have four capable cabinet secretaries and a wider cadre of experienced people in politics, business, and media who would want to join in. "If Ted had been president, I would have volunteered to serve in his administration," Holbrooke said.

Administrations in the White House have come and gone, talks with North Korea have heated up and thawed depending on the direction of pendulum swings, but remaining a steady, familiar American figure on the international scene, is Turner, Wirth says, noting, "Everybody seems to know Ted."

Although Turner has long since abandoned any thoughts of seeking higher office, others note that, as a private citizen, he is more effective. The peace park concept is not novel to Korea and it's not an invention of Turner. He gives full credit for its genesis to a few friends, including Mandela, the man who summoned his services. The former president of South Africa and Nobel Peace Prize winner helped hatch the concept first in his home region along with the late Anton Rupert, director of World Wildlife Fund–South Africa, and the late Prince Bernhard of the Netherlands.

Shortly after the new millennium began, Mandela, being physically unable to jumpstart talks in Korea, personally asked Turner [and by extension Wirth and Finley] to take the lead. Mandela is respected in both Koreas. As he stepped away from public life and entered his ninth decade, he had an instinct about Turner's capabilities. Maretha Slabbert, a Mandela aide who works for the Nelson Mandela Foundation, says, "Mr. Mandela holds Mr. Turner in high regard."

Following his release in 1990 after spending twenty-seven years behind bars for resisting and trying to overturn apartheid in South Africa, Mandela and Mozambique president Joaquim Chissano became intimately involved with establishing transfrontier conservation areas along the common borders of South Africa, Mozambique, Swaziland, and Zimbabwe.

One of the best known, a pet project of Mandela's, is Great Limpopo Transfrontier Park, an area that includes Kruger National Park, considered the Yellowstone of southern Africa. Once upon a time, the Limpopo region was a remote site of lawlessness, ruled by poachers, bandits, and smugglers. Today, it is a destination for nature travelers desiring to see the continent's iconic species.

After Great Limpopo was forged and the region subsequently designated a UN World Heritage Site, it attracted attention from a group of people who wanted to spread peace parks around the globe, essentially incubating them in tension-filled areas. The Peace Parks Foundation was established in 1997, and among those enlisted by Mandela to help promote it were Turner and his staff, Queen Noor of Jordan, English billionaire Richard Branson, and other prominent individuals and corporations.

Mandela had been impressed by Turner's idiosyncratic, out-of-his-own-pocket creation of the Goodwill Games. Mandela also was familiar with another endeavor of Turner's—that of cultivating international environmental journalists in the developing world. Mandela met some of Turner's protégées—young black reporters from southern African countries who had been invited to Atlanta as part of an annual media fellowship program. Mandela realized Turner's reach was different from any other media executive. There was also the matter of Turner's gift to the UN, which caught Mandela's attention when it was explained to him by his friend Kofi Annan.

In all, there are over 188 environmentally and culturally sensitive areas—set among 112 countries around the world—that reside at the intersection of geopolitical conflict. The most visible regions of opportunity are the two Koreas; the Kashmir region around the Siachen Glacier between Pakistan and India; and the disputed territory between Israel and Palestine. Annan calls peace parks a green glue.

"I'm not a diplomat, but I view the peace park initiative in Korea as a way to move beyond polarization," Turner says. "If we could prevail in winning permanent peace and one day help the Koreans achieve reconciliation, I think there'll be hope for solving serious conflicts elsewhere. If we don't succeed, well . . . I don't like to think that way."

Jimmy Carter, who was awarded a Nobel Peace Prize for helping to broker a truce between the Israelis, Palestinians, and Egyptians—and who helped free an American prisoner in North Korea—praises Turner's work at the DMZ. "It's a good niche for him to be in and he is being advised by very, very bright people," Carter says. What is most needed, from Carter's perspective, is finding a path for North Korea to re-enter the international community in a way that offers its leaders and people pride instead of shame. His advice to Turner is the same as Mandela's: Ignore partisan demagogues who live in the past; persevere; champion a different model of engagement.

Following Turner's initial foray to North Korea, the neoconservative American pundit Laura Ingraham went on FOX News and pilloried him for even traveling there. She implied during an appearance with Bill O'Reilly that he was a loose cannon treacherously consorting with what George W. Bush had labeled a member of the "Axis of Evil." One of Ingraham's books is titled *Shut Up & Sing: How Elites from Hollywood, Politics, and the UN are Subverting America.* Turner and his cohorts are mentioned as being part of a conspiratorial cabal.

"I think it's pretty clear that Rupert [Murdoch, owner of FOX News] and his newspeople have their way of thinking about the world and ways that news organizations should be run, and I have mine," Turner says. "I don't wish Rupert ill. All of us will be judged on our actions."

A generation ago, Turner had been similarly criticized by ideological predecessors of Ingraham. Turner courted dialogue and friendship with then–Soviet leader Mikhail Gorbachev at the height of the Cold War when Turner created the Goodwill Games and expanded his media operations into the USSR—the first American newsgathering organization to do so. Further, he once spent a day duck hunting and talking baseball with Cuban dictator Fidel Castro outside Havana while endeavoring to open a CNN bureau on the island. If he were still in command of his former twenty-four-hour news channel, he would want a newsroom, he says, in Pyongyang, Korea, and Tehran, Iran.

"I caught flack from people who said I had no business going to North Korea after President Bush and Vice President Cheney declared the country to be our sworn enemy. The same things were said after I visited with Castro and Gorbachev, too," Turner says, just days after he flew home across the Pacific.

"We went at the request of Nelson Mandela. I don't know many people who would turn down a call for help from him. We agreed that if we refocus the way we think about the DMZ, to see the beauty of things inside of it that both sides share in common, it could help defuse tension. Well, it certainly can't hurt. It's better than counting the ways each side can blow the other up. Besides, nobody I know, or have ever met, doesn't care, deep down, about wildlife. Everyone at some point in their life has been a kid, and kids naturally love animals. But more important than helping animals is helping kids."

～～

The isle of Hispaniola in the northern Caribbean is a landscape of contrasts. It is the place where the Columbian colonization of the New World began at the end of the fifteenth century and now, dividing it, is a line reminiscent in some ways of the Korean DMZ. This point of demarcation isn't military but, in Turner's mind, environmental. Turner has sailed its perimeter and flown over it in Bison One dozens of times, studying the landscape from above.

Two countries share Hispaniola. On roughly one-third of the island, Haiti is largely deforested of trees, rife with poverty, and pockmarked with barrenness from natural resource overexploitation. Its larger neighbor, the Dominican Republic, is alive with foliage and has a thriving tourism and agricultural export economy. The average life expectancy in the Dominican Republic is almost seventy-four years and rising; in Haiti it is sixty-one and falling, in part also related to a relatively high prevalence of HIV/AIDS. The average income in the Dominican Republic is around $9,000 annually while in Haiti it is less than $2,500.

Haiti gained its independence when residents of African descent brought there as slaves to serve French overlords rebelled in 1804. On the surface, Wirth notes, one could point toward Haiti and the Dominican Republic as classic contrasts of political theory writ large. The country without environmental regulation has run amok. Four of every five Haitians, among nine million people, persist on less than $2 a day. "What chance do the kids of Haiti really have?" Turner asks.

A vicious cycle has been created between human desperation and environmental destruction. Arguably, this former French colony, upon achieving independence, could have become a Libertarian oasis, one wherein lack of regulation spawned a vision of free-market environmentalism. But political corruption, pillaging of resources, and lack of laws—as well as a tax base to pay for basic services—have resulted in a primitive infrastructure. It's Libertarianism, absent sensible government, run amok. Large swaths of its subtropical forest have been toppled, causing soil erosion, severe flooding during rainstorms and hurricanes, and desertification. No trees mean poorer soils for growing crops, no shade to keep temperatures down, changes in water cycles, and no wood for construction. It means a loss of biological diversity that brings dividends ranging from insect problems to a marring of the beautiful Haitian landscape. Ecological poverty translates into human poverty.

The Dominican Republic, on the other hand, still has much of its subtropical forest. Its attractiveness has paid dividends as cruise ships have brought a sustainable flow of tourist revenue. It's true: the United States played a role in propping up dictatorships in Haiti friendly to American interests during the Cold War. Still, without a real rule of law, crime rates have been high and recent political instability has served as a disincentive to outside investment. In 2004, UN peacekeepers were dispatched to Haiti to try and restore order over rampant lawlessness and killing.

Wirth had been to Haiti during his tenure in the Clinton State Department and as a member of Congress during the years of the Haitian boat lift, a period when thousands fled the country bound for the Florida Keys, the closest US beachhead 750 miles away.

The UN was making small incremental progress, with the help of former president Clinton, when the 2010 earthquake struck. Within hours after the 7.0 temblor hit the capital, Port-au-Prince, the UN Foundation board, at the urging of Turner and Wirth, pledged $1 million in immediate relief, and it helped hasten other humanitarian contributions that quickly surpassed $100 million. Bison One, Turner's plane, was used to bring some of the first doctors, medical supplies, and journalists to the island hours after the earthquake.

The truth, Turner and Wirth say, is that Haitian civilization, after centuries of exploitation, needs to be reconstructed, not solely with bricks and mortar, but reforestation, sustainable farming, energy sources, and engagement, not abandonment, from the rest of the world.

"Unless we address economic sustainability within an ecological context, as we were encouraged to do in the Brundtland Report, Haiti is a sign of more things to come, and not as an exception," Turner says.

Lester Brown believes he is right. "One of the things I think about is where our global civilization is today," Brown says. "What might undermine it?"

As Brown was working to update his masterpiece, the book *Plan B: Rescuing a Planet Under Stress and a Civilization in Trouble*, he started to more closely examine the concept of failed states, with Haiti being a classic example of dysfunction, a breakdown of society, lawlessness, and environmental devastation, but there are many more in Africa and Asia.

"We've got a phenomenon under way now that is of concern to me. Ten years ago, thinking about how climate change could exacerbate environmental degradation which could accelerate the number of failed states wasn't part of our vocabulary. And now it is something that is common," he says. "How many failed and failing states do you have before you have a failed civilization? I don't know the answer, but it's a question we should be asking. We could reach a point of no return, just as with global warming, and because of it."

Wirth resents the assertion that the international body is "enabling" poverty, which is to say, paternally throwing good money at problems with no capacity to actually fix them. UN critics have characterized it as a "handout" entity that strong-arms donor countries into making billions of people dependent on their benevolence.

Scratch beneath the veneer of those arguments, however, and Wirth says that a sizeable number of businesspeople around the world, who have partnered with UN efforts, realize the fallacy of such thinking. Turner and Wirth both point to Rotary International, the venerable umbrella for local business club chapters that has marshaled a strategy to eradicate polio from the face of the Earth, sponsor water development projects, elevated the profile of micro-lending programs, and devised a platform for mentoring young business leaders.

Wirth says Turner appreciates the conundrum the UN faces on a daily basis. On the one hand, it is assigned to help bring order to chaotic, dysfunctional, and dangerous nation-states sometimes ruled by armed thugs and dictators. On the other hand, it has no real authority to address issues that are the host government's responsibility, since UN peacekeeping and humanitarian endeavors are neither mercenary nor licensed to serve vigilante roles. And, on top of it, the main members of the Security Council have veto authority when it comes to interventions and what form those interventions take. That's not the UN's fault, Wirth says; it's the rules that have been handed to it and those rules need to be changed.

Often as a result of its archaic governance, the UN has had to sit by while witnessing unspeakable human rights abuses, as in Rwanda, the Congo, Darfur, and Cambodia. It's easy to be a cynic, and Wirth asks what country would willingly want to be tasked with the UN's duties. Week after week, responding to the worst kind of natural and human-caused disasters, trying to coordinate delivery of food, water, shelter, and medicines, working with nongovernmental charities to keep orphaned youngsters out of harm's way and exploitation, and being the first on the ground in the aftermath of earthquakes and tsunamis.

Even for the most callous American who would prefer that the United States revert to an isolationist policy, he says the UN's role, from a rational economic perspective, is inestimable. "Ted has the gift and the curse of being able to anticipate what the future will look like. There is a dark side to humanity when we get stressed and things get tough," says Australian paleontologist Tim Flannery. Flannery is a well-known activist in calling upon global leaders to address climate change.

"The lesson of history that he understands is that when resources are scarce, we turn on our fellow human beings. That's my greatest fear with climate change. What's required to combat it is that we adopt a common spirit now. If we leave it until it's too late and stresses become too large, it will make it ever more difficult to maintain law and order."

The American dream is not originally *American*, Turner says; it's a universal desire for all parents to ensure a better life for their children. Parents will go wherever opportunity presents itself. Ironically, America herself was created by a confluence of native people and refugees.

The desire to survive creates unstoppable forces that cannot be contained by barbwire or guards posted along a border. Neither Turner nor Wirth is opposed to strengthening security along the US border with Mexico, but until the root causes of the movement of people is addressed, it will remain a turbulent, unsolvable issue.

"You cannot halt a tide of refugees, any more than you can stop a rising tide of water. Environmental conditions, poverty, and oppressions put people on the move," Wirth says. "There is a moral imperative that is embedded in our consciousness. Ted recognizes this."

For Annan's final speech as secretary-general, he selected the Truman Presidential Library in Independence, Missouri, as the venue. He wanted to point out how the future was circling back into the eddies of history.

Annan intoned, "As President Truman said, 'the responsibility of the great states is to serve and not dominate the peoples of the world.' He showed what can be achieved when the US assumes that responsibility. And still today, none of our global institutions can accomplish much when the US remains aloof. But when it is fully engaged, the sky's the limit."

Then he issued what Annan calls a "Turneresque warning" to those who believe the United States has cocooned itself in a posture of unilateralism:

"My friends, our challenge today is not to save Western civilization—or Eastern, for that matter. All civilization is at stake, and we can save it only if all peoples join together in the task. You Americans did so much, in the last century, to build an effective multilateral system, with the United Nations at its heart. Do you need it less today, and does it need you less, than sixty years ago? Surely not. More than ever today, Americans, like the rest of humanity, need a functioning global system through which the world's peoples can face global challenges together."

In 2010, UN secretary-general Ban Ki-moon approached Turner with another task. He asked him to serve on the UN Millennium Development Goal Advocates along with Columbia University professor Jeffrey Sachs, Muhammad Yunus, and others. The primary goal is to cut in half the number of people whose income is less than $1 a day, fating them to lives of extreme poverty. Other priorities are ensuring that children everywhere receive education into their teenage years and improving literacy, particularly in women who suffer from a number of gender inequities.

Turner has become an especially outspoken crusader in the cause of women's rights. According to statistics assembled by the UN and other organizations, one out of three women around the world has been beaten or suffered some kind of abuse in her lifetime. Women aged fifteen to forty-four are more at risk of dying from rape and domestic violence than from cancer, vehicle accidents, war, and malaria. Half of the women in the world don't have the same rights as men. Turner intends to put a stop to that.

"If we had more women in positions of power, the world would be more peaceful, it would be more loving and caring, and it would be more beautiful," Turner says. Other goals are to reduce infant mortality and improve health care for mothers, reverse the spread of HIV/AIDS and malaria, give more people access to safe drinking water, and promote conditions where sustainable market economies can prosper. Why was Turner one of only a few businesspeople chosen by Secretary-General Ban? Because the UN Foundation was already working on these priorities and engaging with others to achieve them.

Here are just a few examples: The UN Foundation has awarded 533 grants totaling more than $170 million to promote empowerment of girls and women around the world. "The board very early on realized that if we don't invest in women, we weren't going to eliminate poverty," says UN Foundation CEO Kathy Calvin. "What we're seeing is when you give a girl a chance to stay in school, it delays marriage and it delays childbirth.

When you invest in a woman, that money stays in her family; it goes into the community. It educates her children. And we begin to change the world. We're not about charity. We're about change."

The UN Foundation also has targeted $50 million at treating and reducing the incidence of HIV/AIDS. It has distributed more than six million insecticide-treated bed nets to prevent malaria through its award-winning Nothing But Nets program, contributing to a 50 percent decrease in malaria cases since 2000. This has changed the life expectancies and trajectories of millions of families. The foundation has delivered $200 million in conjunction with partners like Rotary International and the Bill and Melinda Gates Foundation, in the cause of polio eradication. It has helped cut the number of measles cases by 78 percent. With the UN Foundation's help, more than one billion children have been immunized against diseases that would otherwise be fatal or debilitating. It has also spearheaded an alliance that aims to make available one hundred million energy-efficient and clean-burning cook stoves as an alternative to wood stoves and campfires that have caused millions to die from lung ailments and hastened deforestation. To combat climate change, foundation efforts have funneled $75 million into clean energy initiatives throughout the world.

Turner becomes overtly giddy when discussing just the latest campaign carried out with UN-friendly partners—to bring electricity and light into the homes of 1.4 billion people in the coming decade. Power won't be passed along transmission lines from distant coal-burning plants, but from mini, cutting-edge solar panels the poor can mount on the rooftops of huts and metal shanties. He calls it "the next best evolution of Thomas Edison." "Here we are in the twenty-first century, and a huge percentage of the world's population doesn't even have reliable electricity," he says. "Think about the shame of that. We're going to give them better lives by enabling them to go off the grid of dirty power and be able to see at night with clean, renewable energy. It chokes me up to think about all those kids who will be able to read." Having this seemingly simple innovation in their lives, he says, will change the future of entire families and communities. "It's the spark of hope."

⌁

Today, the UN is again under attack from American neo-con isolationists, Wirth says. And Turner realizes that it's necessary to stand in defense, like Horatius.

The UN Foundation is hailed worldwide for being one of the organizations making a difference. In 2010, twelve thousand people applied for fifty-eight full-time positions. To explain how and why it has succeeded, Wirth refers to Annan's counsel that the Foundation needed to "move from projects to problems, especially problems without passports."

And it's done that. It hasn't been easy. Wirth points to the fact that on both ends of the Earth polar icecaps are melting. Soaring global financial debt is leading to unprecedented social unrest. Species have begun disappearing at an accelerating rate that ecologists say bears a resemblance to what happened during the last major extinction episode. Fisheries are collapsing. There are shortages of fresh water. Crops are failing. Millions are malnourished. Women are still enslaved by lack of education, chauvinism, and lack of opportunity. Meanwhile, the number of humans on our planet could rise from seven billion to ten billion later in this century, putting unprecedented strain on nature's ability to deliver sustenance. Each of these issues happening simultaneously is a prescription for growing tension between nations, some of which possess weapons of mass destruction.

Yet for Wirth and Turner, their interest is elemental. Wirth speaks about changing trajectories of human lives. Turner will deliver the last batch of his pledged funding to the UN Foundation in 2014. Wirth says that even during his days of traumatic financial turmoil, he never backed away from his commitment, and would have sold off his most beloved ranches before abandoning the UN. It is because of Turner's involvement that the Foundation has invested more than $2 billion to date to mobilize global change by leveraging campaigns with other government and non-government partners. According to Wirth, it has placed "some big bets" on causes that have huge humanitarian impacts—augmenting what the UN could do on its own.

Richard Holbrooke wanted to make clear, in an interview a few months before he tragically died, that Turner did not stop with his donation and launching of the UN Foundation. As a fiscal conservative, he wanted to have America clear its books. "This is a story that needs to be told because I think it illustrates, as much as any other, what kind of guy Ted is," he said.

With regard to his revulsion over the United States refusing to pay its UN dues, Turner had begun working backchannels on Capitol Hill with a fellow southerner, who had been both a friend and foe over the years, the late US senator Jesse Helms, an espoused Republican segregationist from North Carolina.

Some years earlier, a younger Turner had left a positive impression on Helms when he said that programming on television needed to change, and the salacious degrading content cleaned up. Helms also bore a grudge against CBS and its program *60 Minutes* because he believed it was biased and pandered to liberals. Helms had been intrigued when Turner made a bid to take over the Tiffany Network, even though it failed.

Helms even lobbied the Reagan White House on behalf of Turner's request to open a bureau in Havana because he believed that free-flowing information would hasten the downfall of Fidel Castro's government.

The two men, however, sparred over the UN. Helms had led the charge in Congress to withhold US dues until the UN engaged in a wholesale restructuring. Helms didn't believe the UN should be involved with promoting family planning, abortion, and contraception to confront the global population crisis. Further, he thought the US dues, figured according to Gross National Product, were disproportionately high.

Enter then US ambassador to the UN Holbrooke. A dear friend of then Delaware senator (and now vice president) Joe Biden, Holbrooke knew that Biden got along well with Helms. Biden carried forward a two-part proposition backed by Holbrooke and Turner: If the UN made an overt commitment to undertake reform *and* reduce American dues, would Helms lift the freeze?

The so-called Biden-Helms accord, brokered with approval from the State Department in the final weeks of the Clinton presidency, brought an end to the controversy. Part of the overhauls that needed to occur, readily acknowledged by Annan, involved better coordinating of UN activities to avoid redundancy, to make its budget more efficient, and to instill a tougher code of accountability.

This is precisely some of the terrain that would be addressed by the UN Foundation. But there was another sticking point: The new formula for calculating US membership dues and reducing them, as insisted upon by Helms, resulted in the UN still being left $34 million short in its budget for the following year.

"Who got us out of this mess by coming to the rescue?" Holbrooke asks. "Who do you think?"

The latter half of 2000 would be a traumatic one in American society. With division soon to deepen in the wake of the presidential election between Bush and Gore, it was uncertain what a new administration or Congress would make of the UN starting in red ink.

Holbrooke, along with Wirth, Turner, and the rest of the UN Foundation board, had been meeting at the Waldorf-Astoria Hotel in New York when Holbrooke relayed word of a sticking point involving resolution of the United States paying its dues to the UN.

Getting the United States to pony up its dues had been a nasty struggle. Republicans had control of Capitol Hill and would soon control the White House. Wirth remembers how the events played out, largely without public knowledge of what was going on. Through his tortuous work with Helms and others, including one-on-one discussions with more than 170 UN ambassadors, Holbrooke had forged agreement on changing the formula for every country's payment of dues to the UN, Wirth explains. But because of a technical problem related to fiscal versus calendar years, the multibillion-dollar agreement was coming up $31 million short. As 2000 drew to a close, it looked like the complicated deal might fall apart.

Holbrooke and Wirth had known each other since the 1960s, and the ambassador had brought Wirth into the negotiations. Since he knew about the crucial "funding gap," Wirth wanted to bring the UN Foundation board into the discussion. The fall of 2000 was an extremely hectic time for Holbrooke, Wirth remembers. The United States was going to chair the Security Council, Holbrooke was going to feature a precedent-setting focus on AIDS, and he also had to plan for the transition to a new US administration. Wirth knew that getting significant time on Holbrooke's schedule would be very difficult, so he arranged that the UN Foundation would hold its board meeting in a conference room just down the hall from Holbrooke's apartment (the US Mission) located in the Waldorf Hotel. "The thought was that maybe we could catch Holbrooke on the fly and bring him into the board meeting," Wirth said.

The strategy worked, and the rest is history. Holbrooke joined the board meeting, and sitting next to Turner, explained the complex negotiation, ending with a frustrated description of the pending and dangerous funding gap that could cause the entire deal about the United States making good on its dues to unravel.

Wirth describes Turner's reaction: "After listening to Holbrooke's account, Ted said very simply, 'I think I can figure out how to solve this. The Foundation can't pay off a debt, but I can make a personal contribution to the US government to cover the difference! When else has a private citizen paid off an obligation of the government and kept a whole international operation operating? I'll do it!'"

The board was, as ever, delighted to be a part of Turner's vision and generosity, Wirth notes. "And Holbrooke was absolutely ecstatic—a great big grin on his face, he hugged Ted and ran out of the room, on his way to the UN to seal a deal that had been in the works for years."

Wirth adds, "Ted's personal gift was the final piece of a hugely complex international negotiation, returning the UN to sound fiscal balance, and solving the gnawing problems of the US arrears, which had stimulated Ted to start the Foundation in the first place."

Holbrooke says the gesture floored him. "I was frankly shocked by the generosity of it. The amount was significant, on top of the $1 billion pledge he had already made as well as his efforts to get the US out of arrears, and here was Ted willing to give again."

Turner told Holbrooke that he didn't want any press releases issued or any to-do made of it.

"Are you sure you want to do this Ted?" he asked, locking eyes with Turner. "Because you know, this has to come from you and not from me. Under law, as a civil servant representing the United States government, I cannot lobby a private entity. That would be illegal."

Turner grinned. Later, Wirth handed a check from Turner to John Negroponte, the new US ambassador to the UN under President George W. Bush in early 2001. The ceremony took place in Kofi Annan's office and a photo today hangs prominently in the UN Foundation office in Washington.

In the aftermath, Holbrooke broke a promise—"the only time I've ever broken a promise in my friendship with Ted"—by refusing to keep it quiet.

He appeared as a guest on PBS *NewsHour* with Jim Lehrer three days before Christmas 2000 to reflect on his tenure as UN ambassador. He used the air time to mention Turner's deed of a few weeks earlier.

Reporter Terrence Smith asked Holbrooke about the symbolism of a superpower, the most prominent member of the UN, having been unwilling to meet its commitment to the international organization, and that it came down to an individual citizen, more or less, bailing out the government.

"What does it say?" Holbrook responded. "It says different things. It says that this is a great country where people can make great gestures. And this one is more than a normal bequest of a philanthropic nature. This is a highly leveraged, highly targeted and really visionary gift and it will make a huge difference. I think we should all be grateful to Ted Turner."

Smith asked, "Does it not reflect a very deep-seated skepticism on the part of the Congress, certainly about the United Nations and about paying its bills? Normally we would pay our bills through the government."

"Well, it is a very unusual arrangement. I don't think there is any precedent at all," Holbrooke said. "The United Nations is an indispensable but deeply flawed organization. It is valuable to the United States, and the United States is invaluable to it. We need to reform it. What you're talking about now is just a tiny tip of the iceberg towards the reforms which are necessary."

A full decade has passed since Holbrooke made those remarks. He recalled them nostalgically while riding in a limousine bound for a meeting in Washington, DC, with President Obama, Vice President Biden, and their national security staff before embarking to Afghanistan and Pakistan.

Holbrooke had hoped, at the dawn of the new millennium, that the UN would not have to deal with any more Sierra Leones, Rwandas, and Bosnias. "They happened again," he said, "only under different names, and there will be more."

From Darfur in Sudan to Haiti, and with a trail of natural and human disasters strung out in between, including earthquakes, tsunamis, civil wars, and terrorists on the run, the world has not moved one inch closer toward the day when the UN is no longer needed, he said, only the opposite. The enduring lesson is that disaster, human- or nature-caused, always strikes the poorest hardest.

Holbrooke says that Turner couldn't have selected a better person than Wirth to serve at the helm, for he, like Turner, is not an individual who suffers fools gladly. He mentions the passing of Helms who died, at age eighty-six, on July 4, 2008. And he repeats a Turner observation that compassion is a pathogen that needs to reach pandemic levels and continue to spread. Indeed, it infected Helms and it became evident in the senator opening up his heart and becoming friends in the eleventh hour of his life with Paul David Hewson, better known as Bono, lead singer of the rock band U2.

Bono convinced Helms that, just as the United States needed to support the multifaceted work of the UN, it had a moral obligation and a religious one to be more charitable. Helms threw his support behind a bill to send hundreds of millions of dollars in US aid to fight HIV/AIDS in Africa. Together with private efforts of the Bill & Melinda Gates Foundation and the Clinton Foundation, and including the help of the UN Foundation, more medicines are being distributed and investments made in HIV/AIDS-related research than ever before. One night at a concert in Atlanta, Bono crooned happy birthday to Turner as a way of saying thanks. "I really admire Bono even more so for his activism than his music," Turner says. The rock star has said that Turner has a remarkable ability to be relevant.

A few years ago, Turner had a stack of orange bumper stickers made. They are fastened to each of his vehicles as well as those of his children. They state simply, "Save the Humans." Annan says that after seeing them on Turner's hybrid compact car in Atlanta, at Turner's properties in the West, and in Argentina, he asked for a few himself. The more that he considers the double-entendre of the message, the more determined he is to spread it as a slogan.

"Yes, in terms of biodiversity, we can think of saving all of the other species, but what we are really doing when we care for another creature, we are saving ourselves," Annan says. "Have we realized that the path that we are on is one of destruction? This question will hang in the air and be asked until we realize we have to live in harmony with nature. Hopefully, it will not be too late. No higher life form is able to persist when it has a discordant relationship with its environment. Look at Easter Island or, more recently, Haiti. I don't think the message has gotten home yet."

CHAPTER SEVEN

Flash Point

(Preventing Nuclear Ground Zero)

"The guy who brought down Communism wasn't Ronald Reagan. It was Ted Turner. With CNN being available to TV viewers in the Eastern Bloc countries, people in Russia and the rest of the Soviet Union saw how we live in America. They caught glimpses of a free society and wanted one for themselves. I don't know if Ted realized fully what he was doing, but it had a huge impact. Let's see what he can do with nuclear weapons."

—T. BOONE PICKENS

Snow tumbles in Boston a few weeks before Christmas. Meteorologists had earlier in the morning announced a 30 percent chance of flurries, and so, based on that hard evidence and probability, the good citizenry of greater Beantown prepared for a dump.

Now, in mid-afternoon, the whiteout descends.

Along the Charles River in Cambridge, Harvard University professor Graham Allison has been busy with another kind of prognostication. He believes there is a greater than 50 percent chance that over the next ten years a major American city will be attacked by terrorists detonating some kind of nuclear bomb. He isn't reading a weather map; he's an expert in deciphering other kinds of patterns.

If Allison's warning does not jar the senses, then consider another assessment from a different data cruncher, American financial investment guru Warren Buffett. The Oracle of Omaha, known for his unflappability, believes the likelihood of an atomic assault may be even higher.

Around the corner and down the street from Allison's campus office, another man sits in a room at the Charles Hotel. Lounging comfortably in stocking feet and undershirt, Mikhail Sergeyevich Gorbachev is absorbed in thought, writing over a table lit by a dim lamp. He jots notes into a bound pocket-sized tablet with distillations on the root causes of factors influencing Allison's and Buffett's arithmetic.

The previous evening, Mr. Gorbachev, once one of the most powerful men in the world, met with a business-tycoon-turned-citizen-activist who flew into town to hear him speak.

Ted Turner said, "That's what you do for your friends. You support them, stand by them, especially when they're right."

The man in the hotel makes it clear that it was important having his *droog* (a colloquial word meaning "close friend" in Russian) present in the audience. Their association, a fact that surprises a lot of people, goes back a generation.

"We don't see each other enough. I'll never forget those days I spent with Ted in Montana."

The highest human virtue, Gorbachev asserts, raising an index finger and having his thoughts translated by interpreter Pavel Palashchenko, is compassion forged by trust, knowledge, and heart.

For a time, as the leader of the so-called "Evil Empire," Gorbachev possessed the means to complete half of the equation for mutually assured global destruction. He and a circle of military advisors in the former Soviet Union could, if they felt provoked, have pushed the proverbial button and launched a full-scale nuclear attack on the United States, wiping America from the map.

Besides obliterating a perceived antagonist, such an exchange would have meant the end of the world as we know it. Years after meeting with Ronald Reagan in the Icelandic city of Reykjavik, Gorbachev still is bothered by how agonizingly close the two came to reaching historic accord on a plan that would have committed the military superpowers to total *elimination* of their nuclear arsenals. At the height of the Cold War, in 1986, the United States had tens of thousands of warheads and the Soviets about forty-five thousand—many an order of magnitude more powerful than the first and last devastating bombs deployed on human populations at Hiroshima and Nagasaki in 1945.

Gorbachev traveled to Cambridge hoping to jumpstart the process of correcting that missed opportunity, which he considers, to this day, his greatest personal failure. He is doing what he can to encourage the two former enemies to stay in negotiations and not settle for saber rattling or token gestures. He counts his *droog*—Ted Turner—and Turner's co-chairman of the Nuclear Threat Initiative, former US senator Sam Nunn, as being critical catalysts for one day achieving what Gorbachev and Reagan did not get done.

"My hope is that one day zero nukes will be left on the face of the Earth," Turner says. "I'm a peacenik who would like to see complete eradication. Well, okay, maybe we can keep a couple of missiles if we ever need them to stop an asteroid or battle aliens from outer space."

He is being wry, he confesses, but adds, "I'm dead serious when I say there is no rational reason why we need nuclear weapons for military purposes. The more that we have, the more likely it is that one goes off accidentally or that the material used to make the warheads falls into the hands of bad guys."

During the 1980s, there was the infamous incident when US missile command went to highest alert after radar mistook a flock of geese for incoming Soviet missiles. More recently, an Air Force jet took off from North Dakota bound for Louisiana and, by mistake, carried six *armed* nuclear bombs in its payload. A simple malfunction of the aircraft or a crash caused by weather could have resulted in disaster.

"But that's just the tip of the iceberg," Turner says. "The more I've learned, the more I realize that, but for the grace of God, we've dodged a number of nuclear bullets. We've been playing Russian roulette."

"What I love about Ted is that he has natural smarts, sincerity, plain-spokenness and yet profound courage," Gorbachev says.

"And," he adds, "he is *relentless*."

Nuclear disarmament has been more than a sideline interest for Turner. While he credits Nunn, Allison, and others for "giving me an advanced understanding" of the grim realities of the issue, he says it has been Gorbachev, whom he met in Moscow at the height of Cold War tensions in the 1980s, who turned his education into a nagging passion that will not let him rest.

"Ted was one of the few Americans who reached out a sincere hand of friendship to me and my countrymen when no one else would," Gorbachev says. "These things you never forget."

Turner's maxim: Friends don't blow each other up.

———

It is now several months after Turner flew into Boston to rendezvous with Gorbachev. He is alone in Atlanta at the end of a grueling business day, following nonstop meetings with members of his staff. The final event of the afternoon was him meeting with journalists from around the world who have won internships at CNN. Even though Turner doesn't own the cable channel anymore, he still enjoys getting together with the international contingent of young reporters. It is as much a matter of *them* seeking him out—he is, to them, an American enigma.

True to form, high in his office eyrie, alone as the sun sets, he begins to riff.

"America hasn't had any of her great cities deliberately destroyed by human hands since the Civil War. 9/11 was terrible, absolutely horrendous, but it could have been worse."

He is musing in a state of mind his friends call "the zone"—a mental space in which he is partially engaged in a conversation at hand and adrift in other possibilities that only he can see. That's where his reputation for aloofness comes from, but it doesn't mean a lack of focus.

He paces now and stops before a large picture window looking out upon Centennial Park, the heart of Atlanta. Thanks to his friendship with the late cosmologist Carl Sagan, Turner says he has come to realize that chaos is a fundamental operating principle in the universe.

"There is only so much we can control. We as a species on this planet have lulled ourselves into believing that order and calm are the norm. We can't control what the heavens throw at us. As Carl often said, until we establish a colony somewhere else in the solar system, we need to use our brainpower and focus our attention on preventing avoidable human catastrophes here on Earth."

Moments earlier, Turner concluded a short crosstown telephone call with Sam Nunn, the former US senator from Georgia who arrived back in the Big Peach following a trip to meet with Russian colleagues in Moscow.

Nunn is known globally not only for his knowledge of military affairs, having been chairman of the Senate Armed Services Committee, but also for his levelheadedness. In Nunn's call with Turner, he vented frustration.

It is the waning months of the George W. Bush Administration. Nunn has rejected invitations from Democratic and Republican moderates to have him run as an Independent candidate for president.

Partisan wrangling had complicated efforts to get the US and Russia to ratify the new Strategic Arms Reduction Treaty (START). Nunn considered the accord essential to compelling the former Cold War adversaries to scale back the number of nuclear weapons in their arsenals and stockpiles. (It would later be ratified in 2010 though the debate over the role of having atomic, biological, and chemical weapons available as tools of mass destruction continues to flare as a political issue.)

More worrying, Nunn told Turner, he feared that crucial opportunities for preventing nuclear doomsday materials from falling into the hands of terrorists may have been squandered.

A consummate brooder, Turner took a gallows humor poke at the Department of Homeland Security's color-coded warning system. "What level of risk are we under today, Sam? Is it red, orange, blue, or pink?"

Nunn answered sternly: "Ted, I don't think we can afford to think about nukes with a threat level that is ever *unelevated*. We've just been damned lucky."

After Turner bid Nunn adieu for the night, he stood at the window above Luckie Street and shared what he was thinking. Hardware that commemorated triumphs in his earlier life glittered in various corners of the room, mementos from winning the America's Cup yachting race and his former baseball team, the Atlanta Braves, taking the World Series. In some ways, he regards them as superficial relics that will mean even less "if we don't resolve the big important stuff."

"Wouldn't it be a shame if this is as good as it gets? The time we're living in now may come to be recounted in history as the happiest, richest, most peaceful and civilized there ever was. I know it's an arbitrary year, but in 2060—that's half a century from now—my own grandkids may look back and conclude, 'They had it all, but they let it slip away.'"

❧

Nunn and Turner have stood together in the former Soviet Union, in the backs of dilapidated nuclear facility warehouses, holding nuclear materials that could be turned into agents of mass horror. Outside Moscow, they've sat in the actual chair where Gorbachev and his successors literally had a red button in front of them for triggering a nuclear war. And they know the consequences of a small amount of highly enriched uranium, plutonium, or other materials finding its way into the wrong hands.

Illustrating the anxiety he shares with Nunn, Turner holds forth with a tale, for now a purely hypothetical one. It begins ironically enough with a thought of serenity, a tranquil carefree afternoon in Midtown Manhattan.

"I love New York, except when the Braves are playing the Mets or Yankees," he says, his blue eyes lighting up at the memory of regular visits he's paid to the city for various business endeavors, yachting events, and forums associated with the United Nations.

"People say I own a lot of land, and it's true, I do. We've got somewhere around two million acres. But you know what? The twenty-two acres that comprise Rockefeller Center, just as an example, are worth a lot more, in a dollar amount, than all of my real estate combined. That's because it's located in one of the cradles of modern civilization."

Most experts dealing with the nuclear threat use disaster scenarios to make a point. Turner's is based upon conversations he has had with Allison, the noted public policy expert at Harvard University's John F. Kennedy School of Government and former assistant defense secretary.

Turner asks the listener to imagine a balmy day in April. A nice one after a long winter. Central Park is a picture of tranquillity. Workers take late lunches, cutting out early from cubicles. Times Square is its usual electric hive of humanity just before rush hour. Mobs of tourists pose in front of landmark marquees and billboards, taking snapshots for posterity. Street musicians and thespians perform next to food vendors.

"Some of those folks are hungry for a real meal and find their way over to my Ted's Montana Grill restaurant on West 51st Street for a bison burger or steak," Turner, ever the showman, says grinning, then adding that his eatery is only a few blocks away from where his pal and fellow

Montana ranch owner, David Letterman, broadcasts his late night television show at the Ed Sullivan Theater.

How glorious New York is, Turner says. "It's the cultural capital of the world. For us, it's what Athens, Rome, and Constantinople represented in their primes."

Among the frenetic bustle on this otherwise placid day, he describes a van creeping forward in bumper-to-bumper traffic. The vehicle's driver pulls in front of a modest high rise near Broadway and Seventh Street. Hazard lights on, the motorist appears to be making a routine delivery.

Impatient cabbies are logjammed behind the vehicle and honk their horns. Passersby on foot, dammed up at a crosswalk, shout insults. A policeman walks to the window to tell the driver to shoo on because his rig is disrupting the orderly flow of things.

"The driver is a nobody," he notes, explaining that his protagonist has no wealth or influence, yet he's carrying the accumulated power of the ages. Economic desperation, hopelessness, perhaps misplaced religious zealotry—all of it combined with a hatred for American foreign policy and imperiousness—have brought him to this turning point.

"He doesn't believe he has anything to live for. And the rest of the world has indicated to him that it doesn't care."

The man's hand is twitching. He grins at the attending officer. From this nano-instant forward, Turner says, everything that is great and secure about Manhattan, America, and the world will inexplicably change.

"All that our civil society represents, all of our progress and dreams and thoughts about the future, based on our accomplishments of the past, will disappear. And we can't ever go back. There isn't a do-over. We ignored the wake up calls. The hard work that our ancestors put in to build a better world for us is all for naught. What we gave our grandchildren ... was ... *complacency.*"

He becomes quiet, halting his narrative. Choked up, he shakes his head. He is thinking about missed opportunities now—in the present—not only with nuclear security but every major environmental issue where the empiricism of science, he says, is being ignored.

He cites the biodiversity crisis portending a sixth major species extinction episode, global human population soaring to nine billion by the middle of this century, climate change cooking the interior regions of America where he has several major bison ranches, and rising seas, meanwhile, likely to inundate coastal areas, essentially repeating the effects of Hurricane Katrina, sparking massive human exoduses that will affect billions around the world.

He composes himself and continues.

The van driver, carried forward by a series of small individual decisions fueling a feeling of alienation and resentment, compresses his index finger. There will be no surviving eyewitnesses interviewed in the aftermath of this Ground Zero, only accounts of a searing flash observed from afar. It will become part of the lore of human storytelling.

Like an exploding star, the van carrying a nuclear suicide bomber vaporizes before the blast can break out past the sound barrier. The concussive amplitude fans the superheat created by a split atom. The energy released reaches tens of millions of degrees Fahrenheit. No, this weapon didn't originate in a Russian silo.

Riding a typhoon of fire, debris, and shrapnel, the shockwave accelerates to six hundred miles an hour, down the steel, concrete, and glass canyons of the West Side. Buildings within a wide radius are reduced to smithereens. Rockefeller Center, Carnegie Hall, the Empire State Building, American Museum of Natural History, the Metropolitan Museum of Art, and Madison Square Garden now cease to stand but as skeletons; the oasis of Central Park resembles the aftermath of Hiroshima, he says.

And then, the conflagration spawns a secondary inferno. A convection cloud of dust and smoke mushrooms twenty thousand feet—almost four miles—into the sky. Commercial pilots in the air, their planes jolted by turbulence, will say they thought it was a volcanic eruption.

Particles rain down over much of Manhattan Island with deadly radiation wafting across the East and Hudson Rivers into other boroughs and New Jersey, he says. Following the first wave—the nuclear blast—and the second—the firestorm—and then a third—radiation—comes a fourth, a tsunami of primordial human panic on the perimeter.

"Less than ten seconds have passed from the moment the police officer made eye contact with the terrorist," Turner says.

Hundreds of thousands of people are dead and an equal number, at least, will perish within a half mile of Times Square from their wounds or exposure. Hundreds of thousands more will become deathly ill in the weeks that follow.

"*We* know, but on the ground no one knows for sure yet what has happened," Turner says, trying to think how the news media would respond.

Television and radio stations scramble to go live with broadcasts, but the electromagnetic pulse of gamma rays has knocked out local communication.

The mayor of New York hastily tells the civil defense staff—that is, if the mayor and civil defense staff are capable—to activate the emergency protocol for a controlled evacuation that was prepared in the wake of September 11, 2001.

Masses of people scurry from pummeled buildings onto streets and try to flee. Emotion overwhelms calls for rational calm. It is the confusion of 9/11 times ten.

Waterways are radioactive. Wall Street, the nerve center of the American economy, has been transformed into a post-industrial midden.

If it is Manhattan that has been struck, and not Washington, DC, Turner says, the president of the United States and his military commanders will want to formulate a swift and decisive response. "There will be an urge to fire back, to retaliate, but the question is at whom?"

One of the first frantic phone calls made from the White House will be to Moscow to prevent a potential exchange of warheads, hoping that the failsafe protocols between the two nuclear superpowers work. If the nuclear explosion has occurred in Moscow, the process will be reversed.

The bomber was not acting on behalf of a nation. He was born in the womb of the world's have-nots, the class of humanity, Turner says, that many Americans dismiss as out of sight, out of mind, out of impact on their lives.

At Harvard, Allison has contemplated and written about the effects of just such a scenario. He says the detonation of a ten-kiloton nuclear bomb in Times Square, as Turner describes, would obviously not merely alter the nebulous concept of the future.

"Ted and Sam Nunn and I have spoken about the real impact, the worst of which, if you can believe it, wouldn't be the physical devastation. The real blow would be to our human psyche. As bad as 9/11 was, this would be unthinkable."

Allison goes on with his explanation of social disruption, "Our society, in fact the basis of civilization, has been predicated on having reliable, predictable expectations about the future, expectations that enable you to rationally plan and think ahead. This has been the key to sanity. In the aftermath of this trauma, it would be gone."

He pauses, then adds, grimly, "especially if those responsible for the first bomb had a second one with plans to use it."

Allison has a sobering website—www.nuclearterror.org/blastmaps .html—at which readers can plug in their own zip code and see the scale of devastation were a Dragonfire bomb detonated in their own community.

"I've learned that we need to be scared," Turner says. "Whatever it takes to shake us into consciousness. Some of the same people who try to diminish the nuclear threat never thought an event like 9/11 would be possible either."

Turner himself says that it has been a long personal journey for him to reach this point. Nunn recalls an evening over drinks with Turner in

Atlanta when they discussed an existential question: What do you do when you know something terrible could happen without your intervention?

"You might be able to prevent it—or you might not; the result isn't clear, but you know that without doing something, the likelihood of it happening increases dramatically," Nunn says. "The question is: Would you act?"

—⁓—

Turner has a false reputation for being purely impulsive. He has a penchant for wanting to act fast, yes, when he believes he has sufficient information before him, but impetuous, no. At every stage of his life, he has demonstrated a knack for surrounding himself with enormously gifted people not known for making rash decisions.

The man who planted a seed of obligation in Turner's mind, at least as it pertained to nukes, was Tim Wirth. In early 2000, Turner was given an episode of *60 Minutes II* to watch, a segment that focused on nuclear weapons threats.

Turner was riveted. Afterward, he phoned Charlie Curtis, a senior administrator helping Wirth run the UN Foundation, and asked him to give a blunt assessment of what he knew based on his own contacts within the intelligence community.

"I told Ted, 'If you think the strategic posture of the US and Russia, with both countries still having warheads pointed at each other, is scary, I'll tell you something that is *really scary* and that's the vulnerability of nuclear and biological material to theft by those who want to do us harm.' Of course, this was just prior to 9/11."

Curtis, former defense secretary William Perry, and Nunn had developed contacts with Russians who shared their concerns about nuclear security not only in Soviet republics but across a roster that has grown today to include North Korea, Iran, and Pakistan. Curtis said the problem was getting anyone to listen outside the usual channels.

"Ted had made it clear in several speeches he had given that his ambition was to totally eliminate nuclear weapons from the face of the Earth in his lifetime," Curtis said.

Turner, he noted, had just given $1 billion to found the UN Foundation on behalf of humanitarian problems. "He said he wanted to have an impact on nuclear dangers, too. And he wasn't just saying it. He was serious. The growing risk of terrorists getting their hands on nuclear weapons or materials shook him up. He instantly saw what the potential outcome of it would be."

Turner, who was neither a nuclear expert nor a politician, asked fellow Georgian Nunn in the months *before* 9/11: "What can I do?"

He told the former senator that if a catastrophe ensued, "then I wouldn't be able to live with myself if I had been in a position to do something and hadn't. I would spend every moment for the rest of my life dealing with regret."

Sometimes, governments need a push, and this forms a fulcrum in the Nuclear Threat Initiative's genesis story. Turner approached Nunn with the idea of launching a private organization to help reduce these dangers to present and future generations. As a private citizen, Turner could not affect direct diplomacy between nations. That's left up to elected leaders.

But Nunn was involved with former lawmakers, cabinet secretaries from both Republican and Democratic administrations, counterparts from the old Soviet Union who had become friends, and a range of diplomats.

"I think we could have an impact if we worked the back channels," he told Turner.

Turner, Nunn, and former NTI president Curtis (today succeeded by respected nuclear expert Joan Rohlfing) undertook a six-month "scoping study" with experts around the globe to determine whether a nongovernmental organization could have an impact with the space that exists between different nation states. They determined that a private organization could indeed make a difference if it comprised the right people. NTI was established in January of 2001—supported by a pledge of a quarter of a billion dollars' worth of AOL Time Warner stock from Turner.

NTI does not function like the garden-variety think-tank or policy center typically nested on a university campus. It is respected by both national defense hardliners and veterans of the nuclear freeze movement. Why? Because just as Reagan and Gorbachev did, it believes a safer world, free of nukes, is possible.

Co-chaired by Nunn and Turner, its board of directors includes former US military and governmental leaders, Russian experts on security, members of the UK parliament, and academics and political figures from countries such as China, Japan, Jordan, India, and Pakistan. NTI also counts former US secretaries of state George Shultz and Henry Kissinger as important allies. The esteemed circle of statespeople includes more than sixteen former secretaries of state, defense, energy and former joint chiefs of the military who served under both Democrat and Republican presidents.

"It's a powerhouse group of individuals," says former US senator Alan K. Simpson, who is troubled by how partisan wrangling is stymieing America's ability to address dangers that need unified cooperation.

Today, NTI engages governments and thought leaders at the highest levels to improve global nuclear materials security and build a consensus for reversing reliance on nuclear weapons, preventing their proliferation from falling into potentially dangerous hands, and ultimately ending them as a threat to the world. NTI's positions have been core elements of President Obama's nuclear policies, appearing throughout his landmark speech in Prague in April 2009.

Obama said in that address:

Today, the Cold War has disappeared but thousands of those weapons have not. In a strange turn of history, the threat of global nuclear war has gone down, but the risk of a nuclear attack has gone up. More nations have acquired these weapons. Testing has continued. Black market trade in nuclear secrets and nuclear materials abound. The technology to build a bomb has spread. Terrorists are determined to buy, build or steal one. Our efforts to contain these dangers are centered on a global non-proliferation regime, but as more people and nations break the rules, we could reach the point where the center cannot hold.

Now, understand, this matters to people everywhere. One nuclear weapon exploded in one city—be it New York or Moscow, Islamabad or Mumbai, Tokyo or Tel Aviv, Paris or Prague—could kill hundreds of thousands of people. And no matter where it happens, there is no end to what the consequences might be—for our global safety, our security, our society, our economy, to our ultimate survival.

Some argue that the spread of these weapons cannot be stopped, cannot be checked—that we are destined to live in a world where more nations and more people possess the ultimate tools of destruction. Such fatalism is a deadly adversary, for if we believe that the spread of nuclear weapons is inevitable, then in some way we are admitting to ourselves that the use of nuclear weapons is inevitable.

Turner proudly circulated copies of the speech because he knew NTI and friends had the ear of the president, who said at the 2010 Nuclear Security Summit attended by Nunn, Allison, and their cohorts: "The single biggest threat to US security, both short-term, medium-term and long-term, would be the possibility of a terrorist organization obtaining a nuclear weapon."

For Nunn, his knowledge is based on experience. When he accepted the prestigious Hessian Peace Prize in Wiesbaden, Germany, in June 2008 for his work with NTI, Nunn shared a story. In 1962, when he was a twenty-four-year-old staff lawyer for the House Armed Services Committee, Nunn was sent on a three-week fact-finding trip to tour NATO bases in Europe. It coincided with eruption of the Cuban Missile Crisis.

As Nunn notes, if President Kennedy had elected to take out Soviet missile sites in Cuba, the prevailing fear was that it would trigger a nuclear war. Military bases in Europe would have been on the front lines of attack by Soviet weaponry.

"The fact that the fate of the world in the early 1960s was on the shoulders of a few people from both sides who had only moments to decide whether to launch, made a deep and lasting impression on me," Nunn explains. "The survival of humankind has got to rest on firmer ground than that. From this early period of my life, I have been dedicated to doing everything possible to increase warning time for both sides and to take other steps to avoid the chance of nuclear war."

At Ramstein Air Force Base during his visit there long ago, the senior commander for US Air Force operations in Europe at the time told Nunn that if the conflict broke out, he had only a few minutes to scramble all of his aircraft loaded with nuclear weapons. The planes would be primary Soviet targets because they were designed to deliver the first death blows to the enemy.

Pointing to the interview of former defense secretary Robert McNamara in Errol Morris's documentary *Fog of War*, Turner and Nunn say civilization has been dodging bullets on nuclear security for too long. McNamara, who served under Kennedy, spoke of the tension that erupted with Soviet leader Nikita Khrushchev over missiles in Cuba. Shortly before he died, McNamara warned that "rationality will not save us" if we are counting on it being an effective stopgap to nuclear war or terrorism.

He told Morris: "I want to say, and this is very important: at the end we lucked out. It was luck that prevented nuclear war. We came that close to nuclear war at the end [of the Cuban missile crisis]. Rational individuals: Kennedy was rational; Khrushchev was rational; Castro was rational. Rational individuals came that close to total destruction of their societies. And that danger exists today. The major lesson of the Cuban missile crisis is this: the indefinite combination of human fallibility and nuclear weapons will destroy nations. Is it right and proper that today there are seventy-five hundred strategic offensive nuclear warheads, of which twenty-five hundred are on fifteen-minute alert, to be launched by the decision of one human being?"

Reflecting on McNamara's words, Turner asks, "What if the future of the world rested on the intellectual capabilities and demeanor of people like Sarah Palin or Donald Trump or Michelle Bachmann?"

A dozen years after the Cuban missile crisis, Nunn was back in Europe touring NATO facilities again, this time as a newly elected US senator. He was alarmed to learn that NATO forces were prepared to use short-range battlefield nuclear weapons at a moment's notice if it appeared the Soviets were going to invade Western Europe. Even the *appearance* of an invasion could trigger grave consequences if actions were misinterpreted.

"The bottom line is that in the event of a war, we would have, by necessity, moved up the ladder of escalation very rapidly," he explains. "I spent much of my time in the Senate working to strengthen the conventional forces of NATO, so we could move away—both operationally and psychologically—from a strategy that emphasized first strike capability with tactical nuclear weapons."

Although the philosophy shared by the Reagan Administration was controversial in some quarters, including the nuclear freeze movement, Nunn believed adamantly in a strong defense and mutually assured destruction—MAD—as the best deterrence.

"The premise was simple: If you know you're going to be obliterated whether you launch your weapons first or last, you have a profound incentive never to use them at all. It was an understanding that we and the Soviets reached during the 1980s and for the time, it was effective. No one wins in a nuclear war." It is contingent, however, on dealing with rational minds on both sides of the equation.

After the Soviet Union splintered, at the very end of Mikhail Gorbachev's tenure, rogue members of the Russian military attempted a coup d'état that resulted in Gorbachev being placed under house arrest. "As President Gorbachev was released from house arrest following the failed coup, a Russian friend contacted me and said I needed to make an urgent trip to Moscow to meet with the new Russian leaders and President Gorbachev himself," Nunn explains.

In previous meetings, Nunn always found Gorbachev to be candid and direct. "As I left the meeting, I asked him, 'Mr. President, did you retain command and control over the Soviet nuclear weapons during the coup attempt?'"

President Gorbachev looked away and did not answer. "That was enough for me," Nunn says. "Gorbachev was rational, but it was not clear who was in charge of the nuclear arsenal. The Soviet Union was coming apart. I believed that the end of the Soviet empire would speed the march of freedom and reduce the risk of war, but I left Moscow convinced that it would also present a grave global security challenge."

Nunn trusted Gorbachev, but soon Gorbachev was out. Boris Yeltsin, known for his heavy drinking and erratic behavior, was now in charge. The fact that individuals like Yeltsin could find themselves in command of weapons that could end civilization is one of the reasons why Turner regards nuclear weapons on hair-trigger alert among the most serious threats to humanity's survival.

After the Berlin Wall fell, Turner admits that he lulled himself into believing nuclear dangers had diminished.

However, Nunn noted that the level of risk could be seen as even more perilous, because, to this day, the United States and Russia still have thousands of weapons pointed at each other. "We still have the risks associated with the large nuclear arsenals in the United States and Russia, coupled with the dangers of weapons or materials getting into the hands of terrorists," he says.

Before Nunn retired from the Senate in 1997, he teamed with Senator Richard Lugar (R-IN) to sponsor foresighted, bipartisan legislation known as the "Nunn-Lugar program," to help the former Soviet republics secure and destroy their excess nuclear, biological, and chemical weapons. At the time of the break-up of the Soviet Union, there was enough highly enriched uranium and plutonium stockpiled in warehouses to make between forty thousand and sixty thousand nuclear weapons. The material was scattered across 250 buildings in fifty different locations and eleven time zones. Plus, there were biological agents and chemical weapons, and thousands of scientists who knew how to harness them, many suddenly out of work after the Soviet Union collapsed.

The Nunn-Lugar legislation facilitated the dismantling of thousands of warheads in Russia, the removal of weapons from Ukraine, Belarus, and Kazakhstan, and, notably, it made money available to pay the salaries of out of work engineers who perfected weapons of mass destruction that were never used.

In the post–Cold War world, Nunn said conventional wisdom saw fears about a nuclear exchange abating. Aside from the dangers of engagement between nuclear superpowers, the risk of a regional nuclear conflict has increased. Nunn points toward North and South Korea, Pakistan and India, and Iran and Israel as potential flashpoints.

But the biggest hobgoblin for Sam Nunn—"And it scares the bejesus out of me as well," Turner says—is the specter of not one bomb reaching the hands of terrorists, but two, or more.

"Were they to get their hands on one bomb or able to assemble all of the pieces of a bomb, there is little doubt that they would use it," Nunn says. "It's horrible to think of an American city being hit, but there are other scenarios that would drag us and the rest of the world into a deeper nightmare."

Nunn says it would commence a chain reaction of responses that would be difficult to contain, not only militarily. "Forevermore, humanity would be scared not only by what happened but be gripped in the paralysis of what *could* happen again. This would shake us to our core."

"If they had *another* bomb and say, held another city hostage and then detonated it, you would never again know when the terrorists are bluffing or not."

The effects would be massive flight from other likely target cities causing further unrest. Turner sees a parallel between the disarray caused by a nuclear event and the flight caused by climate change if coastal areas are inundated by rising seas and breadbasket regions turned into deserts. And while partisans try to cast doubt on the science behind climate change, there is little debate, within government intelligence circles, that the terrorist pursuit of fissile material is real.

In his book, *Nuclear Terrorism: The Ultimate Preventable Catastrophe,* Graham Allison included example after example of illicit attempts to obtain nuclear material, and his file full of attempts and misses continues to grow. In a follow-up interview with me, he notes how an officer in the Russian Navy in 1993 burglarized a storage facility housing fuel for nuclear submarines and left with pieces of reactor core containing ten pounds of highly enriched uranium. A year later, by accident, police in Czechoslovakia discovered eight pounds of processed uranium in a car in Prague. And in 2000, Georgian nationals had two pounds of the same valuable material when they were arrested near the city of Batumi. The odds alone would suggest some uranium or plutonium has slipped away. Securing it at its source of production and implementing a detailed and guarded line of provenance is a far safer and more efficient calculation than relying on stolen material somehow being discovered as it moves through a porous gauntlet. Certainly, terrorists know there are plenty of places to shop.

Allison is revered by leaders in both political parties and has been a master in devising war games scenarios, including those involving potential conflict with a nuclear Iran or North Korea. After Allison's book was published, Turner received a copy. He cancelled appointments and ploughed through it in an evening.

"I couldn't sleep," he says.

Turner wondered if it was wise to publicly disclose how bad a nuclear event would be. A few colleagues said it could "give terrorists ideas," make citizens scared, or induce a panic. Others accused Allison of exaggerating the threat, being a Cassandra and writing a jeremiad, but he, as a former assistant secretary of defense during the Clinton Administration, is used to hearing from those who try to minimize the danger.

In fact, Allison says, in the years prior to the al Qaeda attacks on New York City and Washington, DC, the Central Intelligence Agency picked up chatter exchanged among terrorists who fantasized about hastening their own "American Hiroshima."

Osama bin Laden put out feelers, attempting to buy highly enriched uranium from agents in South Africa as far back as 1992. Chechen separatists, with cells operating in Russia and many of the former Soviet republics where former nuclear labs sat idle, were also contacted by al Qaeda representatives who wanted to acquire bomb-building materials and enlist nuclear engineers to package a device. Commandeering airliners and crashing them into the World Trade Center, Allison says, was actually al Qaeda's second choice. "With regard to the plane attacks, some of us believed that terrorists could turn aircraft into missiles. We discussed it in the 1990s, but we were dismissed as being alarmist and fanciful. How do you surpass the terror that you inflicted on 9/11? You return to your original game plan, which is staging a nuclear event."

In the NTI office along Pennsylvania Avenue before he retired and was succeeded by Rohlfing, Curtis said: "If there were to be a nuclear terrorist attack on Washington, we'd be sitting now somewhere near probable ground zero. We are equidistant between the White House and the

World Bank, both potential targets. We are only as secure as the weakest link. I've seen too many weak links to feel comforted."

The only reality more frightening than knowing how utterly unprepared America is to deal with nuclear terrorism is how complacent society has been in its denial, a state worsened by political sparring, Turner says.

"Am I supposed to derive comfort from assertions that we are doing all we can when I know it's not the case?" he asks. "We couldn't even stop two terrorists from nearly taking down a pair of commercial aircraft, one guy who stuffed explosives in his shoe and the other guy who lit himself on fire as he tried to ignite material smuggled aboard in his underwear. Had it not been for their own incompetence, we would have had two more planes taken out in midair and hundreds of innocent people dead. If we can barely prevent the amateurs from succeeding, how are we going to stop the professionals with nukes? It's the fear of them executing a plot that makes me want to crawl into the fetal position."

Fully a year *after* Turner stood in his Atlanta office and described a hypothetical doomsday event in Times Square, Faisal Shahzad, who had connections to the Pakistan Taliban, drove a car loaded with explosives to almost the exact same point as Turner's fictional van bomber. A homemade bomb, fabricated of tightly packed gunpowder, had been in the vehicle Shahzad drove, but failed to ignite. According to investigators, Shahzad had three other potential New York City targets to pursue if he had been successful in Times Square: Rockefeller Center, Grand Central Terminal, and the World Financial Center across from 9/11 ground zero. It is unclear if he was acting as a loner or on behalf of a group using him to probe security.

With thousands of US and Russian warheads still aimed at one another across the Atlantic, and newer members of the nuclear club facing border tensions, Gorbachev believes the level of danger is higher than ever before. His concern extends to bombs that can be fabricated from stolen weapons-grade material, their construction aided by experts from former Soviet labs who, in financial desperation, could be wooed by handsome amounts of money.

"If the processes in the nuclear sphere continue as they are now," Gorbachev has said, "one hundred years from now humankind will be no more." He suggests that given social instability rising in many dangerous corners of the world, the real horizon line for possible nuclear disaster, if it's not confronted, is not a century from now but imminent.

Why does the world need to rally together? This is one compelling reason, he says.

"Ted's been pretty low key about talking to the media about his work with nuclear issues," Nunn says, summoning an anecdote. "Because he may not openly divulge this story, I will. It speaks to his character."

After the terrorist attacks of September 11, 2001, Turner was reeling. His marriage to Jane Fonda had ended and a granddaughter had died months before.

Turner and Nunn were rapidly moving forward, establishing NTI based on a commitment of $250 million worth of AOL Time Warner stock. Turner was, after all, the largest shareholder of the newly merged company. By the start of 2002, however, the AOL securities had plummeted and lost nearly 80 percent of their value, decimating Turner's net worth, nearly forcing him to sell some properties, and threatening the commitment he had made to NTI. With much of his personal fortune tied up in land and other investments, he had little free cash.

Turner doesn't remember exactly what he was doing when Nunn telephoned him. But he remembers where he was—at the Flying D Ranch in Montana. He had just come in from fishing on Cherry Creek.

"Ted had always said, 'If there is something I need to do, tell me.' I told Ted that one of those moments had arrived," Nunn says, recalling their conversation.

NTI had been contacted by an official with the US State Department about the Vinca Institute of Nuclear Sciences near Belgrade. The research reactor had approximately two and a half bombs' worth of poorly secured, highly enriched uranium vulnerable to theft by terrorists.

The US government was working with concerned officials from Serbia and Russia to remove the material, but the Serbs would not release the highly enriched uranium unless they received international assistance to address problems related to 2.4 tons of highly radioactive spent reactor fuel at Vinca and to decommission the Vinca research reactor altogether.

"The US government lacked the authority to fund such work and asked NTI to contribute to a joint project," said Curtis.

NTI committed up to $5 million to catalyze a project that allowed the United States, Russia, and Serbia to remove the highly enriched uranium. Turner, Nunn, and Curtis convened quickly by conference call to approve NTI's role.

Turner never hesitated in making the money available, Nunn says, even though the stock he had pledged to NTI was blocked from sale at the time. Turner met with Taylor Glover, his chief financial manager who has turned the juggling of his boss's priorities into an art form. It would require some more juggling, Glover said, but they could get the money.

"I don't want to sound melodramatic. I'm not a melodramatic person, but the threat was dramatically real," Nunn explains. "That amount of material, if used to make bombs, could have taken out the center of two US cities."

In an overview about the nuclear threat written by M. J. Zuckerman for the Carnegie Corporation titled "Nuclear Doomsday: Is the Clock Still Ticking?," the authors note how former vice president Dick Cheney, while serving as defense secretary, said that accounting for even 99.9 percent of Russia's active and former nukes wasn't good enough.

"That's because if you do the math," the report pointed out, "99.9 percent of the Soviets' estimated 22,000 tactical nuclear weapons would leave 22 weapons unaccounted for, each with yields ranging from 0.5 kilotons to 2 kilotons, the equivalent of from 200,000 to 800,000 sticks of dynamite."

The bad guys likely knew the stuff at Vinca was there, he added. Intelligence sources had picked up chitchat in central Asia about al Qaeda wanting to do something that would be more spectacular and rack up more casualties than 9/11.

Turner flew back to Montana to try and put his thoughts at ease. He spent the next several days fly fishing and horseback riding. On August 22, 2002, he received word from Nunn that the mission at Vinca had gone according to plan.

News of the "dramatic, military-style operation" with special commandos used to address "one of the world's most dangerous nuclear repositories—a large and unusually vulnerable stash of the kind of weapons-grade uranium that would be prized by . . . terrorist groups such as al Qaeda" ran on the front page of the *Washington Post*.

"Ted wasn't looking to receive praise or get a thank you plaque from the State Department," Nunn said. "He gave $5 million out of his pocket, at a time of extreme personal financial difficulty, to basically put bomb making material and a nuclear reactor to bed. They don't build monuments to people for this kind of philanthropy. What we both got was one more night's rest."

The operation reinforced the urgent need for action, and the US government created the Global Threat Reduction Initiative, which has since repatriated more than forty nuclear bombs' worth of highly enriched uranium from dozens of countries.

Several years after the Vinca episode, Nunn and Turner traveled to Kazakhstan, taking a tour of a drab, rusty warehouse that just as well could have been an abandoned steel mill in Pittsburgh. It was Ust-Kamenogorsk in central Asia. Given its security status related to nuclear weapons production, it had been one of the Soviet Union's "closed cities." Since the end of the Cold War, it has become notorious as a crossroads for smugglers, drug and arms traffickers, and other criminals. Gorbachev told them to be careful.

NTI was working with the Kazakhstan president and his government to rid the country of nuclear weapons usable highly enriched uranium. The plan was to take the material to the Ulba Metallurgical Plant and blend it down to fuel for use in nuclear power plants. When they visited Kazakhstan, they had been told the job was nearly complete but, while walking around the facility and asking questions, the pair saw tubes containing highly enriched uranium. They were guarded, but Turner thought the protection didn't seem commensurate to the risk.

"Are you kiddin' me?" Turner reacted (saying he actually used more colorful language). "Hell, Sam, you and I could walk out with this right now and give it to terrorists. Here we are in a part of the world that is known for being dangerous, on the backdoor of where a war is being fought against people who want to do us harm, and the material is just sittin' there. If this is the front line of defense protecting millions of people from harm, the world is in serious trouble."

Nunn said close calls that prevent trouble from happening are the ones the public seldom hears about. Indeed, as Allison points out that Russia has improved nuclear security over the past decade, he worries about Pakistan, which he calls "a ticking nuclear time bomb." "It has the most rapidly expanding nuclear arsenal and the one most vulnerable to collapse or breach," he says. "A theft or hijacking of nuclear material or a device would come from an insider, such as a terrorist or sympathizer working in a facility or from outsiders, such as a careful planned external attack like the one that targeted a nuclear facility in South Africa in 2007." He can cite a litany of recent incidents as harrowing as those at Vinca.

Allison presented a paper for a forum sponsored by the Council on Foreign Relations. The title of the event was: "How Likely Is a Nuclear Terrorist Attack on the United States?" Allison wrote, "Al-Qaeda spokesman Suleiman Abu Gheith has stated al-Qaeda's objective: 'to kill four million Americans—two million of them children—and to exile twice as many and wound and cripple hundreds of thousands.'"

Michael Levi, a policy expert on nuclear and climate change issues as well as author of the book *On Nuclear Terrorism*, argues, correctly, that such a tally could be reached in a series of smaller installments. "Our national security would benefit from insights into how to prevent such events," Allison noted. "But ask yourself how many 9/11s it would take to reach that goal. Answer: 1,334, or one nuclear weapon."

While serving together on the board of the Coca-Cola Company, headquartered in Atlanta, Nunn had a number of conversations about nuclear threats and NTI's work with Warren Buffett, the billionaire founder of Berkshire Hathaway and humanitarian.

Buffett is a consummate numbers guy. He's been influenced by Turner's constant leaning on the wealthy of the world to give back more to society and he has acted on his own conscience by joining Bill and Melinda Gates in making disease vaccination in poor countries a major emphasis of their multibillion-dollar push of philanthropy. One of their major partners is the UN Foundation.

"Warren, like Ted, keenly understands the dynamic between managing risk by reducing the odds and then paying the price if things go wrong," Nunn says.

Turner is often quoted as citing a fifty-year horizon line—for addressing nuclear proliferation, climate change, and the population crisis. Fifty years isn't an arbitrary figure. In fact, Buffett lends it credence.

He applied the same theorems to the risk of Armageddon that have been used in the business world. He did it in the company of Nunn, and the former senator has never forgotten it. As an advisor to NTI's board of directors, Buffett figured that:

If the chance of a weapon of mass destruction being used in a given year is 10 percent and the same probability exists for fifty years—the chance of getting through the fifty-year period without a disaster is .51 percent (roughly one-half of 1 percent).

If the chance can be reduced to 1 percent each year, there is a 60.5 percent chance of making it through fifty years. This means that if we make it ten times harder for terrorists or nations to use a weapon of mass destruction in any given year, we can make it 120 times less likely that we will suffer from a use of these weapons for the next fifty years.

Buffett was intrigued by the important but low profile activities of NTI, impressed by Turner's philanthropic zeal, and moved by the fact Nunn, a political moderate, was at the helm. Seeing NTI's agenda, he became a significant contributor with a multimillion-dollar donation.

"Ted can't do it alone. He needs help from those most in a position to give him help," Nunn said. "Warren recognized it. More outside funders need to get involved. If you're a businessperson, it's in your best financial interests to make sure nuclear terrorism doesn't occur."

Nunn knew that NTI needed to do something bold to raise awareness about these dangers, something that would capture the attention of citizens. In 2005, with the support of the Carnegie Corporation and the MacArthur Foundation, NTI partnered with writer and director Ben Goddard to produce *Last Best Chance*, a film dramatizing the risks from nuclear weapons and materials.

The short docudrama tracks the journey from an unguarded warehouse to a rogue nuclear engineer and then portrays a bomb being smuggled across the US border from Canada in a van. The forty-five-minute film debuted on HBO and clips of it aired on *Nightline* and

Meet the Press, CNN and FOX, and other networks. More than one hundred thousand copies have been ordered from a special website, www.lastbestchance.org.

For months, practically every guest who visited Turner in Atlanta or one of his properties was treated first to dinner and then prevented from leaving until they had given him an hour to watch *Last Best Chance.*

Turner regards the triad of foundations he created as ripe opportunities for "cross-pollinating" ideas to better the problem-solving. Recycling weapons-grade nuclear materials into power sources is a means to address climate change by burning less coal. And it can help make America less dependent on fossil fuels produced by unstable political regimes in the Persian Gulf.

Reid Detchon, vice president of climate and energy issues with the UN Foundation, helped launch an offshoot called the Energy Future Coalition, considered one of the most progressive proponents of alternative energy in Washington. Two domestic pilot initiatives spun off of the UN Foundation via Energy Future Coalition are promotion of a smart grid aimed at maximizing efficiency in transmitting power, and "25 X 25," pushing to have 25 percent of US energy needs met by alternative, sustainable, homegrown energy sources by 2025.

Both initiatives, partially funded by the Turner Foundation, enjoy bipartisan support from governors and members of Congress as well as being endorsed by farm and ranch groups, organized labor, forestry companies, power cooperatives, banks, restaurants, car companies, and universities. "Reid is working at the intersections where real breakthroughs are possible," says Mike Finley of the Turner Foundation.

At his office in the nation's capital, Detchon explains Turner's involvement. "I would describe him as a rainmaker, both on the nuclear and energy fronts. He has used his money and influence to seed the clouds, enabling organizations to get off the ground. What's good for the environment is also good for national defense."

—⁓—

"Frankly, we're in a deep mess," Turner says. "The only way for us to find our way out of these problems, if indeed we can, is to design a map to help ensure that everyone moves in the same direction. Once we get our bearings, I'm convinced not only that we'll find solutions but that we'll be able to move on them quickly."

Turner says none of the major survival questions facing humanity can be confronted in isolation from one another. They all are intricately linked. "The nuclear issue," Turner says, "is fundamentally an environmental one in the damage it would cause and in the catalysts that trigger it. People who live in desperately impoverished environments are more apt to resort to doing desperate things. Why do people in other countries want to do harm to the Western world? Because we are rich and they are poor. They resent us not for being wealthy but for being arrogant and insensitive to their misery. Why do I support the UN? Because, like it or not, its mission is to help all people achieve lives of dignity."

If serious headway is ever to be made in the fight against global warming—if we want to follow, for instance the advice of NASA's chief climate specialist, James Hansen—then coal-fired power plants must be phased out. Alternatives must be found. That's far easier said than done. The state of Wyoming, America's largest coal producer, is now planning to export massive amounts of coal to China, which is opening old-style, coal-burning power plants at the rate of about one every couple of weeks. At the same time, some members of Congress are refusing to push for a carbon tax to regulate CO_2 emissions in America, based on the fact that China is reluctant to curb its coal consumption, which is being fed by US suppliers.

In recent years, Turner has been engaged in serious discussions with his old friend from the 1980s, Texas oilman and corporate raider T. Boone

Pickens, about investing in a new power grid, one that would carry energy produced by wind, solar, and natural gas (the latter being a cleaner-burning transition fuel, helping us move away from coal and oil).

Turner had long been ambivalent at best about nuclear power because of concerns over storage of waste. He sought out the opinions of Lester Brown, and from experts at General Electric, which has a nuclear power division.

"Every option has to be on the table, but if we're going to pursue nuclear power as a real part of the solution, we have to be smart. And if it can be a tool for reducing the nuclear threat, then we will have accomplished something significant," Turner says. "But we shouldn't create one monstrous problem by trying to solve another."

Nuclear power is no magic bullet and certainly it is expensive and messy, but being open-minded about its development as an energy source enables the discussion to move beyond those who say coal is irreplaceable and new nations becoming armed is unavoidable.

The international low-enriched uranium fuel bank concept, promoted by NTI and adopted by the International Atomic Energy Agency (IAEA) in 2010, has promise. More and more nations are seeking peaceful nuclear energy to meet their development needs and are weighing available options to determine what will be the most secure and most economical way to ensure a reliable supply of nuclear fuel in the event of a supply interruption. The fuel bank will make commercial nuclear fuel supplies more secure by offering nations reliable access to a nuclear fuel reserve. If their supply arrangements are disrupted, those countries would have access to a fuel reserve under impartial IAEA control. This would make a country's voluntary choice to rely on the market more secure. It also makes this facet of the nuclear issue—the desire to find reliable power mechanisms—a tool for building bridges instead of becoming implements of war.

Tensions could be reduced if economic sanctions are lifted in exchange for those countries mothballing their weapons ambitions and agreeing to rigorous inspections while receiving expertise and materials to have state of the art nuclear power facilities. In fact, they could serve as prototypes.

If the technology is mass-produced and offered as an alternative to coal plants, especially in China, nuclear threats, climate, and energy would be attacked at the same time. China is presently opening a new coal-fired power plant at the rate of about one every week.

~·~

Amid the bleakness, is there reason for hope? "Robert McNamara in *Fog of War* talked about luck playing a role in dodging nuclear disaster during the Cuban missile crisis," Turner says. "We can't count on luck, but I've always believed that in business, as in life, you create your own luck."

There are two mountains being ascended for Turner; the first is the nuclear escarpment riddled with peril, anxiety, and worry; for this trip, Nunn is the guide and pathfinder. Whenever they escape together to a ranch or plantation, Nunn says that he and Turner come back with a greater appreciation for smaller victories. As a result of the Nunn-Lugar program, for instance, the blending down of old Soviet nukes and warhead materials has produced a peace dividend. More than five hundred tons of uranium and plutonium from former warheads have been converted into fuel for US nuclear power plants, Turner says.

NTI initiatives have markedly reduced nuclear dangers, a fact broadly acknowledged by government and security experts.

"When you calculate that 20 percent of all electricity in the United States comes from nuclear power plants, and 50 percent of the nuclear fuel used in the US comes through this agreement, you have an interesting fact," Nunn adds. "Today, roughly speaking, one out of every ten light bulbs in America is powered by material that twenty years ago was in Soviet missiles pointed at us and our friends."

Even after his financial reverses in 2002, Turner was able to give approximately $80 million of the $250 million pledged to the Nuclear Threat Initiative. The gift is one of the largest charitable contributions to reducing nuclear dangers in history.

Turner often considers the words of Albert Einstein: "The discovery of nuclear reactions need not bring about the destruction of mankind any more than the discovery of matches." He also has a favorite expression that he has applied equally to his careers in business and humanitarian causes: If negotiations fail, change the scenery, and if that doesn't work, change the chemistry of the people involved. "Look at the nuclear arms talks in Reykjavik," Turner says. "After years of making little progress, Reagan and Gorbachev went to Iceland and they came within an eyelash of agreeing to eradicate our nuclear arsenals."

In 2010, President Obama and Russian president Dmitry Medvedev agreed to "reset" relations between the two countries and moved toward a new accord. It will result in each nation slashing its number of warheads by a full one third. And China has expressed an interest in reductions. UN Secretary-General Ban Ki-moon called it "an important new milestone."

Standing at the window of his office in Atlanta, Turner says he has more than his conscience to answer to. "I am more fearful of how my grandkids will judge my actions than I am of having to defend myself before God. We have to answer for their future, and if we don't intervene to address some of these threats now, we will have failed them."

CHAPTER EIGHT

Ark of the Underdogs

"The mistake we make is when we delude ourselves into believing that we don't need nature in our lives, and that we can contain or ignore her at will, treat her as an entity separate from us. Our existence depends upon us being better listeners and observers and caretakers. We need to allow her back into our lives."

—TED TURNER

Swinging open a screen door, releasing the aroma of roasting pheasant from the kitchen behind him, Ted Turner steps out onto a prairie farmhouse porch to soak in a sunset. With a glass of wine in his hand, he leads his guests on a short trek into the backyard. "I've got a surprise for y'all," he says.

Removing a set of binoculars from around his neck, Turner passes them over to his companions, then directs everyone's attention to a small divot in the South Dakota sod. "Oh missus praaairie dog," he calls out playfully. "Won't you come out of your hole and introduce us to your family?"

Mike Phillips grins from the sidelines. Next to him is Turner's youngest child, Beau, who now is in his forties. "The boss," Phillips says, "is in his element."

At Turner ranches in South Dakota, Kansas, and New Mexico, staff and biologists from the Turner Endangered Species Fund have brought

prairie dog colonies back to life for Turner's enjoyment, and, more importantly, as a critically important step in restoring the grasslands of the
Great Plains. While it's true that many agrarians on the high plains curse
the native ground squirrels as vermin—they're considered competitors
with grazing livestock—Turner reminds his guests that his fondness for
the creatures is shared with one of America's Founding Fathers.

"How can you disagree with the opinions of a man credited with
writing the Declaration of Independence?" he asks rhetorically.

After Thomas Jefferson became president in 1801, he famously dispatched Meriwether Lewis and William Clark on a mission to map the
lands acquired from France in the Louisiana Purchase. Mid-journey,
Lewis and Clark sent a gift, via canoe, back to Washington, DC. The
living postcard—a prairie dog—provided no small amount of amuse-
ment for the naturalist chief executive. Jefferson reportedly even aspired
to allow a colony to take up residence on the newly christened White
House grounds.

Turner sees Jefferson as a forerunning ecologist. In 1797, Jefferson
wrote, "For if one link in nature's chain might be lost, another and another
might be lost, till this whole system of things should evanish [*sic*] by
piece-meal."

"How many prominent business executives know what a *keystone species* is?" Phillips, director of the Turner Endangered Species Fund, asks.
"How many can boast that they are actively involved in restoring two of
them—the prairie dog and bison?"

Phillips says that Turner's fascination with prairie dogs is based on
their individual characteristics and their role as crucial underpinnings in
a huge food pyramid. "In a way, Ted and prairie dogs have much in common," he says, watching Turner tell his guests how important the gopher-
sized rodents are. "To exercise their greatest influence, each must operate
on a large scale."

The next morning, Phillips and resident ranch biologist Kevin Honness arise early for a walk across a broad rippling peneplain of grassland. "This," Phillips says, "is what many of America's 310-million-plus citizens would consider to be geographical nowheresville. They don't think about the prairie outside of Pierre, South Dakota. In fact, most don't even know it exists. You either drive through it or fly over it. But it's important and it's someplace special to Ted."

Sparse and vacant, the Dakota prairie has been hemorrhaging people, emptying out in a trend that runs counter to the human population growth overwhelming other parts of the world. Turner believes this trend presents an opportunity for nature.

Wading into a swale of knee-high brome, Honness, who operates a scientific research station for TESF on the ranch, warns Phillips to mind the rattlesnakes. Months from now, this outing will be recalled as one of the last joyous memories one man will have of the other. Human longevity will prove short. In this immediate abbreviated span of it, however, Honness and Phillips are trying to catch a glimpse of evolutionary forces that Turner has assigned them to study and then share their findings. In a way, they're to Turner as Lewis and Clark were to Jefferson.

After a ten-minute walk, they arrive at their destination: a bona fide rodent metropolis that dwarfs the quaint scene viewed the previous night behind Turner's farmhouse. Hundreds of conical mounds are embedded in the matted surface of Earth, the surrounding grass nipped short by bucked teeth to a level of manicured smoothness. It resembles a golf course putting green, but is less lush. Turner's neighbors would consider it a "moonscape." Here, ecological function takes precedence over the ground's immediate ability to fill a beef cow's belly with grass.

Scientists call this a glimpse into "rewilding." As a private citizen, Turner's prominence in the movement of rewilding—given his two million acres—is unmatched. Indeed, his portfolio has earned him a reputation as a kind of modern-day Noah.

The Turner Endangered Species Fund has focused on recovering more than twenty species on Turner land. "When you're small," Phillips says, "you have to try to be mighty." Over the years, the TESF has leveraged Turner's investment perhaps fifty fold, adhering to a multiplier effect similar to that of Tim Wirth, Sam Nunn, and Mike Finley at the UN Foundation, Nuclear Threat Initiative, and Turner Foundation.

Phillips cofounded the endangered species initiative along with Ted and Beau Turner. All five of the Turner children sit on its board of directors and each has taken to promoting imperiled species conservation. Phillips was hired away from a job as a senior scientist in Yellowstone where, during the 1990s, he led the historic reintroduction of gray wolves. Prior to that he carried out the historic reintroduction of red wolves to the southeastern United States.

TESF has been a major force in influencing the way conservation is approached in America by building public-private partnerships. And it has attracted attention around the world, in some ways borrowing from NASA's mantra of "faster, better, cheaper." The US Fish and Wildlife Service recently called it a "Recovery Champion." "Recovery Champions are helping listed species get to the point at which they are secure in the wild and no longer need Endangered Species Act protection," the Fish and Wildlife Service's national director Dan Ashe said. Most of the laudable collaborations with private landowners only apply to one or two species, but with Turner it extends to an array of species and properties.

Dr. Michael Soule, an eminent figure in conservation biology circles, says that TESF offers a model worthy of emulation by other property owners who want to make a contribution to wildlife preservation but are leery of government red tape. "We're like 'The Little Train That Could.'" Turner says. "If you believe you can make something happen, then you're already halfway there."

When TESF was first founded, its funding was several fold greater. The collapse in AOL stock value, however, forced a major reevaluation of how resources could be applied. Scrapped were plans to restore California condors to a Turner ranch in New Mexico and wood storks to Avalon Plantation. More important than throwing money at the plight of a species, Phillips says, is having property where animals can have safe, abiding havens. Phillips, the former US civil servant and an active Montana legislator, notes that government agencies can be well intended but they are challenged by bureaucratic regulation that prevents them from being light on their feet. In recent decades, government agencies also have been paralyzed by lawsuits brought by both environmental organizations and resource extraction groups.

Turner's come a long way from those days at Hope and Avalon Plantations when he set those cougars and bears free.

As Ashe of the Fish and Wildlife Service notes, some of Turner's ranches figure prominently at the center of a strategy to recover one of the rarest land mammals in the world. The black-footed ferret was once written off as extinct. But by reestablishing prairie dogs at his ranches in South Dakota, New Mexico, and Kansas—animals that ferrets need to survive—Turner is providing four of the ten venues the US Fish and Wildlife Service says it will take to achieve a minimum baseline of biological recovery.

At Turner's Armendaris Ranch in the Fra Cristobal Mountains of New Mexico, a wildly successful, multi-decade project to restore endangered desert bighorn sheep today accounts for about 40 percent of the sheep in New Mexico and was the principal reason that the New Mexico Department of Game and Fish was able to remove the species from the state list of imperiled species.

At his Ladder Ranch, the wetland habitat and a corresponding captive breeding program account for a significant portion of the recovery numbers for Chiricahua leopard frogs in that part of the Southwest. At the Snowcrest and Flying D ranches in Montana and Vermejo Park and Ladder ranches in New Mexico, Turner is working with states, federal agencies, and the conservation group, Trout Unlimited, to bring back viable populations of native westslope and Rio Grande cutthroat trout and fluvial Arctic grayling. The westslope cutthroat project at the Flying D gave Montana's state fish more than sixty miles of refugia, helping the state resist calls to have the salmonid protected under the Endangered Species Act. He aims to eventually restore imperiled cutthroat trout to 250 miles of streams and rivers in Montana and New Mexico following decades of destruction. His efforts in this regard are unmatched in the world, earning him highest honors from the American Fisheries Society.

At the historic Avalon Plantation near Tallahassee, Turner has led a novel effort to restore endangered red-cockaded woodpeckers, establishing a pilot program for what other private landowners can do to provide safe harbor to species without fear of being encumbered by regulations. Not only did the Turner organization pioneer a method for reestablishing woodpeckers using nest boxes, but he is complementing it with a massive effort to restore native longleaf pine with a replanting effort now surpassing one million seedlings.

At St. Phillips Island in South Carolina (where Turner in the 1980s was one of the first landowners in the country to place conservation easements on his properties, preventing them from being fragmented by development), he has reintroduced indigo snakes and fox squirrels, and secured beach habitat for imperiled loggerhead sea turtles.

At his Collon Cura ranch in Argentina, he is providing habitat for guanacos, wild cousins of the llama. Through TESF and the Turner Foundation, Turner has also supported private-public efforts to preserve hundreds of other species, from the American elm tree and wild Pacific salmon to Tasmanian devils, European bison, gorillas and chimpanzees in Africa, and cranes in Russia and the two Koreas. He has also provided funds to establish a seed bank for the world's plants in Norway as a way of creating a genetic reservoir for botanical species eminently threatened by human-caused climate change.

~ ~

On this warm October morning at Bad River, Honness and Phillips approach a prairie dog colony to the building sound of whispering maracas. A scattering of diamondback rattlesnakes, almost perfectly camouflaged in the dirt and dry grass, rustle into coils and shake their tails. A few vanish down prairie dog holes. "Rattlers come with the territory," Honness says.

As the men safely verge upon the rodent city center, Phillips notes the gawkers standing on their hind feet. Prairie dog sentries bark from the flanks. "Did you ever get the feeling you're being watched—and heckled?"

Honness and Phillips stand still, waiting. A ferruginous hawk sails out of nowhere into the scene, and then come the singing horned larks, balancing on buffalo grass and stabbing at grasshoppers. Over the span of a half hour, a burrowing owl spouts from an underground nest, a coyote lopes over a rise, and a badger chugs along like a panzer. A troop of pronghorn graze in the distance.

Lifting their heads, the researchers marvel at a broader site: a huge herd of bison that Bad River manager Tom LeFaive has turned loose on this part of the ranch. The bovines in weeks ahead will mow down grass and use their hoof action to churn up the soil. Since the massive continental glaciers left the prairie, bison and prairie dogs have evolved side by side.

"If you want excitement—and I do mean real predator and prey action, hang around a prairie dog town awhile," Phillips says. Having studied lobos, brown bears in Alaska, and Australian dingos, Phillips speaks from authority. "Prairie dogs are keystone species for many reasons, not the least of which is that they are important prey for a suite of predators."

Honness crouches near a burrow, examining a set of human footprints. He's able to discern that the two Turners, Ted and Beau, already have passed through the colony, beating them there by an hour. It was Turner's first stop before setting out on a pheasant hunt with his friend and South Dakota native Tom Brokaw.

"Ted gets energized coming out here. He likes seeing how little actions all tie together. And it's a fascination that he enjoys sharing with his son," Phillips says.

The Turner family understands that the extinction crisis will not be redressed in a short period of time. "They are very determined to put their good fortune to good use," Phillips says. "They're not poseurs. They're acutely infected with what E. O. Wilson terms biophilia, an instinctive bond between humans and the natural world."

"They know that as human growth continues and resource consumption continues, the footprint of our species isn't growing smaller and lighter; it's bigger and heavier. Stewardship isn't a one-time thing where you write a check and call your work done. Like good governance, the need to be involved doesn't stop on Friday. You have to be mindful of it every day, forever. Ted has taught them that responsibility begins with your own land."

Small as it seems in the context of Turner's life, "Spots like this give him as much pride as anything else he does," Phillips continues. "And do you know the reason for it? Because Ted knows that restored nature can persist through the ages."

—⁓—

The objective of the Turner Endangered Species Fund is to restore fauna and flora that might have disappeared or been in decline on Turner land when he bought the properties. TESF's theme is: "conserving biodiversity by ensuring the persistence of imperiled species and their habitats." Those words are closely knitted with the motto of Turner Enterprises Inc., the for-profit umbrella of Turner's business holdings, which is "to manage Turner lands in an economically sustainable and ecologically sensitive manner while promoting the conservation of native species."

In practice, the taglines forge a bold and defiant declaration that has captured attention from policymakers in Washington, DC, and other larger landholders, and resulted in collaborations with government agencies mandated, by law, to prevent species extinctions.

For Turner, being an avowed "eco-capitalist" is about having a corporate social consciousness. His intent is to challenge the misguided perception that species preservation comes at the expense of prosperity and human livelihoods. He calls it a false dichotomy. He has heard fellow property owners charge that having endangered species on their land will run them out of business or impinge their liberty. And there is also a widely held view among environmentalists, he says, that unless government steps in and protects species from extinction, many animals will not survive.

"I am committed to proving them wrong. Species survival should not have to depend on public lands or private lands. An animal should not have to die or live or be considered important depending on whether it's on the Endangered Species list. That's wrongheaded. Conservation isn't a choice between nature and prosperity. It's a combination of both, put together.

"Before I spent time out on the prairie, I had no idea that it could be such an interesting place, so alive with animals. It makes you almost want to cry when you are in the middle of it," he says.

⌖

Yes, to be a prairie dweller, unplugged from gadgetry, is to attain a heightened sentient awareness. He is smitten by the passing southward migration of birds overhead; the cackling of rooster pheasants rising from a dog on point; the sight of bounding deer bucks, darting pronghorn, and bison; the way that angling light paints the prairie in washes of warm, abiding earth tones. Something about it, he says, makes him feel less empty and more connected to the rhythm of life.

He has a ritual of trying to visit prairie dog colonies now spread across five different properties. He often is able to summon, from memory, the exact number of acres each colony occupied at last count. His compulsive directive to the ranch managers is always the same: "Look out for the prairie dogs."

Back at the ranch house, Turner meets with Bad River manager Tom LeFaive.

A jolly man and a biologist by training, LeFaive asks Turner to speculate on when he might finally declare mission accomplished with prairie dogs. Ranchers in the area who despise the critters have been wondering, he says. They don't want to be the recipients of Ted's animals spilling over onto their land—especially animals they've spent so much money and heritage trying to annihilate.

Part of LeFaive's own job responsibility is to raise healthy bison, and he too worries about having enough grass. It's been hard for him to warm up to prairie dogs.

Turner's face fills with a mawkish grin as he contemplates LeFaive's question. It's not tinged with defiance, but conviction. "For now, we keep growing prairie dogs. They have an important place on the prairie, the same as we do."

He understands why his neighbors don't like prairie dogs—they see them as stealers of grass that would go into the mouths of cattle. Turner even has resigned himself to the unpleasant reality that, in order to keep peace and continue his restoration, he needs to honor their request for lethal control. Turner isn't lacking in empathy but he says the discussion of prairie dogs has been one-sided.

"You let the neighbors know, Tom, that we'll do our best to contain prairie dogs inside the border of the ranch. And if they should cross over, and the neighbors don't like it, then they can go ahead and control them. But God, I hate poison. You needlessly kill a lot of other things you don't have to kill when you put poison out there. Let them know that we want to work together on this."

Turner's support of rebuilding prairie dog colonies has been characterized by critics as a fetish. His name is openly cursed by some stockmen who have spent generations trying to make prairie dogs vanish. They would be happy to have the landscape completely cleansed of the native animals.

—⁓—

Within the circle of his own family, "Grandpa Ted's" prairie dogs have been the subject of his grandchildren's show and tell days at schools in Atlanta, Tallahassee, Lexington, Kentucky, and Charleston, South Carolina. Turner's eldest daughter, Laura Turner Seydel, is a board member of Defenders of Wildlife, an organization that, for decades, has been trying to bolster protection for prairie dogs. And Turner's youngest daughter, Jennie Turner Garlington, has been a trustee with the National Fish and Wildlife Foundation, assisting private property owners and government agencies with numerous prairie conservation initiatives.

Why do prairie dogs matter? Once ubiquitous in the West, their colonies were dispersed from the Mississippi River to southern California, from the high plains of western Canada to northern Mexico. Five different species inhabited between eighty and one hundred million acres. Perhaps five billion prairie dogs existed when Lewis and Clark passed through the West. Lewis estimated the numbers as "infinite." Today they exist at less than 5 percent of their original numbers and range. Billions of dollars, marshaled in an arsenal of poison baits, traps, bullets, and habitat modification, have been flung at them with lethal effectiveness. Combined with outbreaks of the wildlife equivalent of bubonic plague—called sylvatic plague, introduced to this continent with European colonization—total annihilation of prairie dogs, at one point, was not inconceivable. Many ranchers and farmers would have considered it a victory.

Ironically, as prairie dog populations have tumbled, the economic prospects of farming and ranching have hardly improved. According to the Worldwatch Institute, a little over a century ago, every $1 that consumers spent on a typical US food item yielded about 40 cents for the farmer or rancher, with the rest split between input and distribution. Today, only 7 cents out of every dollar spent at the checkout aisle goes back to the producer. Seventy-three cents goes into the pockets of those who package and distribute the products.

The poor state of agrarian economics can hardly be pinned on prairie dogs, though they've become a convenient scapegoat. "I think there is room out here to share the land," Turner says, his persistence motivated by an emerging scientific awakening of the niche prairie dogs fill. "And here's what we never hear in discussions. If prairie dogs were such a scourge to rangeland, then how did thirty-five million bison live side by side with them? Why could bison thrive and cows allegedly can't?"

Turner bends the ears to win prairie dog allies among anyone he can corner. Tom Brokaw, the elder dean of the newsroom at NBC, is a proud product of Yankton, South Dakota, down the road. He's also been a Montana rancher, and a close friend of Turner's for decades. He has accompanied Turner to numerous prairie dog colonies and, at Turner's insistence, has become a convert to acknowledging the prairie dog's value. Brokaw isn't alone. Talk to a string of Nobel Peace Prize winners—Mikhail Gorbachev, Al Gore, Kofi Annan, or Jimmy Carter—and each has been regaled with tales about the prairie dog frontier.

Turner says he would gladly give any American president and the US secretaries of Interior and Agriculture a tour. "Ted can tell you anything you ever wanted to know about the prairie dog," Annan says. "Until I met Ted, I never would have thought that prairie dogs could make for an entertaining dinner conversation. Fortunately, he served us bison to eat and not prairie dogs. But I'm serious when I tell you that what I learned from Ted about the importance of these little animals has stayed with me."

Phillips says that what conservation biologists and Turner find compelling is the ecological dividends of prairie dogs from a biodiversity perspective. "The questions often posed are: What is the consequence of losing a species? What is the implication when you put one back?"

Phillips asks. "The rationale you hear is that humans can get by with one less animal or plant. Or maybe a couple here and there. And, after that, maybe a few more. Let them go. Let them wink out, they say. What will it matter? And they ask, 'What value is there to any animal that isn't actively bought, sold or traded in the marketplace?'"

He goes on. "It's true. We don't eat prairie dogs, but other things do. If you wanted, I suppose you could justify the loss of many species until there are only weeds and commercial crops left. In some parts of the prairie, that's exactly what has happened."

The Great Plains has a reputation for being home to God-fearing people. "Sometimes the folks who would have you believe they are the most devout spiritual people are the ones least receptive to thinking about the extinction crisis," Phillips says. "I find it ironic, and Ted and I have spoken about it, that they're willing to turn their backs on their God's creation. As Michael Soule says, 'If you love the creator, you have to love the creation. The two are inseparable.'"

<hr />

During the height of his land-buying phase, Turner started to recognize the importance of prairie dogs as building blocks for wildlife conservation across the windswept heart of America. He invokes the words of Jacques-Yves Cousteau: "Happiness, for the bee as for the dolphin, is to exist. For Man, it is to know existence and to marvel in it."

The consequences of species loss are, in fact, part of a riddle the Turners, Phillips and others have spent decades pondering. Phillips led the field team that in 1986 represented humankind's first effort to restore a major carnivore (the red wolf) that had been extinct in the wild. Then, in 1995, he was tapped to carry out gray wolf reintroduction in Yellowstone some sixty years after the federal government eradicated lobos.

In the absence of wolves, elk numbers in Yellowstone had swelled largely unchecked. Wapiti overgrazed aspen and willow, which affected the abundance of beaver—their hydro-engineering critical to creating marshes. The absence of beaver as wetland builders negatively impacted moose and songbirds and wading avians, some preliminary scientific studies suggest. Coyotes also climbed in number, affecting the abundance of a small pronghorn antelope population.

Mike Finley, president of the Turner Foundation, was there as superintendent of Yellowstone when wolves were brought back. "I would walk through potential aspen groves that were thigh high and nothing more than stunted woody shrubs," he says. "Over time the wolves reduced the numbers of elk but just as importantly changed their browsing behavior. The elk no longer stayed in one location for extended periods hammering the vegetation. When I revisited in 2009 it was stunning to see twelve- to fourteen-foot aspens and willows. The aspens had escaped the browse line of the elk and were now robust. Where there was once one beaver colony there were now eleven colonies benefitting waterfowl and recharging the aquifer."

"Some species reset the deck and alter the natural order of things. Humans do it, and probably so do wolves in many settings," Phillips adds. "Hunters today complain that Yellowstone is no longer the elk factory it was in the days when ranchers outside the park complained there were way too many of them. With wolves back, there is probably a wider range of species beneficiaries, all kinds of scavengers, birds, and mammals all the way down to insects. Whether it's better or not comes down to your own perspective, but if you're not going to have wolves in a symbolic place like Yellowstone, then where? Well, here's Ted Turner raising his hand and saying, 'Hey, I know a place. I volunteer.'"

As a biologist who has specialized in "charismatic megafauna," Phillips is keenly aware how species at the top of food chains command public attention and priority. They are easy to watch, and what they do on a landscape appears to be obvious. But they ride on the shoulders of other animals operating literally at the grassroots level. Smaller keystone species, like prairie dogs and beaver, not only support other organisms but are also indicators of ecological health.

"Prairie dogs provide one of the best illustrations of how ecosystems can unravel," he says. "When people like E. O. Wilson and Jane Goodall and Jeffrey Sachs talk about the world entering the sixth great episode of extinction—the only one I might add, when humans have been present on Earth as a species—they know that some species serve as emblematic triggers. "When they disappear, other species start to vanish. Keystone species are like the foundation of an inverted pyramid. The tippy crown at the bottom holds up the weight of the mass above it."

Turner calls prairie dogs "seed corn" for biodiversity.

All five species of prairie dogs have so declined in number that each has been proposed for protection under the federal Endangered Species Act. There is the white-tailed prairie dog (*Cynomys leucurus*) that occurs at the highest elevations, generally along the Rocky Mountain Front; Gunnison's prairie dog (*C. gunisoni*), that are found in four Southwest states; and Utah prairie dog (*C. parvidens*) that inhabit the steppes of the Beehive state and are classified as a threatened species. Finally, Mexican prairie dogs (*C. mexicanus*) are limited to 4 percent of historic range and are critically imperiled south of the US border.

The most widely distributed, the black-tailed prairie dog (*C. Ludovicianus*), enjoys sanctuary at Bad River and a couple of other Turner properties. Black-tails historically were found in at least eleven western states. They were recently rejected for receiving protection from the Fish and Wildlife Service. Their status is a matter of huge public controversy.

Some two hundred years ago, black-tails inhabited at least seventy-four million acres (roughly the size of thirty-five Yellowstones). As late as the nineteenth century, a single community of prairie dogs in the Lone Star State numbered four hundred million strong. In terms of total prairie dog distribution among four different species, black-tails alone are esti-mated to have numbered five billion around the time that the Declaration of Independence was drafted in Philadelphia.

Michael Gilpin, one of the world's foremost authorities on wildlife demography, determined the animals were not really persecuted until the 1930s. He found documentation suggesting that the administration of Franklin Delano Roosevelt enlisted thousands of Americans hungry for work during the Great Depression to wage a full-blown assault on prai-rie dogs. They fanned out across the nation's midsection carrying backpacks loaded with eighty pounds of poison, shoveling it down burrow holes. By the early 1960s, prairie dogs inhabited less than four hundred thousand acres.

Today, the Fish and Wildlife Service, based on estimates from states determined to prevent federal protection, says black-tails are found on 2.4 million acres, which means they are seven times more numerous than in the 1960s but still more than 98 percent depleted since the end of the nineteenth century.

Many observers, including Gilpin and Jonathan Proctor (now an ecologist with Defenders of Wildlife), say the Fish and Wildlife estimate of currently occupied habitat is inflated. It may actually be half of what the agency says it is, if not less.

Turner passes along a little arithmetic. Biomass, in terms of available energy resources (e.g., food), is what a collective population of a species represents to another. Turner takes the historical estimate of five billion prairie dogs and multiplies it by two pounds (the average weight of a typical adult prairie dog) to arrive at ten billion self-sustaining pounds of biomass feeding a community of other animals. The current estimate of twenty-four million black-tails would yield forty-eight million pounds of biomass.

Turner wonders aloud about the net effect of reducing prairie dogs to just 2 percent of their historical distribution and its effect on the car-rying capacity of the prairie. "It's obvious, isn't it?" he asks. "The prairie is starved of prairie dogs."

Conservation biologist Gilpin did his own back-of-the-napkin computation. That ten billion pounds of prairie dog biomass was equal to the total biomass of the two hundred million humans alive on the planet in 0 AD.

— ～

Right now, as one reads these words, prairie dogs are being attacked again. State and federal laws allow them to be liberally killed on public and private land. Poisons are used to kill large numbers of prairie dogs, the absence of which impacts predators and scavengers because less sustenance is available for them. Shooting with lead bullets is very popular. Tragically, because lead is highly toxic, shooting prairie dogs equates to indiscriminate killing of non-target animals that consume the carcasses of dead prairie dogs. Turner opposes indiscriminate killing of any kind, and the use of lead ammunition for any reasons is prohibited on his ranches.

This quiet war against prairie dogs persists at the same time that the US federal government and states are spending hard-earned tax dollars every year trying to rescue species that rely on prairie dog colonies for food and shelter.

Turner isn't the only person who likens the earlier eradication campaign "to a form of genocide." But he is certainly the best known. His conclusion is shared by the leading conservation biologists in the world, who liken the assault on prairie dogs to the strategy of applying biocides like DDT to control insects after World War II without a full understanding of its effects.

DDT caused staggering declines in non-target animals, including bald eagles (the nation's symbol), peregrine falcons, and other species. The story of its toll formed the narrative of Rachel Carson's seminal 1962 book, *Silent Spring*, that arguably marked the advent of modern environmental awareness. The rapid loss of bald eagles served as a catalyst for getting DDT banned and passing the Endangered Species Act (ESA) into law. Back in the 1970s and '80s when Turner's children were in high school, he handed them copies of *Silent Spring*. "It was the first book that Dad gave to me and said, 'Read it, it will make you smarter,'" his eldest child, Laura Turner Seydel, says.

If Mike Gilpin had his druthers, he would see a major span of short and mixed grass prairie revert back to Indians, bison, and prairie dogs, overtaking monoculture and cows. But this vision, of course, is not practical. If the objective is to have a measurable impact on the ground, talk has to move beyond daydreaming to action. And Gilpin's track record with pondering the fates of imperiled species is extensive. He was among the select team of experts who made the call to pull the last twenty-two remaining California condors out of the wild in 1987, preserving their genetics instead of allowing the birds to fade into certain oblivion, or as conservationist Kenneth Brower said, letting them wink out on their own, "extinction with dignity."

Gilpin has watched the pattern repeated time and again: expanding human populations fragment wildlife habitat, leaving species to persist only in remnant shards until they vanish into silence. And he is not hopeful, given current trends in the world, that prairie dog and bison will ever re-attain the full ecological function they had on a grand scale.

"Unless . . . ," Gilpin says, stopping mid-thought. "Unless something happens in the market that gives us a radically different orientation to the environment from the one we have." He points to the work of British ethologist and evolutionary biologist Richard Dawkins, author of the provocative 1976 book, *The Selfish Gene*, in which Dawkins introduced the concept of meme (pronounced *meem*). A meme, by his definition, is an idea, behavior, or style that spreads from person to person within a culture.

Dawkins proposed that species may evolve by passing genetic material, as espoused by Charles Darwin, with such things as environmental factors and competition gradually shaping the form that plants and animals take.

But another factor affecting survival is that of the *meme:* In other words, do societies possess traits that predispose them to survival or extinction? The gist is that human collective behaviors have parallels to species' abilities to perpetuate themselves. Values are passed along like DNA from one generation to the next. Hence, for example, a society that is culturally indoctrinated to pursue land-use practices, that, say, result in chronic environmental degradation, possesses a meme that predisposes them to fail compared to customs that emphasize living well below the threshold of resource depletion. This is also postulated by Gilpin's friend, Jared Diamond, in his important book, *Collapse.*

In the animal kingdom, including humans, Gilpin has noticed across time that species which have customs—or memes—that control their populations, prevent inbreeding that harms their genetics, and avoid risky behaviors such as wars and unhealthy living that might jeopardize their survival, tend to last over time. Another iteration of a meme is a cultural tradition that eradicates species based on a continuously reinforcing value system. Unless something happens that triggers believers to abandon it for another way of thinking about those species, they are doomed to perish.

Prairie dogs have a meme that involves females practicing infanticide as a form of population control, in addition to other social practices that prevent incest and environmental degradation.

On a macro, human-behavioral scale, Gilpin sees Turner as a possible meme; a man who is challenging destructive, culturally indoctrinated customs in the West that have resulted in nature being subdued, tamed, diluted, and extirpated. By actions, he is showing that profits can still be derived while being more tolerant and ecologically sensitive, that broad, deep, and enduring value requires much more than a maximally favorable fiscal bottom line. It places him, potentially, at the forefront of a new tradition that emphasizes real eco-sustainability, not some half-baked notion of it.

This kind of meme, which is expressed by Turner and only a few others, has broad implications. In 2012, Turner sponsored a summit of large private landowners that collectively have dominion over millions of acres. They wanted to know more about how he does what he does.

"The question is what effect he has on others who are in a position to make a difference. Will they follow? Can Turner's ethic be adopted by enough people that it starts a shift?" Gilpin asks.

One way or another, Gilpin says, the human species will discover that it cannot violate the fundamental laws of evolution. Organisms cannot outstrip the resources that sustain them and engage in behaviors focused on individual selfish interests at the expense of the species.

He, like Turner, heeds the warnings of Paul Ehrlich about the population explosion and the age-old predictions of the Reverend Thomas Robert Malthus. Ehrlich wrote the 1968 book, *The Population Bomb*, that Turner says has influenced where he focuses his energies: on nuclear nonproliferation, protecting biodiversity, addressing climate change by promoting alternative energy, and reversing human population by elevating poor people out of poverty but without accelerating resource consumption.

There are seven billion humans now, at least nine billion projected by the middle of this century, and at the present rate of resource depletion it will require another Earth and a half to meet the demand for raw materials. Since no other Earth is in sight, it means scaling back human numbers, over time, to between five hundred million and 1.5 billion, two billion at the most, Ehrlich says, a range that members of the political right and commentators on FOX News consider heresy. Turner isn't proposing heavy-handed eugenic intervention or laws prohibiting breeding, but rather support for women's rights, access to birth control, and standard of living improvements, including health care, all of which have shown to serve as factors in reducing the number of babies women have. It would be achieved incrementally over generations. The last century showed that countries with high quality of life—not necessarily tied to high levels of resource consumption—have lower birth rates.

As Ehrlich adds, parents who have two children actually are below the replacement rate. Turner notes that as much as he loves his *five* children, he *would* strictly adhere to the two-child rule today. Devil's advocates have rightly pointed out that he also flies in a private jet, logging millions of miles during his career and contributing exponentially more than a small legion of average Joes ever will to climate change in terms of emissions from their transportation vehicles. These are two huge contradictions to which Turner replies that he has no defense, other than to point out that he is managing his land to serve as sinks for collecting greenhouse gas emissions well in excess of the total emissions of all Turner activities. He is capturing more carbon than he is creating by a ratio of seven to one.

Turner contends that the risk of being a hypocrite should not prevent one from doing more good than harm. "Whether you're rich or not, we all need to do our part. I make decisions and if they are harmful, I will correct them or more than make up for them. I ain't perfect but you don't need to be perfect to take positions to make you a better human. You just can't be a coward."

Challenging the status quo is unsettling to those invested in defending it, but it's myopic to ignore the compelling evidence of science that demands humans change their behavior, former US vice president and Nobel Peace Prize recipient Al Gore, perhaps the world's best known crusader on climate change, tells me.

"Owing to his forays into cable television, this isn't news to Ted. Sometimes, it results in him being on the receiving end of ad hominem attacks. Believe me, I know ad hominem attacks when I see them. For doing what Ted Turner has done, never pursuing things based on whether they are popular but rather whether or not they are right, I love the guy."

Gore, like Turner, travels in jet aircraft, in private planes. He drives a car, lives in a house, eats meat, consumes material goods, and has no dreams of being a Neo-Luddite. "People are always going to take potshots no matter what you do," he says of the "shoot the messenger" syndrome. "If you allow your critics to define you, addle you, then you are destined to do nothing. I know that I can never live a perfect life in the eyes of some others, but that doesn't stop me from being conscientious and striving to do a little better tomorrow than I did today. Ted is someone who typifies that philosophy."

Turner has no business card, but in his wallet he carries around a printed one-sided copy of "Eleven Voluntary Initiatives by Ted Turner":

I promise to care for planet earth and all living things thereon, especially my fellow human beings.

I promise to treat all persons everywhere with dignity, respect, and friendliness.

I promise to have no more than one or two children.

I promise to use my best efforts to help save what is left of our natural world in its undisturbed state, and to restore degraded areas.

I promise to use as little of our non-renewable resources as possible.

I promise to minimize my use of toxic chemicals, pesticides and other poisons, and to encourage others to do the same.

I promise to contribute to those less fortunate to help them become self-sufficient and enjoy the benefits of decent life including clean air and water, adequate food, health care, housing, education and individual rights.

I reject the use of force, in particular military force, and I support United Nations arbitration of international disputes.

I support the total elimination of all nuclear, chemical and biological weapons, and ultimately the elimination of *all* weapons of mass destruction.

I support the United Nations and its efforts to improve the conditions of the planet.

I support clean renewable energy and a rapid move to eliminate carbon emissions.

Yes, Turner has been confronted with his contradictions, especially with points 3 and 5. That's why he consciously tries to use his resources to radically reduce his carbon footprint in other ways, he says. He is managing his ranchlands in ways that keep the plant life and soil healthy in order to maximize natural carbon sequestration; that's why he buys carbon credits; that's why he sanctioned an energy audit to identify places in his operation to be more efficient; that's why he's invested millions of dollars in alternative energy, and it's why, among other things, he supports Turner Foundation efforts to help achieve large systemic changes, such as partnering with the National Restaurant Association to change the way the industry does business in more than a million eateries, helping local entrepreneurs achieve savings through energy and water conservation and by scaling the use of best practices geared to sustainable resource use. He's also promoting a parallel initiative with national hoteliers.

"In 1938 when I was born, the world had around two billion people. We've just sailed through seven billion and we're headed toward nine or ten billion during this century," Turner says. "That's a three and a half time increase of the world population in just my lifespan. That's insane. Today, two billion of those seven billion people are undernourished and we're already seeing stressed resources."

Turner and Ehrlich agree that small, feel-good measures carried out by individuals add up, but unless such things as recycling, wind and solar power, fuel efficiency in autos and homes, are scaled to incorporate hundreds of millions and billions of citizens, it won't matter. Game over. Whales were saved only because electricity brought a better way to illuminate the night.

"We're going to run out of everything," Turner says. "The fossil fuel industry says we've got enough oil and gas to last one hundred years. A hundred years! That's no amount of time at all. And where will we be with another two or three billion of us in fifty years, not including the billions in China and India who are taking their cues from how we live? We need to lead."

Ehrlich says that relying on the promise of technological fixes to rescue civilization from large-scale environmental problems is folly, particularly when the issue is compounded by the stress of demand for basic resources by a population that continues to rise.

"Ted is absolutely right to make the connection between all four of his focus areas," Ehrlich says. "Population affects resource depletion and uses land to grow food, which reduces habitat for native plants and animals. If you throw climate change or a nuclear disaster on top it, we're flirting with serious trouble. You have to address all four moving parts. But population is the big elephant in the room."

If humans do not consciously make an effort to reduce population, nature will find a way to get the reduction done, Gilpin says. Ehrlich praises Turner for trying to keep the discussion about human population and its impact on nature alive, even though it opens him to constant ridicule. As a leading thinker in conservation biology based at Stanford University, Ehrlich points to Turner's use of bison as a retro tool for bettering biodiversity and integrating it into a supply side model of promoting healthier eating. It's a radical departure from the prevailing agricultural model of crop monoculture, intensive use of herbicides and pesticides, water use, and pumping livestock full of antibiotics, and it is complementary to sustaining predators at the top of the food chain.

"I've always been an admirer of Ted's. I like his direct approach. If the objective is protecting biodiversity, he goes out and buys it himself, then protects it, or he makes his land available to bring biodiversity back and he is using native species to make it profitable, without taming bison through heavy-handed animal husbandry," Ehrlich says.

"If you want to call that a meme more likely to predispose human survival, and I think you could, it's a damned good one."

Billionaire John Malone, the CEO of Liberty Media, is a close friend of Turner's, going back to the days when they made cable television a fixture of American life. He says Turner's green ethics have rubbed off on him. Like Turner, Malone has used his fortune to buy land—a whopping two million-plus acres, with the aspiration of bypassing Turner and being the biggest individual landowner in the country. He accomplished that feat in 2011.

Based on conversations and lobbying he's received from Turner, Malone has put a huge swath of his property under conservation easement. "We haven't made a move to bison yet. We're running some cattle but we're doing it in a way that is mindful of the range and the watersheds," Malone says. "You can't be around Ted and not be affected by what he's doing."

Malone joined several large landowners at Turner's Flying D Ranch recently, with the idea of doing for wildlife conservation on private land what the growing fold of magnanimous billionaires are doing for eco-philanthropy. And their efforts won a glowing endorsement from E. O. Wilson.

As for whether Turner is a potential meme—an agent of change—and whether the TESF is a useful model that others might duplicate for protecting biodiversity, this, too, has attracted influential emulators.

Thomas Kaplan refers to Turner as his green role model. "Ted Turner is the one. He is the intellectual and practical leader of this new wave in conservation. I am a follower, albeit a passionate one."

A more recent self-made billionaire, Kaplan has launched two private conservation initiatives that he says mirror the objectives and functions of the Turner Endangered Species Fund.

One is an idea inspired by his daughter's interest in snakes called Project Orianne. Kaplan has purchased a large property in southern Georgia where, as with Turner's efforts on St. Phillips Island, staff biologists are reintroducing indigo snakes. Secondly, and based on his own fascination with the ecological role of big cats as apex predators, he has hired some of the leading field biologists in the world to spearhead his effort. Called the Panthera Corporation, it is aimed at protecting lions, tigers, jaguars, cheetahs, leopards, mountain lions, and snow leopards. Heading up the restoration effort (with a focus on field research and on expanding protected areas around the world) is George Schaller and zoologist Alan Rabinowitz.

"There's no doubt in my mind that the gauntlet he threw down with his contribution to the UN had an impact. And so, too, with the Turner Endangered Species Fund and his other foundations. He said people who have the good fortune of making money should use their wealth and power to do good during their lifetime. Anything else, he said, was considered a cop-out. His challenge turned heads. I know it did because it caught my attention," Kaplan says.

Specifically and poignantly, Turner had the courage to call upon people he considers to be his friends, guys like Bill Gates and Warren Buffett, telling them it's too late to wait until one is dead and leave your intentions up to heirs to carry out. "He said the world has big issues that we must contend with now—issues that might be unsolvable later," Kaplan explains. "That kind of appeal made a lot of sense to me. And the way he involves his children made me start thinking how I, too, can involve my family."

A generation younger than Turner, Kaplan is confident, soft-spoken, and possesses a similar, golden-boy mystique. He made his fortune based upon an ability to predict the locations of some vast veins of precious minerals. The New Yorker makes no apologies for his shrewd talents as a natural resource capitalist and notes that the proceeds have allowed him to try and do good on behalf of the environment.

Like Turner, his academic pedigree was not forged by pursuing an MBA at a prominent business school and then ascending the corporate ladder. This Oxford-educated liberal arts major studied history in England and wrote his PhD dissertation on a rather arcane subject: the relationship between tin and rubber markets in colonial Malaysia and the role of British politics in influencing the extraction of those raw materials.

Kaplan applied that knowledge and, using geological studies, was instrumental in uncovering some of the largest mineral deposits in South America. Taking his profits, and remembering Turner's admonishment to plutocrats, he searched for examples. He was intrigued by TESF.

Through Project Orianne, Kaplan tethers his daughter's name to meaningful conservation. The indigo snake has a wide range and is a voracious forager. It lives in habitats that people want to see preserved. Ninety percent of the habitat being protected for indigo snakes overlaps with the habitat necessary to protect imperiled gopher tortoises; the indigo snake also resides in forests suitable for longleaf pine restoration. It's the keystone species concept being repeated.

The Turner Endangered Species Fund, too, is studying the correlation between tortoises and snakes, as both species are slated for recovery at Avalon Plantation.

As for his cat work, led by Dr. Alan Rabinowitz, Kaplan would like to move faster with expansion of jaguar range, but he has encountered hurdles, just as Turner's enthusiasm for restoring gray wolves to the southern Rockies has been tempered by political resistance.

"I am sympathetic to his frustration with the slow pace of getting wolves back on the ground at his ranches in the Southwest," Kaplan says. "I built my own company on being impulsive, and he epitomizes [that same sensibility] with his record. Both of us believe in rapid decision-making and expect our associates to fall in behind us quickly."

In private business, he says, one can do that because the owner sets the tone and the agenda. In wildlife conservation, it doesn't work that way. "Let me correct that," he says. "It *rarely* works that way. I assumed at the beginning that everyone in the nongovernmental arena of wild-life conservation was a saint equipped with a halo and wing. I never expected to encounter so much bitchiness and backbiting and competition, detracting from the main objective. There are excellent groups out there, but sometimes the conservation movement is as dysfunctional as government can be. That's why I moved forward with founding Project Orianne and Panthera."

In his book *Outliers*, in which he makes specific reference to Turner, writer Malcolm Gladwell explores the ways that nonlinear experience serves as a presage to the rise of perceived genius. He talks about the importance of repetition—doing things over and over again, at least ten thousand times to lay the groundwork for accelerated mastery. And how collaboration with others is often the essence of great achievement. Two indispensable ingredients are natural talent and raw ambition. Certainly, Turner's uncanny percipient abilities, namely his knack for creatively marshaling—and *leveraging*—all available assets—provided fodder for Gladwell's research.

In another essay for the *New Yorker* magazine, Gladwell described Turner as fitting the classic profile of an entrepreneurially minded "predator" who is not a free-wheeling risk taker but a man exceptionally capable of assessing risks and perils in the hunt for opportunity. If Gladwell's analysis is correct, then the very same prowess Turner possesses for making money as a capitalist, he wields as a humanitarian and environmentalist in reading dangers in the road ahead. He is using his shrewd, risk-averse instincts to advise humanity to take a safer course.

Turner's rise by connecting the world via satellite beams is as unlikely as Kaplan moving from the don track at Oxford to launching a phenomenally successful hedge fund that hit the jackpot with a number of mineral ventures. Both appeared to bet everything they had on ideas that hit pay dirt. But Turner in fact is far more rationally calculating than his former public persona sometimes let on. Kaplan can relate to Turner in the way he applies business sense to saving nature.

"It's one thing to be the only one out there doing it. It's another when you inspire others who take what you've done and put their own spin on it," Phillips says. "I think what Mr. Kaplan is doing with Project Orianne and Panthera are hugely laudable efforts and they have the potential to do some real good. As someone who has spent some time around large carnivores, his cat project is most impressive."

Turner says he is flattered by Kaplan referencing him, and it is clear they share a similar philosophy. They like to act fast, they rue excessive regulation and the slow pace of how governments work, they see advantages in private property, and they believe that meaningful conservation will only persist if it has an underpinning of economic sustainability. In other words, they don't want to whimsically throw money at a problem. And they want their efforts to continue to produce dividends beyond their lifetimes. What Kaplan found attractive about the way Turner works is that Turner indulges his own intellectual curiosity by approaching philanthropy from a number of different angles, including finding top people in their fields to collaborate with. It was a style that spoke strongly to Kaplan's own humanities-style of learning—bringing together ideas across a variety of academic disciplines—that he had developed at Oxford.

"Looking at his work from a macro standpoint, I think it is one of the great inspirations in philanthropy," he says of Turner. "Although we may have some political disagreements, I think we are kindred in our intentions."

Pausing, Kaplan adds: "Turner's statements have sometimes seemed over the top. But whether you believe in an afterlife or not, he should be judged on his actions. If it were up to me, he's going to heaven. His proactive stands have made him an iconoclast, but an iconoclast worth emulating."

The recent book *Wildlands Philanthropy: The Great American Tradition* is a magnificent coffee table tome by Tom Butler that pays homage to eco-philanthropists mostly of the past, many of whom used their fortunes to protect land that, in many instances, was committed to public ownership.

The cost of the book was underwritten by Doug and Kris Tompkins, former outdoor clothing company executives who have set aside an unprecedented preserve in the Patagonian region of Chile. Their place is not far from Turner's estancias in Argentina. A sweet little foreword is offered by Tom Brokaw, who knows not only Turner and the Tompkinses but also Yvon Chouinard, founder of the outdoor clothing company Patagonia, a benefactor to conservation and promoter of One Percent for the Planet.

All are varying examples of a new era of eco-capitalists who are using their money to be more supportive of nature conservation. There is a passage in Brokaw's essay that most certainly is a direct reference to Turner. "I detect among my friends a growing consciousness to treat the land as they would a piece of rare art. That is, something not just to be collected but to be conserved and shared in its original, undiminished state. The rewards go well beyond whatever tax benefits are to be realized. A protected piece of nature is a legacy of deeply satisfying proportions."

Back, then, to prairie dogs. Turner says that environmentalism in the twenty-first century must necessarily be about overcoming long-held biases that created an adversarial relationship between humans and the land. Prairie dogs are a testament to the gulf that exists between cultural mythology and scientific knowledge. It "astounds him" to think how close an enlightened culture came to erasing a linchpin of prairie ecology without realizing the grave mistake it was making.

Dr. John Hoogland, known colloquially around the world as "Mr. Prairie Dog," and whose work was the subject of a documentary film made by Turner Broadcasting System, has devoted four decades to researching the much maligned animals. Only at the end of the twentieth century did science begin to achieve traction in reversing the hatred toward prairie dogs that had similarly permeated attitudes toward wolves, grizzly bears, sharks, and big cats around the world.

"Turner's been a quiet prairie dog ambassador but his impact has been gargantuan," Hoogland says. "If nothing else, his interest causes other influential people to pay attention."

The plight of prairie dogs can be extrapolated to other species, and they badly need a champion beyond biologists and environmental groups, says Hoogland. "With bison, he's gone off the grid of the beef industry. And he's been able to show that the same private property rights argument used to subdue nature can be leveraged in reverse to pursue biologically informed management." Hoogland praises the good work of nongovernmental, nonprofit organizations like The Nature Conservancy, which has helped restore prairie dogs on its own system of reserves, but Turner's work with TESF, and as a private individual, makes him unique.

A fascinating but obscure book, edited by Hoogland, *Conservation of the Black-Tailed Prairie Dog: Saving North America's Western Grasslands*, influenced Turner. Researchers Natasha Kotliar, Brian Miller, Richard Reading, and Susan Clark share Turner's observation of the prairie dogs' keystone role. "Some species sporadically and opportunistically capitalize on the benefits provided by prairie dog colony-sites, whereas others have stronger associations," they write. "Several species that associate closely with colony-sites are endangered or declining, so that a continued decline in prairie dog numbers might further imperil [them]."

There are a number of animals known to either depend on prairie dog colonies or closely associate with them. The first is the American bison, itself a keystone. Bison and prairie dogs evolved together on the short and mixed-grass prairie. Bison keep the grass lower and the habits of prairie dogs nurtured the kinds of nutritious grasses that bison liked to eat. Bison found prairie dog colonies attractive venues in which to wallow, rubbing off their wooly winter hair and covering themselves with dust to repel biting insects. In turn, the brutes left behind dung that fertilized the soil, churned by millions of sharp hooves tromping over it. Other species associated with prairie dog colonies include pronghorn (antelope), golden eagle, American kestrel, chestnut-collared longspur, ferruginous hawk, American badger, black-tailed jackrabbit, horned lark, killdeer, coyote, deer mouse, eastern cottontail, northern grasshopper mouse, striped skunk, thirteen-lined ground squirrel, white-tailed deer, eastern meadowlark, western meadowlark, horned lark, Texas horned lizard, ornate box turtle, prairie rattlesnake, western diamondback rattlesnake, western plains garter snake, Great Plains toad, tiger salamander, plains spadefoot toad, and Woodhouse's toad.

Mirroring the panoply of species that converge at water holes during the dry season in Africa, prairie dog colonies play the role of eco-centers. The dens of prairie dogs serve as burrows for other species. The way vegetation is pruned and foraged upon by prairie dogs yields a nutritious smorgasbord garden that is attractive to other grazers (including cattle). The engineering of dens leads to more water being trapped in the soil. And the short and mixed-grass prairie where prairie dogs establish settlements attracts predators and prey.

Phillips says that natural adaptation and survival of the fittest, when played out over millennia, create animals that are suitable for their setting.

For bison and pronghorn to persist over thousands of years, they had to have a way to outwit predators. They also had to endure harsh prairie conditions—periods of extreme cold and heat, variations in rainfall, and both finding adequate nutrition in plants and, by their habits, creating the natural salad bar.

There are three additional species associated with bison and prairie dog ecosystems—black-footed ferret, mountain plover, and burrowing owl. The fates of these species have tracked closely to prairie dogs. All three, plus the swift fox, have been beneficiaries of TESF. Climate change, Turner says, could radically alter the ability of landscapes to support species, making large chunks of secure habitat ever more valuable in the decades to come. His commitment to saving the black-footed ferret, Phillips says, serves as a classic case study.

⌒

Within the lexicon of imperiled species conservation, there is a phenomenon known as "The Lazarus Syndrome." It applies to species written off as extinct but then rediscovered. By the late 1970s, the US Fish and Wildlife Service, following years of fruitless searching to find just one animal, was preparing to formally declare the black-footed ferret an extinct species, joining company with the passenger pigeon, the ivory-billed woodpecker, and the dodo.

"Ferrets vanished primarily because of one singular factor: the persecution and rapid disappearance of black-tailed prairie dogs," Phillips says. "Prairie dogs are what ferrets eat. The loss of one causing the loss of the other is a perfect cause and effect relationship."

By grace of miracle, Wyoming earned a place on the Lazarus map, for it was in the badlands near Meeteetse that a remnant black-footed ferret was spotted by accident on September 26, 1981. As the tale goes, ranchers John and Lucille Hogg found a dead mink-like animal near the dog food dish of their blue heeler, Shep, who had killed it. Upon closer inspection by a taxidermist, the carcass was positively identified as a black-footed ferret. Researchers turned up more ferrets and suddenly the species had risen from the dead.

Over the last three decades, the Wyoming Game and Fish Department, along with other state, federal, and private partners, has done heroic work to get ferrets removed from life support. The goal is to have fifteen hundred ferrets back on the ground in ten or more free-ranging separate populations. The challenge is finding enough suitable prairie dog colonies where ferrets can be transplanted with modest expectations of survival.

Ferrets, too, have complex interactions with each other and they, like prairie dogs, are highly susceptible to sylvatic plague. It is the wildlife equivalent of bubonic plague, which left millions of humans dead during the Dark Ages. And while bubonic plague can be cured if diagnosed and treated early enough in humans, sylvatic plague is a death sentence for prairie dogs and ferrets.

Establishing ten different ferret populations is dependent upon having ten large self-sustaining prairie dog colonies. To decrease their vulnerability to a catastrophic disease outbreak, the Fish and Wildlife Service wants them to exist in geographical separation.

That's where TESF comes in. Turner has voluntarily offered to let two or more of his ranches with prairie dog colonies serve as ferret-release sites. At Vermejo Park Ranch, TESF's Dustin Long also has worked closely with the Fish and Wildlife Service to propagate ferrets at a captive breeding facility. In essence, Turner is not only offering ferrets a safe haven but also he is using the ranches to serve as a platform to assist the federal government and ultimately restore ferrets so they can be removed from the Endangered Species list.

"I know that when Ted Turner first said in print that prairie dogs were going to share the range with his bison, some considered it heresy. In fact, if you can believe this, it has practically been illegal in some states, because of laws passed by legislatures, to move ahead with protecting prairie dogs on one's own land," Hoogland says.

"Prairie dogs, which are mentioned in Lewis and Clark's journals, haven't enjoyed wildlife status, yet they are one of the most important prairie animal there is. They've been grouped within the same category of rats, locusts, and mosquitoes. That's how deeply engrained the cultural bias against them has been."

Turner knows his ranch managers are in a tough spot when they go into nearby towns for supplies and interact with locals who still believe the only good use of prairie dogs is as target practice for sighting in hunting rifles. Some of those who partake in shooting prairie dogs for sport refer to them colloquially as "pink mist," which is what happens to them when they are struck by a rifle bullet.

"Ninety percent of ranchers in the West will tell you they hate prairie dogs," Hoogland says. "The two most common justifications they invoke are that prairie dogs compete with their livestock for forage, which is partially true, and that cows break their legs when they step into the holes of prairie dog dens, which is a tall tale based on Spartan anecdotal information and is, in fact, very, very uncommon."

He adds, "Ranchers Smith, Jones, and Nelson will tell you that prairie dogs are a scourge because that's what their daddies told them, and their grandfathers and great-grandfathers before them. It is a perception that got formed and reinforced over 150 years. Old beliefs die hard, even when they are misinformed. I don't expect that we'll see a major sea change in attitude over the next ten years but a more enlightened understanding is slowly taking hold."

He notes that while prairie dog colonies can reduce the amount of forage available to cattle, studies show that cattle, like bison historically, actually are attracted to forage around colonies at certain times of year, especially spring green-up. Plants there are not only nutritious and tasty, they are available to cattle earlier.

"When Ted speaks of prairie dogs' right to exist and points out their value, some call it blasphemy," Hoogland adds. "But you know what? Ted Turner is right in looking past that, and he has a lot of courage."

A corollary to Phillips's question—what is the consequence of losing a species—is this: What is the consequence of intervening to save a species?

—~—

In this middle of nowhere, standing in the city center of a prairie dog town, and with the footprints of Turner visible in the soil next to the other animal tracks, one has to wonder: How did Turner get here?

How did a boy, emotionally estranged from his parents, raised in a strict prep school, forced to leave college prematurely, having embraced free-market capitalism to make billions in advertising and media, becoming creatively adept at thriving in the city, a pathological wanderer, preternaturally wary of trusting in intimacy—how did a person like this find his way to this intellectual terrain?

When the question is posed directly to Turner, he says, "This is where I always wanted to be. I just didn't know it."

"It's difficult to predict where fate leads a person," Phillips says, describing the day when he first presented Turner the idea of creating an entity to push recovery of imperiled species.

Turner was intrigued after Phillips prepared a white paper showing how Turner's portfolio of lands could accomplish what government typically doesn't. "Ted," Phillips said, "you could give voice to imperiled species that have no voice and establish a badly needed example of the importance of private land based on two simple but critical notions: restoration is an alternative to extinction and coexistence with the federal Endangered Species Act."

Once Turner agreed to back it financially and *emotionally*, he convinced Phillips to leave his government service job. Phillips proposed that they call it "The Noah Project." It was a name that Turner rejected because he did not want it to have overt religious connotations.

"Ted was adamant. He said he had nothing against the Bible. He believed, and rightly so, that caring about the plight of endangered species should appeal to anyone," Phillips says.

Together with Turner, Jane Fonda, and Beau, they settled on the "Turner Endangered Species Fund" and hit the ground running. Turner was excited about the prospect of having wolves on the Flying D and Phillips told him the only way they would get there is if they happened to wander there out of Yellowstone, which he said was likely.

The blueprint for TESF in the late 1990s was ambitious, and given that Turner was planning to generously underwrite it to the tune of millions of dollars annually, not unrealistic. From sea level in South Carolina to the nearly fourteen-thousand-foot peaks in the Sangre de Cristos on the border of Colorado and New Mexico, from Bozeman to Patagonia and Tierra del Fuego in Argentina, Turner issued a simple mandate: "Identify species that need a helping hand and be that hand."

Phillips established contacts with his friends in the Fish and Wildlife Service to make Turner's ranches possibly available for restoration of California condors. Down at Avalon Plantation, they planned to use part of a picturesque wetland that resembles a French landscape painting as a rookery for endangered wood storks.

Phillips knew that for endangered species, by definition time is of the essence. Between 1998 and 2002 as the Fund grew by leaps and bounds, the vision of private land as beachheads of security for countless imperiled species came into inspiring focus.

But then the AOL Time Warner deal happened, and when it turned into a fiasco by August 2002, Turner had to scrap his plans. Phillips released 40 percent of his staff, talented scientists who had become important friends, and for over a year he and Turner considered daily how the Fund could emerge from the crisis in a manner that honored the spirit and intent of its founding.

Consider: the $10 million that Turner lost every day over two years would have paid for a lot of things. Just a day's worth of losses might have funded a proposed decade-long plan to restore California condors to New Mexico. With the Turner Foundation poised to channel huge sums of money to TESF, the tentacles of recovery could have reached the Kamchatka Peninsula—the geyser-filled area known as "the Yellowstone of Russia"—where efforts were under way to safeguard some of the last wild salmon runs in the world, to the jungles of Rwanda in a big way where wild gorillas are hanging on by a thread, to saving the American chestnut tree, stopping the loss of amphibians, and pollinators.

The aftermath of the AOL Time Warner stock collapse was a time of personal and professional soul searching for Phillips and Beau Turner. They began exploring how the availability of Turner's land—more than his money—could make a difference in conservation.

After the AOL Time Warner crisis passed, and Turner cut his ties with the conglomerate (stabilizing his net worth at just shy of $2 billion), Phillips, Beau Turner and Turner Foundation president Mike Finley established an aggressive agenda, albeit retooled. "We came out of the AOL mess with a sharpened focus. We decided to leverage Ted's investment to achieving not only the best outcomes we could, for the amounts of money involved, but Ted made it clear he wanted to lead by example," Phillips says. "Of course, the geographical spread of his lands and his ethic are assets worth more than any amount of money."

Long before TESF was even established, the first two imperiled species that Turner lent a helping hand to were loggerhead sea turtles nesting on the shore at St. Phillips Island and a group of indigo snakes and rare squirrels that were released there back in the 1980s. Those efforts coincided with him putting two of the first major conservation easements in the country on the island and nearby Hope Plantation.

Along with indigo snakes and squirrels, plus prairie dogs, ferrets, and swift foxes, the Turner Endangered Species Fund is involved, across the country, with pioneering private restoration of red-cockaded woodpeckers, desert bighorn sheep, gray and Mexican wolves, westslope cutthroat and Rio Grande trout, Aplomado falcons, Chiricahua leopard frogs, long-leaf pine, willow riparian ecosystems, bolson tortoises, and hundreds of other mammals, birds, fish, reptiles, and amphibians—as well as thousands of species of plants, insects, and native microorganisms—that find shelter on Turner properties. He also has welcomed grizzlies to his land in Montana and supported research on Tasmanian devils in Australia, an effort to restore European wisent (bison) in Poland and Russia, and guanacos in Argentina.

In 1987, ecologist William Newmark published a paper in *Nature* that took wildlife managers of public nature preserves by storm. He noted that even in the cases of big national parks like Yellowstone, development pressures from the outside were converting them into ever-shrinking islands; current conservation strategies were insufficient. And in a follow-up paper in *Conservation Biology*, he noted that twenty-nine mammal populations had vanished from western national parks.

Newmark is revered as a thinker. He was asked to take a look at the last twenty years and conjecture on where Turner fits into the big picture. "Private landowners can play a very important role in landscape-wide conservation strategies."

Turner's lands function as fountainheads of life, and prairie dogs provide the most vivid demonstration of Turner's contributions to restoration ecology. In less than fifteen years, Turner went from having around twenty thousand prairie dogs on less than one thousand acres—inherited when he bought his properties—to more than a quarter of a million spread across ten thousand acres. The notable population growth was the result of a well-considered restoration effort that involved translocating nearly fifteen thousand prairie dogs to unoccupied habitat. In typical Turner fashion, the project is the largest restoration effort ever conceived for the species.

"It wasn't long after Dad moved full steam ahead with bison that he realized from reading natural history studies that prairie dogs needed to be factored into the management equation. In many places they go together," Beau Turner says one evening on a porch in South Dakota. "Those little animals found a soft spot in Dad's heart and when he gets settled on a cause, he refuses to give up."

For Turner, it *is* personal: "I know what it means to be an underdog. I know how difficult it can be when the status quo isn't ready to accept the ideas you espouse. Until you are vindicated, it can be a lonely struggle. Prairie dogs are the ultimate underdogs. We as a species have treated them horrendously, as worthless pests, and we almost wiped them out, just as we almost exterminated bison. They are pretty amazing and important creatures, but it is the prairie where they live that has paid a huge price."

Heroic intentions aside, Ted Turner will be the first to acknowledge that life is full of surprises. Nature is full of contradictions that test human patience and mental aptitude. Certainly, there's something about prairie dogs that defies pat generalities.

The flats of Vermejo Park Ranch in New Mexico can be breezy and hot. It's one of the places where Turner intends to proceed with expediting both wind and solar energy development. His largest solar array has hundreds of thousands of panels. In recent years, as the wind blasts through, the ranch has also produced something else: Huge dust storms have caused townsfolk living nearby in tiny Maxwell to complain. The airborne dirt has been catapulted off the surface of bare ground within Vermejo's expanding prairie dog colony. Turner's general manager of western properties, Russell Miller, talks about the discussions held over the mandate of the Turner Endangered Species Fund and the for-profit motivations of Turner Enterprises.

The conundrum presented by the prairie dogs, whose numbers have had a deleterious impact on vegetative ground cover, presents real world problems known to other western ranchers. Turner, Miller says, roots himself on the progressive side of reality and sees the problem not as a setback but as a learning opportunity, and one that will play out over years and seasons.

"In many ways," Miller says, "the challenges at Vermejo represent a perfect storm." Previous unintentional overgrazing at the ranch by previous cattle operators and then with Turner's bison, combined with years of drought and the desire by the Turner organization to expand prairie dog numbers, have created immediate ecological problems that must be addressed.

Mark Kossler, Vermejo's manager and a truly progressive thinker about the science of sustainable rangeland in the West, notes that on pasture where prairie dogs have proliferated, the amount of cool season grassland has declined from 10 percent to 1 percent. That's a huge decrease.

It has necessitated that those pastures be given a rest. Bison have been pulled from the premises and moved to other parts of the ranch. "It's kind of interesting and ironic, isn't it, that here you have two keystone species that evolved together on the plains—bison and prairie dogs—and in order to have one, we have to temporarily remove the other," he says.

Of course, historically bison would have simply migrated to more accommodating range. But the West of the twenty-first century is defined by land ownership patterns and social sensibilities that call for proactive management schemes by livestock operations like Vermejo's.

When precipitation returns and those grasslands show recovery, bison most likely will return to the portion of the ranch reserved for prairie dog recovery, but for now they are temporarily exiled. And, in the meantime, Turner approved something that cut against his desires.

Dustin Long, the on-the-ground biologist at Vermejo working with prairie dogs and helping to set the stage for establishing a wild population of black-footed ferrets, has strategically employed nonlethal methods—and lethal only as a last resort—to continue the spread of a colony that covers nearly eight thousand acres.

Rangeland systems are dynamic, and in order for humans to reside on them, hard choices have to be made. For Miller, it comes down to the tenets that guided him nearly a quarter century ago when Turner tasked him to find properties that would be suitable for holding bison: Land. Soil. Grass. Water. Where one becomes lacking, it affects the others. The dilemma at Vermejo, however, is a microcosm within the macro picture of the West, particularly a West that, according to the best scientific models, is likely to soon be distressed by altered precipitation patterns and potentially rising temperatures due to climate change.

The interior of the West, from the middle part of this century forward (if not sooner), is projected to encounter less precipitation, less snowpack in the mountains, likely spottier rainfall and hotter average temperatures. The higher the average temperature, the more precipitation that is required to stave off desiccation in the landscape. The more that landscapes broil, the less cold season grass, and the less grass the more barren soil and dust storms. Where prairie dogs and bison fit into the altered future is still unknown. Generally speaking, the bigger the landscapes that species have access to, the easier it is for them to survive. Of course, the still-unanswered question is whether agrarians on private land will ever be willing to share their pasture with prairie dogs.

On the other hand, there are many scientists who believe that, given their resiliency on the plains, bison will provide far more advantages than cattle. Turner figures that the more bison that are out there, the more likely that the people raising them will be forward thinking, which means greater tolerance for prairie dogs and, in turn, better conditions for other forms of prairie wildlife. "Ted finds these kinds of discussions to be enormously stimulating and fascinating," Phillips says.

When Turner acquired Vermejo in the 1990s, about seventy-five hundred prairie dogs occupied about five hundred acres. Today, more than one hundred twenty thousand prairie dogs occupy over eight thousand acres. And yet, Vermejo lags behind Bad River and the Z-Bar Ranch in Kansas in the number of prairie dogs it supports.

Conservationists have cheered Turner's prairie dog program and the benefits it has brought to wildlife, including providing some of the best habitat in the West for black-footed ferret reintroduction. But range specialists affiliated with the livestock industry have joined neighboring ranchers in condemning prairie dogs.

"Prairie dogs challenge conventional wisdom that native species always live in balance with their habitats," said the late Joe Truett, a respected ecologist who had been TESF's senior expert on the ground in the southern Rockies before he died in 2011. "Over time, they may actually abuse rangeland by measures that, for many decades, have been embraced by conservationists. In particular, they reduce the condition of the range and in so doing, often dramatically lower its ability to sustain even prairie dogs or any other grazers. Unawareness of this leads to nonsensical statements by some conservationists such as 'We need more prairie dogs and fewer cattle because cattle overgraze the land.'"

Turner is a booster of prairie dogs, Truett says, but his advocacy doesn't override his better judgment. In fact, Truett says that all land managers, be they private or public, must prescribe what they want the range conditions to be. It's not a question of whether humans should intervene and tinker.

At Bad River Ranch, Honness, Phillips, Truett, and Beau Turner were presented with a conundrum as they attempted to restore swift foxes live-captured in Wyoming and Colorado and transplanted in holding facilities prior to release. Swift foxes represent little threat to humans or livelihoods, a point made as TESF worked to obtain cooperative agreements with dozens of different federal and state agencies and private landowners.

"Swift foxes don't eat livestock, they don't show up around henhouses on farms, they don't take down game animals, and they are definitely not a safety risk to people," Phillips says. "They eat mice and voles and prairie dogs, and they should be regarded as friends to ranchers who want a natural form of rodent control."

They also have two formidable predators: coyotes and, to a lesser extent, golden eagles. After acclimating to their new surroundings, transplanted foxes were released from protective enclosures positioned astride of prairie dog colonies. Slowly, they started establishing dens, and eventually a few mated pairs produced litters of kits. However, coyotes preyed upon foxes with abandon. Their survival rate also was affected by another variable: the height of grass. The taller the brome, the less of a clear sightline they had for spotting coyotes and evading them.

So Honness and Phillips had an idea: Enlist bison to mow down the grass and eliminate the knee-to-waist-high patches that gave coyotes places to lie in ambush. The experiment, which involved killing coyotes to reduce their density in swift fox reintroduction areas and moving bison through those same areas to graze intensively and keep the grass short, started paying dividends.

When the swift fox experiment began, Phillips said, "We had to knock the hell out of the coyotes at the beginning. Coyotes have tremendous reproductive potential, however and the amount of resources required to keep their numbers subdued is like pouring water into a bucket with a hole in it."

Further, because Bad River offers highly adaptive coyotes ideal habitat, it was clear that coyote control would have to be perpetual. The decision was made to halt coyote control and leave foxes to make it on their own. It was a valuable lesson learned.

Historically, the prairie was a dynamic system with ebbs and flows of wildlife distribution that followed the hooves of bison and the expansions and subtractions in the size and number of prairie dog colonies, he explains.

"Without large numbers of nomadic bison, we've lost an important element. You can try to replicate it with bison on a big ranch, and you could emulate the grazing patterns of bison if you were a cattle rancher, but it requires vigilance. And more than that, if you are a cattle rancher it demands that you re-examine some of the things you are doing, including the killing of prairie dogs. A lot of stockgrowers out there aren't averse to having swift foxes, but they're worried that prairie dogs will cost them money."

In the end, given a cost-benefit analysis, coyotes may ultimately win. Of course, if there were wolves at Bad River, there would be fewer coyotes and more swift foxes, but it would not please surrounding ranchers. To make it clear, Turner has no intention of advocating that wolves be restored to South Dakota. Although if wild lobos from the northern Rockies found their way on their own to Bad River or Vermejo Park Ranch in Colorado, he would welcome them.

—◦—

Turner says he's intrigued by the level of informed debate he is hearing from members of his staff. In the past, many such disputes would have resulted in extreme action one way or the other—to the benefit of livestock and the detriment of wildlife, or vice versa.

"I don't want an organization of yes-men," he said. "Sometimes there simply isn't a definitive answer. If a ranch manager or biologist doesn't know the answer immediately, that's okay, but I want them to go look for an answer, and arrive at a conclusion as honestly as they can. And then we need to move forward, not sit on our hands. . . ."

The dividends of prairie dogs are irrefutable, Truett said. "If we, and by 'we' I mean the American people, can embrace restoring large areas with native species like prairie dogs, we will have demonstrated our willingness to forgo yet more blind pursuit of things that have huge downsides for the ecological diversity, benefits and aesthetic appreciation native species provide." He also acknowledged that by employing bison as a replacement for cattle—a species that evolved with prairie dogs—Turner has offered a third way of thinking about the age-old polemic.

By design, Turner has positioned his lands to be fulcrums for discussing big ideas. Even when he's not on the premises, he's allowing the ranches to serve as backdrops for tantalizing and controversial discussions.

In mid-2000, a group of leading conservationists gathered at the Ladder Ranch to discuss a topic called "post-Pleistocene rewilding" and to focuses on what would happen if large animals that disappeared from North America thirteen thousand years ago were brought back—Ice Age creatures such as woolly mammoths and mastodons, giant sloths, saber-tooth tigers, camels, cheetahs, and an assortment of other creatures.

"It was all purely conceptual revolving around the concept, 'what if?'" Phillips says. "It was brainstorming with ecologists whose whole careers have been spent thinking about extinctions and how ecosystems operate, what we've lost, and how you put things back together again."

Fireworks erupted when an essay was published in *Nature* written by Josh Donlan from the Department of Evolutionary Biology at Cornell University, and a distinguished list of others. The essay proposed that people think about animals that have vanished and replacing them with rough equivalents, i.e., bringing African cheetahs to the Great Plains in place of vanished American cheetahs, the predators responsible for turning pronghorn antelope into such fleet runners.

"This 'Pleistocene rewilding' would be achieved through a series of carefully managed ecosystem manipulations using closely-related species as proxies for extinct large vertebrates, and would change the underlying premise of conservation biology from managing extinction to actively restoring natural processes," they wrote.

The media, however, interpreted it another way. Tinged with snide sensationalism, some reporters implied that Turner was behind a plot to put long-extinct, lethal meat-eating animals back into the West. Calls for interviews flooded in, leaving Turner's staff in Atlanta struggling to confront the hysteria. Eventually, it blew over, but there was still a lingering impression of Turner as an eccentric mischief maker, even though he never attended the Ladder meeting.

It turned out to be much ado about nothing. "Hell," Turner said, bemused, "it sure led to a lively discussion for a while, didn't it?"

"On a very basic level, what people don't understand is that Ted already has engaged in rewilding of a creature that has ancestral roots in the Pleistocene, and that's the bison," Phillips says. "If he could, he would have reintroduced another, the California condor. The whole point was that conservation biology has been placed in a reactionary posture where we are always on the verge of writing an obituary for species, seldom are we given a chance to get them out of the emergency room."

TESF operates on big physical landscapes and theoretical, sometimes controversial, canvases. The paramount conundrum and one related to the issue of rewilding is this question: Restore to what? What *period* in time? What ecological condition? What result that can be sustainable and replicable, its results non-fleeting in the twenty-first century?

How far back does one wish to go—to the end of the nineteenth century? Pre–Lewis and Clark? Before Columbus, European diseases, the arrival of the horse? Or maybe one aspires to recede further in time to say, the end of the Pleistocene Epoch after the major continental glaciers retreated into the north, opening up more places for wildlife to disperse?

Of course, if one really wanted to be radical, Phillips says, you could think Jurassic and Triassic, isolating the DNA extracted from a fossilized bone or frozen in a piece of amber, and attempt to genetically engineer a dinosaur.

Ruminating about options is clever and mind-blowing, especially over a couple of glasses of wine, but Phillips says temporal regression isn't what Turner is after, at least as it pertains to a specific year; rather, the answer for "*Restore to what?*" lies in determining what land condition and level of ecosystem *function* is possible.

Land, after all, isn't a clean blank canvas; it comes replete with texture, and is the accumulation of all the previous decisions made by humans who have lived on it.

Turner has the means to pour a lot of money down an *Alice in Wonderland* rabbit hole. He could isolate himself behind the veiled curtains of various terrestrial Xanadus. He could pretend that the rules of society do not apply to him.

"Ted isn't naïve, he certainly isn't a recluse, and he's not running away from the obligation he feels toward the larger world. If anything, it's the opposite," Phillips says. "He wants to leave things better than he found them. He has done more for humanity with an environmental focus than any other person, living or dead. Is his ego in play? Sure it is."

❧

Turner aims to be the first to achieve private-land, conservation milestones that many have said were impossible. "More than that," Turner says, "I want to do it to inspire, to demonstrate what can be done if you are willing to try. If other landowners feel motivated, then they too can apply whatever knowledge we've gathered or lessons learned and make their own contribution."

Phillips remembers congratulating Turner at the outset of a novel approach for restoring red-cockaded woodpeckers, a waning denizen of southeastern pine forests. The restoration project, led by biologist Greg Hagan, is now held up as a prototype for private-public collaboration and is substantiating the value of the US Fish and Wildlife Service's "Safe Harbor" program. Safe Harbor provides incentives for private landowners that welcome or tolerate imperiled species on their land.

"That's great, Mike," Turner said, "but we commonly do things first, before anyone else, whenever it's possible."

Not long ago, Turner was at the Ladder Ranch standing next to manager Steve Dobrott, the former federal quail biologist. Turner held the equivalent of a dinosaur in his hand.

It was a bolson tortoise (*Gopherus flavomarginatus*), also known as *tortuga grande* in Mexico, and mentioned specifically in Josh Donlan's controversial essay in *Nature*. It had likely been gone from the United States for millennia. "For all the fears associated with Pleistocene rewilding, here was an example of the real thing, a relict animal that had winked out in the Chihuahuan Desert and Ted was giving it a new home," Phillips says. "It's a pretty cool creature, it's not a threat to anybody, and now it has a new champion. How many times do you have a chance to bring a species back from the edge of oblivion?"

Resembling the desert tortoise of the Mohave Desert, bolsons were only discovered by science in Mexico in 1959. Relatives of the famed Galapagos tortoise, it is thought that, at most, the number of wild tortoises in Mexico (their last stronghold) is in the thousands.

In 2006, twenty-six tortoises were brought to the Ladder from a captive breeding facility, the Audubon Appleton-Whittell Research Ranch, in Elgin, Arizona. Within five years, the Fund had perfected husbandry and breeding techniques and the captive population included over two hundred animals. Reintroductions to restore wild populations through the species' prehistoric ranges may soon be under way.

"To those of us who have worked in biology as a career, you dream of having an opportunity to do something like this just once," Dobrott says. "Ted is making them happen all the time. I don't think he really understands the impact he is having and the potential that he has to create a dovetail effect."

As Turner hunted quail with Finley, Wirth, and NBC newsman emeritus Tom Brokaw at the Ladder, Dobrott and I peeled away.

Just beyond our drainage is another draw that contains a bubbling spring, a harbor for imperiled Chiricahua leopard frogs. Further, the tranquil meander of Las Animas Creek has been a venue for bringing back native Rio Grande cutthroat trout.

West in the Gila National Forest, the famous American conservationist, Aldo Leopold, worked to have the Gila's spectacular interior protected as the nation's first wilderness, so that future generations would know and share the aboriginal wonder that would become ever in smaller supply.

Leopold may also have been motivated by penance. Years before, as a young US Forest Service ranger, he had shot and killed one of the last known wild wolves in New Mexico, a mother lobo with young pups at her side. His own hand, he was forced to reconcile, had been on the trigger of a culturally supported annihilation of a species. Standing over the mortally wounded predator, he watched the green fire of existence fade from her eyes.

Mexican wolves today are back in the Gila. And a captive breeding facility, sanctioned by the US government, resides at a discreet location on the Ladder as part of a unique private-public partnership.

Where the boundary of the Ladder Ranch ends, the Elephant Butte Reservoir, a vast artificial lake holding back the Rio Grande River, appears. On the other side of the water, a former cattle operation, the Armendaris, entered into Turner's portfolio in 1994.

Unruly, its topography includes an island mountain sub-range, the Fra Cristobals, where the Fund, with special oversight from Turner's youngest son, Beau, is committed to reestablishing a population of imperiled desert bighorn sheep. Success sometimes requires killing cougars to minimize predation pressure. "This isn't Disneyland out here. Sometimes you have to make tough calls. You have to decide what you value more," says Armendaris manager Tom Waddell.

Skirting the scorching bottom of the desert floor is the four-hundred-year-old pathway, El Camino Real de Terra Adentro. A special subsection of the trail is Jornado del Muerto, or "Journey of the Dead Man." A sea of mesquite, cacti, and playas during wetter climates, the one-hundred-mile-long corridor, despite its appearance, is actually more alive than it seems.

"It's not a desert of death, despite its reputation," Waddell says. "Ted has proved it to be otherwise."

Along Jornado del Muerto, Turner is actively working with the Peregrine Fund and the US Fish and Wildlife Service to recover the endangered aplomado falcon. Nearby, a jumble of ancient volcanic lava also is home to a world-renowned bat cave, a small prairie dog colony, and a small commercial bison herd. All are under Waddell's vigilant watch.

To enhance the baseline understanding of the ranch and the Chihuahuan Desert ecosystem, Waddell has chaperoned no fewer than one hundred different scientific research projects dealing with everything from mountain lion predation on bighorn sheep to prairie dog survival and assessing how many different kinds of neotropical birds use the ranch seasonally. It's become a living laboratory for budding university ecologists to learn from seasoned veterans.

In New Mexico, Turner is proactively involved in helping to restore species to their native habitat. In Montana, he's been more aggressive.

The Flying D has become home to the largest single pack of wolves in the Lower 48 states. More than twenty members strong, it has established its territory in the ranch interior, not far from where Phillips cut wolf tracks long ago.

"Wolves found their way here," Val Asher, Turner's resident wolf biologist, says. "If you're a wolf, this is probably the closest thing to paradise."

Wolves, however, are costing Turner money. Through active monitoring of the animals since 2003, biologists estimate that wolves have killed several dozen bison. In market terms the combined value of those animals is significant, particularly if they were owned by mom and pop ranchers.

A percentage of those losses is just called the "cost of doing business." But there is also grumbling from those who operate the lucrative guiding and hunting operation at the Flying D. Despite a cost of $14,000 or more for individual hunters seeking the chance to harvest a trophy bull elk, on average more than thirty hunters a year partake.

And while there is debate over whether a decrease in the number of large elk bull has occurred since the arrival of wolves, the number of wapiti overall still fits within the desired population parameters of between fourteen hundred and twenty-two hundred elk.

"A few other ranchers in the West have exhibited tolerance for wolves, but none has demonstrated the patience that Ted has," Asher says. "He's been willing to accept losses of commodity animals and allow time to collect more data before any kind of compensatory action is taken." By compensatory, she means pulling the trigger of a gun.

Asher is lean, hardy, and prescient. Hired by Turner at Phillips's recommendation, she cannot stand accused of creating a rose-colored picture of *Canis lupus*. At her hand dozens of wolves have died. Prior to this job, she worked under a collaborative arrangement between the US Fish and Wildlife Service and a division of the US Department of Agriculture called Wildlife Services.

Should the day ever arrive when Turner gives the go-ahead to reduce wolf numbers on the Flying D, Asher's recommendation will be to strategically remove certain pack members. Such a strategy could be carried out with cooperation from the guides and outfitters who stalk elk and it could be based upon science and the standards of fair chase.

In 2012, three wolves were shot and killed just outside the Flying D by hunters in full compliance with Montana's big game laws. Turner didn't rue the losses. He accepted that they were roaming beyond his protection the moment they crossed the ranch's boundary.

Turner's own son, Beau, an avid sportsman, is in favor of culling the size of the pack.

Meanwhile, the intelligence being gathered at the Flying D is significant, Asher says. While wolf research being conducted in Yellowstone National Park, at two million acres, represents the largest effort of its kind, the work at the Flying D is novel because the tracking of pack behavior is happening on a piece of private land large enough to contain an entire pack.

"I don't see this as an either/or. What if I want to grow bison and wolves?" Turner asks. "How much would I be willing to pay to have a healthy wolf pack on the ranch?"

He doesn't have to say it, but his thoughts are drifting to the cougars and bears turned loose at Avalon Plantation a generation ago—to that failed experiment. Here he has a laboratory that has been likened to an American version of the Serengeti and he's able to do what no one else before him has.

Yes, he admits, there are advantages to having lots of money, but Turner points out, as he has often, that he has no intention of throwing it away. "I'm making an investment in wolf carrying capacity," he says. "Wolves had been gone from the ranch for what, a century, after living here for at least ten thousand years? I'm not in a rush to make them leave again."

Kevin Honness loved working for Ted Turner, and being challenged by Mike Phillips to leave his own mark in science. He succeeded. His contribution wasn't earth-shattering, but it was transformative. Together with his wife Kristy Bly-Honness, he and some of Turner's ranch managers and understudies perfected a technique for humanely live-capturing and transplanting prairie dogs into former rangeland to recolonize.

A few months after Phillips and Honness spent several days together with Ted and Beau Turner in the field visiting swift fox release sites and counting the acreage of prairie dogs, Phillips and Honness strolled along the Bad River.

Honness said that tracing the water's path on foot and, better yet, via kayak or canoe during higher water, was akin to cracking open a journal of geological and paleontological history. Routinely, he would find aboriginal arrowheads in the uplands and remains of bison. He felt connected to the current. And, on a couple of occasions, he was able to share his passion for exploring with Turner.

"Let me know if you find anything interesting," Turner had told him. "I'm always excited to hear what you turn up."

During the early summer, following a winter of heavy prairie snow and spring rain, Honness dropped Phillips an e-mail. He was excited to be floating the Bad River at high water through the riparian forest. It was a wildlife lover's dream, a true safari experience, he told Phillips. Honness was thrilled to be restoring the swift fox and cataloguing their interaction with prairie dogs, making his own contribution to the understanding of prairie ecology.

A few weeks later, Honness and a fresh crop of college interns who joined the swift fox and prairie dog projects set out to float the Bad River below the field station. The students were in a canoe and Honness in a one-man kayak. At a bend in the river, things went horribly wrong. Somehow, Honness got swept into a hydraulic created by a fallen tree. He became submerged and drowned.

He was just forty-five. The Turner organization was stunned by his death. An easterner, it had been his dream to live and work in the West. "He was an impressive young man," Turner said. "I always enjoyed the conversations I had with him. He did some great work. We had a lot of fun in the field."

Phillips is normally a stoic. But in speaking about Honness, his voice cracks. And he says the biologist's impact lives on, in the insights he gleaned from figuring out how to restore swift fox. The data have been published and are being used to guide conservation efforts elsewhere.

"These are the ways that people establish legacies," Phillips says, paraphrasing a maxim that he hears often from Turner. "What you did in the past becomes passé. The things you do that can continue to be applied are how you reach into the future. That's one kind of legacy, another is family."

In the book she wrote with Thane Maynard and Gail Hudson, *Hope for Animals and Their World: How Endangered Species Are Being Rescued from the Brink*, noted primatologist Jane Goodall places Turner within a category of conservationists that she calls "pathfinders." They are people who refuse to accept that species are doomed. She cited a recent study produced by the International Union for the Conservation of Nature that concluded at least a quarter of mammal species are headed toward extinction in the near future. "And tragically, for many, there may be little that can be done," Goodall notes. "There is an old maxim; 'Where there is life, there is hope.' For the sake of our children we must not give up, we must continue to fight to save what is left and restore that which is despoiled. We must support those valiant men and women who are out there doing just that."

CHAPTER NINE

Bloodlines

"I am proud to be an American and I love making money, but money alone can't buy happiness or ensure success or improve your self-esteem. You know what? Generosity can. Given the problems we are facing, we can't allow people in the top 1 percent to barricade themselves away and not acknowledge that serious human pain and suffering exists on a massive scale in the world. But we can alleviate much of it if we all rally together. Every one of us can be a hero to somebody. All we need to do is step forward."

—TED TURNER

ALL FIVE TURNER CHILDREN HAVE SEEN THEIR FATHER CRY—HE BE-comes so maudlin sometimes that he'll weep during nature documentaries—but never so hard as when he summoned them together for a meeting of the Turner Foundation board of directors and said he had let them down.

In 2002, as his finances were crashing toward their lowest point, necessitating that the foundation invoke a temporary freeze on charitable giving, he accepted responsibility for what he believed was a colossal failure.

Turner himself could not have known, at what was the lowest ebb in his life, that the following decade would bring some of his most satisfying achievements; his complete awakening, if you could call it that, involved opening himself up in his personal human relationships. By 2002, the Turner Foundation had left a mark by broadening the diversity of the environmental movement. Turner's children had reason to be proud; they weren't mere voyeurs.

But some of them may have been fraught with uncertainty, intuiting that their father had fallen into a funk, that his plight could potentially domino down to the philanthropic efforts, nullifying the forward progress. They should have known better.

Led by their father's rally, the foundation has been involved in some groundbreaking initiatives to unite millions of entrepreneurs involved with the restaurant and hotel industry to realize enormous cost savings by being more fuel efficient in their operations and utilizing fewer resources. Yes, Turner gained a second—or perhaps a third—mighty wind in his sails after that long night at the Flying D. It's the fulfillment of another desire.

⌁

During the years when he was building CNN and TBS, Turner read the writings of Andrew Carnegie, who warned it was a mistake to leave heirs with vast amounts of money without a sense of obligation to give back to society. He also attended a seminar on philanthropy in Washington, DC. He sat next to a man, a retired executive, who, like Turner, had explored a number of different options and settled on the family foundation model as a way to approach charity. Both men, a generation apart, had heard horror stories about how children with trust funds squandered the resources. The executive, whom Turner doesn't name, explained to him that a foundation enabled him to get emotionally closer to his children, to share a common interest in doing good. He also knew his relationship with his offspring, impacted by his own emotional distance, could use some mending.

What Turner heard appealed to him, so he called his children together in a meeting and told them what he had in mind. "I wanted them to realize that even a decent chunk of money can get lost quickly if you're not careful. This might sound kind of cornball, but I've honestly felt good all my life giving money away. It's a feeling I wanted them to know. And remember, you don't have to be rich to know the feeling. America is the most charity-minded nation on Earth."

Turner's first experiment with a foundation, the Better World Society, ended in 1991 after a six-year run. It had been a vehicle to help underwrite the cost of expensive environmental programming at TBS and its sister channels. The effort enabled Turner to assemble an impressive board of world leaders who remain good friends to this day. They became his partners in tackling global environmental problems. But the model for the Better World Society required that the organization solicit outside funding, which compromised its effectiveness; fund-raising saps creative energies that would otherwise be applied to addressing problems on the ground.

Turner realized that to accomplish everything he wanted, he would have to provide much of the financing himself. The Turner Family Foundation was established in 1991. The following year its first executive director, Peter Bahouth, took the reins. Bahouth certainly did not fit the profile of the typical foundation strategist. He had risen through the ranks of Greenpeace, the feisty global environmental organization perhaps known for its sharp elbows and acts of civil disobedience, most notably in battling whaling ships on the high seas as well as protesting at nuclear bomb-making facilities. Laura Turner Seydel, who worked as a Greenpeace staffer fresh out of college, was aware of Bahouth's respect among grassroots conservationists and lobbied for his hiring to her father, who also elicited the thoughts of Jane Fonda. Both Seydel and Turner admit that Bahouth pushed him out of his comfort zone.

In 1990, after the *Exxon Valdez* oil tanker ran aground in Prince William Sound, Alaska, sullying the ocean ecosystem with millions of gallons of crude oil, Bahouth, then executive director of Greenpeace USA, seized the moment. He joined activists in New York City and gave a rousing speech in front of the Exxon building. Then he went to work organizing protests against the felling of old growth forests in the Pacific Northwest and helped organize "Redwood Summer," a movement that involved tree sit-ins to stop logging companies.

"Peter kind of had this fearless mystique about him," Turner Seydel remembers. "He was young, around the same age as me and my siblings, and I took a liking to him. When you are young, direct action is appealing because it's a way to channel your enthusiasm."

Turner and wife Jane Fonda listened as the Turner kids made a case for Bahouth's hiring. Bahouth's instincts were driven by idealism. Only eldest son Teddy Turner dissented; he was convinced that many environmentalists are too idealistic and not rooted in the reality of how the business world works. He says his attitudes started to change when he worked for his father in the Moscow office of CNN and witnessed firsthand the dysfunction of Soviet-style communism and the suppression of a market economy. Ultimately, Bahouth was hired.

With Turner offering to pump tens of millions of dollars into the grant-making capability of his new foundation, word of its launch created an instant sensation in the nonprofit world of grassroots organizations. Bahouth says the five Turner children were determined to light a spark in the environmental movement.

The Turner Foundation, under Bahouth, took a cloud-seeding approach, gifting tens of millions of dollars to a vast range of conservation groups selected by Fonda, Turner, and his children. Indeed, countless organizations that came into being on the strength of Turner Foundation funding still exist today.

"Ted's kids were clearly kind of cautious around him because they had not been involved much in seeing how he worked in making business decisions that landed him on the covers of magazines and in profiles by *60 Minutes*," Bahouth says. "They didn't know what standing *they* had with their dad."

Turner made it clear that democracy would rule. Each child had a vote, plus Turner, plus Fonda made seven. Bahouth was merely there to serve as facilitator of discussions about groups seeking money.

Bahouth said, "I told the kids outside of Ted's presence, 'Come on, speak up. This is why your dad wanted *you* to be a board member and not one of his famous friends. *You* need to step up. Whatever resides in your heart as far as causes you say deserve support, you need to back it up with evidence showing how that organization can succeed. He expects you to be an advocate for what you believe in. He wants you to persuade him.'"

Bahouth has a theory: "Ted Turner actually enjoys being in the thick of chaos. The parent in him wants his children to battle because it makes them more adept in advocating for causes, better at group problem solving and in respecting each other's opinions. The egotistical side of Ted doesn't mind having circumstances when civility breaks down and he is called to intervene." Turner has been known for causing commotions in his negotiations over the years, and getting rises out of people by saying provocative things, but Bahouth's thought is that, more often than not, it's calculated.

Mike Finley, the current Turner Foundation president and CEO who succeeded Bahouth and brought the entity to a whole new level, observes, "To me, the mark of a good parent is listening to what your children have to say, hearing them out even when you disagree, even when your experience tells you that the organization should be going in a different direction. As painful as it is to observe, you have to let them make mistakes."

Both Bahouth and Finley agree that when it comes to the way the Turner Foundation has done business, going through an intensive screening process in deciding which environmental and humanitarian causes to support, Turner has seldom, if ever, been domineering. "I've learned a lot," Turner himself says. "I have more appreciation for movements that begin at the grassroots level. Very often, change happens when those at the tops of governments and organizations implement at a larger systematic level, but it starts at the bottom."

"Shortly after he hired me to run the foundation, Ted made it clear that he wanted it to be a vehicle for doing good environmental work, but just as important to him was that it brought him and his children together," Bahouth says. "He wanted them to experience the satisfaction that comes with giving money away and the discrimination that is necessary when you do it. Ted knows that philanthropy, when its motivations are misguided, can become a weapon that does more harm than good."

The kneejerk assumption every Turner child encounters from others is that, because of their father's wealth, they are less sincere or committed, or that they have an endless trove of money to appropriate. There have been days, when interacting with others, when they never knew for sure if they were being solicited to assist based on the strength of their ideas or because they were riding coattails.

"Ted is well aware of the intimidating presence he has," Finley says. "That's why he increasingly is taking a step back and playing more of a quiet, supportive role. He is proud of his kids and he wants their work to be recognized."

He adds, "I think they now understand why he implemented the austerity measures at home when they were growing up. He wanted them to not feel coddled but understand that sacrifice can lead to more opportunity."

Bahouth notes that "an interesting and wonderful" expansion of empowerment occurred in the kids' demeanors from quarterly meeting to meeting.

"Ted very quickly learned to like being challenged by his family. It gave him a sense of what each of them was made of," he says. "Their dad might have been an imposing figure to them in the past but as the strength in them grew he became less so and, as a result, I think they felt a deeper mutual connection. That doesn't often happen with grown children and parents."

This is precisely what Turner had hoped for. The foundation, Fonda says, became a vehicle for Ted to bond with his kids in ways that never happened with his own father.

⸺

Part of the kids' responsibility in preparing for a vote is intensively researching the environmental issues at hand. Invariably, as they visited sites to better understand a given organization and its issues, they became outraged by some of the callous disregard for wildlife and special places. In their early advocacy, each would compile a litany of problems and resources being destroyed. As Turner listened to it, he thought of how he felt that evening on board the *Calypso* with Cousteau.

"Sometimes, the number and magnitude of problems seems so over-whelming," he says. And when his kids became cynical, he would pipe in and say that maybe their motto should be, 'There is no hope, the world is doomed, but, then again, we might be wrong.'"

All of the kids go about grant-making in a different way. Finley says Laura would rather give money to fifty different groups and spread it around as seed stock. Teddy tends to want to give fewer grants and more money to conservative groups and initiatives in the Southeast. Rhett always applies strict fiscal scrutiny and, given his work as a professional photographer and filmmaker, is visually oriented in thinking about problems and solutions. Beau has more faith in people who are willing to apply elbow grease, and has a special affinity for sportsmen and women. And Jennie, from being both a professional journalist and board member on other conservation organizations, has a keen knack for thinking about how investments can be leveraged.

Teaching his children by example, Turner demonstrated the kind of resolve he had when refusing to pull environmental-oriented program-ming at CNN and TBS. Once, the Turner Foundation gave $20,000 to an upstart grassroots recycling coalition pushing for beverage makers to ensure all bottles, cans, and plastic containers could be recycled. Atlanta-based Coca-Cola opposed it.

The Turner kids ran into friends of theirs working for Coke management in Atlanta who chided them for supporting groups that they considered anti–free enterprise. As Turner learned about Coke's grumbling and heard his kids complain about being socially scorned, he replied, "You go back to Coke and let them know that if a multibillion-dollar company is freaked out by our little $20,000 donation to a group trying to do the right thing and help make their customers' lives better and with a better planet, then next time our donation to the recycling group is going to be $40,000! And we're going to keep upping the ante."

Today, Coke touts its own recycling efforts as an example of its green chops and environmental responsibility.

Part of Turner's somewhat misleading reputation for being a dyed-in-the-wool, far left–leaning environmentalist has to do with the causes supported by the Turner Foundation. When it was launched, the timber wars were flaring in the Pacific Northwest and Alaska. The foundation directed monies to groups trying to save old growth forests from clear-cutting. Some of the money supported groups that helped activists stage sit-ins. Other grants went to groups that tilted a skeptical eye toward globalism, believing it would merely expand the power of multinational corporations.

One of the groups that benefited, the Ruckus Society, championed various forms of civil disobedience. When press accounts pointed out that the Turner Foundation backed such groups, Turner himself came under fire. While some of Ruckus's goals conflicted with his own notions of civil disobedience, he said he was willing to take the heat and support the decisions of his children, who outvoted him and steered the group funding.

As the decade went on, Teddy Turner, too, resisted giving money away to what he considered to be more radical environmental elements.

Teddy's ideology aligns with some of the talk show hosts on FOX News. Still, he told the *Atlanta Journal Constitution* in 1997 of his father: "In business, he's always been able to see the whole big picture. What he saw in environmentalism is that the big picture is pretty bleak. We're all going to kill ourselves eventually. That's why the 'Save the Humans' slogan of the Turner Foundation is absolutely perfect, because if we save ourselves, we save everything else and vice versa. It all works together."

The year after Teddy made those comments, in the wake of Turner giving the United Nations $1 billion, the Turner Foundation gave away a total of $25 million, up from $1.7 million in grants its first year.

"We were able to operate in kind of a quick strike capacity and respond to fast-evolving issues if we needed to," Bahouth says. "Often, we were the first funder getting into a fight, important sometimes because if the resource extraction companies saw that the Turner Foundation was there from the beginning, it could change the behavior of how they acted toward local groups. More than having the money sometimes, the groups felt empowered to have Ted Turner and his kids standing behind them."

Bahouth helped the Turner Foundation establish a scattershot pattern of involvement on issues ranging from pollution to population. A joke that pops up occasionally around the holiday dinner table relates to Turner's tireless promotion of "population stabilization," a euphemism for slowing the rate of human reproduction, encouraging people to have smaller families. As the father of five children from two different mothers, and with conventional population control strategies aimed at encouraging family sizes of two children or less, he routinely is asked by his critics which of his three children he would do without?

He responds that as recompense—"No father would give up one of his children," he says—he is pouring as much money as he can to organizations seeking to lessen the ecological footprint of society.

Reflecting on the impact that Cousteau had on his own sons, Turner searched for a way to inspire kids. While the Turner Foundation was still in its nascency, Turner and his two women lieutenants at TBS and CNN, Barbara Pyle and Pat Mitchell, were working with filmmakers to make environmental documentaries. From that springboard, Turner funded the novel animated cartoon series, *Captain Planet*, implemented by Pyle. It created a sensation.

The genesis for *Captain Planet* grew out of conversations Turner had with Lester Brown, as well as the realization that with the aging of such seminal figures as Jacques Cousteau, Jane Goodall, and other eco-heroes, there was an urgent need to reach young people. Turner owned the Hanna Barbera children's cartoon library and noted there wasn't much of a green message in *Yogi Bear, The Flintstones,* and *Scooby-Doo.*

"Lester told Ted we need to make the time to train and inspire the next generation of students. You can't be asked to solve problems unless you know what they are and have had time to think about them," Pyle explains. "With Ted, you could see the light come on . . . what Lester said really got his mind turning."

Contrary to rumors, Turner says he never thought of himself as being the prototype for the green-skinned spirit created when five Planeteers put their rings together.

Each week on Saturday morning, they battled and foiled polluters, poachers, and other villain despoilers of the natural world. "I don't see Planeteers as a group of politically correct wimps or as saboteurs," Turner says. "They're eco-warriors holding the bad guys to account. The Planeteers make it cool to be green."

Pyle's vital role in the 113 *Captain Planet* episodes that extended over six seasons, Turner says, was as "birth mother" who refined the story lines and moved them through production with animators and the actors enlisted to provide the character voices. She and Nick Boxer came up with scripts and ran them by Turner.

Says Pyle, "We predicted so much stuff, so many real disasters before they happened. We based one episode on an oil spill around Big Sur where Ted has a house and lo and behold it aired preceding the *Exxon Valdez* disaster. As some in the company wondered whether this was a good investment, Ted defended it. When people in the company expressed concern that it might be a waste of time and cost too much money, Ted said, 'Let's give it chance.'"

Captain Planet left its mark on what Pyle calls "the millennial generation"—those kids who were passing through childhood and adolescence at the turn of the century. She receives correspondence every week from young adults who said they were influenced by the series and now want their kids to view it.

Captain Planet and the Planeteers also left Rush Limbaugh apoplectic. And the fact that Limbaugh was so worked up that he felt compelled to sound off about the eco-cartoon characters on his syndicated radio program was enough to make Turner want to continually air it. That Limbaugh was ranting about Turner's fictional kids attempting to save the Earth from polluters meant free publicity.

That it was reaching millions of real kids each week was great; that it has hundreds of thousands of fans on Facebook today—among kids who grew up and became ardent environmentalists—even better.

"This," Turner says, "is the best reward of all. Limbaugh and people like Glenn Beck today might not appreciate what a clean and healthy environment means, but the kids understand. And they represent the future of the world. Plus, they're going to outlive Limbaugh and Beck."

Ayn Rand in *Atlas Shrugged* lampooned the notion that people of fortune should feel any sense of altruistic duty to help save humanity. Consumer advocate turned presidential candidate and novelist Ralph Nader, conversely, proposes that the only way doom can be averted is if the wealthiest of plutocrats channel their resources. In his recent eco-thriller novel, *Only the Super-Rich Can Save Us*—which won critical praise from

Lewis Lapham, business guru Tom Peters, and actor Warren Beatty—one of Nader's do-gooder protagonists is Turner himself. Nader venerates Turner as a catalyst because of his real-life deeds, but part of his plot was inspired by having been a fan of *Captain Planet*.

As the third person narrator, Nader writes, "It was no surprise to anyone that Ted Turner, the 'Mouth of the South,' was the first to speak. 'The world is going to hell in a poverty handbasket,' he declared."

Today, an energetic outfit called the Captain Planet Foundation, wholly separate from the Turner Foundation, is dedicated to funding high-quality, hands-on environmental education programs that bring nature into classrooms and youth into nature. Over the past two decades, foundation programs have reached more than eight hundred thousand students worldwide. The organization has leveraged millions of dollars to fund experiential learning across a gamut of focus areas: watershed education and water quality monitoring; wetlands, riverbank, and native flora restoration; air quality and climate change study; creating pollinator gardens; recycling; how to compost organic waste; and others.

"Our main focus isn't just on textbook learning. It's experiential; it's applying the ideas students learn in school to hands-on application to the world they inhabit," Turner Seydel says. Where does food come from? The kids come away with a healthy respect for how it is grown, she notes. Where does water come from and why is it important to not pollute? Students make trips to local rivers and sewage treatment plants. How important is it to recycle? It becomes clearer when they visit a landfill. "We're talking about environmental literacy, understanding how different aspects of their lives are intermeshed. It's important for kids to know that, as citizens, they have enormous power in creating the kind of world they want, which is the underlying message of Captain Planet and the Planeteers," Turner Seydel adds. "There's a lot of negativity out there. We don't want young people to be filled with cynicism. We're trying to ignite inspiration."

Barbara Pyle, who brought the cartoon series to life, is working with Turner Seydel, her siblings, and Captain Planet Foundation executive director Leesa Carter, a nationally recognized nonprofit leader and environmental educator, to resurrect the profile of eco-warriors for a new generation. Captain Planet, as an icon, still maintains a nostalgic fan base of more than 550,000 Planeteers spread around the globe and interconnected through a page on Facebook.

The cartoon series has been translated into twenty-three languages and has aired on TV in over one hundred countries. "You'd be surprised where you find the Planeteer faithful. They're in Africa, Asia, equatorial South America, and in the Far North," Turner Seydel says. "Dad had a sense of how Captain Planet would catch on twenty-five years ago. He always said that it just needed some time."

"When I go back and watch those old episodes, two things strike me," Ted says. "First, they're even more fun today than when they first ran. And secondly, they're more timely and relevant. We're dealing with the same issues, the same clashes between heroes and villains and the only thing that's different is that with climate change breathing down our necks, the stakes are higher."

The Bahouth era of the Turner Foundation, combined with the crisis created by the collapse in AOL stock value, gave way to a need for dramatic change in direction. It's been ushered forth by former civil servant Mike Finley.

During his three and a half decade career wearing a National Park Service ranger uniform, Finley met every US president going back to Richard Milhous Nixon. He would go on to testify before Congress on a number of high-profile natural resource controversies. He ascended through the ranks of America's most trusted government agency and attained three of the most prestigious management posts, becoming superintendent of Everglades, Yosemite, and Yellowstone national parks.

Finley, many said, was on the fast track to one day being named Park Service director. But tripping him up was one obstacle he could not overcome—his outspokenness and fidelity to uphold the environmental laws of the land when politicians would have preferred he bend them.

People who work for Turner tend to reflect his own values. The legacy of the National Park Service going back to the era of Theodore Roosevelt, John Muir, and Stephen Mather, Finley says, is about standing up to special interests that either wanted to destroy or exploit the country's natural resources, parks, and public lands.

For a while early in his rangering, Finley was a dutiful foot soldier. But by the 1980s, he was tired of watching parks suffer from political kowtowing. In 1986, during the Reagan Administration, he was put in charge of looking after the Everglades, celebrated as "the river of grass." Long before he arrived in Florida, Finley had been told the ecosystem was in trouble due to attempts to drain and divert water on behalf of developers and the powerful sugar cane industry that was polluting the Everglades.

In fifty years, the number of wading birds had plunged from 2.5 million to just 250,000. More than a dozen animals and plants were classified as endangered, and the mystical Florida panther was barely clinging to survival. As the Everglades were drained, some fourteen hundred miles of canals were dug, transforming a vital wetland system into a Florida version of the concrete-bottomed Los Angeles River. It was the largest public works project funded by the US government outside of the Panama Canal.

Finley raised hackles and turned heads while he was in the Everglades. One prominent Florida environmentalist said Finley, in part due to his willingness to take on sugar cane growers, was the best superintendent in the history of Everglades National Park. Reflecting back to those years in the 1990s, he says, "That same argument has been used over and over again. 'If you protect a place, it's gonna put people out of work.' Almost without exception, the opposite proves to be true. When you protect nature, people want to live near healthy ecosystems and get out into the middle of it because it makes them feel better about being alive. Conservation doesn't destroy prosperity, it creates it."

Apart from the obvious positive monetary metrics such as revenue generated through ecotourism, he says it's the subtle elements of "eco-system services" that serve as the underpinning. "What you don't see or appreciate is the natural resource systems that are protected and result in further economic benefit," he explained to me. "These species such as blue crab, spiny lobster, and shrimp are often born and raised in the protection of the park, but leave and are harvested by private parties in accordance with state law. The existence of the park literally provides food for human consumption and income for fishermen and crabbers. They are nature's gifts to society, only possible through a well-managed and protected ecosystem."

Just months later, Park Service director Jim Ridenour transferred Finley to yet another hotbed of controversy, Yosemite in Northern California. Far away in the Sierras, he was assigned to sort out a long festering dispute over the future of seven-mile-long Yosemite Valley that had become clogged with traffic congestion and foul air. "I told a reporter with the *L.A. Times* that the sound of passing buses was louder at my house in Yosemite Valley than the urban noise I heard in Miami," he says.

Ultimately, politics stymied much of his work in Yosemite, but his efforts at restoring the Merced River and reducing the footprint of development earned him the number one posting in the service, the superintendent post of Yellowstone. "All of this was my preparation for going to work for Ted," he says.

In America's first national park, Finley was thrown to the wolves. Literally. He and his wife, Lillie, started unpacking their bags at Mammoth Hot Springs in November 1994 and within a few months, fourteen wolves were being released in the park, the first step in a now famous predator restoration project that made conservation history.

Besides the controversial release of wolves, another politically charged row was brewing. A Canadian mining company wanted to build an open pit gold mine on the back doorstep of the park within a stream system that drained into park waterways and upper reaches of the Yellowstone River system. Some colleagues told Finley not to mess with it, but he spoke out against the mine and ultimately, with the backing of President Bill Clinton, Interior Secretary Bruce Babbitt, and conservation organizations, they got it stopped.

Even as these debates raged, Finley got a call from Turner who asked if he and Jane Fonda could come up to the park and see the wolves.

"Ted had been reading about them in the newspaper and supported the reintroduction. He was hoping they could take a look at them," Finley says of the visit in summer 1995. "I was somewhat familiar with him, certainly with Jane's film work, and told them to come on up."

The couple was escorted out into the Lamar Valley where lobos were being held prior to release. Turner and Fonda fed them in their acclimation pens and then returned to have dinner themselves at Finley's house. Turner and Fonda were impressed by Finley's steely nerve with the mine debate and, as Turner says, his passion and fluency on global topics.

Within a few months, Phillips left his park job to work for Turner. Turner and Fonda stayed in touch with Finley. Finally, after Bahouth left the Turner Foundation, Finley got a call on Christmas Eve 2000. It was Turner offering him a job for the fourth time.

The Turner Foundation was in a period of transition and in need of a strong rudder. Turner and Fonda were splitting up, the Turner kids were older, and their collective grasp of grant-making had matured.

Finley finally said yes, and he now heads one of the most effective eco-charities in the world. His estimate is that over thirty-five hundred

Together at the 4,878-acre Red Rock Ranch, Turner and Jane Fonda designed a cabin that spoke to their modest, rustic tastes. Forged of recycled wood and found stone, it's not only a hub for fly fishing but a place where Turner invites world leaders to discuss global challenges. TODD WILKINSON

Off Turner's back door at the Flying D Ranch rise the wild Spanish Peaks—one of the reasons he instantly fell in love with Montana a quarter century ago. The 113,000-acre Flying D is the largest tract of private land in the greater Yellowstone region, and home to all of the original native species that existed there at the end of the last Ice Age.

Even Turner has contended with the proliferation of natural gas exploration in America. Split estate laws allow others to develop resources beneath the ground he owns. By working with the energy company, however, natural gas development at Vermejo Park in New Mexico is viewed as a model for blending resource extraction with protection of natural values. TODD WILKINSON

Dustin Long, a biologist with the Turner Endangered Species Fund, holds a baby black-footed ferret in a captive breeding facility at Vermejo Park Ranch, a resource that provides critically endangered ferrets for release in the wild, on Turner ranches as well as elsewhere.
TODD WILKINSON

With a herd of bison 55,000 strong and spread across six western states, Turner is the largest bison rancher in history, innovatively using the animals as ecological tools to restore healthy landscapes and turn a profit.

Desert bighorn sheep, released in New Mexico's Fra Cristobal Mountains, have established Turner's sprawling Armendaris Ranch as a robust foothold for the iconic animals. The bighorn herd was restored to such a level that it is now providing high-value, recreational hunting opportunities.

Turner's youngest son, Beau, shares his father's passion for the outdoors. Making his home in Florida, Beau helps to manage wildlife on all of Turner's properties. Here, at Avalon Plantation near Tallahassee, he oversees a controlled burn, an important agent in southeastern forest ecosystems. Turner is carrying out one of the largest private revitalization efforts of longleaf pine in the country. TODD WILKINSON

As seasoned field men, the late Joe Truett (above, in white baseball cap) and Kevin Honness (with swift fox) played instrumental roles in helping the Turner Endangered Species Fund pioneer new approaches to wildlife conservation on private land. They would find pleasure knowing their work outlasted them. TODD WILKINSON (left)

Giving wild wolves a home on his properties has long been a Turner dream. Here, he peers through a spotting scope at members of the Beartrap Pack that have taken up residence on the Flying D Ranch in Montana, living among bison and elk herds. Since December 2002, with twenty-plus members, the Beartrap Pack has been one of the largest in North America.

Turner is undertaking some of the most ambitious aquatic conservation programs in America, aimed at nurturing native fish and restoring riparian ecosystems. Both westslope and Rio Grande cutthroat trout have been given new homes on Turner ranches. Costilla Creek, a tributary of the Rio Grande, is one stretch among the more than 150 river miles that have been healed in several states.

Every year in Denver, Turner brings the Atlanta management staff of Turner Enterprises, Inc., together with TEI management staff and ranch managers from the West. The group, which he affectionately calls "my posse," is treated as an extension of his family. It's a diverse mix. Pictured, front row (L to R): Magnus McCaffery (Turner Endangered Species Fund Senior Biologist), Mike Phillips (TESF Executive Director), Beau Turner (TESF Chairman), Ted Turner, Rutherford Seydel (General Counsel and Turner's son-in-law), Bill Shaw (VP Human Resources), David Withers (Director of Finance), Phillip Evans (VP Communications). Back row (L to R): Tom Waddell (Armendaris Ranch), Dave Dixon (Snowcrest Ranch), Alan Oborny (Blue Creek Ranch), Dusty Hepper (McGinley Ranch), Dr. Dave Hunter (TEI Veterinarian), Josh Marks (Legal Counsel), John Hansen (Assistant General Manger), Bob Biebel (TEI CFO), Gus Holm (Asst .Manager Vermejo Park Ranch), Keith Yearout (Z Bar Ranch), Steve Dobrott (Ladder Ranch), Tom Bragg (Deer Creek Ranch), Mark Kossler (Manager Vermejo Park Ranch), Terry Purdum (Spikebox Ranch), Neil Lawson (Turner Ranches Wildlife Director), Carter Kruse (TESF Senior Fishery Biologist), Johnny Covey (Fawn Lake Ranch), Danny Johnson (Flying D Ranch), Aaron Paulson (Red Rock Ranch), Tom LeFaive (Bad River Ranch), Russ Miller (VP/General Manager of western ranches). Not pictured: Taylor Glover (TEI CEO), John Hurd (Bluestem Ranch), and Jack Shell (Bar None Ranch).

Ladder Ranch Manager Steve Dobrott holds a bolson tortoise hatchling that will be given a home on Turner lands. The bolson has heretofore been extinct in the US for over ten thousand years. TODD WILKINSON

These two bumper stickers adorn many of Ted Turner's vehicles. TODD WILKINSON

Turner says that having a relationship with the land has given him and his staff a profound sense of humility. Here, Turner's Vice President/General Manager of western ranches Russ Miller and assistant GM John Hansen walk through the sea of open space at a bison ranch in the Sandhills of Nebraska.

The front lawn of Turner's Estancia La Primavera along the Rio Traful in Argentina's Patagonia region has an exceptional, late-afternoon view of the mountains. TODD WILKINSON groups have, to date, received nearly $360 million in Turner Foundation grants, not including some special ad hoc projects. "Ted has really tried to be a silent partner," Finley says. "And even in communities where there might be hostility to him because of some of the things he has said over the years, he will say, 'That's okay, we can still give that community money. People don't have to like me. That's not a requirement. If our funding can help get a project done that wouldn't otherwise, then maybe people there will want to do more.'"

Finley has magnified the Foundation's reach even more by working closely with Tim Wirth at the UN Foundation. During the AOL Time Warner stock free fall, both men recognized the huge benefits of attacking problems by building campaigns around issues and developing nontraditional partnerships.

"When I first arrived at the Turner Foundation our budget was approximately $50 million a year. After the AOL Time Warner loss, we reduced our budget by over 75 percent. It resulted in not only a smaller staff but it meant a different strategy for maximizing the effectiveness of our funding," Finley says. The foundation went from an open process where groups submit proposals to an "invitation only" business model where the foundation reaches out to appropriate nonprofits demonstrating innovation. "Ironically, we are now a leaner, more agile, and focused foundation."

An organization that bears Finley's signature and Ted and Beau Turner's blessing, for instance, is the Theodore Roosevelt Conservation Partnership (www.trcp.org) founded to empower the original American conservationists—hunters and anglers. It was launched with pivotal leadership provided by the late and legendary Jim Range, who served as key advisor to former US senator and majority leader Howard Baker of Tennessee. Range was an ardent Republican and indefatigable hook and bullet conservationist.

TRCP, as it is called, reflects the Turner organization's affinity for Theodore Roosevelt, and it champions protection of habitat while striving to get more kids out in the field to experience hunting and fishing. "Our research had shown that there were approximately forty million Americans who hunt and fish. Most of these outdoor enthusiasts do not belong to the typical national organizations that the Turner Foundation funds such as Defenders of Wildlife or the National Wildlife Federation," Finley explains.

"These are good groups, but they did not resonate with the more conservative hunting and fishing crowd. Our goal was to give a political voice to the millions of people who love the outdoors, who see the benefits of clean water and clean air and want to protect the lands and waterways of this country."

TRCP seeks to unite people who love the great outdoors rather than being pettily divided by interests applying an ideological litmus test, says Whit Fosburgh, president and CEO of TRCP. "Ted, just as Jim Range did, cherishes the strength and value of pulling people together around their common values rather than trying to deliberately fragment them along the lines of their differences. The hunting and fishing community is like a microcosm of the country. We live in different areas but we all feel called to the outdoors."

Sacred too is the responsibility of motherhood and looking out for the health of their babies. The Turner Foundation has been instrumental in raising awareness about the plight of pollinators linked to pesticide spraying. Concern about honeybees, which are essential workhorses in the multibillion-dollar fruit and produce industry, piqued a greater curiosity about the proliferation of chemicals in the environment that get ingested into the human body, a special interest of Laura Turner Seydel and her sister, Jennie Turner Garlington, both mothers. The Turner Foundation supports the Environmental Working Group that has catapulted bioaccumulation of toxic household chemicals to national attention, and locally in Atlanta it supports Mothers & Others for Clean Air, a coalition of eight environmental and public health organizations.

"It's the first time that public health groups in Georgia have come together alongside environmentalists to look at how outdoor air quality affects the well-being of at-risk communities, especially children," Turner Seydel says. "It's a vulnerable population." And the approach being adopted there is being emulated in other states.

As Turner Seydel learned about how chemicals can disrupt the endocrine system, crucial to the human immune system in fighting off diseases, she also became fluent in the cause of an escalation in kids suffering from asthma and chronic respiratory illness. Together, Ted Turner, Laura Seydel Turner, and her children all had blood work done to see the level of exposure as carried across generations. Startling, the adults had a wider array of agents because of longevity but the children had higher percentages of synthetic toxins in their system—something that should be of concern to all parents in the twenty-first century. Another fascinating correlation is that Jean-Michel Cousteau, son of the late Jacques-Yves Cousteau, notes that longer-lived marine life also bio-accumulates toxic agents in its fatty tissue. "It all relates to the stuff floating around in the water and air we're taking in and don't even realize," Turner Seydel says.

Gerald L. Durley is a pastor at Providence Missionary Baptist Church in Atlanta, the same church where the Reverend Martin Luther King Jr. delivered some of his memorable sermons. Clergyman Durley says there is a subtle element of racism within the mainstream American environmental community. It isn't that environmental groups, especially conservation organizations involved in wildland protection, have ill feelings toward African Americans; it's that they assume blacks, Hispanics, Asians, and American Indians have no interest in nature-related experiences synonymous with Caucasian America. The same applies for ethnic groups being involved in activism.

"In order to attend the dance, you first have to be asked," Durley says. "My advice for the environmental organizations is that you make an invitation to people of color to get involved in environmental organizations. If you get kind of an indifferent response, don't walk away. Come back again, seek out the right people. Call me and I'll help put you in touch with the right individuals. We in the black community aren't uninterested in environmental issues. We're starved of attention."

Someone else in Atlanta who increasingly is making a connection between biblical scripture spoken from the pulpit and the importance of healthy outdoor environs in parishioners' lives is minister Bernice Albertine King, the second daughter and youngest child of the late and legendary Dr. King. She was only five years old when her father was tragically killed. She describes herself today as one of Turner Seydel's friends and students, enamored with the concept of "creation care," i.e., the notion that those who believe in God have a duty to be caretakers of the natural world. And she has no doubt that had her father lived, he would be embracing environmentalism as another important facet of social justice and civil rights.

For her part, Turner Seydel commends King and Durley. She is hoping to get the multiracial *Captain Planet* cartoons running nationally on television again because they reach kids in the home. She also is using the Captain Planet Foundation to encourage young inner city students to pursue careers in the sciences.

Durley says that Seydel, like her father, is a green *missionary* who recognizes the nurturing sanctuary quality of parks and the pastoral countryside. From their ongoing interaction, Laura helped Durley and King realize how climate change threatens to affect the lives of those in the pews at Providence Missionary Baptist and other churches. "Urban temperatures are likely to rise. We could be facing water shortages. There could be an expansion of tropical diseases shifting north," Durley says.

Durley and King have served as key catalysts in rallying together ministers and parishioners around Atlanta to see showings of director

Davis Guggenheim's *An Inconvenient Truth,* which featured Al Gore, and HBO documentary *Too Hot Not to Handle.* Both of these projects were spearheaded by the noted climate change activist Laurie David, who came to Atlanta and screened the films. Durley and King say they started to see connections that weren't readily apparent before.

After Turner Seydel handed them copies of Richard Louv's book, *Last Child in the Woods* (about the growing pandemic of "nature deficit disorder"), Durley says, "It hit me over the head like a brick. I felt like he was speaking to me and to the families of kids in my congregation. The environment is a civil rights issue that has not been on our radar screen."

Withdrawing into the safety of their living rooms based on an irrational fear of the outdoors, and becoming entranced by video games rather than plugging into the colorful sights, smells, and sounds of living things, is a problem for many, many inner city youth.

"So much of learning is passed down parent to child and teacher to child," Laura says. "We have generations of people who have been cut off from regular contact with nature. It's awfully hard for a child to develop an awareness if no one is exposing it to them and telling them about what they're seeing and letting them know they can have a safe inspiring place."

No segment of the Turner Foundation's work resonates more personally with Turner than its support of the Turner Youth Initiative, Finley says. As the reach of Turner's land empire grew, he was sensitive to the prevailing perception of many wealthy outsiders coming into regions to recreate—essentially to take from local communities and benefit from them—without offering goodwill in return.

The Turner Youth Initiative has given millions of dollars in grants to a huge array of grassroots projects led by young people in the communities near Turner's properties. Projects have gone out to more than half a dozen states, as well as villages around his estancias in Argentina.

A shining recent example is a $60,000 grant in Bozeman that has given way to the "bio-bus," says Bob Buzzas, who worked with Mike Finley's daughter, Devon, in overseeing projects in Montana. "Bio-bus is an exemplary illustration of what I love most about the work of the youth initiative," Buzzas says. High school kids came up with an idea to create literally a green bus that operates as a portable greenhouse growing vegetables that travels around from school to school touting the value of healthy eating and teaching kids how they can grow gardens at home. An old bus was overhauled and retrofitted with environmentally friendly greenhouse glass, plant boxes, and a rain water collector.

"The lesson that the Turner Youth Initiative tries to impart is never sell kids short. He sees young people taking the virtues espoused in *Captain Planet* and putting a human face on them," Ms. Finley said one afternoon in Helena, Montana, where students from Helena High School were working with administrators to create a more youth-friendly lounge next to the cafeteria. "Recipients of grants have opened youth centers, radio stations, worked in facilities for senior citizens, designed skateboard parks, conducted exotic weed control, started popular energy conservation and recycling projects, and showed their parents, in some cases, what responsible citizenship is," Finley says.

Students are required to draft a business plan and create a structure for administering the money, carrying their projects out to fruition. No adult meddling is involved, which initially left some "helicopter" parents in local communities, accustomed to micro-managing their kids' activities, feeling uneasy.

Some of the money, in South Carolina near Hope Plantation, has been used to create a safe after-school environment for kids in areas where gang crime is a problem. Tutors await youngsters of all ages when they get off the bus, help them with school work, give them something to eat (knowing it might be the last healthy meal they have until the morning), and allow them to play and just be kids.

Other efforts have involved recycling drives, park projects, and bicycle banks in which abandoned bikes are collected from local police departments, fixed up, and then distributed free of charge to other kids around the community. Some have failed from disorganization; others have led to lasting benefits.

"I remember in the beginning, going back a number of years after Ted first arrived on the scene in Montana. We did encounter a bad perception of him from some local people," Buzzas says.

"We rolled out some teenager-led projects that went through fits and starts. Some people said that Ted was merely trying to buy himself goodwill. What the parents didn't realize is that the possibility of hitting and missing with some of the projects was anticipated. In fact, that was the whole point, Ted's point."

The unofficial mandate handed down from Finley and the Turner children is that the foundation has a low profile. It's fine that the kids gain publicity for *their* efforts but they are not expected to deliver a sound bite for the Turner family. Turner himself doesn't see the work as a gamble or a waste. He calls it "some of the best millions of dollars I've ever invested."

As he likes to say, "We're trying to give the kids in these towns a license to fail. Money that's available for kids is in short supply everywhere. What's important is not that they succeed, but that they dream and *try to succeed* and give it their best with few strings attached. The most important lessons I've learned in my life have all come from failure and disappointment. For every victory there were ten times as many smaller defeats and sometimes some pretty big ones. It's the same philosophy I've tried to take with my own kids. Real confidence that holds up under challenges doesn't come from doing easy things or those you are good at. It comes from figuring out how to succeed by expanding your repertoire."

It's true for the Turner kids as well. Rutherford Seydel, Laura's attorney husband, arrives at their Buckhead home, "Ecomanor," in a hybrid vehicle. He has an hour before attending a meeting in Atlanta organized by the Energy Future Coalition. Now, he stands in front of a kitchen wall console, like Spock from *Star Trek*, taking readings from all of the sensors on the *Enterprise*.

The console is futuristic and cutting edge: It enables the Seydels to know how much solar energy was produced that day on the roof, how much water and electricity was used, temperatures in different rooms, and how that translates into saving money. It is the brain of an organic home that has elements that live and breathe. "If the kids leave a light on or the faucet running before they leave for school, we know," he says.

In 2003, high winds blew through Atlanta and sent a two-hundred-year-old southern oak crashing down on the roof of a cottage they had hoped to use as guest quarters. The damage was so significant that they saw it as an opportunity to retool their footprint.

Ecomanor (www.ecomanor.com) cost $1.5 million to build, 10 percent more because of its green engineering figures, but a sum well within the norm of what properties of similar size go for in Buckhead. They found collaborators with a number of green material companies, and after Ecomanor was built, started giving public tours.

Their energy costs are now between 80 and 90 percent below those of a comparable home, and they see savings in their water bill as well. During the recent drought in Atlanta, underground cisterns that served as catchments for rare rain enabled the couple to have water for their landscaping, at the same time a watering ban, using municipal supplies, had been imposed on Atlanta residents. Climbing to their rooftop attic and stepping outside in a crow's nest viewing area, Rutherford points to the solar panels and says that he hopes to one day make money by selling excess electricity back into the grid.

"What people don't realize is that alternative energy will enable citizens, wherever they live, to become eco-entrepreneurs. I don't know what is more conservative than striving to be self-sufficient and turn a profit by being smart," Rutherford says.

"We need to give Americans a means to make better, more informed choices," Rutherford says. "I'm not emphasizing this point to justify what Laura and I have done. I'm trying to suggest that pointing fingers and demonizing people doesn't work. Gentle persuasion works better, showing that you can actually save money by making smarter environmental decisions. If people can see part of their own lives reflected in what we are doing, it makes them much more willing to listen."

The tradeoff that Laura and Rutherford made in constructing Ecomanor has to do with sacrificing privacy and putting a target out there for critics to aim at. They've heard the rebukes: that it is a monument to their own egos, too big, too lavish, completely unnecessary, and, in the end, sending the wrong message.

Chuckling, Rutherford says, the perception is that progressive environmentalists are turning into lifestyle cops, inflicting their own Orwellian version of social Darwinism. "But it's not true," he says. "At the end of the day, if we are parents with a conscience, we know there is a responsible direction we need to go."

One of the reasons they open their home to tour groups is to help others understand the practical application of energy efficiency and environmentally friendly design. "When people see it in action, they know they can do it themselves."

Laura acknowledges that part of her motivation was to show her father that she could be pioneering in her own way, too. "Dad casts a pretty big shadow," she says. "He's a pretty competitive guy who is used to leading, and if he has the opportunity to do something first, he would rather do it than wait for someone else. At the same time, he is incredibly supportive of us kids finding our own niches."

Some of the lessons learned from Ecomanor have been availed to Turner as he pursues construction projects on his western properties, including an adobe home in the Chihuahuan Desert of New Mexico that employs both thermal and solar heating and cooling.

Maybe the most effective weapon the Turner Foundation is using to reach people is food, by working with George McKerrow, cofounder of Ted's Montana Grill Restaurants, now in fifty locations across the country.

"If you have access to multiple platforms for reaching people, as Ted does," Finley says, "Why not use them?"

Beyond noting the benefits of eating healthy meals, Finley and McKerrow are using the cachet of Turner to tout how reducing waste and energy use in eating establishments saves proprietors money and helps reduce America's carbon footprint.

"It's great to tell individual citizens to change out the light bulbs they use at home for energy efficient ones, but where you really get gains is when groups like the National Restaurant Association tell their members that by adopting environmental measures as part of their best business practices it enhances their own prosperity and shows their patrons they care about the impact they are having on local communities," Finley says.

"Ted is just as excited about a little start-up company like Ted's Montana Grill as he was about starting a new network or buying the Braves. He likes the challenge of being in a new venture and watching it grow and mature. He always finds a new angle on old ways of doing things," McKerrow says. "For him, it always comes back to doing something on behalf of the environment."

McKerrow talks about how Turner's influence has caused him to assess how to run a restaurant with things he didn't think much about when he earlier built the LongHorn Steakhouse concept into national prominence.

"We get approached all the time. We had a bottled water purveyor approach us with a very attractive packaging. My response was, 'Sorry but how much fuel is being used to transport one bottle halfway around the world.' The other thing we frown on is plastic. We try to set the tone with our suppliers, with our dining customers and give our competitors something to look at. The best way to drive an innovation in the restaurant business is to have a profitable operation based on the ideas you are espousing."

In 2012 McKerrow told the *Atlanta Journal Constitution,* "At Ted's Montana Grill, it took us ten years to be an 'overnight success.' Ted's capital is the only reason we're here. The recession hit and we lost 20 percent of our sales. We had to close underperforming locations. Ted never gave up. He could have bailed out. We started losing a couple of million dollars a year, and he had to give us the money to keep the doors open."

Perseverance paid off. "Now, we are becoming a profit center," McKerrow said. "Our goal is to double the size of the company to eighty-eight restaurants by 2021. We'll do it all with internally generated cash."

"Dad does not tell us how to live our lives, except to say that if you're going to do something, be passionate about it, and if you have a choice between doing what's good or bad for the environment, do the good thing," Laura Turner Seydel says. "What's in a person's heart and conscience never lies."

~⌐~

On Ted Turner's desk in Atlanta rests a copy of a book that a friend had passed along, *1,000 Places to See Before You Die: A Traveler's Life List.* He flips through a couple of pages. He doesn't have a bucket list of things he needs to do or posh resorts to be pampered at, or any human wonders to see in order for him to feel complete. He has a different set of destinations in mind.

And he's already given a lot of thought to what will happen after he's gone. Money, he knows, can make people do funny things. He has no desire to hover over his children as a specter, but he does want the natural empire he's built to stay intact and flourish, to not be busted up in probate.

He trusts that his children will honor this wish. He also has instructed his financial chieftain Taylor Glover to draft his will, specifying that all properties, upon his death, be subsumed into the Turner Foundation, to be overseen by its trustees—his children—and a few selected administrators, with the hope that it will involve his grandchildren and their children and so on. Two-thirds of his estate is tied up in land and related investments. And he does not want the momentum that he's gathered to eliminate nukes, enable the UN, promote biodiversity protection, and confront climate change to perish, either. That's why he's taking steps to plan for how the initiatives will continue and remain funded after he is gone. "Philanthropy needs to try and be self-perpetuating," Turner says.

Many have asked what will happen to the UN Foundation? Wirth says Turner will not allow the positive gains for humanity to be ephemeral. "The board of the UN Foundation is now working to assure the organization's long-term sustainability, beyond 2014 when Ted's financial commitment will be completed," Wirth says, noting that it doesn't mark the end of Turner's involvement. "He is constantly assessing the variables, plotting trajectories, thinking about where the planet and humans will be in 2038, which would be a century from his own birth, and in 2050, 2100—beyond the reach of his own life."

For Turner, metrics of success with his charity work and results accomplished through land stewardship are how he holds himself accountable and tries to reconcile his personal actions with his admittedly own romantic visions. The changes that he has helped usher forward on behalf of healthy living things—human and animal—are his trophies now.

He doesn't remember when he crossed the threshold from being the hunter of stags to becoming admirers of them solely through binoculars. It started to happen sometime in his late fifties when he lost interest in killing anything larger than a quail. He is contented listening to the stories that come instead from the lips of Beau.

Turner has no control over how his children interpret the places that give him meaning—he knows that—but he hopes they will be able to feel his presence in them after he is gone. He wants his children to go looking to find them on the properties. Like the Enchanted Forest at the Flying D.

"They won't find my places; they'll discover their own and when they do, I hope they choose to do something about it, get fired up and try to make a difference," Turner says. "That's all that any one of us can do, to go wandering and try to find ourselves."

~~~

David Getches, the late dean of the law school at the University of Colorado–Boulder, related an anecdote to me about a raft trip down the Yampa River with Turner, Tim Wirth, and a few other committed conservationists. The Yampa descent was a glorious float among friends.

The river brimmed with snowmelt in late spring. A gorge in front of them pinched the roaring current tighter, revealing fins of whitecaps. There was a notorious stretch of challenging rapids awaiting them, amid a gauntlet of massive submerged rocks and dangerous undercurrents. At a spot upstream, the boat was guided to shore so that rafters could walk down and assess a patch that, over the years and by caprice of nature, had claimed the lives of capsized boaters.

Some of the younger floaters bounded back to the craft, eager to let fate play its hand. Turner, who had survived Fastnet in 1979, thought about the run in the context of earlier escapes and the odds of maximizing his years during this last stretch of his life.

"I'm going to pass," he said, making his calculation. "I'm going to find a high spot and watch the rest of y'all go through."

He picked his way to promenade above the river and watched the boat crash through without flipping and then met his crew on the other side of the Class IV whitewater.

"Why didn't you want to run it, Ted?" Getches asked, knowing that he was speaking to America's original Captain Courageous.

For most of his life, Turner the intrepid one would never have hesitated. He, after all, had for years clung to the notion that dying during an adventure was the chisel that writes a noble epitaph for young men.

He looked Getches in the eye. It was not a glance of fear, Getches said, but "sublime wisdom . . . he accepted his *senescence*."

"I want to see my grandchildren grow up," Turner said. "I want to fight for the environment *with them*."

"I don't know where he *was* in his thinking before, earlier in his life, but Ted's obviously focused now on the things he still wants to accomplish, the risks that are worth taking," Getches says. "He values the years he has ahead. He is curious about how all of this, the bigger picture, is going to turn out."

CHAPTER TEN

Parting Aspects

"I think Ted is thinking more about his legacy and, like the rest of us, the finite number of years remaining and what he wants to do with them. He is far from finished, and he will always be one of the people I feel most privileged to have met. In our times together he never fails to make me laugh and make me think. A great novelist would be hard-challenged to have invented a character like him."
—NBC News anchorman emeritus, conservationist, and citizen Tom Brokaw

So. *Who. Is.* Ted Turner?

When pressed for an answer, I look to the different aspects of a Turner I have come to know. There's the lesser-known Turner chronicled in these pages, the environmentalist and the philanthropist. There's also the apocryphal character, the man whose name is regularly appropriated in the interests of telling an unflattering story. This is Turner as he's perceived by his enemies and detractors. There's the Turner fiercely devoted to his inner circle, the warm and generous eccentric who values his relationships above almost all else. This is Turner as he's known to his friends and family. There's the Turner who *might* have been, and there's the Turner who *will* be, whose presence will be felt for years, perhaps generations, after he's gone. In order to fully grasp such a complicated personality, you need to somehow keep all these aspects in mind at once.

In considering the *apocryphal* Turner, I think about a conversation I had with his youngest son, Beau.

"Has Dad been obnoxious and outrageous sometimes? All my life," Beau said during a hike at Avalon Plantation in Florida. It was spring, just after the end of quail hunting season, and Beau was helping to ignite controlled fires, burning away the underbrush in order to spur new, more robust plant growth to keep the land rejuvenated. "What more do you need to know?" Beau asked. "Did he say things we wish he wouldn't have sometimes? Absolutely. Goodness gracious, he once insulted Pope John Paul by making a Polack joke. How many people do you know who have had to make a personal apology to a pontiff?"

There is a paradox involved here. How many people have the standing to make headlines by a slip of the tongue, and yet will, if circumstances demand, issue statements of contrition?

"In a way, I suppose it's kind of humorous. If he didn't say things that some people find outlandish, he wouldn't be who he is," Beau explains. "Dad will make utterances sometimes just to get a reaction—to wake people up. And you know what? More often than not, when it comes to issues facing the world, his instincts are right. On the other hand, there are stories about things Dad did or said that simply aren't true."

Turner has, for whatever reason, attracted more than his fair share of damaging apocrypha. In Montana, where I live, a story about how he was ejected from a local restaurant went viral on the Internet, was even repeated by lawmakers on Capitol Hill, and was broadcast on the Rush Limbaugh radio show. It goes like this:

During the early 1990s, Turner and Fonda were in Montana driving their Range Rover between the Bar None and Flying D ranches. It was summer, around dinnertime. En route they stopped at Sir Scott's, a steakhouse located in the tiny farming community of Manhattan.

Fonda and Turner were said to have strolled imperiously through the front door and informed the hostess they needed a table for two, pronto. The maître d' let them know there was a forty-five-minute wait, and their name would be added to a list.

Fonda glared at the waiter. "Do you know who we are?"

"Yes. But you're still going to have to wait forty-five minutes."

Fonda and Turner were so accustomed to getting the red carpet treatment that they demanded to talk with management.

When restaurant-owner Scott Westphal appeared, he asked: "We're obviously busy tonight. How may I help you?"

"Do you know who we are?" Turner and Fonda demanded.

"Yes, I do. But you're still going to have to wait, just like everybody else."

Fonda and Turner made a scene that riveted the attention of everyone in the establishment.

Westphal, now irritated, could no longer maintain his politeness. "Do you know who *I* am? I am the owner and a Vietnam veteran. Not only will you not be able to get a table ahead of my dear friends and neighbors here, you will not be eating in my restaurant—not tonight or any other night. Now get the hell out of here and goodbye!" Westphal raised his arm and pointed toward the door.

Fonda and Turner drove away, never to be seen again. As the legend goes, the entire restaurant erupted into cheers. Westphal was transformed into a folk hero for putting Hanoi Jane and her wealthy blowhard husband in their places.

A satisfying story, particularly if you were already predisposed to dislike Turner. But here's the thing: It *never* happened. I spoke with Scott Westphal, owner of Sir Scott's Oasis.

Westphal, a good and decent man (and too young to have served in Vietnam), chuckles when asked to describe what *really* happened. Fonda and Turner did show up at Sir Scott's for dinner one fine summer evening—as they had done several times before. They kept returning because they liked the food, atmosphere, and being able to converse with real people who have no affectations. And that particular evening, there was indeed a lengthy backlog of diners. Turner and Fonda were polite and low-key, however, and when they heard about the wait, they simply mentioned to the hostess that they were sad but they couldn't wait. They would return some other day.

What does Westphal make of Turner, a fellow restaurateur with his Ted's Montana Grill chain? "As a businessman, I respect everything he's accomplished. He's definitely an American success story. I know some of the ranchers don't care for him, but whenever he and his wife came in, they were like anyone else."

The Sir Scott's tale is one of several pure fabrications that involve Turner. Among some of the other doozies? That Turner is involved in an international conspiracy with the United Nations to undermine America's sovereignty and impose a New World Order that would destroy private property rights. That he's enlisted Kofi Annan and Belgian pilots in their blue UN helmets to secretly fly Canadian wolves to his ranches in New Mexico. That he's opposed to the Second Amendment, and doesn't support men and women in military uniform. That he's secretly a Communist or Socialist, and doesn't pay taxes. And on and on. Turner and his organization no longer try to refute these false assertions—they are prolific and tinged with schadenfreude—but like so much information on the Internet, the more that something goes viral, the more the masses believe it. Believing myths is inherent to modern tribal identity.

The second aspect of Turner involves Turner the friend, the compatriot, the loyal supporter.

"The most interesting things in life, and often the most important relationships in life, happen by accident," asserts Mikhail Gorbachev.

Gorbachev's first introduction to Turner was in 1986, two years after CNN opened its Moscow Bureau, the first US media organization to win approval from the Soviets.

Turner was in the Russian city to help promote the Goodwill Games. Turner remembers thinking, as he sat with Gorbachev, how many Americans had such a distorted, maligning view of the Soviet leader. "Here was this very gracious, very thoughtful man who loved his country and loved his wife and daughter, who valued pretty much the same things I did. He wasn't happy about the nuclear tensions. He didn't believe in Communism, not really. He wasn't interested in blowing us up. He was an agent of change. I told him that Reagan was in a tough position, that he was unlikely to budge on reducing the number of nukes, but that if he [Gorbachev] took up the idea, it *could* happen."

A rising political star, Gorbachev had become general secretary of the Communist Party a year earlier. He remembers how strange it seemed to him and his colleagues in the Politburo that this young headstrong entrepreneur—Turner—at the height of escalating anxiety with the West, wished to extend a hand of friendship.

KGB intelligence officials wondered about Turner's motivation. He behaved so differently from the Americans they had encountered in Washington and at negotiating tables. Was he a secret CIA agent? Was he playing sophisticated psychological mind games?

Chuckling, Gorbachev told me it took some studying of Turner before he realized, "Ted was simply being sincere. He was being who he *is*."

Despite enduring ridicule from some in the United States (who claimed regular reporting from Moscow would be a ruse for spreading Communist propaganda), Turner insisted that CNN tell stories about real life in the USSR. Not long afterward, the other three US networks followed suit.

Turner sent his own son, Teddy, to help with the news gathering. The gesture moved Gorbachev. To him, it was "heartening." No man would send a beloved child to a place he believed was the domain of an enemy.

Gorbachev was also struck by the international flavor of CNN's reporting, its lack of blatant, over the top American chest beating; it transcended what Gorbachev's colleagues expected would be Yankee propaganda. Gorbachev himself became an avid watcher of CNN. Sizing Turner up in hindsight, he confesses: "I liked him from the start."

The pair met again and again. "He was a very likeable capitalist who showed what you can do in this country through hard work," Gorbachev says, partially in jest. "And in addition to becoming rich, you can also speak your mind." Turner, he realized, was an ambassador for the virtues of free speech.

CNN was in Iceland when Gorbachev famously met with Reagan at the seminal moment when both sides of the Cold War were prepared to accept total elimination of nuclear weapons. It could have happened, Gorbachev notes, except that Reagan and US negotiators refused to give up the Star Wars Missile Defense program (which was ultimately abandoned after billions of US tax dollars were spent). Today, there are lingering tensions between the United States and Russia over a proposed missile defense system in Eastern Europe.

Widely hailed outside his own country, Gorbachev would be the last general secretary of the Communist regime, a position dating back to Vladimir Lenin in 1922. For ending oppression, Gorbachev was cheered in the United States and Western Europe but vilified in his own country by Communist Party loyalists for going too far.

Turner is puzzled, he says, by the way Gorbachev is viewed. Despite setting his society free, he is pilloried by old party hardliners, perhaps because freedom ended their autocratic authority.

"I don't think Americans ever fully realized how much Mikhail risked for himself, for his family, and the sacrifice he made to his own popularity by taking the courageous stands he did," Turner says. "And he is a man today who has a rare perspective into one of the most important chapters of world history."

"Ted reminded us all, using CNN, that apart from politics, there are far more inspiring things that unite us," Gorbachev said. "After I stepped down [following the breakup of the Soviet Union] and became a free man, my relationship with Ted blossomed. We found that both of us were linked by our enormous interest in nature and the environment. At that time, and with time, I came to understand the most important thing about Ted: He is a person who is not seeking personal gain, who is not trying to seek profit at every opportunity."

Gorbachev credits Turner with helping him realize how social instability increases wherever there is resource plundering that leaves landscapes and people impoverished.

In the 1990s, Gorbachev had job offers from a number of multinational companies. And he could have easily enlarged his personal net worth simply by going on the lecture circuit full time, receiving six- and seven-figure amounts for speaking appearances. Instead of leaving his country, he committed himself to staying in Moscow and, in 1994, Gorbachev founded Green Cross International (known as Global Green in the United States), hoping to help ignite a global environmental movement among world leaders. He planned to base it in a proposed new building in Moscow that would also house the Gorbachev Foundation. He channeled all of the money he received for winning the Nobel Peace Prize into the building and new organizations. Money for construction also was pledged by a few entities in Switzerland and Russia.

Pat Mitchell, who today is CEO and president of the Paley Media Center in New York and who also served as CEO of PBS, was in those days working for Turner in Atlanta, heading up TBS/CNN's award-winning documentary film division. As the Gorbachev Foundation was getting off the ground, Turner sent Mitchell to Moscow to lend organizational assistance.

"When I visited him in Moscow, his office at the time was no bigger in size than a closet," Mitchell says. "He had stacks of important historical documents in boxes and he said that mounds of other personal records had been confiscated by the Russian government and locked in the Kremlin. He wanted to create a repository, to have all of it collected together in one place, both as an act of transparency for the Russian people and for historians of the future to pore over. He wanted that repository to be in the Gorbachev Foundation."

Gorbachev himself persuaded Mitchell and her husband Scott Seydel to sit on the US board of Global Green that has offices in several American cities, including hurricane-devastated New Orleans, where Global Green has helped residents with construction of new homes.

The battering of the emerging free market economy in Russia, however, took a toll on Gorbachev. He was too proud to solicit help from friends, and money pledged for the foundation building—an edifice that would become roughly parallel in its symbolism to constructing a US presidential library—did not materialize.

Gorbachev felt isolated, abandoned, and betrayed. He refused to accept donations from shadowy business figures in his home country because of favors they might ask of him. He sunk into a personal depression, he says. A site and a building with only a roof and shell stood as a testament to his inability to realize its completion. It was personally humiliating.

A few months later, at a Global Green event in Los Angeles, Turner flew out to introduce his friend to the audience. Turner could tell something was bothering Gorbachev. After persistent prying, Gorbachev revealed that some Swiss contributors did not follow through on their pledge for the foundation. Mitchell shares the details of their exchange.

"Well, how much do you need?" Turner asked.

Gorbachev demurred, trying to change the subject.

"No, I'm serious, Mikhail. What will it take to complete the building the way you want it?"

At last, and only with strong-arming by Turner, did Gorbachev reluctantly divulge the amount of the shortfall in the construction budget: several million dollars.

"Ted handled it really well," Mitchell said. "He didn't make a big deal out of it, but he wanted to get it resolved for Gorbachev's peace of mind and for his own. He wrote Mikhail a check, told him that friends need to be there for each other, and insisted he take it to fulfill the important role that the foundation was meant to play."

There was no press release issued because that's not how friends operate. Turner reached out when others did not, Gorbachev remembers, saying, "The biggest donation came from Ted. Without him, we wouldn't have been able to complete the building."

To not honor a true "freedom fighter" that risked everything, as Gorbachev had been, would be a travesty, Turner says. "He deserved to be treated with respect."

In the United States, Gorbachev had seen the impact of charitable giving, American style. He was awed, he said. Such a tradition did not exist in Russia. Gorbachev had hoped his foundation would become an example for how his countrymen might think about the value of private philanthropy and giving back to society as an obligation of one's own prosperity.

Turner and Mitchell were invited to attend the dedication of the new structure in Moscow. "Ted did not want any acknowledgment. He wanted it to be President Gorbachev's day to be honored," Mitchell says. Still, Gorbachev paid homage to his American *droog* and today, if one looks closely in the courtyard of the Gorbachev Foundation, there is a plaque under a tree, thanking Turner in Russian and English.

In reaching out to a person he considered a great man, Turner didn't realize that Gorbachev aspired to imitate him, to embrace the Turner Foundation as a template. It is a spirit of empowerment that goes back to his interaction with Cousteau.

Amid his incessant travel, filled with public speaking appearances, shuttle diplomacy, and fund-raising in support of philanthropy, there are few tangible examples of private individuals creating a roadmap to follow. Turner is the one Gorbachev invokes when he talks with world leaders. Why? Because of the range of interrelated projects he funds.

"This is a man who knows how to make money, but more importantly he is a visionary who knows how to spend it right," Gorbachev says. "Ted will tell it like it is and in particular, if there is a need to defend something or someone out of principle, he will do it. I am proud to say I regard Ted as one of my best friends."

The former KGB careerist who had, at times, evinced an intense poker face in his talks with Reagan at Reykjavik, smiles again. He recounts a visit to Turner's ranches in Montana. He shares the tale of meeting a Turner friend, a magpie named Harry. The corvid had fallen out of its nest at the Snowcrest Ranch, then was hand-raised by Turner and his staff. He was charmed seeing the way that Turner interacted with the avian member of the crow family, a species known for its intelligence.

Turner recalls how Harry joined Gorbachev one morning at the breakfast table, sat on his shoulder, and beak-tapped his forehead. (The bird is still alive but now resides at the Beartooth Nature Center in Red Lodge, Montana, his viewers surely unaware of the prominent group of human friends he made along the way.)

Mostly, Gorbachev says, he was impressed to learn about the kinds of environmental restoration efforts occurring on Turner's properties at a time when many natural landscapes around the world are unraveling. He mentions the planting of a million longleaf pine seedlings at Avalon Plantation in Florida to restore the native forest and absorb carbon dioxide.

"On another property [the Armendaris Ranch] he is protecting bats!" Gorbachev says, becoming more animated and enthusiastic.

From their visits together, Gorbachev proudly has made a point of becoming conversant about the ecological niche bats fill. "Preserving hundreds of thousands of bats on just one property!" he says. "And, of course, Ted is raising and saving bison. He may even try to help rescue the bison of Europe!"

Unknown to many Americans, he relates, is that Turner's popularity around the globe stems from him calling himself an *internationalist* who embraces different cultures, religions, and customs.

When Gorbachev delivered his lecture in 1991 upon accepting the Nobel Peace Prize, he said: "Today, peace means the ascent from simple coexistence to cooperation and common creativity among countries and nations. Peace is a movement towards globality and universality of civilization. Never before has the idea that peace is indivisible been so true as it is now. Peace is not unity in similarity but unity in diversity, in the comparison and conciliation of differences. And, ideally, peace means the absence of violence. It is an ethical value."

"We have discovered often that policies are not enough. We need to build a new world order that will sustain life on Earth and unite the efforts of all nations," he added later in our conversation. "But foremost we need to make the kind of change that is needed tangible in people's minds. This is what Ted, on his ranches and through his philanthropy, is trying to do."

The threat of armed conflict and nuclear terrorism is heightened by nations attempting to wall themselves off in self-exile from the rest of the world, he says.

"What happens is that sometimes there are insulting attitudes expressed on the outside, and inside of that wall those words are meant to incite. But we forget, the people on either side of the wall have the same dreams. No matter where we live, we all have God's gift of life, we're all children of one peaceful loving God, but we can express those beliefs differently," Gorbachev says. "People like Ted may not adhere to a single religion, but as I know him, he believes in the spirit of humanity. That's his religion. And I don't think any god would fault him for that."

The next facet of Turner is the Turner who might have been.

Today, and while he is loath to admit it, it pains him to watch the decline of CNN in the content and ratings wars, the news channel that he birthed, nursed to global respectability, and transformed into the standard bearer for international coverage of world events. More than a decade after he was usurped, not a day goes by when former colleagues and faithful CNN viewers aren't pining for his return. He holds no personal ill will toward his onetime rival and ideological nemesis Rupert Murdoch.

Murdoch's reputation has been sullied plenty of late with the hacking scandal involving his newspapers in Britain. "No one has ever accused me or my company of illegally stealing private information and no television network I ran was operated to, so destructively, divide a country for partisan reasons and destroy any confidence that citizens have in America." Turner refuses to identity FOX by name but it should be implicit.

No one in television today fills the niche that Turner did. The fact is, he loved his role as a self-made media man. He appreciated the good it allowed him to do in the world. Although he says that he's had a fully satisfying life involved with other endeavors, a turn of events erased his ambition of bringing the role of news to an even higher plane.

"I don't say this to be dramatic, but one tragic part of Ted Turner's life—and it is nothing short of a tragedy—is what happened in wresting him of his power to complete the revolution in television he had envisioned."

Sharing the comments above, John Malone, founder of Liberty Media and a valued Turner friend, is referring to the blockbuster deal at the end of the twentieth century that brought together Time Warner Turner and Internet company AOL.

Malone still has strong feelings of revulsion for how Turner lost control of the media properties he spent his life building. He was with Turner the day that news of his ouster reached him. It didn't arrive in person, nor in a phone call, but via a fax sent to him at the Ladder Ranch in New Mexico.

Turner and Malone, it should be noted, have the same kind of trusting friendship as Turner and Gorbachev have. As Turner notes, he and Malone "were involved in cable TV before cable was cool." Both became billionaires because of their vision in bringing it mainstream.

In 2012, Malone earned the title of largest private landowner in America, overtaking Turner. He is effusive, however, in praising Turner for transforming the way he thinks about the environment and conservation and land. Because of Ted Turner, John Malone told me, he realizes there is no legacy more profound than how one treats the Earth because it reaches beyond generations.

If Turner had remained in media, and overseen the news media elements of Time Warner and AOL after the merger, Malone believes there would be a different tenor today in America. Turner, he says, would have devoted considerable resources, including his own wealth, to using television and print communication to foster a better and farther reaching dialogue about the problems facing America and the world—be it the debt crisis, the influence of lobbyists in politics, climate change, overpopulation, poverty in the developing world, or nuclear security. He would have assembled a dream team of newspeople and statesmen and women to moderate discussions.

Pat Mitchell, chief executive of the Paley Media Center, says Turner's removal confirms another irony: "We hear a lot about social corporate responsibility today. Ted invented that concept when he gave television a green conscience. We can only imagine what good might have come from him having the forum and resources to promote civility in America and foster goodwill."

The AOL Time Warner merger made Turner incredibly wealthy almost overnight, and when the stock value collapsed he also experienced one of the largest slides of fortune in human history. Even more painful than losing the money, Malone says, was Turner knowing that the orchestrators of the merger, Gerald Levin representing Time Warner Turner and Steve Case, founder of AOL, had frozen Turner out from any senior management role in the new company. But they could never tell him of their intentions to his face.

"I told him after reading the fax. I said, 'Ted, I'm sorry to inform you of this, but, friend, you just got screwed,'" Malone says.

Today, AOL Time Warner is a topic Turner seldom discusses, even among friends. He does note that Levin made a general apology in the newspaper, although he has never expressed his contrition personally to Turner, nor has Case reached out.

But Levin told the *New York Times* in response to decisions that cost Turner and fellow shareholders billions: "I was the CEO. I was in charge. I'm really very sorry about the pain and suffering and loss that was caused. I take responsibility."

"I don't care what Jerry Levin says. He double-crossed Ted Turner, pushed him out of television, and we are the worse for it," says John Malone.

"To call the transaction the worst in history, as it is now taught in business schools, does not begin to tell the story of how some of the brightest minds in technology and media collaborated to produce a deal now regarded by many as a colossal mistake," wrote reporter Tim Arango in the *New York Times* on January 10, 2010, on the occasion of the tenth anniversary of the AOL Time Warner deal.

Turner isn't bitter, just disappointed. He had dreams of what he would have done with the money, spending it on efforts to totally eradicate polio from the face of the Earth, getting mosquito nets into the hands of every family in malaria-prone regions of the world, amping up efforts to rescue species, battling poverty, promoting solar and wind and decommissioning nuclear weapons facilities, perhaps even incentivizing the Koreas to join hands in a peace park.

On top of it, if he had been in charge of programming at CNN, he would have used the airwaves to educate millions of viewers. And he had a fantasy of recruiting the best broadcast talent and experienced people skilled in statecraft to host debates on issues of the day. TV, Turner said, should be used to resolve serious problems, not make them worse. With an arsenal of cash, he is convinced he could have made it work.

"I'd like to forget it," he said of the AOL Time Warner saga in his interview with the *Times*. "That's what goes through my mind. I almost didn't do this interview because I didn't want to dig it up again. Let it pass into history. The Time Warner–AOL merger should pass into history like the Vietnam War and the Iraq and Afghanistan wars. It's one of the biggest disasters that have occurred to our country."

❦

Who is Ted Turner? Winner or loser? A reader's conclusion based on what kind of ledger? The final essential piece of the puzzle in arriving at an answer must necessarily address the Turner to come, the man who will still exude an influence after he's gone. And it won't be in television or technology.

What will happen when Ted Turner dies? It's a question I've received more often than any other. Will everything that he's tried to accomplish be all for naught? Will it vanish just as his physical presence is destined to disappear? Will he be forgotten like Charles Foster Kane?

It's a question that's worried Turner himself, even as far back as those days when he sat in a Washington, DC, seminar and first thought of establishing the Turner Foundation. He called upon his estate planner, Bob Biebel, one more time to help him plot his final moves.

Turner has crafted a document that is part of his will, giving instructions to his five children. He does not wish to merely leave them with a financial fortune. He wants them to carry on the stewardship he started, and yet put their own stamp on decisions that can affect, positively, the outcome of the world.

Decades ago, Turner helped to ignite the conservation easement movement in America, which gives property owners tax breaks for agreeing not to develop their land and preserve elements of nature for the common good. As part of a new landmark partnership he's invented with The Nature Conservancy, Turner has taken that idea to a whole new level.

Most of Turner's two million acres of land, extending across nearly two dozen properties, would be bequeathed to The Turner Conservation Trust, a sibling to The Turner Foundation. And The Nature Conservancy would serve as a "conservation guardian"—a watchdog—ensuring that the integrity of the land be maintained in perpetuity. The aim is to approach sustainability in such a way that the triple bottom line will be defended. Again, the "triple bottom line" refers to financial balance sheets, protection of the environment, and benefits to local and larger communities. "I believe the triple bottom line is our only hope," Turner says. "We need to promote an accounting system that produces human wealth, safeguards the wealth of nature, and benefits society rather than making problems worse."

A written preamble reads in part: "The purpose of the Turner Conservation Trust will be to demonstrate how large ranches and other lands can be managed to achieve the objectives of conservation, renewable energy and other compatible uses, such as ecosystem services, in a way that is financially sustainable. It is hoped that the demonstration of such an approach to land management will show other owners . . . that there is a better way to manage their resources—a new model of land management that combines the best land conservation practices with renewable/sustainable commerce that minimizes impact on the land, while generating revenue that can be used to sustain the ranch. This new model of land management is currently being defined and refined by Turner ranches, the

Turner Foundation and the Turner Endangered Species Fund under the direction and leadership of Ted and his family. After Ted's death, his family, through the Turner Conservation Trust, will continue this work. The trustees will work alongside The Nature Conservancy and other entities in securing the success of this project and disseminating the results in an effort to replicate the model as widely as possible."

Noteworthy is that while Turner's net worth today is slightly north of $2 billion, he has, considering all of his combined philanthropic contributions and the conservation plans for his lands, given away a monetary amount equal to his fortune, and it is the fortune that will be used to make his eco-humanitarian philanthropy self-perpetuating.

"I have no delusions about achieving immortality," Ted says, "but it's sure been a lot of fun living this life. There have been some rough patches but we made it through. We fought our hardest. That's all we can do."

Not long after the black wolf appeared to Turner in his dreams, he and one of his friends were driving up a back road behind his Montana home when a real lobo, its coat as dark as night, appeared. Turner and his companion got out of the vehicle and watched it for a long time at exceedingly close range. It evinced no fear and showed Turner no malice. It made his heart race with excitement.

Some human residents on the perimeter of the Flying D would like to see the ranch's pack exterminated, or at least have its numbers severely slashed. But Turner is making a stand for wolves and for all kinds of other underdogs. He says his burgeoning relationship with the environment has made him think differently, to see himself in its reflection. Where once he had a bumper sticker made that read, "Save the Humans," his new slogan is, "Save Everything."

On the same porch where he once looked into the starlight and thought of taking his own life, he now joins family members and friends in a little revelry. Fresh on the heels of a visit to the wolf den over the next ridge, Turner's guests stand listening as Ted cups his hands around his mouth and offers a primal baying up into moonlight.

A few minutes later, from that distant knoll, a wolf howls in reply. And then comes another.

Acknowledgments

Writing this book has taught me profound lessons about the character of individual people.

In the hardcover version of *Last Stand,* I shared this observation once made by Ernest Hemingway: "If a writer knows enough about what he is writing about, he may omit things that he knows. The dignity of movement of an iceberg is due to only one ninth of it being above water." The iceberg analogy with Ted Turner holds. Indeed, the essence of many things resides in what was previously unseen. The challenge always is to illuminate the surface while revealing what lies below or is hidden in shadow, for it is the shadow that often defines who people, great or not, really are. As any writer knows, we write to understand, to try to compile a more complete picture of our subjects, to minimize potential blind spots and eliminate surprises. Revelation comes from distilling down everything that you know and absorb into the elements that you believe are essential.

I am grateful to Ted Turner for opening himself up. We discussed a multitude of aspects to his life that are not in this book. He gave me unconditional, unlimited access, knowing up front that my intent was neither to write a hagiography nor to produce a shameless, tabloidy "tell-all." This book is instead about a complicated man's exploration of bid ideas, the motivations behind them, and what action or inaction could mean for our lives and future generations on Planet Earth in this century.

Many, many people were generous in providing insights into Turner and his well-known and lesser-understood idiosyncrasies. I cannot possible name every individual here, though I should note that a large number are quoted or referenced in the preceding pages. To one and all, I am deeply thankful for your help and cooperation.

The research and writing of *Last Stand* has been a journey of unforeseen twists, turns and discoveries as I surveyed the iceberg. Some things I could never have anticipated at the onset. I have come to understand more about Turner and his world since the first edition of *Last Stand* appeared. Over the lengthy span in which the book came together, my two children, Carter and Natalie, went from being grade schoolers to young adults. They literally grew up hearing stories about their dad's encounters with Turner, the wide arc of his life, and people in it. They witnessed how the final book moved from abstract concept to a human portrait hopefully drawn with myriad dimensions.

I am indebted to them and my wife, Jeanne, for indulging me with time spent away, and support as I agonized through aspects of this book that, from start to finish, engulfed eight years. I also thank those courageous selfless individuals—you know who you are—who believed, unwaveringly, in this book before and after its publication. I toast you here and now.

Books become records and in a way archives of remembrance that speak not only to specific time frames but they set the stage for thinking about the future. Going back a couple of decades to the first interview I had with Turner, I've learned that the most valuable asset a person can have isn't money, nor fame, adulation, position, nor a checklist of accumulated material things, including land, but time to make a difference. The world is full of poseurs. Those who are truly selfless, who don't have personal agendas to make themselves look bigger or appear more important than they are, stand out. As an expression of how fleeting and fragile time is, several remarkable people whom I interviewed for this book have since passed on. They deserve our remembrance: Richard Holbrooke, Jim

Range, Joe Truett, David Getches, Johnny Godley, Russ Peterson, Bob Wussler, Kevin Honness, and Clarence "Curly Bear" Wagner.

At Lyons/Globe Pequot, special mention must be directed to Allen M. Jones, my gifted, discerning editor from the West who provided a clear-headed, even-keeled, and indispensable role in helping me pare back and tighten the manuscript. Originally, *Last Stand* stood at more than 195,000 words; the book in your hands is some where in the range of 130,000 words. The 65,000 words you do not see does not mean they are not fascinating, important or relevant.

Here, I need to thank Carolyn and Johnny Godley and Ray and Joanne Tudor who graciously hosted me at Hope Plantation and St. Phillips Island in South Carolina and who, over many years, served as anchors in Ted Turner's life and that of his family. A long chapter on what those two properties, which were managed by the Godleys and Tudors did not make it into print but readers should know they were crucial in Turner's evolution as aneco-capitalist-humanitarian.

At Turner Enterprises Inc, I am grateful in particular to these people: Debbie Masterson in Atlanta; Karen and Jim Averitt in Bozeman, Montana and Russ Miller,who recently retired as general manager of all of Turner's properties in the American West. Each of them has been a pillar in Turner's personal life and I thank each for helping me overcome obstacles to make this book happen.

At Lyons/Globe Pequot, I thank Erin Turner, Meredith Dias, Laurie Kenney and Amy Alexander. In terms of individuals who provided especially important perspective were Rutherford and Laura Turner Seydel, former US senators Sam Nunn and Tim Wirth, Mike Finley, Taylor Glover, former US President Jimmy Carter, former Soviet President Mikhail Gorbachev, Lester Brown, former UN Secretary-General Kofi Annan, Jane Fonda, Tom Brokaw, former Vice President Al Gore, John Malone, Charles Curtis, Graham Allison, Pat Mitchell, George McKerrow, Barbara Pyle, Jean-Michel Cousteau and others.

In addition, I thank Taylor Glover, Cathy Gwin Tim Flannery, Paul Ehrlich, T. Boone Pickens, Dan Flores, Joe Gutkoski, Fran and Deborah Popper, Wes Jackson, Leon Neel, Mike Clark, Pavel Palazhchenko, Sally Ranney, Katie Distler Eckman, Teddy Turner, Cynthia MacDonald, Kristine Witherspoon, Mike Gilpin, Dan Goodman, Catherine Crier, Dennis Glick, Bob Buzzas, Paula Beswick and colleagues at the Bozeman Public Library which made *Last Stand* the One Book-One Bozeman selection, Ariana Paliobagis and the great staff at Country Bookshelf, Ray Rasker, Elena Cizmaric (who shot the cover image for the book!), Baldwin Harris, Beau Turner, Rhett Turner, Jennie Turner, Devon Finley, Phillip Evans, Carl Pope, Steve Topping, Terry Anderson, Kalee Kreider, Pat Clancey, Bruce Farling, Rick Peterson, Randal Dutra, John Felsing, Alex Diekmann, Al Zelver, Michael Soule, Ed Bangs, Doug Smith, L. David Mech, Steve Duerr, Greg Hagan, Bill Newmark, John Hoogland, Ilse-Mari Lee, Jim Webster, Lisa Robertson, Bill Burke (co-author of the Turner memoir Call MeTed), Brian Kahn, Tim Sandlin, Gerald Durley, Bernice King, Susan Clark, Thomas Kaplan, Tim Crawford, Jim Peterson, Brian Schweitzer, Peter Bahouth and others.

Finally and certainly not least, are those who gave me priceless assistance on every one of Turner's landholdings, enterprises and related endeavors involving bison. They are the trust folks whom Turner regards as extended members of his own family: Russ and Marcia Miller, Mike and Linda Phillips, Tom and Linda Waddell, Steve and Janie Dobrott, David Hunter, Barb Killoren, Dave and Linda Dixon, Mark and Pat Kossler, Tom and Irma LeFaive, Keith and Eva Yearout, Danny Johnson, Carter Kruse, Carolyn Godley and her clan, Ray and Joanne Tudor, John and Jaynee Hansen, Frank Purvis and his clan, Raymond Bass, Bud Griffith, David Withers, Marv Jensen, Dustin Long, George Richards, Chris Francis, Rob Arnaud, Jim Dorn, Ray King, Val Asher, Todd Traucht, Neil Lawson, Josh Marks, Bob Biebel, Dusty Hepper, John Hurd, Tom Bragg, Alan Oborny, Terry Purdum, Johnny Covey, Jack and Gail Shell, Brian and Diane Ward, Bob and Laurie Dineen, Ty Ward, Dave Carter, Jim Matheson, Magnus McCaffery, Aaron and Alisha Paulson, Malcolm and Trudy Deane, Pablo Rehbein, Ronnie Olsen, and Gustavo Olsen—the Norwegian-Argentine boatman/fishing guide who was there with me on the Rio Collon Cura that autumn day when Turner put down his fly rod and started to wax/reflect on the most closely guarded aspects of his life.

Appendix

Turner Foundation, Inc.
TFI Grantees as of September 13, 2012
Total Giving to Date: $358 million

Grantee Names

1000 Friends of Florida
1000 Friends of New Mexico
10000 Years Institute
20/20 Vision Education Fund
2041 Foundation Incorporated
A Better Hometown Community
A Friends House
A Territory Resource
Academy for Educational
  Development
Academy Theatre
ACLU
Action Canada for Population
  and Development
Action Health Incorporated
Adelante Resource Conservation
  and Development Council
Adolescent Pregnancy Coalition
  of North Carolina
Advocacy Arts Foundation
Advocates for Youth
African Wildlife Foundation
Africare
AID Atlanta
Alabama Rivers Alliance
Alan Guttmacher Institute
Alaska Center for the
  Environment
Alaska Conservation Foundation
Alaska Forum for Environmental
  Responsibility
Alaska Marine Conservation
  Council
Alaska Public Interest Research
  Group
Alaska Wilderness League
Alaska Wildlife Alliance
Alberta Wilderness Association
Alder Volunteer Fire Department
Alfred B. Maclay, Jr. Private Day
  School
ALIMAR
All Saints Episcopal Church

Alliance for Affordable Energy
Alliance for Justice
Alliance for Nuclear
  Accountability
Alliance for School Choice
Alliance for the Rio Grande
  Heritage
Alliance for the Wild Rockies
Alliance for Water Efficiency
Alliance Theatre
Altamaha Riverkeeper, Inc.
Alternative Energy Resources
  Organization
Alzheimer's Disease & Related
  Disorders Association, Inc.
Amazon Alliance for Indigenous
  and Traditional Peoples of the
  Amazon Basin
Amazon Watch
American Association for the
  Advancement of Science
American Bird Conservancy
American Birding Association
American Cancer Society , Inc. -
  Georgia Chapter
American Cancer Society, Inc. -
  Illinois Chapter
American Cancer Society, Inc. -
  South Carolina Chapter
American Chestnut Foundation,
  Inc.
American Council for an
  Energy-Efficient Economy
American Farmland Trust
American Fisheries Society
American Forests
American Heart Association, Inc.
  - Florida Chapter
American Heart Association, Inc.
  - Georgia Chapter
American Hotel & Lodging
  Educational Foundation
American Indian Institute
American Jewish Committee
American Land Institute

American Lands Alliance
American Littoral Society - Cape
  Florida Project
American Littoral Society -
  ReefKeeper Int'l Division
American Lung Association -
  Atlanta Chapter
American Lung Association -
  DC Chapter
American Lung Association of
  the Southeast, Inc.
American Medical Women's
  Association
American Museum of the
  Moving Image
American Music Scholarship
  Association
American Oceans Campaign
American Red Cross
American Rivers, Inc.
American Saddle Horse Museum
  Association, Inc.
American Saddlebred Special
  Commission
American Sail Training
  Association
American Solar Energy Society
American Thoracic Society, Inc.
American University
American Whitewater
American Wildlands
Americans for Equitable Climate
  Solutions
Americans for Our Heritage and
  Recreation
Americans for the Environment
American's Wildlife Association
  for Resource Education
American-Scandinavian
  Foundation
America's Watershed Landkeeper
America's Wildlife Association
  for Resource Education
Amigos Bravos, Inc.
Amigos of Earth

353

Amory Lovins-Consultant
Anchors Away
Ancient Forest International
Andrew J. Young Foundation, Inc.
Androcles Society
Animal Health Trust US Ltd.
Animal Protection of New Mexico, Inc.
Antarctica Project
Anti-Defamation League
AOPA Foundation, Inc.
Apalachicola Bay and Riverkeeper, Inc.
Aperture Foundation, Inc.
Appalachian Center for the Economy and the Environment
Appalachian Trail Conference
Appleseed Foundation/Montana Law Center
Aquidneck Island Trust
Arcadia Wildlife Preserve, Inc.
Argentina's Ornithological Association
Arid Lands Project
Arizona Board of Regents
Arizona Center for Law in the Public Interest
Arizona Fraternal Order of Police Foundation, Inc.
Arizona Memorial Museum Association
Arizona State University - Department of Anthropology
Arizona State University - School of Human Evolution and Social Change
Arizona-Sonora Desert Museum
Armed Forces Foundation
Arms Control Association
Armuchee Alliance
Artemis Common Ground
Artemis Wildlife Foundation/ Common Ground
Asian Pacific Environmental Network
Associated Builders and Contractors, Inc.
Association for Vulsurg
Association of Small Foundations
Athens Land Trust

Athens-Clark Heritage Foundation
Atlanta Anti-Eating Disorders League
Atlanta Audubon Society
Atlanta Ballet, Inc.
Atlanta Bicycle Campaign
Atlanta Botanical Garden
Atlanta Boy Choir
Atlanta Children's Shelter
Atlanta College of Art
Atlanta Community Food Bank
Atlanta Education Fund, Inc.
Atlanta Hawks Foundation, Inc.
Atlanta Historical Society, Inc.
Atlanta History Center
Atlanta Housing Authority
Atlanta International School, Inc.
Atlanta Lyric Theatre
Atlanta Neighborhood Development Partnership
Atlanta Outward Bound Center
Atlanta Partnership for Arts in Learning
Atlanta Resource Foundation
Atlanta Ronald McDonald House Charities, Inc.
Atlanta Symphony Orchestra
Atlanta Women's Foundation Inc.
Atlanta-Fulton County Zoo, Inc.
Atlantic Salmon Federation, Inc.
Audubon Nebraska
AVSC International
Bank Information Center
Barrett Memorial Hospital Foundation
Bass and Howes
Bat Conservation International, Inc.
Bay Area Nuclear Waste Coalition
Beartooth Nature Center
Beaufort County Open Land Trust, Inc.
Beaufort High School Theatre
Belgrade Youth Forum
Beltline Partnership, Inc.
Better World Fund
Better World Society
Bide-a-Wee Home Association
Big Brothers Big Sisters of Galatin County

Big Brothers Big Sisters of Metro Atlanta, Inc.
Big Sky Wildcare Raptor Center
Big Sky Youth Empowerment
Big Sur Arts Initiative, Inc.
Big Sur Land Trust
Big Sur Learning Project
Big Wild Advocates
Bighorn Institute
Bill Fish Foundation
Biodiversity Legal Foundation
Biodiversity Project
Bird Emergency Aid and Kare Sanctuary
Black Women's Wellness Center
Blackfeet Reservation Development Fund, Inc.
Blackfoot Legacy
Blenheim Foundation
Blue Mountain Clinic, Inc.
Bluegrass Conservancy, Inc.
Bluewater Network
B'nai B'rith International
B'nai B'rith Youth Organization
Boggs Rural Life Center, Inc.
Boone and Crockett Wildlife Conservation Program
Boulder-Lhasa Sister City Project
Boy Scouts of America - Atlanta
Boy Scouts of America - Coastal Carolina Council
Boys & Girls Club of America
Boys & Girls Club of Sierra County
Boys & Girls Club of the Big Bend
Boys & Girls Clubs of Lowcountry, Inc.
Boys Farm
Bozeman Deaconess Foundation for Gifting
Bozeman Public Library Foundation, Inc.
Bozeman Youth Initiative
Bread for the Journey
Bridger Clinic
Broad River Watershed Association
Broadwater County Social Services Committee

Brookings Institution Center on Urban and Metropolitan Policy
Brooks School
Brookwood School
Brown Bear Resources, Inc.
Brown College
Buckhead Baseball, Inc.
Buenos Aires National Wildlife Refuge
Buffalo Field Campaign
Business Executives for National Security Education Fund
Business for Social Responsibility Education Fund
Business Leaders for Sensible Priorities Information Fund
California Association of Resource Conservation Districts
California Public Interest Research Group Charitable Trust
Callanwolde Fine Arts Center
Callaway Gardens
Calvert Foundation
Camp High Harbor
Campaign for a Prosperous Georgia
Campaign for America's Wilderness
Canadian Parks and Wilderness Society - BC Chapter
Cancer Research Foundation Capacity, Inc.
Caprock Partners Foundation
Captain Cooper Parent Club
Captain Planet Foundation, Inc.
CARAES Lowcountry Modeling
CARE
Caribbean Conservation Corporation
Carmel Unified School District
Carolina Art Association
Carolina Farm Stewardship Association
Carrie Steele-Pitts Home
Carter Center
Cascade County Historical Society
Cashiers Historical Society, Inc.
Castle-Crown Wilderness Coalition

Catalina Island Conservancy
Catawba River Foundation, Inc.
Catawba-Wateree Relicensing Coalition
Catholics For a Free Choice
Cenozoic Society, Inc.
Center for a Sustainable Coast
Center for a Sustainable Economy
Center for Adolescent Reproductive Health
Center for Arms Control and Non-Proliferation
Center for Biological Diversity
Center for Clean Air Policy
Center for Climate Strategies
Center for Commercial - Free Public Education
Center for Community Development
Center for Constitutional Rights
Center for Defense Information
Center for Democratic Renewal and Education, Inc.
Center for Development and Population Activities
Center for Energy Efficiency & Renewable Technologies
Center For Environmental Citizenship
Center for Environmental Politics
Center for Health, Environment and Justice
Center for Immigration Studies
Center for Independent Documentary, Inc.
Center for International Environmental Law
Center for Marine Conservation
Center for Media and Democracy
Center for Neighborhood Technology
Center for Policy Alternatives
Center for Public Interest Research, Inc.
Center for Reproductive Rights
Center for Research on Population and Security
Center for Resource Management

Center for Resource Solutions
Center for Resourceful Building Technology
Center for Rural Affairs
Center for Science in Public Participation
Center For Study Of Responsive Law
Center for the Advancement of Women
Center for Watershed Protection
Centers for Disease Control and Prevention Foundation
Central Baptist Church
Ceres, Inc.
Chancellor International Wildlife Fund
Charleston Community Sailing, Inc.
Charleston Day School, Inc.
Charleston Stage
Charleston Waterkeeper
Chastain Horse Park LTD
Chatham Academy
Chattahoochee Hill Country Conservancy
Chattahoochee Nature Center, Inc.
Chattahoochee Riverkeeper, Inc.
Chattanooga Chamber Foundation
Chattooga Conservancy
Chattooga Land Trust
Chattowah Open Land Trust
Chayil, Inc.
Chesapeake Bay Foundation
Chesapeake Bay Youth Conservation
Child Development Centers of the Bluegrass
Childkind, Inc.
Children's Blood Foundation, Inc.
Children's Healthcare of Atlanta Foundation, Inc.
Children's Home Society of Florida
Children's Museum of Atlanta, Inc.
Children's Museum of the Low Country
Children's Scholarship Fund
China Women's Hotline

Choice USA

CHRIS Kids, Inc. Christ Episcopal Church

Christian Emergency Help Center

Church Health Center

Churches' Center for Theology and Public Policy

Cimarron Public Schools

Cincinnati Zoo and Botanical Garden

Circle of Friends Celebrating Life, Inc.

Citadel

Citizens Against Nuclear Trash

Citizens Campaign on Dioxin & Synthetic Hormone Disrupters

Citizens Coal Council

Citizens' Environmental Coalition

Citizens for a Better Flathead

Citizens' for Clearinghouse for Hazardous Waste

Citizens For Environmental Justice

Citizens Fund

Citizens Trade Campaign Foundation

Citizens Vote, Inc.

City Lore, Inc.

City of Atlanta

City of Gordon

Clark Atlanta University

Clark Fork Coalition

Clarkston Community Center Foundation, Inc.

Clean Air Cool Planet, Inc.

Clean Air Council

Clean Air Network

Clean Air Task Force, Inc.

Clean Air Trust Education Fund

Clean Energy Group, Inc.

Clean Water America Alliance

Clean Water Fund

Clean Water Network, Inc.

Clemson University - Dept. of Biological Sciences

Climate Institute

Coalition for Clean Air

Coalition for Environmentally Responsible Economics

Coalition to Abolish Slavery & Trafficking

Coalition to Restore Urban Waters

Coast Alliance

Coastal Community Foundation of South Carolina

Coastal Conservation Association Florida

Coastal Environmental Management Program

Coastal Georgia Land Trust

Coastal Mountains Land Trust

Cobb County Public Schools Educational Foundation, Inc.

Cold Mountain, Cold Rivers

Collective Heritage Institute

College of Natural Resources University of California, Berkeley

Colleton Prep

Colorado Conservation Trust

Colorado Division of Wildlife

Colorado Environmental Coalition

Colorado NARAL Foundation

Colorado Public Interest Research Foundation

Columbia University: Columbia Earth Institute

Columbus Citizens Foundation

Common Cause Education Fund

Common Ground Project

Commonweal

Communication Works

Communications Consortium Media Center

Communities for a Better Environment

Community Action Agency of Southern New Mexico, Inc.

Community and Indian Legal Services of Northern New Mexico

Community Environmental Management, Inc.

Community Foundation of Central Georgia

Community Foundation of Greater Greenville

Community Foundation of Jackson

Community Foundation Serving Monterey County

Community Housing Resource Center

Community Networking Resources, Inc.

Community Office For Resource Efficiency

Community Rights Counsel

Community Youth Advisory Council

Community Youth Initiative Advisory Board, Inc.

Comprehensive School Health

Concerned Citizens for Nuclear Safety

Concerned Women for Family Planning

Concerts for the Environment

Congress for New Urbanism, Inc.

Congressional District Programs, Inc.

Congressional Sportsmen's Foundation

Conservation Foundation - National Office

Conservation Fund - Alaska Office

Conservation Fund - Colorado Office

Conservation Fund - National Office

Conservation Fund - Southeast Regional Office

Conservation International

Conservation Research Institute

Conservation Society

Conservation Trust of Puerto Rico

Consultative Group on Biological Diversity

Consumer Federation of America, Inc.

Consumer Policy Institute

Consumers Choice Council

Container Recycling Institute

Cool Girls, Inc.

Co-op America

Cooper Union for the Advancement of Science and Art

Coosa River Basin Initiative, Inc.

Coptic Orthodox Patriarchate Diocese of Southern United States
Coral Forest
Coral Reef Alliance
Coral Restoration Foundation, Inc.
Corporation for Enterprise Development
Corporation for Olympic Development in Atlanta
Corporation for the Northern Rockies
CorpWatch
Council for Quality Growth, Inc.
Council on Economic Priorities
Council on Foundations
Court Appointed Special Advocates
Craighead Wildlife Environmental Research Institute
Crazy Horse Memorial Foundation
Create Your Dreams
Creating Pride Atlanta, Inc.
Culinary Hospitality Educational Foundation
Cuyin Manzano
Cystic Fibrosis Foundation
Dallas Austin Foundation, Inc.
David Suzuki Foundation
Decatur First United Methodist Church
Defenders of Wild Cumberland
Defenders of Wildlife, Inc.
Dekalb County Partners in Education Foundation
Dekalb County Public Schools Foundation, Inc.
Del Agua Institute
Delaware Community Foundation
Delta Junior Sailing Association
Delta Society
Delta Waterfowl Foundation
Democracy South
Design Industries Foundation Fighting AIDS
Desktop Assistance
Development Center for Appropriate Technology

Dia de la Mujer Latina, Inc.
Dian Fossey Gorilla Fund
Dikembe Mutumbo Foundation
Dine'CARE
Disabled Sports USA
Dogwood Alliance
Dolphin Project
Dona Ana County Colonias Development Council
Don't Waste Arizona
Dos Margaritas
Ducks Unlimited, Inc. - Bismarck Chapter
Ducks Unlimited, Inc. - Charleston Chapter
Ducks Unlimited, Inc. - Marietta Chapter
Ducks Unlimited, Inc. - Memphis Chapter
Ducks Unlimited, Inc. - Tallahassee Chapter
Duke University
Duke University Primate Center
Dukes Foundation Corporation
Dyslexia Research Institute, Inc.
E. River Elementary School
EAGLE
Earth Action Network/E-Magazine
Earth Challenge
Earth Communications Office
Earth Council Foundation - US
Earth Day Network
Earth Force
Earth Island Institute, Inc.
Earth Policy Institute
Earth Restoration Alliance
Earth Share
EARTH University Foundation
Earthbond
Earthjustice - Juneau Office
Earthjustice - Midwest Regional Office
Earthjustice - Northern Rockies Regional Office
Earthjustice - NW Regional Office
Earthjustice - Oakland Office
Earthlaw
Earthlife Canada Foundation
EarthRights International
Earthworks

Eastlake Community Foundation
Ebenezer Baptist Church
Eco Educators, Inc.
ECOlogists Linked for Organizing Grassroots Initiative
Ecology Center, Inc. - Berkeley Office
Ecology Center, Inc. - Missoula Office
Economic Policy Institute
Ecotrust
Edisto Island Open Land Trust
Edmund S. Muskie Foundation
Educational Broadcasting Corp.
Egleston Children's Hospital/ EN-ACTE Program
Eisenhower World Affairs Institute
Ellijay Wildlife Rehabilitation Sanctuary, Inc.
Elton John AIDS Foundation
Emory University
Emory University - Michael C. Carlos Museum
Emory University School of Law - Turner Environmental Law Clinic
Emory University School of Medicine - Dept. of Psychiatry
Emory University School of Medicine - Office of Development
Endangered Species Coalition
Endangered Species Project
Endowment of the United States Institute of Peace, Inc.
Energy Foundation
Energy Research Foundation, Inc.
Enersol Associates, Inc.
Engender Health
Enterprising Environmental Solutions, Inc.
Entrepreneurial Department
Environment California Research and Policy Center
Environment News Trust
Environmental and Energy Study Institute
Environmental Background Information Center

Environmental Careers Organization
Environmental Community Action, Inc.
Environmental Defense Fund, Inc. - New York Office
Environmental Defense Fund, Inc. - North Carolina Office
Environmental Defense, Inc. - National Office
Environmental Defense, Inc. - Rocky Mountain Office
Environmental Education Media Project for China
Environmental Educational Alliance, Inc.
Environmental Enterprises Assistance Fund
Environmental Film Festival in the Nations Capital
Environmental Fund for Florida, Inc.
Environmental Fund for Georgia, Inc.
Environmental Grantmakers Association
Environmental Health Fund, Inc.
Environmental Justice Fund
Environmental Justice Resource Center at Clark Atlanta University
Environmental Law Institute
Environmental Media Association, Inc.
Environmental Media Services West - Northwest Office
Environmental Policy Project/ Georgetown University Law Center
Environmental Protection Information Center
Environmental Research Foundation
Environmental Solutions International
Environmental Support Center
Environmental Systems Protection Fund
Environmental Working Group
Eos Institute
Equestrian Events, Inc
Equilibres et Population

Essential Information
ETV Endowment of South Carolina, Inc.
Evaro Community Center Inc
Everglades Foundation, Inc.
Exodus
Eyak Preservation Council
Fairness & Accuracy in Reporting
Faith Presbyterian Pre-School
Families First
Family Health Productions
Farm Aid, Inc.
Farmworker Association of Florida, Inc.
Farmworker Network for Environmental and Economic Justice
Fashion Cares
Federation of Southern Cooperatives
Feminist Majority Foundation
Feminist Women's Health Center, Inc.
Fernbank, Inc.
First Nations Development Institute
First Scots Presbyterian Church
First United Methodist Church
Five Valleys Land Trust, Inc.
Flathead Land Trust
Flint Riverkeeper, Inc.
Florence Fund
Florida Audubon Society
Florida Biodiversity Project
Florida Certified Organic Growers and Consumers
Florida Defenders of the Environment
Florida State University
Florida Stewardship Foundation
Florida Water Environment Association
Florida Wildlife Federation
Forest Conservation Council
Forest Guardians
Forest Service Employees for Environmental Ethics
Forest Stewardship Council US
Forest Trends
Forest Trust
ForestEthics

Forward Arts Foundation
Fossil Fuels Policy Action Institute/Sustainable Energy Institute
Foundation Center
Foundation for Global Sustainability
Foundation for International Environmental Law & Development
Foundation for Medically Fragile Children
Foundation for North American Wild Sheep
Foundation for Public Broadcasting in Georgia, Inc.
Four Corners Institute
Frank Foundation CAI
Franklin Institute
Friends Committee on National Legislation Education Fund
Friends of Buenos Aires National Wildlife Refuge
Friends of FAI-The Italian Environment Foundation, Inc.
Friends of Fondo per l'Ambiente Italian
Friends of Hawaii Volcanoes National Park
Friends of Pritchard Island
Friends of Raven Run, Inc.
Friends of Scotland
Friends of the Africa Foundation
Friends of the Bitterroot
Friends of the Earth
Friends of the Earth - Japan
Friends of the Owls
Friends of the River
Friends of the Wild Swan
Friends of Yosemite Search and Rescue
Frisco Creek Wildlife Rehabilitation Center
From Darkness to Light Program
Full Gospel Tabernacle
Fulton-DeKalb Hospital Authority - Grady Memorial Hospital
Fund for Investigative Journalism, Inc.
Fund for Southern Communities
Fund for Wild Nature

Fundacion Aguas Patagonicas
Fundacion Vida Silvestre
Argentina
Funder's Network for Smart
Growth and Livable
Communities
Funders Network on Population,
Reproductive Health and
Rights
Future Harvest
G&P Foundation
Galapagos Conservancy, Inc.
Gallatin Gateway Youth Group
Gallatin Valley Land Trust
Game Conservancy Trust
Ganados Del Valle
Garden Club of Georgia
Garden County Schools
Gateway Youth Group
Geltaftan Foundation, Inc.
George West Mental Health
Foundation, Inc.
Georgia Aquarium, Inc.
Georgia Association for Pri.
Interim
Georgia Battlefields Association
Georgia Boy Choir, Inc.
Georgia Campaign for
Adolescent Pregnancy
Prevention, Inc.
Georgia Conservancy, Inc.
Georgia Conservation Voters
Education Fund, Inc.
Georgia Council for
International Visitors
Georgia Department of Natural
Resources
Georgia Department of Natural
Resources/Sapelo Island
Georgia Ensemble Theatre
Company
Georgia Environmental Council
Georgia Environmental
Organization
Georgia Environmental Policy
Institute
Georgia Forestwatch, Inc.
Georgia Historical Society
Georgia Initiative
Georgia Interfaith Power &
Light, Inc.

Georgia Law Center for the
Homeless
Georgia Legal Watch
Georgia Organic Growers
Association
Georgia Organics, Inc.
Georgia Poultry Justice Alliance
Georgia Public
Telecommunications
Commission
Georgia Recycling Coalition, Inc.
Georgia Restaurant Council, Inc.
Georgia River Network, Inc.
Georgia School-Age Care
Association, Inc.
Georgia Solar Energy
Association, Inc.
Georgia Southern College
Foundation
Georgia Southern University
St. Catherines Sea Turtle
Conservation Program
Georgia Southwestern College
Foundation, Inc.
Georgia State University
Research Foundation
Georgia Tech Foundation, Inc.
Georgia Tech Research
Corporation
Georgia Transplant Foundation,
Inc.
Georgia Trust for Historic
Preservation
Georgia Urban Forest Council
Georgia Wand Education Fund,
Inc.
Georgia Watch
Georgia Wildlife Federation
Georgia World Congress Center
Authority
Georgians for Children, Inc.
Georgians For Choice
Georgians for Clean Energy
Georgians for Transportation
Alternatives
German Foundation for World
Population
Get Challenged
Gettysburg National Battlefield
Museum Foundation
Gila Resources Information
Project

Girl Scout Council of Northwest
Georgia, Inc.
Girl Scout Troop # 266
Girl Scouts Council Northwest
Georgia, Inc.
Girl Scouts of Carolina Low
Country
Girl Scouts of Greater Atlanta,
Inc.
Girls Incorporated - New York
Office
Girls Incorporated of Greater
Atlanta
Give 2 Asia
Glamorama
Glen Canyon Institute
Global Environment & Trade
Study
Global Environmental Options,
Inc.
Global Exchange
Global Fund for Women
Global Green USA
Global Greengrants Fund
Global Security Institute
Global Stewardship Initiative/
Aspen Institute
Glynn Environmental Coalition,
Inc.
Good Wood Alliance
Goodwill Industries of North
Georgia
Goodwill Industries of the
Coastal Empire
Gorbachev Foundation
Government Accountability
Project
Grand Canyon Trust
Grassroots Recycling Network
Great American Station
Foundation
Great Bear Foundation
Great Lakes United
Greater Atlanta Chamber
Foundation, Inc.
Greater DC Cares
Greater Gila Biodiversity Project
Greater Yellowstone Coalition,
Inc.
Green Fire Productions
Green Seal
GreenLaw, Inc.

Greenpeace Fund
Groundwater Foundation
Group for Cultural Diversity
Grupo de Tecnologia Alternativa S.C.
Guana Area Intracoastal Network
Gulf Coast Environmental Defense
Gulf Restoration Network
Guy Harvey Ocean Fund, Inc.
Gwich'in Steering Committee
H. John Heinz III Center for Science, Economics and the Environment
Habitat for Humanity
Hands On Atlanta
Hank Aaron Chasing the Dream Foundation, Inc.
Haralson Coalition for Children, Youth & Families
Harbor Historical Association of Georgetown
Hardtner Community Foundation
Harrison Schools
Harvard School of Public Health
Haven
Hawaii Natural History Association, LTD
Hawks Aloft
HawkWatch International, Inc.
Headley - Whitney Museum, Inc.
Headwaters Resource Conservation and Development Area
Health Care Without Harm
Health Sciences Foundation
Healthy Child Healthy World, Inc.
Hearts of the Valley
Heartwood
Helena Education Foundation
Hells Canyon Preservation Council
Help Argentina
Henry A. Wallace Institute for Agricultural and Environmental Policy at Winrock International
Henry Clay Memorial Foundation

Henry Street Settlement
Henry W. Grady Health System Foundation
Heritage Foundation, Inc.
Herreshoff Marine Museum
Hesperia Museum and Nature Center
High Hope Steeplechase Association, Inc.
High Museum
Highlander Research & Education Center
Historic Charleston Foundation
Historic District Development Corporation
Historic Ricefields Association
Hooker County Community Foundation, Inc.
Horatio Alger Association of Distinguished Americans, Inc.
Horizon Theatre Company, Inc.
Hornocker Wildlife Research Institute
Hudson Riverkeeper Fund
Human Resource Development Council
Humanitarian Aid Relief Fund, Inc.
Hygeia Foundation
ICLEI-Local Governments for Sustainability USA
Idaho Environmental Education Association
Idaho Rivers United
Idaho Sporting Congress
Idaho Wildlife Federation
Independent Press Association
Independent Sector
Indian Law Resource Center
INFORM, Inc.
Inland Empire Public Lands Council
INOCHI
Institute for Advancement of Journalistic Clarity
Institute for Agriculture and Trade Policy
Institute for America's Future
Institute for Civic Renewal
Institute for Conservation Leadership

Institute for Energy and Environmental Research
Institute for Fisheries Resources
Institute for Georgia Environmental Leadership, Inc.
Institute for Local Self-Reliance
Institute for Policy Studies
Institute for Regional Education
Institute for Transportation & Development Policy
Institutes for Journalism and Natural Resources
Interdenominational Theological Center, Inc.
Interfaith Council for the Protection of Animals and Nature
Interhemispheric Resource Center
Intermountain Planned Parenthood, Inc.
International Center for Research on Women
International Center for Technology Assessment
International City/County Management Association
International Crane Foundation, Inc.
International Forum on Globalization
International Indian Treaty Council
International Institute for Energy Conservation
International Marine Mammal Project
International Planned Parenthood Federation/Western Hemisphere Region
International Ranger
International Ranger Federation
International Rescue Committee, Inc.
International Rivers Network
International Snow Leopard Trust
International Study for Animal Rights
International Union for Conservation of Nature

International Wilderness
Leadership Foundation
International Wildlife Film
Festival
International Wolf Center
International Women's Health
Coalition
International Women's Media
Foundation
International Yacht Restoration
School
InterTribal Bison Cooperative
Iowa State University
IPAS
Island Press - Center for
Resource Economics
Italian American Business
Council, Inc
Izaak Walton League of America
J.W. Fanning Institute for
Leadership c/o University of
Georgia Foundation
Jackson Hole Conservation
Alliance
Jackson Hole Wildlife Film
Festival
Jacksonboro Community Center
Jacksonville Community
Foundation
Jacksonville Film and Television
Commission
Jacksonville Sailing Foundation
Jacksonville University
Jacksonville Zoological Gardens
James Levine Co.
Jane Fonda Center at Emory
University
Jane Goodall Institute
Jane Goodall Institute for
Wildlife Research, Education
and Conservation
Jefferson County Board of
County Commissioners
Jefferson County High School
Jefferson County Humane
Society, Inc.
Jefferson County Youth Council
Jekyll Island Foundation
Jewish Family Services, Inc.
Jewish Federation of Greater
Atlanta
Jobs and Environment Campaign

Joseph E. Lowery Institute for
Justice and Human Rights
Jules Verne Adventures USA
Junior League of Houston, Inc
Juvenile Diabetes Research
Foundation International
Katy Prairie Conservancy
Kearney Area Community
Foundation
Keep a Child Alive
Kentucky Educational Television
Foundation, Inc.
Kentucky Environmental
Foundation
Kentucky Horse Park
Foundation, Inc.
Keystone Center
Kidz 1st Fund
Kiwanis Youth Foundation of
Monticello Florida
Klamath Basin Rangeland Trust
L S B Leakey Foundation
Labor Community Strategy
Center
Lady Bird Johnson Wildflower
Center
Lake Allatoona Preservation
Authority
Lake Pontchartrain Basin
Foundation
Land and Water Fund of the
Rockies
Land Institute
Land Trust Alliance, Inc.
Land Trust for the Little
Tennessee, Inc.
Lanier Partners of North Georgia
Latin American Association, Inc.
Lawyers' Committee for Civil
Rights Under Law
League of Conservation Voters
Education Fund
League of Wilderness Defenders
League of Women Voters of Los
Angeles - Education Fund
League of Women Voters
Population Coalition
Legal Environmental Assistance
Foundation
Leukemia & Lymphoma Society,
Inc. - Hunt Valley Chapter

Leukemia & Lymphoma Society,
Inc. - Mt. Pleasant Chapter
Lexington Cancer Foundation,
Inc.
Lexington Hearing and Speech
Center, Inc.
Lexington Public Library
Foundation, Inc.
Life Net
LifeLine Animal Project, Inc.
LightHawk - Lander Chapter
LightHawk - San Francisco
Chapter
Lima Public Schools
Little Red Schoolhouse
Educational and Community
Center, Inc.
Little Traverse Conservancy
Livable Communities Coalition,
Inc.
Logan Heights Family Health
Center
Lookout Mountain Conservancy
Lost Boys Foundation
Louisiana Environmental Action
Network
Lovett School
Lowcountry Open Land Trust,
Inc.
Lula Lake Land Trust
MacGillivray Freeman Films
Educational Foundation
Maclay
MADRE
Make It Right Foundation
Make-A-Wish Foundation of
Georgia and Alabama, Inc.
Malpai Borderlands Group, Inc.
Maple Women's Psychological
Counseling Center
Marcus Autism Center, Inc.
Marie Stopes International
Marine Conservation Biology
Institute
Marine Conservation Biology
Institute
Marine Mammal Center
Markey Cancer Foundation, Inc.
Massachusetts Audubon Society
Maynard Jackson Youth
Foundation, Inc.
McCallie School

McKenzie River Gathering
Foundation
Meals on Wheels of Atlanta
Median Island International
Men Stopping Violence, Inc.
Mercy Corps
Methodist Home of the South
Georgia Conference
Metro Atlanta YMCA
MEXFAM
Michigan Environmental
Council
Middle Georgia Wilderness
Institute
Mikal Kellner Foundation for
Animals
Military Toxics Project
Mineral Policy Center
Mineral Policy Institute
Minnesota Medical Foundation
Minnesota Organization
on Adolescent Pregnancy
Prevention
Mission Wolf
Missoula Center for Responsible
Planning
Missouri Botanical Garden
MLK Jr. Center for Non-Violent
Social Change
Montana Association of
Churches
Montana Audubon
Montana Community
Foundation
Montana Conservation Corps
Montana Conservation Science
Institute
Montana Department of Fish
Wildlife & Parks
Montana Environmental
Education Association
Montana Environmental
Information Center
Montana Fish, Wildlife and
Parks
Montana Fishing Outfitters
Conservation Fund
Montana Historical Society
Montana Human Rights
Network
Montana Land Reliance
Montana Outfitters & Guides
Association

Montana Parks Association
Montana Public Interest
Research Foundation
Montana River Action Network
Montana State University -
Biology Department
Montana State University -
Department of Land Resources
and Environmental Sciences
Montana Wetlands Trust
Montana Wilderness Association
Montana Wildlife Federation
Montanans for Choice
Monterey Bay Aquarium
Foundation
Morehouse School of Medicine
Morris Brown College
Mothers and Others For a
Livable Planet
Mount Sinai School of Medicine
of New York University
Mountain Conservation Trust
Mountains Education Program
Movement for the Survival of the
Ogoni People, USA
Ms. Foundation For Women
Mule Deer Foundation
Multiple Sclerosis Foundation
Museum of Television and Radio
Museum of the Rockies
Mythic Imagination Institute
Nanakila Institute
NARAL New Mexico Education
Fund
NARAL Pro-Choice America
Foundation
NARAL Pro-Choice Georgia
NAS - Appleton Whittell
Research Ranch
National Abortion Federation
National Academy of Sciences
National Affordable Housing
Network, Inc.
National Alliance for
Community Trees
National Arbor Day Foundation
National Association of
Plumbing-Heating-Cooling
Contractors
National Association of Clean
Water Agencies
National Association of
Conservation Districts

National Association of State
Conservation Agencies
National Audubon Society -
Alaska State Office
National Audubon Society, Inc. -
Florida State Office
National Audubon Society, Inc. -
National Office
National Audubon Society, Inc. -
New Mexico State Office
National Audubon Society, Inc. -
New York State Office
National Audubon Society, Inc. -
South Carolina State Office
National Black Arts Festival, Inc.
National Black Women's Health
Project
National Buffalo Museum
National Campaign for Pesticide
Policy Reform
National Campaign for
Sustainable Agriculture
National Campaign to Prevent
Teen and Unplanned Pregnancy
National Catholic Rural Life
Conference
National Cattlemen's Foundation
National Center for Appropriate
Technology, Inc.
National Center for Learning
Disabilities
National Congress For
Community Economic
Development
National Council for
International Health
National Council of Churches
of Christ
National Council of Jewish
Women, Inc.
National Environmental
Education and Training
Foundation
National Environmental
Education and Training
Foundation, Inc.
National Environmental Trust
National Family Planning
& Reproductive Health
Association
National FFA Foundation, Inc.
National Fish and Wildlife
Foundation - National Office

National Fish and Wildlife Foundation - New York Office
National Fish and Wildlife Foundation - South Carolina Office
National Fish and Wildlife Foundation - Southern Region Office
National Forest Foundation
National Forest Protection Alliance
National Foundation March of Dimes
National Foundation March of Dimes
National Governors' Association - Center for Best Practices
National Marine Sanctuaries
National Multiple Sclerosis Society - Georgia Chapter
National Museum of the American Indian
National Network of Abortion Funds
National Network of Grantmakers
National Park Foundation
National Park Service
National Parks Conservation Association
National Pipeline Reform Coalition
National Practitioners Network for Fathers and Families
National Public Radio
National Recycling Coalition
National Religious Partnership for the Environment, Inc.
National Restaurant Association
National Trust for Historic Preservation
National Wild Turkey Federation, Inc.
National Wildlife Federation - Anchorage Office
National Wildlife Federation - Boulder Office
National Wildlife Federation - National Office
National Wildlife Federation - Northern Rockies Office

National Wildlife Federation - Reston Office
National Wildlife Federation - Seattle Office
National Wildlife Refuge Association
National Women's Health Foundation
National Women's Law Center
Native Action
Native American Fish & Wildlife Society
Native Ecosystems Council
Native Forest Council, Inc.
Native Forest Network
Native Lands Institute
Native Seeds/SEARCH
Natural Resources Defense Council, Inc. - National Office
Natural Resources Defense Council, Inc. - New York Office
Natural Resources Defense Council, Inc. - San Francisco Office
Natural Resources Defense Council, Inc. - Santa Monica Office
Natural Resources Law Center
Natural Science for Youth Foundation
Nature Center Design Network
NatureServe
Nebraska Appleseed Center for Law in the Public Interest, Inc.
Nebraska Community Foundation
Nebraska Farmers Union Foundation
Nebraska Statewide Arboretum
Nebraska Wildlife Federation
Nepenthic Society
Network for Family Life Education / Rutgers University
Nevada Nuclear Waste Task Force, Inc.
Nevada Outdoor Recreation Association
New America Foundation
New Energy Economy, Inc.
New Mexico Community Foundation

New Mexico Department of Game and Fish
New Mexico Environmental Law Center
New Mexico Institute of Mining and Technology
New Mexico Land Conservancy
New Mexico Natural Heritage Program
New Mexico Public Interest Research Group Education Fund
New Mexico Teen Pregnancy Coalition
New Mexico Water Dialogue
New Mexico Wilderness Alliance
Newtown Florist Club, Inc.
Noah's Ark
Noel Foundation
Norma B. Mitchell Dance Organization
North American Arctic Goose Conference
North American Industrial Hemp Council
North American Lake Management Society
North American Wilderness Recovery
North Avenue Presbyterian Church
North Carolina Coastal Federation
North Carolina Community Foundation
North Carolina Outward Bound School
North Carolina State University
North Carolina Sustainable Energy Association .
North Carolina Waste Awareness and Reduction Network
Northeastern CD for Watermark Association of Artisans
Northern Plains Resource Council
Northern Rockies Conservation Cooperative
Northwest Ecosystem Alliance
Northwest Environment Watch
Northwest Georgia Healthcare Partnership

Nuclear Age Peace Foundation
Nuclear Control Institute
Nuclear Information and
  Resource Service
NW Energy Coalition
Oakhurst Community Garden
  Project
Ocean Alliance: Whale
  Conservation Institute
Ocean Conservancy
Ocean Foundation
Oceana, Inc.
Oglethorpe University, Inc.
Oglethorpe Wild Land Trust
Ohio Valley Environmental
  Coalition
Okefenokee Wildlife League,
  Inc.
Oklahoma City, OK / Oklahoma
  City Community Foundation
Olusegun Obasanjo Presidential
  Library Foundation in the USA
OMB Watch
One More Generation
Open Space Institute
Openlands Project
Oregon Environmental Council,
  Inc.
Oregon Natural Desert
  Association
Oregon Natural Resource
  Council
Oregon Trout
Organic Consumers Association
Orion - The Hunters Institute
Orlando Science Center, Inc.
Ossabaw Island Foundation
Our Children's Earth Foundation
Outdoor Activity Center, Inc.
Owens Foundation
Owl Research Institute
Oxbow Meadows Environmental
  Learning Center
Ozone Action, Inc.
Pace University School of Law
Pacific Aviation Museum Pearl
  Harbor
Pacific Environment
Pacific Fleet Submarine
  Memorial Association, Inc.
Pacific Institute

Pacific Institute for Women's
  Health
Pacific Primate Sanctuary
Pacific Rivers Council
Palouse-Clearwater
  Environmental Institute
Panthera Corporation
Parent to Parent of Georgia
Parent-to-Parent
Park County Environmental
  Council
Park Pride Atlanta, Inc.
Parks & Recreation Foundation
  of Northeast St. John's County
Partners for DeKalb Parks
Partnership Project, Inc.
PATH Foundation, Inc.
Pathfinder International
PAX, Inc.
Peace Lutheran Church
Peachtree Road United
  Methodist Church
Pedals for Progress
Pedestrians Educating Drivers
  on Safety
Penn Center
People for the American Way
  Foundation
Peregrine Fund, Inc.
Performing Arts Program for
  Youth
Pesticide Action Network North
  America Regional Center
Pets Are Loving Support, Inc.
Pew Center on Global Climate
  Change
Pew Charitable Trusts
Pheasants Forever
Philanthropic Collaborative, Inc.
Philliber Research Associates
Phoenix Academy Theatre
Physicians for Social
  Responsibility
Piedmont Hospital, Inc.
Piedmont Park Conservancy
Pierre Healthy Communities -
  Healthy Youth
Pinchot Institute for
  Conservation
Pirates Alley Faulkner Society,
  Inc.
Planet 21

Planet Green Foundation
Planned Parenthood Affiliates of
  Michigan
Planned Parenthood Federation
  of America
Planned Parenthood of Alaska
Planned Parenthood of Los
  Angeles
Planned Parenthood of
  Minnesota/South Dakota
Planned Parenthood of New
  Mexico, Inc.
Planned Parenthood of New
  York City, Inc.
Planned Parenthood of Northern
  New England
Planned Parenthood of South
  Carolina
Planned Parenthood of
  Southeastern Pennsylvania
Planned Parenthood of the
  Atlanta Area
Planned Parenthood of the
  Rocky Mountains
Planned Parenthood of the St.
  Louis Region
Planned Parenthood of Western
  Washington
Planned Parenthood
  Reproductive Health Services
Planned Parenthood Southeast,
  Inc.
Planning and Conservation
  League Foundation
Ploughshares Fund
Pocono Environmental
  Education Center
Points of Light Foundation
Polynesian Voyaging Society
Population Action International
Population Coalition
Population Communication
Population Communications
  International, Inc.
Population Connection
Population Council
Population Institute
Population Reference Bureau
Population Resource Center
Population Services International
Porter-Gaud
Poseidon, Inc.

Powder River Basin Resource Council
Prairie Plains Resource Institute
Predator Conservation Alliance
Prescott College
Preservation Project Jacksonville, Inc.
Prickly Pear Land Trust
ProChoice Resource Center
Profamilia
Professional Impact
Professional Logging Contractors of Maine
Program for Appropriate Technology in Health
Progressive Technology Project
Project Concern International
Project Underground
Pronatura Peninsula de Yucatan A.C.
Protovotonic Institute
Providence Learning Center and Development Corporation
Providence Missionary Baptist Church
Proyecto Lemu
Public Education Center
Public Employees for Environmental Responsibility
Public Health Institute
Public Interest Projects
Public Lands Action Network
Public Media Center
Quality Deer Management Association
Queens College Center for the Biology of Natural Systems
Quest Foundation
Quivira Coalition
Rabun Gap-Nacoochee School
Rachel's Network, Inc.
Radio and Television News Directors Foundation
Rails-to-Trails Conservancy
Rainforest Action Network
Rainforest Alliance, Inc.
Rainforest Foundation International, Inc.
Rainforest Foundation, US
Random House
Raptor Resource Project

RARE Center for Tropical Conservation
Raton Recreation & Education Council
Red Hills Horse Trials, Inc.
Red Lodge Zoological Society
Red Wolf Coalition
Redefining Progress
Reef Relief
Refugees International
Regeneration Project
Regents of the University of Michigan
Regents of Universities
Regional Alliance for Conservation Policy in Latin America and the Caribbean
Religious Coalition for Reproductive Choice Educational Fund
Renewable Energy Policy Project
Renewable Northwest Project
REP Environmental Educational Foundation
Reporters Committee for Freedom of the Press
Reproductive Health Technologies Project
Research, Action and Information Networking for the Bodily Integrity of Women
Resource Service Ministries, Inc.
Resources for Global Sustainability
Resources for the Future
Rest The West, Inc.
Reuse Development Organization
Revelry of Racing for Bluegrass Boys' Ranch
Rhode Island School of Design
Right From the Start Medicaid Project
Rio Grande / Rio Bravo Basin Coalition El Paso
Rio Grande Restoration
Rio Pueblo/Rio Embudo Watershed Protection Coalition
River Network
River Watch Network
Riverkeeper - New York
Robert F. Kennedy Memorial

Robert W. Woodruff Arts Center, Inc.
Rockefeller Family Fund
Rocky Mountain Bird Observatory
Rocky Mountain Elk Foundation - Atlanta Chapter
Rocky Mountain Elk Foundation - National Chapter
Rocky Mountain Institute
Rome Chamber Music Festival at Vill Aurelia, Inc.
Ron Clark Academy, Inc.
Rosa & Raymond Parks Institute for Development
Rose Foundation for Communities and the Environment
Roswell Clean & Beautiful
Rotary Foundation of Rotary International
Round River Conservation Studies
Ruby Valley Hospital Foundation, Inc.
Ruckus Society
Rural Advancement Foundation International - USA
Russian Academy of Sciences
Sacred Earth Network
Safe Alternatives for Our Forest Environment
Safe Energy Communication Council
Safely Treating Our Pollution
San Francisco State University Foundation
San Juan Citizens Alliance
Sandhills Area Foundation, Inc.
Sandhills Development Corporation
Santa Fe Canyon Preservation Association
Santa Fe Public Schools Self-Awareness & School Support
Sapelo Island Cultural and Revitalization Society
Satelife
Sautee-Nacoochee Community Association
Savannah Riverkeeper
Savannah Science Museum

Save America's Forests Fund
Save Our Bosque Task Force
Save Our Children
Save Our Wild Salmon
Save The Bay, Inc.
Save the Children Federation
Save the Manatee Club
Save the Peconic Bays
Saving America's Mustangs
Saving Places for Atlanta's Community Environments, Inc.
Sayre School
Scenic America
Schenck School
School of the Building Arts
Sci Trek Museum
Scottish Rite Children's Medical Center
Sea Turtle Restoration Project
Second Chance Animal Rescue & Adoption
Self Reliance Foundation
Senior Citizen Services of Metropolitan Atlanta, Inc.
Sequoia ForestKeeper
Service Organization for Youth
Service Over Self
Seva Foundation
Seven Stages Theatre
Seventh Generation Fund
Sexuality Information and Education Council of the US
Shakertown at Pleasant Hill Kentucky, Inc.
Shands Teaching Hospitals and Clinics, Inc.
Share Our Strength, Inc.
Shepherd Center
Sheridan Public School District #5
Sherman Park Community Development
Sierra Club Foundation
Sierra Club Foundation of Canada
Sierra Club Legal Defense Fund
Sierra Club Legal Defense Fund - Canada
Sierra County Arts Council
Sierra Youth and Education Council
Simon Wiesenthal Center

Sinapu
SisterLove
Sitka Conservation Society
Sky Island Alliance
Skyland Trail
Small Woodland Owners Association of Maine
Smart Growth America
Smithsonian Institution
Smithsonian Migratory Bird Center
Smithsonian Tropical Research Institute
Snake River Alliance
Snook Foundation, Inc.
Snow Leopard Conservancy
Social and Environmental Entrepeneurs
Society for Ecological Restoration
Society of Environmental Journalists
Solar Electric Light Fund
Solar Energy International
Sonoran Institute - Northwest Office
Soque River Watershed Association, Inc.
South Carolina Aquarium
South Carolina Campaign To Prevent Teen Pregnancy
South Carolina Center for Birds of Prey
South Carolina Coastal Conservation League, Inc.
South Carolina Department of Natural Resources - Marine Resource Division
South Carolina Environmental Law Project
South Carolina Environmental Watch
South Carolina Forest Watch
South Carolina Maritime Heritage Foundation
South Carolina Waterfowl Association
South Carolina Wildlife Federation
South Central Community Foundation

South Dakota Community Foundation
Southeast Alaska Conservation Council
Southeast Alaska Indian Cultural Center
Southeast Energy Assistance
Southeast Energy Efficiency Alliance, Inc.
Southeast Land Preservation Trust
Southeast Watershed Forum
Southeastern Charity Horse Show
Southeastern Council of Foundations
Southeastern Horticultural Society, Inc.
Southeastern Louisiana University
Southern Alliance for Clean Energy
Southern Appalachian Biodiversity Project
Southern Appalachian Forest Coalition
Southern Appalachian Highlands Conservancy
Southern Christian Leadership Conference Women's Organizational Movement for Equality Now
Southern Coalition for Advanced Transportation
Southern Environmental Law Center, Inc.
Southern Organizing Committee for Economic & Social Justice
Southern Partners Fund
Southern Rockies Ecosystem Project
Southern Rural Development Initiative
Southern Utah Wilderness Alliance
Southface Energy Institute, Inc.
Southwest Community Resources
Southwest Cultural Preservation Project
Southwest Environmental Center

Southwest Natural and Cultural Heritage Association
Southwest Network for Environmental and Economic Justice
Southwest Research and Information Center
Southwestern Endangered Aridland Resource Clearing
Southwestern Medical Foundation
SouthWings
Special Olympics of Montana
Special Olympics, Inc.
Spelman College
Sportfishing Conservancy
St. Anne's Day School
St. Johns Riverkeeper
St. Jude's Children's Research Hospital
St. Luke's Episcopal Church
St. Mary's College of Maryland
Starkey Hearing Foundation
State Botanical Garden of Georgia
State Family Planning Commission of China
Stroud Water Research Center
Sundance Best of the Fest
Sundance Institute
Surface Transportation Policy Project
Surfrider Foundation
Susan G. Komen Foundation, Inc.
Sustainability Institute
Sustainable Atlanta, Inc.
Sustainable Cotton Project
Sustainable Development Institute
Sustainable Energy Coalition
Sustainable Settings
T.J. Martell Memorial Foundation
Tall Timbers Research, Inc.
Tallahassee Memorial Hospital Regional Medical Center Foundation
Tampa Baywatch
Taos Land Trust
Taxpayers for Common Sense
Teach for America

TechRocks
Teen Reproductive Health Services of Grady Health System
Tennessee Aquarium
Teton Regional Land Trust
Teton Science School
Texas A&M Foundation
Texas A&M University
Texas A&M University - Kingsville
Texas Fund for Energy and Environmental Education
Texas Wild
The 5 Gyres Institute
The Agape Foundation
The Arch Foundation for the University of Georgia, Inc.
The Atlanta History Center
The Atlanta Opera
The Bhutan Foundation
The Boat Company
The Breast Cancer Fund
The Cabinet Resource Group
The Center for Living Democracy
The Children's Christmas Party of Jacksonville
The Community Foundation for Greater Atlanta, Inc.
The Cumberland Island Museum
The Day Shelter for Women & Children
The Exploration Foundation
The Film Society of Lincoln Center
The Future of Hunting in Florida, Inc.
The Great Land Trust
The Green Belt Movement
The Group for Cultural Documentation
The Kentucky Hemp Growers Cooperative Museum & Library
The Keystone Center
The Lands Council
The Larry King Cardiac Foundation
The Leukemia & Lymphoma Society - Jacksonville Chapter
The Lexington School

The Marine Fish Conservation Network
The Methodist Home for Children and Youth
The National Italian American Foundation
The Natural Step
The Nature Conservancy
The Nature Conservancy - Altamonte Florida Chapter
The Nature Conservancy - Arlington Chapter
The Nature Conservancy - Georgia Chapter
The Nature Conservancy - Global Marine Chapter
The Nature Conservancy - Hawaii Chapter
The Nature Conservancy - Minneapolis Chapter
The Nature Conservancy - Montana Chapter
The Nature Conservancy - New Mexico Chapter
The Nature Conservancy - North Dakota Chapter
The Nature Conservancy - South Carolina Chapter
The Nature Conservancy - Southeast Regional Office
The Nature Conservancy of Canada - BC Region
The North American Water Office
The Resource Foundation
The SOC Education Fund, Inc.
The Study Hall
The Sweetheart Ball
The Tributary Fund
The UCLA Foundation
The University of Tasmania Foundation USA
The Wellness Community
The Western North Carolina Alliance
The Wolf Fund
The Women's Museum
Thedfore & Mullen Volunteer Fire Departments
Theodore Roosevelt Conservation Partnership, Inc.
Third Millennium Foundation

Thomasville Antiques Show Foundation, Inc.
Thomasville Community Resource Center
Thomasville Cultural Center, Inc.
Thoroughbred Charities of America
THRIVE
Thunderbird
Thurgood Marshall Scholarship Fund
Tides Center - Minneapolis Office
Tides Center - National Office
Tides Center - San Francisco Office
Tides Foundation
Tierra Del Fuego
Tonantzin Land Institute
Torah Day School of Atlanta, Inc.
Town of Lima
Townsend Social Services Committee
Toxic Comedy Pictures
Tree New Mexico
Trees Atlanta, Inc.
Trees, Water & People
Tri-State Coalition for Responsible Investment
Tropical Forest Management Trust
Trout Unlimited - Foothills Chapter
Trout Unlimited - Madison-Gallatin Office
Trout Unlimited - National Office
True Colors Theatre Company
Trumpet Awards Foundation, Inc.
Trust For Public Land - Atlanta Office
Trust for Public Land - Bozeman Office
Trust for Public Land - National Office
Trust for Public Land - San Francisco Office
Trust for Public Land - Tallahassee Office

Trust for Public Land- Santa Fe Office
Trust for the Future
Trust to Conserve Northeast Forestlands
Trustees for Alaska
Truth or Consequences, NM - Jornada RC&D
Tulare County Audubon Society, Inc.
Tule River Conservancy
Turner Endangered Species Fund, Inc.
Turtle Island Restoration Network
U.S. Green Building Council, Inc.
U.S. Public Interest Research Group Education Fund
UGA College of Agricultural and Environmental Sciences
UNICEF - Atlanta Chapter
Unified School District
Union of Concerned Scientists, Inc.
Unitarian Universalist Association
United Church of Christ
United for a Fair Economy
United Kingdom Mission to the United States
United Methodist Church, Board of Global Ministries - Women
United Nations Foundation
United Negro College Fund, Inc.
United States Department of State
United States Sailing Association, Inc.
United Way of Beaverhead
United Way of Metropolitan Atlanta, Inc.
United Way of New York City
United Way of the Big Bend, Inc.
Universidad Autonoma de Chihauhua
University of Alabama, Tuscaloosa
University of California Berkeley - Museum of Vertebrate Zoology
University of Colorado Indian Law Clinic

University of Denver
University of Florida Foundation/Archie Carr Center
University of Georgia - Institute of Ecology
University of Georgia - Office of Public Service & Outreach
University of Georgia Foundation
University of Georgia Research Foundation, Inc.
University of Georgia School of Forest Resources
University of Georgia/Vinson Institute of Government
University of Hawaii Foundation
University of Kansas Center for Research
University of Maryland Medical System Foundation, Inc.
University of Maryland, Center for Environmental Science
University of Montana
University of New Mexico
University of South Carolina - Beaufort
University of Southern California
University of Spiritual Awakening, Inc.
University of Tampa
University of Tennessee - Dept. of Ecology & Evolutionary Biology
University of Texas
University of Wisconsin-Madison
University of Wyoming - Department of Zoology and Physiology
Upper Canada Educational Foundation
Upper Chattahoochee Riverkeeper Fund, Inc.
Upper Gila Watershed Alliance
Upstate Forever
Urban Training Organization of Atlanta, Inc.
Useful Wild Plants
Usher's New Look, Inc.
USS Missouri Memorial Association, Inc.
Vail Valley Foundation, Inc.

Valenti International Foundation, Inc.
Valentine, NE - Nebraska Community Foundation
Valhalla Wilderness Society
Valley Community Clinic
Vanguard Public Foundation
V-Day
V-Day Atlanta
Video Action
Villa Traful
Vital Ground Foundation
Volunteers of America
Volusia Friends of the St. John's River
Voyageurs National Park Association
Walterboro, SC - Coastal Community Foundation of SC
WAMC/ Public Radio
War Child USA
Washington Environmental Alliance for Voter Education
Washington Office on Environmental Justice
Water Information Network
Waterkeeper Alliance, Inc.
Western Canada Wilderness Committee
Western Environmental Law Center
Western Governors' Foundation
Western Network
Western Organization of Resource Councils Education Project
Western Resource Advocates
Western States Center, Inc.
Western Sustainable Agriculture Working Group
Wheelock College
Where R U Black Man
Whirling Disease Foundation, Inc.
White Earth Land Recovery Project
White House Project
Wild Alabama
Wild Angels
Wild Candid Survival & Research Center, Inc.
Wild Earth Society

Wild Salmon Center
Wild Things Unlimited
WildAid
Wilderness Society
Wilderness Society - Alaska Office
Wilderness Society - Colorado Office
Wilderness Watch
Wildlands Center for Preventing Roads
Wildlands Project
Wildlife Center of Virginia
Wildlife Conservation Fund of America
Wildlife Conservation Society - Montana Office
Wildlife Conservation Society - New York Office
Wildlife Forever
Wildlife Foundation of Florida, Inc.
Wildlife Rescue Team, Inc.
Wildlife Society
Winter Wildlands Alliance, Inc.
Wisconsin Family Forests
WNET.ORG
Women in International Security
Women's Action for New Directions Education Fund, Inc.
Women's Choice for Boulder Valley
Women's Environment & Development Organization
Women's Opportunity and Resource Development, Inc.
Women's Sports Foundation
Women's Voices for the Earth
Wood Reduction Clearinghouse
Woodrow Wilson International Center for Scholars
Woods Hole Research Center
Woodward Academy
Working Films
World Bank Watch - Latin American Campaign
World Chamber of Commerce
World Media Foundation
World Neighbors
World Piano Competition, Inc.
World Population Foundation
World Resources Institute

World Watch Institute
World Wide Film Expedition
World Wide Fund for Nature Russia - Far Eastern Branch
World Wilderness Committee
World Wildlife Fund, Inc.
Worldwatch Institute
Wounded Warrior Project, Inc.
Wyoming Outdoor Council
Wyoming Wildlife Federation
Xaverian High School
Xerces Society, Inc.
Yale University
Yellowstone Association
Yellowstone Ecosystem Studies
Yellowstone Grizzly Foundation
Yellowstone Park Foundation, Inc.
Yellowstone to Yukon Conservation Initiative
Yellowstone to Yukon Conservation Initiative - Canada
Yellowstone Wolf Recovery Fund
YMCA of Beaufort County
YMCA of Metropolitan Atlanta, Inc.
YMCA of Metropolitan Chattanooga
Yosemite Fund
Young Americans Education Foundation
Young Life
Young Women's Project
Youth Communication: Metro Atlanta
YWCA of Cobb County
YWCA of Greater Atlanta
YWCA of Lincoln
YWCA of the USA
Zapovedniks Environmental Education Center
Zoo Montana
Zoological Foundation of Georgia, Inc. Atlanta
Zuni Mountain Coalition

INDEX

ABOUT THE AUTHOR

Todd Wilkinson has been a professional journalist and author for more than twenty-five years, with assignments that have taken him around the world. He is author of several books, including the critically acclaimed *Science under Siege: the Politicians' War on Nature and Truth.*